Money in Economic Theory

The financial crash of 2008 showed the fragility of the financial system. A key question which surfaced in the aftermath of the global crisis was why economists were unable to predict this crash. This new volume argues that this failure can be attributed, at least in part, to the poor and inconsistent treatment of money and monetary matters in economic theory. The book takes this problem as its starting point, and from there aims to develop a more consistent treatment of the topic.

Here, Hasse Ekstedt affirms that the treatment of money in economic theory has been inconsistent and that the topic of money can in fact be seen as anomalous. He argues that this anomaly depends on deficiencies in the economic theory, which through an equilibrium approach mainly perceives money as an index of measurement.

In contrast, this volume puts forward the case for money as a non-equilibrium concept, and that the stability of money and financial markets are to be sought in social and institutional structures. In particular, the volume discusses the relationship between the market and public bodies, as well as addressing economic and financial stability in general and in relation to the globalized economy, particularly focusing on the problem of structural stability. In doing so, the book offers a new approach both to money and to its role in economic theory.

Hasse Ekstedt is a Senior Researcher in the School of Public Administration at the University of Gothenburg, Sweden.

Routledge international studies in money and banking

Money in Economic Theory

Hasse Ekstedt

Routledge
Taylor & Francis Group

LONDON AND NEW YORK

First published 2013
by Routledge
2 Park Square, Milton Park, Abingdon, Oxfordshire OX14 4RN

Simultaneously published in the USA and Canada
by Routledge
711 Third Avenue, New York, NY 10017

First issued in paperback 2014

Routledge is an imprint of the Taylor and Francis Group, an informa business

British Library Cataloguing in Publication Data
A catalogue record for this book is available from the British Library

Library of Congress Cataloging in Publication Data
Ekstedt, Hasse.
Money in economic theory/Hasse Ekstedt.
  p. cm.
  Includes bibliographical references and index.
  1. Money. 2. Economics. I. Title.
  HG220.A2E47 2012
  332.401–dc23

                                                      2012024569

ISBN 978-0-415-69739-2 (hbk)

ISBN 978-1-138-90125-4 (pbk)

ISBN 978-0-203-07651-4 (ebk)

Typeset in Times New Roman
by Wearset Ltd, Boldon, Tyne and Wear

Contents

Figures

Tables

Preface

Back in days when the Donald Duck series was my prime source of cultural information of society I learnt that a scientist, Gyro Gearloose or someone was a person often standing in front of a blackboard filled with formulas. This person represented a mysterious world beyond and above the ordinary knowledgeable world and when I became a bit older reading about alchemy this feeling was deepened. Nowadays when looking at TV news I can see much the same pattern and this is particularly obvious when it comes to financial news. It is a different somewhat scary world out of which sudden disasters like lightning strikes individuals and societies. Sometimes the radical view of equalizing the financial and economic conditions of states and individual households is taken which often implies a relatively simple ethical analysis of bad guys and good guys, but that also implies that money is something which is given to people, probably by the invisible hand so we end up even in this approach in a mystery. Adding mathematics we then leave the understandable world.

It is obvious that some groups make money on this state of confusion but when we think about it we realize that people in general understand quite well economics, the need of competitive companies, the need of a diversified industry, the need of good internal and external balance, the somewhat complicated relations between foreign trade and internal welfare policy, but when it comes to money and money matters it seems to be something for a few specialists. Why is it so? Is it something particular with money? This question has in fact puzzled me for a long time and that is why I write about money although I have never been regarded myself as a monetary theorist.

Money is a kind of mystery because it is basically an abstraction. It is defined by a sort of social convention and it gets its value from that which furthermore implies that money possesses features which potentially are at variance with each other: medium of exchange, liquidity and the accounting/valuation feature. Thus a ten dollar bill, crumpled in the pocket, represents a link to both an aggregate and a fairly abstract world. I am not saying that money is difficult to understand but it is a bit more complex than at first sight and we have to go through the intrinsic features with some care.

We have to separate money from ordinary commodities on logical grounds and we will use a technique involving Russell's and Cantor's paradoxes. This logical separation leads as usual in logical argumentations to rather trivial results which seem to be evident but yet necessary to keep in mind.

Our discussions will take us to the edge of the political discussion, spring 2012, but our main interest is to spell out evident but important conflicts, which hardly exist, at least not theoretically, in a barter economy but are of utmost importance in a monetary economy.

The author has chosen to start with early economists who saw the birth and the youth of the monetary economy and it has been remarkable to see the utmost importance theorists like Hume, Say and Thornton attached to the role of money in accelerating of the socialization process and changing the structure of the society both culturally and socially. It was like a journey in time and it struck me that if we make a roundabout the world trip today we may actually experience the same kind of journey in time. Perhaps people and politicians in Europe and the USA should pay more attention to this in implementing policies for development whatever that might be. Furthermore it struck me that the joy David Hume and Jean Baptiste Say express with respect to the increased pace of socialization and change of society has today been turned into fear for the future and hostility to changes. In advanced countries like Sweden not few among those who regard themselves as intellectuals seriously claim that the society would become better if we go back to a barter economy and blame money for all the evil. Many in the financial sector if we should judge from interviews on TV seems to be convinced that money making irrespective of methods is what promotes growth and prosperity for the society.

Money in economic theory is somewhat an anomaly. Full understanding of money can never be reached if we are not prepared to give up the stubborn refusal to let in analysis of sociological and cultural structures within economic theory and only that will bring us nearer a serious theory of money as well as economics.

Acknowledgements

First I want to express my respect for my two teachers, late Professors Tor Fern-holm and Lars Westberg. I got in touch with Professor Fernholm in the 1960s when he was already retired. He was both a philosopher and an economist and he taught me the qualitative difference of the monetary economy in comparison with the neo-classical barter economy. Professor Lars Westberg was my teacher, friend and co-writer. He was early affected by the Stockholm School and he also introduced the studies of Gurley and Shaw and performed similar studies in Sweden. All his life he was a student of the interaction between the real and financial spheres of the economy. I have been much dependent on these two outstanding scholars and it is with great pleasure I use in Chapter 7 figures from their respective works.

Dr Angelo Fusari, former Director of Research at the Institute of Studies and Economic Analysis, ISAE, Rome, has been of fundamental help for me at the planning stage of the book when we had in-depth methodological discussions. I am grateful for his support and for his criticism.

My friend Chris Sanders at Sanders Research Associates Ltd has for many years supported my research and I am in great debt to him for all I have learnt from him about the financial world.

Professor Alfonso Palacio-Vera at Universidad Complutense de Madrid intro-duced me to the School of Salamanca and I have benefitted from discussions with him. He has also provided me with appropriate reading on general as well as economic matters from the golden age of the School of Salamanca.

I am grateful to Professor Björn Rombach, Head of School of Public Admin-istration, University of Gothenburg, for reading and commenting on parts of the book and I am also grateful to him for using his administrative flexibility to arrange my lecturing and other duties in such way that I have enough time for my writing.

I am in deep gratitude to my son Fredrik Ekstedt, MSc Maths and BA Eco-nomics, analyst at Swedish Export Credit Corporation. His deep theoretical as well as practical knowledge of the financial market has been of great importance for me and I have learnt much from our discussions. He has also provided me with valuable papers on relevant matters.

Finally I want to thank my wife Barbro Ekstedt, former linguist at the Council of the European Union in Brussels. Reading my text she has put her finger on weak logics and blurred reasoning. I am in deep debt to her and I give her my respect and my love.

All my family, also the little member who will soon appear in this world, is and has been of tremendous importance for me and I give them my devotion and love.

1 Introduction, scopes and methods

"Money makes the world go around" the Master of Ceremonies at Kit Kat Club sings in the musical *Cabaret* and it is probably right. In the Bible we read in Matthew 6:24 "No one can serve two masters, for either he will hate the one, and love the other, or he will be devoted to the one, and despise the other. You cannot serve God and money" (ESV Bible). Why does money make the world go around and what is meant by serving money: isn't money a servant of ours? We quote St Thomas in Chapter 2 and he says that no object is evil in itself, but it is man himself who turns it into evil. But still – how can we become servants to money, it seems to be a kind of addiction?

Money is one of the most powerful concepts in human mind. Early in life we learn its power via weekly allowances, via aunts and uncles handing some coins to buy sweets; children learn quickly transforming different desires into relative prices.

In Wesley Mitchell's paper, "The role of money in economic theory", he ends his paper by saying:

> The current tendency to make money "the centre around which economic science clusters," then, is a tendency to be fostered. For that course promises (1) to clarify economic theory by giving it a better framework, (2) to render economic theory more useful by directing attention to those actual processes with which all serious proposals for governmental regulation and social reorganization must deal, (3) to make economics more realistic and therefore more interesting intellectually as well as practically, and, finally, to make economic theory more profound by orienting the economist for a fruitful study of his aspect of human behavior.
>
> (Mitchell 1916: 161)

These words cut through the sophisticated neoclassical general equilibrium analysis as well as the huge Keynesian modelling as a knife in butter.

Money which has become a theoretical anomaly in main stream modelling is placed in the very centre of the analysis by Mitchell. The fundamental meaning of the economic analysis is the allocation of scarce real resources and the distribution among the agents of the production result, but, to analyse this, the understanding of the different roles of money is essential.

Economics is indeed a remarkable topic within social sciences, since there is a distinct moment of action combined both with a theoretical and a practical possibility of measurement, namely when the very exchange of money for commodities takes place. It is the more interesting since we know that the concept of money also represents the powerful concept of liquidity, normally in its highest form, and furthermore historical, current and future values are expressed in money whether it concerns accounting figures, contractual matters or future expectations. That means that we may actually observe the agents' current choices and also, at least to some extent, the choice between actions now or at a later stage. From an empirical point of view that makes us to a certain degree observe inertia of different kind; we may also link actions to different, both microscopic and macroscopic, events. The interpretations of the very action and its purposes are difficult but at least we have an exact figure whatever it means.

Unfortunately economic theory, and this concerns both neoclassical and Keynesian theory, is often more occupied with a priori modelling of the nature of the agents and/or economic structures, which shuffles around real matters of commodities and production factors but leave the dreams, ethics, institutional matters and idiosyncrasies, strange or not, outside the analysis and this is actually where money is of a prime interest. In creating a machine close to a *perpetuum mobile* more or less founded on the Aristotelian value of labour, the economic science has lost its contact with one of the most formidable powers in history, namely the human imagination and dream. From a scientific point of view the fundamental mistake is the confusion between science of studying *objects* and the science of studying *subjects*.[1]

The essence of this difference is the very ability of the subjects to redefine values and wealth with respect to future actions. Thus the current accounting value of an asset is not *The Value* but an input in the subject's contemplation of the future.

John Commons (1990 [1934]: pp. 413–14) in his discussion on MacLeod's *Economics for Beginners*, touches the point with a needle;

> Yet his negotiable debts are the modern meaning of capital. The economists, said MacLeod, "never made the slightest attempt to bring the subject of Credit and Banking into the general body of the science: in fact, they have given up the whole subject of Banking in hopeless despair." MacLeod resolves this difficulty by shifting the physical things to the future and by substituting mental acts and operation of law which give rise to property rights. If property-rights are themselves credits, then banking is only a special case of the universal principle of buying and selling credits.
> [...]
>   There was a double meaning, says MacLeod, in Adam Smith's usage of the term Wealth. In the first half of his work wealth was defined as "the annual produce of land and labor"; in the second half it was anything exchangeable. Ricardo followed Smith but restricted his meaning to any product of labor designed to be sold.... Hence MacLeod followed what was

included in all their meanings of wealth and made exchangeability the essence of wealth and value. This however, as we have said, confuses wealth and assets.

Furthermore Commons adds "according to MacLeod and the other physical economists who made exchangeability the sole subject-matter of economics, an exact science can be developed only when, like the physical sciences, it can be reduced to mathematical equations". This doesn't mean that we must interpret Commons as hostile to the use of mathematics in economics but what Commons puts his finger on is the absolute need of precise definitions of concepts and this is even more necessary when dealing with a science studying subjects.

The principles of empirical sciences are rather simple and straightforward. We observe somehow inert structures which we try to represent as neatly as possible in logical structures possible to analyse in deductive patterns. These deductive patterns will then in principle govern the mode of observations as well as the interpretation of further empirical observations. The representation however is always dependent on the questions we raise with respect to our observations. That of course means that our pre-understanding, prejudices and other idiosyncrasies play an important role already in the stage of observation; furthermore they play a crucial role in the forming of seemingly empirical structures which are the basis for deductive analysis. This is so in natural sciences, which are to be seen as sciences of objects and probably in a much larger degree in sciences of subjects.

When it comes to economics we additionally have to strive for universal modelling built on a priori axiomatic structures which not only restrict the structures of the deductive modelling but also restrict the empirical observation in the first case. This is indeed remarkable since even the natural sciences have left this stage of development of the scientific analysis.

It is refreshing to read the pious friars of Salamanca, from the sixteenth century, and their analysis of what was actually going on in the Spanish economy, in asking why the performance of the Spanish economy was so bad in spite of the huge inflow of gold to Spain. This gave rise to an intellectually satisfactory analysis of money which later was almost forgotten. Comparing the analysis of the pious Dominican friars of Salamanca with some of the economic analysis today one gets the impression that economic science has been degraded to a more or less religious faith.

Money is a concept easy to understand vis-à-vis relative prices and a budget restriction in a microeconomic setting; however when we introduce the concept of cash balance, we are already in trouble. Cash balances are difficult to handle in traditional optimization problems of the households given consistent preference structure. In a Walrasian setting money appears more or less as a residual. When we look at macroeconomic theory money plays a more prominent role. We discuss interest rates, liquidity preference, quantity of money and velocity of circulation. However when we try to close the theoretical gap between the microscopic and the macroscopic theory the two logical structures are seemingly ill-fit.

One route of thinking is to basically accept the microeconomic theory and its particular form of additive aggregation and add the quantity theory of money which deals explicitly with the quantity and circulation of money. In monetarist theory this has evolved into the interesting solution that as long as markets are free and works properly according to the neoclassical theory we can handle macroeconomic problems of inflation and unemployment solely through manipulating the quantity of money.

However many theoreticians get a gnawing unrest when looking at this reasoning and start to ask whether it is possible to add one theoretical approach to another where the theoretical concepts of the first don't even exist. This has raised questions of whether we really have a consistent theory of money in economic theory.

An early proponent for these doubts is the Swedish economist Knut Wicksell who writes;

> I already had my suspicions – which were strengthened by a more thorough study, particularly of the writings of Tooke and his followers – that, as an alternative to the Quantity Theory, there is no complete and coherent theory of money. If the Quantity Theory is false – or to the extent it is false – there is so far available only one false theory of money and no true theory.
>
> (Wicksell 1936: xxiii)

Unfortunately Wicksell's words are still relevant to a great extent. Thus the almost axiomatic inclusion of the quantity theory in the neoclassical building is a theoretical mystery and furthermore the adding of supposed Keynesian concepts of liquidity and even uncertainty is also mysterious from a logical point of view. Kenneth Arrow and Frank Hahn wrote in the concluding chapter with the title "The Keynesian Problem" of their fundamental study of economic theory in its neoclassical setting, *General Competitive Analysis*: "If a serious monetary theory comes to be written, the fact that contracts are made in money will be of a considerable importance" (Arrow and Hahn 1971: 356–7).

Our quotation from Wicksell expresses the same mood although it is written more than 70 years earlier. The modern portfolio analysis based on the theoretical achievements by Black, Scooles, Merton and Samuelson is indeed interesting but it is based on a completely different form of mathematical structure from the one in the neoclassical theory.

When entering an abstract analysis of the inconsistencies of money and money matters in economic theory our basic approach is that the inconsistencies do not depend on a lack of a theory of money but instead it is the fruit of more fundamental inconsistencies in economic theory.

Scopes of the book

This is not a book about the economic reality, although we often taken examples from and allude to rather common experiences. The author has reached an age where such studies are seen as a contradiction in terms of a comfortable life; furthermore experiences from the business world have effectively increased the state of confusion with respect to what reality, if it exists as a general concept, is.

The title *Money in Economic Theory* tells rather well the main scope. The basic question will be how money is treated in economic theory and this will give rise to methodological discussions on the relevance and implications. Naturally the first question will be "what do we define as economic theory?" followed by "what is money?" However since these two questions call for additional books to be written, the author has taken on a very simple attitude, namely to start the discussion with what we actually tell our first year students about what economics and money are.

The reader might not expect any breathtaking conclusions which lead to new universal theories but more a methodological inquiry of the theoretical treatment of money. Much of what can be said is to a certain extent well known except perhaps for some concepts brought from physics and mathematical logics, but these are just practical tools of analysis.

The conclusion is simple. Economics is not a machine and theoretical approaches striving to create such a machine are not penetrated with respect to the very essence of the concept of money. Thus the bad theoretical apprehension of money in economic theory does not mean that economists do not understand money and monetary matters in the empirical world but that the general economic theory does not allow for a relevant apprehension of money. Thus the so-called mainstream economic theory, which is a mishmash of neoclassical, Keynesian and monetarist thoughts, which by no means need to be wrong in principle, induces us sometimes to do exactly what Commons criticizes, namely mixing up concepts bringing contradictory elements into the same kind of theoretical representation.

That leads our interest from the question of what money really is towards what money is thought to be in conjunction with the rest of the theoretical considerations.

One could say that the expression of the Roman emperor Vespasian, *pecunia non olet*, is at the very centre of our analysis. Another expression which also will follow us is from Luigi Amoroso (1938: 6) "the dead city dominates *through inertia* the living city".

Methodological matters

Our main scope is a methodological study of economic theory vis-à-vis money so the question of which kind of methodology we should use for this methodological purpose is indeed appropriate. We start from the fact that all empirical sciences have to penetrate possible inert structures both with respect to their fundamental dimensions and its dynamics, thus all inert structures have to be formulated in such a way that logical deductions are possible, not necessarily mathematical deductions but still meaningful with respect to causal consequences implied by their existence.

Thus with respect to such deductions we have to start from some form of assumptions which we hold at least temporally and locally for true. Then there appear two problems; the relevance of the assumptions and the consistency of the logical (causal) analysis. For the economic science this is of particular interest since the basic structure to which all other approaches have to relate is actually based on a precise set of a priori assumptions of the agents' behaviour. As implicit in the quote from Commons above, the axiomatic structure focuses completely on the concept of market exchange of commodities and production factors. This means that the sophisticated theory often has difficulties to handle rudimentary problems which are of common character and with which people of no education in either economics or mathematics has to deal in their daily life. One such example is just money. As we shall see even such a trivial concept as cash balances make the very axiomatic foundation quiver.

A philosophical basis for analysis

As said our analysis of money will not be an empirical study of the monetary economy, but a study of the theoretical basis for the concept of money in economic theory. Thus we will start in a study of the foundations of economic theory as they appear in the neoclassical approach and we will ask the simple question "why does money play such a diminutive role of the theory although it seems to play an overwhelmingly important role in the reality?" Thus our basic interest is not the reality in itself but sooner the theoretical picture of the reality and the basic question is what happens to our theoretical approach to money if we change the basic theoretical picture of the economy.

Much has been said about using mathematical/logical approaches in social sciences, suffice to argue here that any *science* asserting some kind of generality has to be logically scrutinized, whether it takes a mathematical form or not. Inertia of causal relations in the physical/social space has an analytical dual in consistent logical structures. Thus we do not question the use of mathematical and logical structures per se, but there is a fundamental problem in using abstract mathematical forms which Wittgenstein discusses in *Tractatus Logico-Philosophicus*, namely the relation between logics/mathematics and reality in scientific theories and enquiries and to focus on some fundamental problems of using mathematics/logics in science. Proposition 6.211 says:

> In real life a mathematical proposition is never what we want. Rather, we make use of mathematical propositions only in inferences from propositions that do not belong to mathematics to others that likewise do not belong to mathematics. (In philosophy the question, "What do we actually use this word or this proposition for?" repeatedly leads to valuable insight).
>
> (Wittgenstein 1974 [1921]: 65)

Ekstedt (2006) illustrated this proposition as in Figure 1.1.

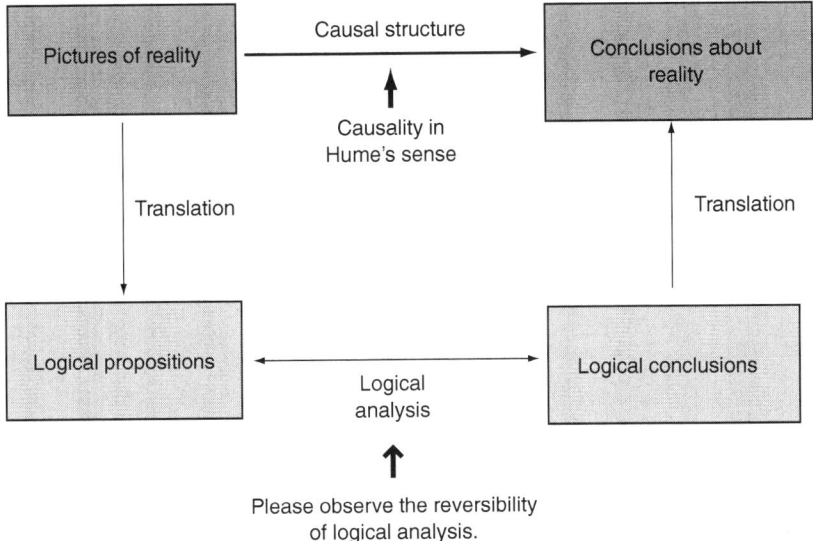

Figure 1.1 Mathematics and reality.

First of all it is important to realize that formal logics and mathematics are languages of a more precise character than the language we use in everyday life. That does not mean that it is generally superior to ordinary language but in relation to certain problems it can be more efficient to use. The particular feature of *precision* of concepts and functional forms can be of great value but not necessarily if we do not pay attention to the implications of this precision with respect to reality. Precision mostly implies that we constrain the dimensionality of a concept but whether or not this is adequate in relation to the studied piece of reality is a matter of judgement with respect to empirical experience. The richness of the ordinary language is of an enormous benefit to us in opening up associations and perspectives which in the end might lead to innovative thinking, something which is lost in the strict logical/mathematical analysis.

In Figure 1.1 it is important to note the difference between the two levels, the causal analysis and the logical/mathematical analysis. Causal structures are always asymmetric and thus irreversible in time, if we stick to David Hume's definition, while logical analysis, if not properly restricted, is reversible.[2] In economics this is a prominent analytical problem called the *Problem of Integrability* which deals with the *principle of revealed preferences*.[3] The appearance of such a reversible effect in dealing with an empirical world is indeed remarkable if the axiomatic structure is supposed to mirror important features of the reality. In relation to money and its use we may suspect that such reversibility is a crucial feature in analysing the axiomatic structure.

When we use logic/mathematics in any science we are extremely dependent on the inertia of the area for scientific analysis. Even appropriate use of the strict requirements of mathematics induces implicit structures into the problem which might be strange to the real problem. Thus when we translate a real problem to a mathematical structure we must squeeze it into a form where we unfortunately have to accept a certain mathematical superstructure which can be very inconvenient to our study of the empirical reality. Thus the inappropriate use of mathematics in empirical sciences seems almost always to appear in frivolous translations of the mathematical/logical conclusions into the empirical study without any attention paid to these mathematical superstructures. An even worse case is when we broaden such conclusions into more general areas, as in economics, and make normative statements about general socioeconomic and political processes.

Our analysis in this book will actually use Wittgenstein's proposition and Figure 1.1 as a kind of methodological foundation for the analysis.

The usage of mathematics

The world created by economic theory is remarkable in many aspects. It is a closed world with precisely defined concepts which basically builds on a kind of Newtonian equilibrium system where the proof of the existence of general equilibrium is the jewel in the crown.

The axiomatic structure per se is consistent and it is both possible and easy to derive hypotheses which are suitable for empirical testing when we develop analytical functions consistent with the axioms.

This has made the neoclassical model, in its precision, an example to follow for other social sciences, and some of its concepts, particularly its definition of rationality, has in fact conquered the world of social sciences and gained an almost undisputed role as "the definition" of rationality. Therefore the criticism of the concept of rationality often takes the form of questioning human rationality *in toto*, claiming irrationality of humans.

Compared to other social sciences economics utilizes mathematical methodology to a much larger extent, which is made possible by the closeness of its axiomatic structure, and sometimes the high degree of mathematical formalization is seen as a sign of the scientific precision of the theory. However there is an ointment in the soup. The closed character makes the definitions of the concepts very narrow and the closeness excludes many aspects of the reality. In natural sciences where the research areas are normally rather inert such exclusions are a minor problem if the researcher is aware of them. In social sciences, however, where we may expect structures to be changing or short lived, exclusion of dimensions of the research area can be fatal if not taken into account.

In the aftermath of the financial debacle of 2008 many important questions have been raised about why economists were unable to foresee the coming disaster. One of the suggested explanations has been the affluent use of mathematics in economic analysis, sacrificing empirical realism to logical elegance. Paul

Krugman, for example, in an article in the *New York Times*, 2 September 2009, partly pursues this line of explanations. This form of criticism is sensible as long as it deals with the malpractice of mathematics, but on the other hand logical structures are necessary in science, irrespective of which kind of science we discuss and some logical structures are more apt to transform to a mathematical language than others. We then regard mathematics as a language where we translate perceived real structures into logical structures and then perform the logical analysis into logical conclusions which are translated into propositions viable for the real world. Thus as we see from Figure 1.1 the translation process is of central importance; the logical analysis in itself is either right or wrong and does not add any information to the original problem.

A fascinating exchange of opinions took place at Salvatore Dali's place in Figueres, north of Barcelona, November 1985, when the Nobel laureate in chemistry Ilya Prigogine met René Thom, the great French mathematician, in a public discussion:[4]

THOM: You should very carefully distinguish between what belongs to mathematical theory and what belongs to real systems. Mathematics has nothing to say to reality.

PRIGOGINE: That's your point of view, it's not mine.

Two giants discussing and we are squeezed in between in our poor efforts to make some economic research; we may take a wise position and say that both are right. But if so, what are the implications? René Thom seems to be right in the very fundamental sense that mathematics is a language and as such neutral to the substance of the analysis. Generally we may analyse the language as such but this analysis should not affect the meaning of what we are trying to say other than possibly increasing the clarity. This is also the fundamental meaning of Gödel's famous paradox. Prigogine may also be right, but then we think more about abstract geometric and topological forms analysed in mathematics which allow us to analyse different complex structures with logical precision and that may also give rise to fruitful inventions of new perspectives in economic science. The reality displays a richness of forms which is overwhelming. The problem is that these different forms interact and create new forms.[5]

Paradoxes

Another virtue of strict mathematical models is when the mathematical/logical analysis evolves into a paradox when we compare it with actual conclusions with respect to the reality. We may then understand that our axiomatic structure is exhausted and we have to scrutinize the precise content of our axioms with respect to the analysed reality in order to see why we achieve the paradox. The result of such a scrutiny seldom affects our apprehension of the reality but gives rise to questions with respect to the axioms. Unfortunately a common form of malpractice is to start the other way around and ask what the paradox tells us about reality.

As we discussed in relation to the proposition by Wittgenstein, squeezing in a problem of the reality into a logical model implies that we trim our picture of reality which on one hand implies that important dimensions of the real problem are left out, but on the other hand we must adopt mathematical feature/restrictions which are often strange to the real problem. Logical models are of great help but must be interpreted with great care. The German philosopher Hans Reichenbach is close to Wittgenstein when he divides the research process into two steps: the *context of discovery* and the *context of justification* (Reichenbach 1938: 7, 382). The context of discovery is about the detection and systemization of inert real structures into a set of presumptions for a deductive analysis and the subsequent deductions. The context of justification is then the systematic control of the appropriateness of the conclusions based on the set of presuppositions, which in the logical treatment rise to the dignity of axioms. This step is also of fundamental importance to analyse the degree of generality of the deductive system.

Any consistent axiomatic structure thus forms a universe in which we are either inside or outside. When we believe in the neoclassical general equilibrium theory we are inside a universe, which has no outside. There cannot be a neighbourhood, which does not belong to the universe irrespective of how close it is. Thus analysing a system from inside conveys certain answers which are consistent with the axiomatic structure, but asking a question from outside the system enters dimensions which are not possible to answer within the system. Think of the classical paradox of the Cretan who tells you that *all* Cretans are liars. What kind of answer do you expect if you ask him "Is that true?"

When we scrutinize the neoclassical theory, we will use two famous paradoxes in economic theory Allais' and Arrow's. The latter is probably the most well known. Both these paradoxes confront the neoclassical theory with particular problems which are prevalent in the real world and receives a paradoxical result vis-á-vis either the theory or the reality. Interpreting such paradoxes could be twofold; either we go on explaining that something is wrong with the reality or that something is wrong with the theory. If we go back to Figure 1.1 we realize that most probably the logical/mathematical analysis is not wrong. Logical mistakes can be made but these are normally short lived. The reality is normally what it is, and causal structures exist independent of whether people care about them or not so that leaves us with the two translation arrows as the crucial factors for the appearance of the paradoxes. Thus analysing the empirical reality on the basis of paradoxes is seldom a fruitful way of gaining insight of the reality but instead we must look at the way we set up the axioms to represent the reality in the logical analysis. As we will see both Arrow's and Allais' paradoxes vanish as logical paradoxes both with respect to the basic axiomatic theory and the subsequent logical analysis as well as any connection between the content of the respective paradox and the reality.

We will base our analysis of the neoclassical theory with respect to money on these two paradoxes and as a matter of fact we aim at destroying any link between the neoclassical theory and the reality so we then approach some sort of a theoretical chaos.

Theoretical chaos?

In our efforts to build up another theoretical picture which hopefully describes the problems we are aiming at, we will use another set of paradoxes from mathematics, Russell's paradox and Cantor's paradox. The reason why we employ these paradoxes is that since we dismiss neoclassical theory as a global theory, which means that any proposition based on the axiomatic structure bears no a priori information of the truth-value of the proposition with respect to the empirical world other than temporally and locally and at the pleasure of the single agent or researcher. Thus neoclassical theory is strictly to be seen as an ad hoc theory vis-à-vis a certain empirical structure. But in such a state of art we must ask ourselves if the reality is totally chaotic or empirical structures are to be seen as fractals with no deterministic content with respect to life time. We may however suspect that this is not the case for a limited analysis in time and space. But if so our destructive activities with respect to the neoclassical theory leave us without useful axiomatic concepts which may be used in a theoretical approach. Thus when we criticize the neoclassical theory in the way we do it is indeed proper to ask; "What do you do with a concept like rationality?" or "Do agents optimize their actions or at least follow other kinds of rules?" and there are several more legitimate questions to ask. The two questions mentioned are of course central in the analysis of money. If we answer no to them we either must go into a kind of chaos analysis or have to add external forces which give rise to regularities in economic actions. The latter is of course possible by assuming a kind of economic/social Darwinism but one may suspect that such a force is not particularly helpful in analysing financial markets and other monetary matters.

Thus we actually keep some parts of the neoclassical axiomatic structure but add the concept of "epistemic cycles". This concept originates in a systematic way in Thomas Brody's *The Philosophy behind Physics* but is adopted for a social and economic analysis in Ekstedt and Fusari (2010). The reason we adopt this concept is that since we reject any global analysis we need a precise concept enabling us to discuss partial regularities and different levels of aggregation. With the help of Russell's paradox we may then derive some conclusions for an economy containing several aggregate levels. Those conclusions are not particularly brave but they will be useful when we discuss the different features of money.

Measures

Money is a measure and to that extent we may use it within the neoclassical theory, but having said that we quickly glance at the other features which we have attached to money. Are they really compatible with respect to the use of money as a measure?

It is a medium of measurement, not a measure and it is not what we measure. The measure we use is often expressed as prices but these prices could be expressed in ounces of gold, kilograms of wheat and so on. What we measure is more difficult to say. Do we use money/prices on an individual level or on an aggregate level? Do we measure some kind of an objective market value of a commodity or the individual desire for a commodity? Will money work as a good medium of measurement whether we measure prices of commodities, wealth or liquidity? As a consequence of this multitude of questions in relation to the purpose of measuring one may ask whether the different purposes affect money as a measure in different ways.

Let us first state that in the analysis of measures in general there are three central aspects to consider with great care; *the actual measure, the medium of measurement* and *the purpose of measurement*. When these aspects have been carefully discussed we are ready to consider the more technical aspects of measures which must be dealt with in order to bring the whole discussion into a mathematical form which then could be transformed into statistical analysis.

Let us look at a general definition of a measure in mathematics.[6]

Definition of general measure

Let us define a measure φ and a set S which consists of subsets $s_1, \ldots, s_n$ where $s_i \subseteq S$; $s_i \rightarrow s_1, \ldots s_n$, then the following conditions must hold:

1 $\varphi \times s_i \leq \varphi \times S$;
2 $\varphi \times (s_1 + s_2) \leq \varphi \times s_1 + \varphi \times s_2$;
3 $\varphi \times (\sum s_i) = \varphi \times \sum s_i$;

These conditions are seemingly rather simple and natural but as we shall see terribly annoying. To actually apply this rather simple general definition we have to consider the three aspects above but also the very structure of the space we are going to measure.

The problem of measurement and measures is of utmost interest to any science and we may say that measuring is the very core of a scientific analysis of the real world. That does not mean that non-measurable aspects of reality are of no importance; in fact they are probably of equal or more importance, but a consistent scientific study of a problem which explicitly contains non-measurable factors, where we cannot even use the dichotomy exist/not exist, is indeed difficult if not impossible. We must thus admit that even the most brilliant scientific conclusions and hypotheses are just a meagre part of the real world of human beings.

Consistent measurement is difficult even with respect to simple comparisons of different phenomena using dichotomized criteria since the logical content of the used criteria is of importance if we are allowed to make a comparison whatsoever. Using words as bigger/smaller in a physical sense requires that we are aware of the dimensionality, length, volume or mass, and these concepts imply different measures and thus may change the relative measurement.

With respect to abstract problems the question of dimensionality often is extremely difficult. This problem is described by Henri Bergson in "Time and the Free Will" where he discusses the bodily sensation when pressing a needle in the palm of your hand. Going from tickling to "hurts a bit" is a qualitative difference, and this becomes even more pronounced when the pain increases from "hurts a bit" to "an insufferable pain" affecting your bodily and mental balance (Bergson 1912: 21–6). Comparing such dimensions along a one-dimensional axis is certainly a philosophical and psychological problem. Technically when we make a "pain scale" for example 1 to 10, we must realize that the steps are discrete and reflect different dimensionalities. Thus when doctors/nurses ask you to rank your pain from 1 to 10 and you answer 5 this may mean something quite different from the doctor's or the nurse's interpretation of the answer, which actually may affect the treatment. Thus we must be careful about the definitions of the consequences in going from 4 to 5 for example.

The Beaufort wind scale is another example of measuring, concerning the strength of wind (1 to 12). In open sea it is relatively easy to define the steps of the scale with respect to physical consequences (given a relatively constant depth), the height of the waves, the structure of the waves, the production of froth and its behaviour in the wind. However using the same scale on land is more difficult since the physical effects depend on the topological characteristics of the area in question.

We ask the reader to consider these two examples with respect to the definition above of a general measure in order to do mathematical calculations. This does not mean that using such scales is worthless, on the contrary, but it requires experienced doctors and nurses to interpret the answers and they probably will use the answer in relation to other bodily and mental signs from the person giving the answer. For the Beaufort scale it is an analogous argumentation.

Thus such measuring scales can usually not be generalized without very specific definitions with respect to each step, which are attached to unambiguous questions and general signs even for unexperienced persons.

Measures have to be regarded with respect to the ultimate purpose of the measuring in a specific environment. There are two sides of the problem of a measure. On one hand the scale has to be defined with respect to some properties of the real world. On the other hand the relation between the actual measures has to be understood in relation to our interpretations in relation to a specific purpose. This gives rise to the question of generalization of a measure.

Clock time is basically based on the fact that the earth revolves around the sun. But its use varies in relation to different purposes. On a universal scale the local time phenomena on earth is of minor importance, also in different micro-sciences where things like half-life for certain substances may form a sort of clock independent of the revolution of the earth around the sun but still these scales are convertible into the more used media of measurement.

The convertibility of different mediums of measurements is dependent on the inertia of the measured structures and in natural sciences such structures are rather easy to find.

However measuring time in a social space–time is completely different. True that the clocks are the same but Ekstedt and Fusari (2010) show that a social time-concept is completely different from the physical, which is a consequence of defining humans as final causes? Consequently it is from a scientific physical/ mathematical perspective difficult, not to say impossible, to find some sort of global time index in social structures defined for individual agents as for aggregates.

Thus, first, in general, we may say that setting up a measure requires a carefully defined space where the measure can be assumed to hold globally, second, in comparing two spaces with the same measure requires that both spaces have the same dimensionality and the third condition is that a particular purpose of a particular measurement must be defined within the frames which are defined for the space that is relevant for the measure.

When we then pass over to economics, we use prices as a measure of the dimension, which the medium of measurement is supposed to measure. Prices are on one hand supposed to reflect some value intrinsic to an item; on the other prices are a relative value of purchase in relation to other commodities. Describing the use of money in this way seems in fact rather close to what is supposed to be the message of the neoclassical theory. If we were satisfied with this imprecise statement, the whole analysis turns out to become an empirical matter close to sociological studies. The neoclassical axiomatic structure however is much more specific since it assures us that for a random agent the link between the inner sensations of value can be uniquely linked to a commodity set in the outside world, and this link is independent of the context.

Thus there is a basic problem in economics with respect to measures. If we choose a theoretical approach where economics is a subset of sociology we risk that we end up in a multitude of temporal and local measures which are non-compatible. On the other hand we actually have a really important thing which is unique to economics compared to other social sciences and that is the very exchange of money for commodities in a broad meaning. This very point of exchange is the very core of economics and it seems that economic science should flock around *money as "the measure"*. The measure of what is more difficult to say but as scientists we have to admit the excitement of scrutinizing such a thing.

We can look at the neoclassical theory as a consistent basis for a measure. However at difference to measures regarding the nature, which we exemplified above, the neoclassical basis build on an a priori axiomatic structure and even worse the measure is only relevant given a particular general equilibrium.

Consequently, to grant that money is to be used in the neoclassical way, neutral and with a value fulfilling a condition of homogeneity of degree zero and consistent irrespective of aggregate level, the neoclassical axiomatic structure is necessary. Hence when we reject the axiomatic structure, money loses the foundation on which it can be used as a consistent measure, given the definition of a general measure. Furthermore conclusions based on the axiomatic structure have no logical relation to the empirical truth value of the proposition even if it is a strictly logical conclusion with respect to the axioms. To have such a logical relation we must first prove that the axiomatic structure has a global relevance.

Economists are sometimes criticized for using concepts as utility, preferences, maximization and optimization. We think that these concepts may well be defended, and we will in fact use them in our suggestion for a different foundation of money. What we criticize is the axiomatic link between what happens in the agent's head and the outside world in the form of a commodity basket. Most probably it is actually sensible to assume a link between the inner sensations of the value with the outer relative value in purchasing terms but this link is not unique, neither in space nor time. However it is realistic to expect that during periods of social and cultural stability when there might be a considerable degree of inertia we may have patterns which work as if the neoclassical axioms were relevant.

Our analysis of Allais' and Arrow's respective paradoxes will lead us to question the nature of the measurable space derived from the neoclassical axioms and consequently we have to discuss more closely the conditions for a money measure.

In fact our fundamental conclusion will be that the concept of money only is meaningful in a general state of disequilibrium. That however doesn't mean that we slip into a chaos but that we need to find the stability creating forces outside what we regard as the normal realm of economic theory.

Measurement and aggregation

Particularly Arrow's paradox concerns the problem of aggregation and this problem is one of the key problems of theoretical conflicts in economic science. The neoclassical theory suggests, given a consistent treatment of the axioms, that we may use additive aggregation and thus optima of all individual agents and the aggregate society will appear at the same price vector. This is the central issue of Arrow's paradox.

When we discuss aggregation and the use of prices (as a measure) the reversibility of the analysis becomes a tricky issue. In Figure 1.1 we make a point of the difference between causal analysis and logical analysis. The former is always asymmetric and thus irreversible in the empirical world while the latter is, unless specific precautions are postulated, symmetric and reversible. Thus in a logical analysis the propositions can be regarded as axioms from which we may derive the former axioms as propositions. A cause may give rise to different effects depending on the environment, but this must be added as basically empirical information.

Aggregation can be performed in many ways. From a mathematical point of view the problem of aggregation is present in derivation and aggregation. Let us look at a simple polynomial derivation/aggregation, in Table 1.1.

The simple example is interesting because the derivation process, when we know the exact function leads to an exact result. The opposite operation, going from a known local solution to the global function is indeed uncertain and requires considerable extra information about the parameters a, b and c. Thus given the figure "6" it is normally very difficult to say anything about the

Table 1.1 Fundamental problem of derivation and aggregation

Derivation	Aggregation
$y = f(x) = x^3$	$Y = F(x) = 6$
$f'(x) = 3 \times x^2$	$F^1(x) = 6 \times x + a$
$f'(x) = 6 \times x$	$F^2(x) = 3 \times x^2 + a \times x + b$
$f''(x) = 6$	$F^3(x) = x^2 + \dfrac{a}{2} \times x^2 + b \times x + c$

structure of $F^3(x)$. However the axiomatic structure of the neoclassical theory makes these two processes reversible.

When we regard measures and particularly money as a medium of measurement we can say that given additive aggregation as in the neoclassical theory we may expect that the measure is of exactly the same character on the microscopic level as they are on the macroscopic. However if we deny the possibility of additive aggregation we also deny reversibility of the derivation/aggregation process and in such a case we are apt to believe that the measure, whatever it is but particularly money, can be used in different ways on different aggregate levels and that there is no common logical ground for money as a measure. In fact if we can reject additive aggregation we have lost the common ground for money as a medium of measurement on different aggregate levels.

Whether we accept the challenges implicit in the quotations from Wicksell and Arrow and Hahn is a bit difficult to say, since we actually do not regard money as a concept within narrow economic frames but a part of the institutional structure of a society and most of all we will claim that the concept of money is not a concept of an equilibrium theory but plays a central part in economic disequilibrium, and a general theory of disequilibrium seems rather impossible to invent.

The general methodological feature

In fact very few approaches in economic analysis are new in the meaning that they stem from the last 50 years. The quantity theory of money is rather explicitly settled by the Dominican friars of Salamanca. They were followed by the so-called bulionists in England during the early nineteenth century with Ricardo as a top name and they were consequently attacked by the anti-bullionists where we find Adam Smith. Somewhere in a middle position we find one of the most interesting historical economists dealing explicitly with money, Henry Thornton, died 1815, who was a banker and in some sense the first Keynesian. He wrote his huge work on paper credit in England in 1802, the year after Jean Baptiste Say's monumental work on political economy was published. Say and Thornton can both be regarded as non-equilibrium economists and give a rather similar view of monetary questions. It is somewhat a mystery that Jean Baptiste Say has become the main figure in general equilibrium theory through his alleged law. In this book we dismiss that opinion categorically and although Keynes' criticism of Say's law in its neoclassical setting gave rise to the interesting and important dimensionality problem in economic theory, Keynes did not interpret Say particularly faithfully and in fact Keynes is completely dependent of Say in his original discussion of the alleged law for the multiplier analysis.

We have chosen to study the earlier analysts rather carefully since they were theorizing from scratch so to say. We thus link our different discussions of the current economy to historical economists in order to understand the development of the theory. This means also that we can establish two types of economic theorizing: those who link economic analysis to a broader social analysis and those who close the economy into a sort of Newtonian equilibrium system.

As it should be we start our exposé of Money in Economic Theory in Aristotle's writings. In relation to Adam Smith it is remarkable to see that Smith does not seem to add anything to Aristotle's analysis of money, save from applying it to the relevant environment of the eighteenth century. However we quoted Wicksell's doubts on the existence of a theory of money which more or less was repeated by Arrow and Hahn and that has triggered a curiosity of why it has become like that. Thus we have dug somewhat deeper in the economic research up to Ricardo. Adam Smith is said to have given birth to economics as a science, something which Jean Baptiste Say does not agree to. According to him the baby was already in the cradle, put there by David Hume, and Smith only nourished it. Anyway since we in this book particularly attack the equilibrium concept it is of value to observe that we may see a line of equilibrium theoreticians from Aristotle (only implicitly) to Smith who explicitly brought in Newton's concept of equilibrium and then to Ricardo who put the theory in a systematic form which was developed by the neoclassicists. But there is also a strong line of what we may call disequilibrium economists, emphasizing the dynamics, from the friars of Salamanca, who to some extent broke with Aristotle and St Thomas, to David Hume followed by Thornton and Say who looked at the monetary economy as an important part of the transformation of the society. Thus the introduction of money also induced a mean which was of substantial importance in the socialization process and consequently money was basically seen as creating dynamics of a non-equilibrium character.

The structure of the book

In Chapter 2 we start with a short review of approaches to money during different historical periods. Thus we start with Aristotle and then jump to the Dominican friars of Salamanca during the sixteenth century and their important question of how the economy of Spain could be so bad despite the huge inflow of gold from America.

We then compare the two eighteenth century giants in England, Adam Smith and David Hume, with respect to their approach to money. Adam Smith's approach was to a large extent taken by Ricardo who developed economics into a kind of Newtonian system, which at those times was the highest form of science. It is however interesting to note the difference in Ricardo's writings before and after the Napoleonic wars, since Ricardo after the wars was involved in the restoration of the state finances in England. As earlier said we then present the two "disequilibrium" economists Henry Thornton and Jean Baptiste Say.

We then end the historical overview with Knut Wicksell who can be seen as on the threshold to the modern analysis.

Chapters 3 and 4 are discussions of the neoclassical theory and the macroeconomic theory respectively and their specific approaches to money. Our hypothesis is that the different examples of ill treatment of money and monetary matters are to be searched in the basic structures of the different approaches attitude to the *real economy*. Thus in fact by defining the structure of the real economy money as a complex concept becomes in a certain way superfluous. In Chapter 3 we analyse the neoclassical approach particularly with respect to Arrow's paradox and by introducing the concept of epistemic cycles we can, by using Russell's paradox, reject additive aggregation and thus we allow for the existence of optimum at given aggregate level independently of other levels. This also implies that money gets a more active role in the theory and we end up in discussing extensions within the neoclassical theory to make the theory more dynamic thus giving room for money. we then arrive at what we call the *mereological rule of thumb*. Chapter 4 is to a great extent devoted to the IS-LM analysis, particularly Hick's first version which laid the ground for the neoclassical synthesis. Subsequently to this we analyse the complex of inflation and unemployment. Particularly we pay attention to permanent unemployment. This will become the basis for discussing the potential conflict between the three intrinsic features of money: medium of exchange, liquidity and accounting/valuation.

Chapter 5 is to be seen as a kind of conclusion with respect to the analysis of Chapters 2 and 3. We particularly discuss the three intrinsic features of money and also the measurement problem, particularly with respect to inflation. With respect to the concept of liquidity we discuss risk and uncertainty.

Chapter 6 deals exclusively with the meaning of concepts of risk and uncertainty and in Chapter 7 we introduce future contracts and here we are able to express the full conflict of the intrinsic features in money and Amoroso's wording on the dead city ruling the living becomes the key issue. In Chapter 7 we also say some words on globalization. Theoretically globalization does not imply any difference in kind of the analysis of money but more in magnitudes. Uncertainty as well as opportunities increase and cultural exchange and friction are causes of new commodity dimensions. Furthermore the nations become partially fragmented since important agents become more dependent on the environment than of the home nation.

Chapter 8 finally is to be seen as a roundup of the book.

This book has no intention to tell "what money really is", we will not reach an ultimate goal to arrive at what Arrow and Hahn call "a serious theory of money". The reason is simple; the very character of money is all the time changing somehow and somewhere, due to the fact that humans are acting subjects, a notion which we must regard with utmost care from a methodological and logical point of view.

We will concentrate on discussing different aspects that concern money as it appears in different theoretical contexts and thereby hopefully be able to pose questions which perhaps can start a journey towards "a serious theory of money". Since we regard human beings as subjects, they are to be regarded as final causes. Also collective expressions of culture are ultimately to be regarded as local and temporal, but having said that there is also in human affairs considerable inertia which makes historical parallels of at least educative value.

Thus we may learn from earlier theorizing and practical experiences but every slice of time has its own characteristic feature, more or less inert, which means that the understanding of money changes with respect to inherent characteristics, due to socioeconomic and legal changes, which also change the very questions which seem to be relevant. This prevents us from developing a grand general theory since the inventiveness of the agents will probably change the foundations for such a theory before it is even settled.

2 The understanding of money

A retrospective glance

Introduction

The question of commodity money, usually metallism, versus chartalism has historically been of great importance and provoked rather intense discussions. Ludwig von Mises, who is one of the illustrious proponents for gold standard, writes (2007 [1949]: 483):

> The struggle against gold which is one of the main concerns of all contemporary governments must not be looked upon as an isolated phenomenon. It is but one item in the gigantic process of destruction which is the mark of our time. People fight the gold standard because they want to substitute national autarky for free trade, war for peace, totalitarian government omnipotence for liberty.

Another drastic view on the nature of money, from our days, 2009, is Katsuhito Iwai (2009: 11, 24).

> Commodity theory asserts that a certain thing functions as a general medium of exchange because it is useful commodity that has a value independent of its use as money. Cartal theory in opposition, asserts that a certain thing serves as a medium of exchange because its use as money is approved by communal agreement or decreed by the head of kingdom or sanctioned by legal order. Although historians of monetary theory have been busy in classifying past authors on monetary matters into these two camps, we now know that both theories are wrong. – This brings us back once again to Keynes' beauty contest. The liquidity of demand deposits is supported by exactly the same bootstrapping process that supports money as money; just as money is money merely because everybody believes everybody else believes it is money, demand deposits has liquidity because every depositor believes every other depositor believes it has liquidity.

Both these views are pretty drastic in their formulations and both are basically built on their respective underlying views of the capitalistic market economy.

Von Mises was a passionate defender of freedom from state oppression and saw the free market as a cornerstone. The year of publishing the book 1949 also makes it easy to understand this after what has happened in Europe.

Iwai is an equally devoted analyst advocating the view of the inherent instability of capitalism, and from the date of the paper 2009 it is perhaps equally easy to understand the vigour of his analysis.

The mysterious money

Although we in the microscopic theory of economics hardly mention money as a theoretical concept, it is easy to link our everyday understanding of money vis-à-vis relative prices and a budget restriction. However when we introduce cash balances, as from everyday experiences, we are already in theoretical trouble; in traditional optimization problem of the households given consistence preference structure, money appears as a residual with respect to prices and can be any of the commodities in the households' basket, thus the cash balance is meaningless.

When we look at macroeconomic theory money plays a more prominent role; we discuss interest rates and liquidity preference, quantity of money and velocity of circulation. However when we try to close the theoretical gap between the microscopic and the macroscopic theory the two logical structures are seemingly ill-fit.

One route of thinking is to basically accept the microeconomic theory and its particular form of additive aggregation and add the quantity theory of money which deals explicitly with the quantity and circulation of money. Monetarist theory has evolved into an interesting solution, which implies that as long as markets are free and work properly according to the neoclassical theory, we can handle macroeconomic problems of inflation and unemployment solely through manipulating the quantity of money, although the used concepts are seemingly contradictory to the neoclassical axiomatic structure.

Consequently many theoreticians get a gnawing unrest when looking at this reasoning and start to ask whether it is possible to add one theoretical approach to another where the theoretical concepts of one don't even exist in the other. This has raised questions of whether we really have a consistent theory of money in economic theory.

An early proponent for these doubts is the Swedish economist Knut Wicksell who wrote:

> I already had my suspicions – which were strengthened by a more thorough study of the writings of Tooke and his followers – that, as an alternative to the Quantity Theory, there is no complete and coherent theory of money. If the Quantity Theory is false – or to the extent it is false – there is so far available only one false theory of money and no true theory.
>
> (1936 [1893] p. xxiii)

Unfortunately Wicksell's words are still highly relevant. Thus the almost axiomatic inclusion of the quantity theory in the neoclassical building is a theoretical mystery and furthermore the adding of supposed Keynesian concepts of liquidity and even uncertainty is indeed mysterious from a logical point of view. In their fundamental study of economic theory in its neoclassical setting, *General Competitive Analysis*, Kenneth Arrow and Frank Hahn wrote in the concluding chapter with the title "The Keynesian Model": "If a serious monetary theory comes to be written, the fact that contracts are made in money will be of a considerable importance" (1971: 356–7).

Our quotation from Wicksell expresses the same mood, although more than 70 years earlier.

The rather recent advancements in financial theory have to some extent widened our understanding of money with respect to future contracts when the modern portfolio analysis based on the theoretical achievements by Black, Scooles, Merton and Samuelson mainly based on thermodynamic models of heath distribution, that is a sort of *diffusion process*, has been developed by Hobson-Rogers, Heston and others into a completely different form of theoretical thinking where the models are calibrated to mirror the actual behaviour in the form of expected values and volatilities, for example on a daily basis, and then used under the assumption of temporal inertia.[1] Thus there are no postulated causes for uncertainty but an effort to catch the gist of the *apprehended uncertainty* of the market which then is used as a basis for future pricing. This gives us a different causal and mathematical structure in comparison with the analysis in the mainstream neoclassical as well as Keynesian theory although it might be seen as a way of handling Keynes' discussions of uncertainty and "degree of rational belief" (Keynes 1962 [1921]: 10–15).

However when entering an analysis of the inconsistencies of money and money matters in economic theory our basic approach is the insight that the inconsistencies do not depend on a lack of an understanding of money per se, but instead it is a fruit of more fundamental inconsistencies in economic theory. The problems of handling money in the neoclassical theory, for example, follow more or less directly from the axiomatic structure of the theory.

As we will see, and this is also to a large extent mirrored in the quotes from von Mises and Iwai; the theorizing on money and money matters is to a great degree dependent on two dimensions which are not necessarily independent of each other: the basic one is the judgement with respect to the inherent stability of the market economy, particularly the capitalistic market economy, and the other is the question of the eligibility of state control.[2] As we understand the latter dimension is partly linked to the judgement of the stability of the market but it also contains the question of using monetary policy for other public goals than stabilization policy, such as allocation of capital by asymmetric interest or quantitative means, and we have also as an example the discussion in the US, during the late 1980s, to relax the conditions for household borrowing as a means to redistribute welfare.

Thus even when we start a very rudimentary discussion on the nature of money in terms of the question of commodity money or fiat money we are stuck in theoretical and ideological superstructures from which it is hard to emancipate.

The quotes from Wicksell and Arrow and Hahn display ambivalence towards the ability of the economic theory to anticipate the full importance of money. We do have theories of prices and interests alongside monetary theory but as we have mentioned there is some unrest whether we really catch the full understanding of the monetary economy in economic theory.

Let us directly establish, as a kind of metaphysical belief, that it is very difficult to grasp the consequences of transforming the global and even regional and local economies into a pure barter economy, thus we implicitly hold as a fact that during a foreseeable time we have to deal with monetary economies both in theory and reality.

When it comes to the physical form of money we may discuss commodity money and fiat money, and also different measures of the money stock but what about such things as plastic cards? Travelling abroad may involve several types of transactions: paying with a debit card linked to an account in your home-country bank, paying with a credit card not linked to any account but based on trust in both directions, paying cash in a foreign country where you get money from a cash machine using a card linked to an account in a bank in a third country, to which you can transfer money from your home-country bank via internet operations. It is certainly a bit more complex than using stones as Keynes gives an example of in the beginning of *A Treatise on Money* (Keynes 1953 [1930]: 14). Thus the modern money transactions to a large extent involve what can be named accounting money, the simultaneous manipulations of accounts in different bodies, to which also can be added the operations on the financial market of derivatives of different kind where the link to physical money sometimes is difficult to detect particularly if we want links to the quantity of money in a specific currency.

The nature of money is indeed changing. The very change of the nature of money provokes of course a discussion of the inherent stability of different money systems. It also provokes the question of who has the ultimate power in a particular system or at least the classical question "*Cui Bono?*"

Some methodological issues

We will not discuss a complete historical exposé over the development of the theory of money, and pass lightly over *secula seculorum* just making stops where we meet some important thinker, who is well established among modern scholars as of importance for modern analysis. Often these thinkers have appeared during profound changes in the life of the societies, when the social change and intellectual revolutions have called for a systematic rethinking.

Few concepts and theoretical approaches are particularly new in economic theory. Concerning money the quantity identity $M \cdot V \equiv P \cdot Y$ was in fact discussed by the Dominican friars of Salamanca in the seventeenth century, David Hume in the eighteenth, Henry Thornton and J.S. Mill in the nineteenth and Friedman in the twentieth. During this time the institutional structures have been radically changed and it would seem quite remarkable if the quantity identity by different assumptions could be transformed into a theory which covered all times.

This actually gives rise to a methodological principle concerning development of theories of which the roots are long back in history. In physics for example the scientific development must be rather strongly related to earlier theoretical achievement though the physical world is rather inert. When it comes to economics however the structure of the society changes socially, institutionally and technically and thus the concepts and theoretical questions in economic science ought to undergo revisions with respect to the understanding of used concepts. More particularly this affects the reading and understanding of historically famous economists. Bertrand Russell (1996 [1946]: 173) when he writes about Aristotle begins

> In reading an important philosopher, but most of all in reading Aristotle, it is necessary to study him in two ways: with reference to his predecessors, and with reference to his successors. In the former aspect, Aristotle's merits are enormous; in the latter, his demerits are equally enormous. For his demerits, however, his successors are more responsible than he is.

These words could be said about any of the economists we are dealing with in this chapter. One example comes to mind, Jean Baptiste Say and his famous/illfamous Say's law, where an interesting and sensitive discussion of the diffusion of money in a society has been transformed to an axiomatic principle for a barter economy. All the famous historical economists that we will discuss in this chapter were often in the centre of political and economic developments of their societies and discussed the current experiences, but they were also aware of achievements in philosophy and most of all they were very aware of the institutional framework in which they were discussing economic theory.

Thus when Hume for instance discusses the quantity theory he does so from his particular world; taking his discussion literally and transforming it unchanged into our world demerits indeed Hume's work, but we cannot blame him but his successors.

In our historical exposé we will watch up for the usual assumed inherent characteristics which seem to be generic in respect of money: *medium of exchange, liquidity/store of value, medium of valuation* and *accounting*.

Aristotle

Money and money markets are old inventions in social affairs and consequently we will find that Aristotle has touched on it quite extensively although a bit reluctantly "The discussion of such matters is not unworthy of philosophy, but to be engaged in them practically is illiberal and irksome" (Aristotle (1990 [334–324 BC]: 452, Bno. 1258[b]).[3]

In his politics he describes the successive growth of barter from simple commodity barter to more complex barter when "inhabitants of one country became more dependent on those of another", and consequently the use of a medium of exchange to simplify the exchange process is practical and even necessary. He looks upon the ordinary market exchange, seen as barter, as a necessity "from the circumstance that some has too little, others too much" (ibid.: 451, no. 1257ª).

On money

The existence of money is granted by a convention to have an equalizing medium of exchange and valuation.

> But money has become a convention a sort of representative of demand; and this why it has the name "money" (νόμισμα) because it exists not by nature but by law (νόμος) and it is our power to change it and make it worthless.
>
> (ibid.: 381, no. 1133ª)

Although Aristotle only discusses metal coins he has a cartalist attitude. Money "becomes in a sense an intermediate; for it measures all things ... how many shoes are equal to a house or to a given amount of food" (380–1, no. 1133ª).

As a basis for the actual relative valuation Aristotle uses the value of labour as an anchor, the exchange values ought to reflect the relative content in a commodity of labour efforts. But he has an interesting wording possibly indicating a sort of market valuation:

> There will, then, be reciprocity when the terms have been equated so that as farmer is to shoemaker, the amount of the shoemaker's work is to that of the farmers work for which it exchanges. But we must not bring them into a figure of proportion when they have already exchanged (otherwise one extreme will have both excesses), but when they still have their own goods.
>
> (ibid.: 381, no. 1133ª–1133ᵇ)

In any case he touches on a sort of *ex ante/ex post* reasoning.

The existence of a medium of exchange also implies that it becomes an intertemporal store of value but the value of money may also be affected. But how about future markets, has he something to say with respect to such modern theoretical inventions?

> And for the future exchange – that if we do not need a thing now we shall have it if ever we do need it – money is as it were our surety; for it must be possible for us to get what we want by bringing the money. Now the same thing happens to money itself as to goods – it is not always worth the same; yet it tends to be steadier.
>
> (Ibid.: 381, no. 1133ᵇ)

Wealth-getting

Introduction of the medium of exchange implies the possibility of retail trade and a new art of getting wealth. Barter as such has nothing to do with "the art of getting wealth". However when the medium of exchange is introduced retail trade developed and so the art of wealth-getting:

> When the use of coin had once been discovered, out of the barter of neces-
> sary articles arose the other art of wealth-getting, namely retail trade; which
> was at first probably a simple matter, but became more complicated as soon
> as men learned by experience whence and by what exchanges the greatest
> profit might be made.
>
> (ibid.: 451, no. 1257[b])

This distinction leads him to distinguish between natural wealth-getting and the acquisition of coins. The former has to do with the management of the household while the latter is linked to retail trade and produces wealth by the exchange process in itself, and he concludes paragraph 1258[b], by saying

> There are two sorts of wealth-getting, as I have said; one is a part of the
> household management, the other retail trade: the former necessary and hon-
> ourable, while that which consists in exchange is justly censured; for it is
> unnatural, and a mode by which men gain from one another. The most hated
> sort, and with the greatest reason, is usury, which makes gain out of money
> itself, and not from the natural object of it. For money was intended to be
> used in exchange, but not to increase at interest.
>
> (ibid.:. 452, 1258[a]–1258[b])

This quote is very important since it led St Thomas d'Aquinas to reject money exchange and craving interest on loans. This ban was lifted by the friars of Sala-manca, during the sixteenth century, which we discuss later. It is also interesting to note that he indicates a possible conflict in the very concept of money.

From Aristotle we can thus draw some conclusions with respect to market actions and money. First, money is a medium of exchange simplifying commodity exchange of vastly disparate kinds of commodities. Second, money is an abstraction which makes it possible to have a common measure for otherwise incommensurable commodities. This measure holds to some extent also for a future exchange operation, although there is no reason that the "value" of money is always constant but undergoes variation. At the same time it is more stable than the exchange values of non-monetary commodities and thus provides some kind of security. A third conclusion is that money is based on conventions and laws and eventual intrinsic value is of no relevance. A fourth conclusion is interesting; the *ex ante* price of the market transactions is not necessarily equal to the *ex post* price and there is a possibility of excess demand/supply *ex post*.

Finally concerning prices he links the relative price of an item to its relative content of labour, which will be basic to just and natural prices (ibid.: 381, no. 1134[a]). This is of importance when we later discuss Adam Smith and his followers.

With respect to the question of chartalism or metallism Aristotle in his distinction between natural money and law money lays down some form of development direction into a more complex society. Thus the use of precious metals represents a prior step in development of the society.

The Salamanca School

The Muslim philosopher Averroes introduced Aristotle's thinking into Europe (Spain) during the twelfth century and Thomas d'Acquina more or less canonized Aristotle's philosophy within the Roman Catholic church.[4] Thus the labour theory of value came to dominate. The church was reluctant to accept a value reflecting exchange conditions since that was close to retail trade, which Aristotle condemns as a form of greediness, searching gain for its own sake.

However in the sixteenth century Spain had a great inflow of wealth, particularly precious metals, from America which more or less forced the intellectuals, particularly in Spain and its leading university of Salamanca, to analyse the ongoing economic dynamics. The inflow of precious metals didn't produce the expected wealth and prosperity, either for Spain or for the majority of its population. Marjorie Grice-Hutchinson begins her book on the School of Salamanca by saying:

> If there was one economic lesson which the whole Spanish nation had learned by the middle of the sixteenth century, it was that the value of money is fickle and that gold and silver are not synonymous with wealth, a lesson made all the more bitter by the high hopes that had attended the discovery of the New World a few decades before. The dream of El Dorado had been followed by a harsh awakening.
>
> (Grice-Hutchinson 1952: 1)

However it provoked analysis and particularly money and money matters were at the top of the agenda in the intellectual centres of the economic analysis of those times. We will mainly follow Marjorie Grice-Hutchinson in the description of the thoughts and use the ancient texts she has added to her analysis. Many of the different authors within the School of Salamanca were friars, mainly from the Dominican orders and consequently the Aristotelian analysis was the basic doctrine and in principle all analysis was checked against the Aquino/Aristotelian foundation. Nevertheless the contemporary economic and political dynamics called for a reconciliation of the doctrines with the facts of the world. Fortunately the friars and other intellectuals of the School of Salamanca were allowed a certain amount of intellectual freedom within the church.

The just price

First of all the School of Salamanca turned the Aristotelian discussion of the just price linked to its content of labour, to a price reflecting the demand/supply conditions. As we saw from the quotes from Aristotle he actually opens a possibility of such an interpretation in his admittance that money value undergoes changes and that there might be *ex post* surplus/shortage and for the pious friars of high intelligence this was a possible interpretation to use and still obey the dogmas of the church.

Luís Saravia de la Calle is very outspoken on the matter of what is to be regarded as a just price.

> Excluding all deceit and malice, the just price of a thing is the price which is commonly fetched at the time and place of the deal, in cash, and bearing in mind the particular circumstances and manner of sale, the abundance of goods and money, the number of buyers and sellers, the difficulty of procuring the goods, and the benefit to be enjoyed by their use, according to an honest man.
>
> (ibid.: 79)

Then he discusses price differences depending on different places and whether the merchandise is abundant or scarce there. He also distinguishes between the place where the goods are situated and the place where the contract is drawn up and signed. Furthermore he points out that "time alone raises or lowers the price of a thing" (ibid.: 80). But most important he completely rules out the Aristotelian "just price" as linked to labour costs:

> Those who measure the just price by the labour, costs, and risk by the person who deals in the merchandise or produce it, or by the cost of transport or expense of travelling to and from their industry, risk and labour, are greatly in error, and still more so are those who allow a certain profit of a fifth or a tenth. For the just price arouses from the abundance or scarcity of goods, merchants, and money, as had been said, and not from costs, labour, and risk. If we had to consider labour and risk in order to assess the just price, no merchant would ever suffer loss, nor would abundance or scarcity of goods and money enter into the question.
>
> (ibid.: 82)

A second text by Domingo de Soto (ibid.: 83–8) arrives at the same conclusions on the proper basis of quotations from Aristotle and Augustine.

Making profit on money exchange

The second point where the reality was at variance with Aristotle and the dogmas of the church was the problem of making profits of money exchange.

Martin de Azpilcueta Navarro (ibid.: 90) accepts the Aristotelian description of the development of money but in making a reference to his own time he observes that

> money of a particular country came to be worth less there than abroad (as today nearly all the gold and silver of Spain is worth less in Spain than in

Flanders and France), there came into being the art of exchange, which is the art of giving and taking one kind of money in exchange for another.

Under these circumstances he realizes that money exchange is a necessity and "benefits the republic to some extent". The theoretical acceptance is taken in two steps vis-á-vis Aristotle and St Thomas. First profits have to be allowed so although "Aristotle disapproved of this art of exchange" and "St Thomas, too, condemned all business whose main object is gain for gain's sake" he claims that "even St. Thomas allows that the merchant's trade is lawful so long as he undertakes it for a moderate profit, in order to maintain himself and his family" (ibid.: 90).

The next step is then to make money-change a respectful business:

> Nor is it true that to use money by changing it at a profit is against nature. Although this is not the first and principal use for which money was invented, it is none the less an important secondary use.
>
> (ibid.: 91)

It might seem astonishing that Navarro could turn so to say 180° and still remain in the church, but a good help for Navarro in his ethical analysis of money exchange was St Thomas' distinction of the goodness or badness of the will. Thus Thomas asks "Is the goodness or badness of action due to its object?" His answer is then

> It seems not. 1. An action does not seem to derive goodness or badness from its object, for the object of an action is a thing, and evil is not in things but in the use of them by sinners, as Augustine says in On Christian Doctrine.
>
> (Aquinas 1998 [1271]: 568)

The value of money

Navarro also explicitly deals with metal money and its value. He gives eight reasons why the money of two countries may have different values of which for our purposes the fourth is interesting. Different countries imply different demand/supply condition both with respect to ordinary commodities and money. Thus Navarro distinguishes between the place from where the commodity is actually delivered and the place where the contract is signed. The latter he regards as the most important since the valuation of money at this place is the decisive factor for the price agreement. He discusses which causes there are for money to rise or fall in value and he mentions four reasons. First, very pious, that it seems to be a law of God and Nature. Second he explains that if money is sold or exchanged by some form of contracts it obeys the law of supply and demand as ordinary commodities. Third, he claims that if there is scarcity of money in one country all other commodities, labour included, will be traded for less money as compared to the situation that money were abundant. Fourth, concerns the relation of gold and silver coins. If there is a shortage of gold more silver coins (or other metals) will be given in exchange. Causes two to four are in fact basic to a kind of quantity theory of money.

Tomás de Mercado's analysis is along Navarro's lines and he underlines the abundance or scarcity of silver. Fransisco Garcia adds another concept to Navarro's analysis, that of whether the money is at a place where it is subject to risk or not.

Why was Spain poor in spite of all the gold?

Martín Gonzáles de Cellorgio was concerned about the reasons why Spain, in spite of the inflow of precious metals, became poor.

> This is because we will not understand the true wealth does not lie in the possession of great quantities of gold and silver (whether wrought, coined or in bullion) which are destroyed as they are consumed, but in the possession of things which, even if they are consumed by use, are yet preserved in kind by the medium of substitution, which enables us to take gold and silver from out of the hands of friends and enemies, just as we negligently allowed them to be snatched from our own.
>
> (ibid.: 108–9)

He doesn't regard money as truly wealth but as a necessity of exchange in foreign trade, and thus he regards a balanced trade as a necessity for sustainability of the wealth of a country and proceeds "If, as the law says, it [money] was invented only to facilitate contracts, then it is the cause and not the effect of exchange" (ibid.: 109). The use of money was not the cause of the poverty in Spain but the misuse since the inflow of precious metals and thus abundance of money facilitated or even opened up the possibility for international trade but this trade should have been effectively paid by exporting other commodities, thus the gold and silver should have been maintaining and increasing the production potentials of Spain, otherwise the money, gold or silver will be "snatched for our hands" with nothing left after the commodities are consumed. He also criticizes the thought that the wealth of the State is augmented by variations of the quantity of money in circulation. The central point in his discussion is to keep money in a stable relation to the supply/demand of commodities, hence Martín González de Cellorgio also provides us with a rudiment of a quantity theory.

However the money exchange in itself was a necessity for foreign trade. The money-price, irrespective of metal-value, was dependent on the relation between the quantity of money and commodity supply/demand and this was in its turn affected by the supply/demand conditions of the money market. Thus what the friars of the Salamanca School point at, is the necessity of an export production which keeps the prices at the international market stable, paying export with precious metals comes to an end because of the decreasing price of these metals in real terms.

Furthermore in international trade the real value of money is the important thing. Thus money exchange will in fact be equilibrating the real value of money in different countries and this would be necessary to stop the outflow of precious metals from Spain though the money value of a commodity there was much higher than in other parts of Europe.

David Hume 1711–1776

Adam Smith is seen as the initiator of the modern market theory and contemporary to Hume. His most famous work *Wealth of Nations* was first published 1776, the same year as Hume died. Thus Hume's *Essays* was published 24 years earlier. Hume and Smith were friends and in a letter, on the death of Hume, to Willian Stracham he expressed his deep friendship as well as high respect for Hume's philosophical thinking.[5] Hume strongly influenced Smith with respect to moral philosophy, while Smith in his economic writings appeared more rationalistic.

Hume and Smith were partly contemporary with Newton, who died 1727. They were both affected by Newton although Hume kept himself more distant to letting Newton influence his philosophy, which was rather sceptical towards general models of humans since he rejected reason as the prime cause of action but advocated that reason was the humble servant of passion. Furthermore his thorough analysis of causality made him sceptical of inductive reasoning.[6] Smith on the other hand was more influenced by the Newtonian equilibrium system, also since it was in the line of Aristotelian analysis of money, which could be developed into a rationalistic analysis.[7] "The invisible hand" discussed by Smith is virtually impossible in Hume's analysis and may be seen as a consequence of Smith's rationalism.[8]

This is also natural from what we earlier said about their respective reception of Newton's synthesis on the laws of physics and its consequences for general philosophical thinking. Irrespective of this however Smith was influenced by Hume in his economic thinking and both were strongly advocating free trade both within and between countries. A free and dynamic market was not only increasing the quantity of commodities but most of all the quality and the diversity of commodities and had both an educative and stabilizing effect on the individual mind as well as in making the society more powerful and stable. However there are, as we will see, distinct differences, which most probably have their root in the differences of their philosophical approaches.

On money

As Adam Smith, Hume sees the industriousness of people and their free disposal of what is produced for own purposes or taking to the market, as the basic wealth of a society. Hume is very outspoken on this subject:

Now, according to the most natural course of things, industry and arts and trade encrease the power of the sovereign as well as the happiness of the subjects; and that policy is violent, which aggrandizes the public by the poverty of the individuals.

(Hume 1770: Essay I Of Commerce: 12)

Regarding money he is affected by Aristotle, and we also see the links to the School of Salamanca.

> Money is not, properly speaking, one of the subjects of commerce; but only the instrument which men have agreed upon to facilitate the exchange of one commodity for another. It is none of the wheels of trade: It is the oil which renders the motion of the wheels more smooth and easy.

(ibid.: 45)

Thus pursuing an Aristotelian setting completed with the Salamanca friars' position on a Quantity Relation of Money. "If we consider any one kingdom by itself, it is evident, that the greater or less plenty of money is of no consequence; since the prices of commodities are always proportioned to the plenty of money" (ibid.: 43). Thus basically the quantity of money affects prices but has no influence on relative prices and the pricing of productive factors, hence money is neutral to the real economy, at least in its everyday use. As a matter of fact this statement by Hume is crucial with respect to the monetarist theory.

However it is also interesting to note that the *real* effect of money is on the relations between the microscopic and the macroscopic level; "It is only the *public* which draw its advantage from the greater plenty of money; and only in wars and negotiations with foreign states" (ibid.: 43, original emphasis).

On foreign trade

Hume is an eager proponent of international trade in developing the country:

> Foreign trade, by its imports, furnishes materials for new manufactures; and by its exports, it produces labour in particular commodities, which could not be consumed at home. In short, a kingdom, that has a large import and export, must abound more with industry, and that employed upon delicacies and luxuries, than a kingdom which rests contented with its native commodities.

(ibid.: 17)

Although Hume presupposes basically gold and silver standard in international trade for the transparency of prices, the import should be paid by export. Furthermore he is aware of the equalizing forces of trade.

A country which is superior in economic wealth to another has an advantage of developing industrial skill at a higher level and thus a more effective industry as a consequence of the harder competition created by the flourishing industry and commerce implying trade at lower profit margins. However this might in time be partly neutralized by the lower prices of goods and productive resources in the poorer countries, which may imply that the sinking profit margins in the richer countries induce flows of manufacturers who open production and business in the poorer countries.

Inflow of money from other countries as was the case when the mines of America were discovered causes a vitalization of merchants and manufacturers, "since the discovery of the mines of the mines in AMERICA, industry has encreased in all the nations of EUROPE, *except in the possessors of those mines*" (ibid.: 48, my emphasis). Here is implicitly a direct recognition of the analysis of the friars of Salamanca only from the other side so to say. Hume's analysis of the roles and effects of money is to a large extent parallel to that which appeared among the friars at the School of Salamanca.

The effect of an inflow of money as a consequence of increased foreign demand is described by Hume as a dynamic process of dispersion of the increased inflow to first merchants and manufacturers who tend to increase the supply thus hiring more labour which vitalizes also the internal markets causing the "new" money to be dispersed in the economy, thus also stimulating new ventures.

On bank money versus gold and silver money

Hume's attitude to bank/credit money is somewhat sceptical; his suspicions against an increase of bank money concern the effects on foreign trade. He means that an expansion of bank money may imply that the international commensurability of prices could be lost. His rejection is also based on the fact that such money will be subject to low or none convertibility in international trade. He is equally doubtful towards public securities which are as readily as the current price of gold and silver. The effects of public securities will thus become negative in the form of inflation and if placed in the hands of foreigners a restriction on the countries' financial affairs (ibid.: 138–42). Hume is advocating a metallist approach but that seems to be more a consequence of lack of international institutions and treaties than a theoretical conclusion.

Hume was however a sort of predecessor of the bullionist doctrine. Gold and other precious metals were themselves victims of market revaluations; thus an eventual intrinsic value was of no importance but the regulated market value. He advocated that the important feature was the constancy relation between the marketed commodities and the stock of money which ultimately was related to a quantity of gold. But the gold was not in the form of meticulous money defined in purity and form, stamped by proper authorities but large quantities of bars. Thus gold was basically a conventional norm but Hume displays not an opinion of money fully convertible into gold, which Smith did, and this was reflected in the later conflicts between the bullionists and advocators for real bills.

On this basis he discusses a form of rudimentary expansive monetary policy, changing the supply of money (coins) irrespectively of the foreign inflow. (ibid.: 51) Since decreasing money stock would set back the enthusiasm and industriousness of the agents Hume suggests a continuous growth of money (coins of less precious metals) of some 2 per cent per annum, which given a real annual growth of 2 per cent would leave the relation of money quantity and commodities unchanged. Thus the saying that Hume advocated a mildly inflationist policy is not correct since, when he describes the diffusion of money out to the market agents, he sees it as a slow process and mainly an effect of a growing market circulation of commodities, which should be the very purpose of the money increase.

In this discussion of the effects of money supply so to say for internal use, he compares different countries and note that those countries in Europe, German and Austrian dominions are taken as examples, who actually have a flourishing industry but where money is scarce or poorly used outside the centres of the country, has a poorly developed internal as well as external trade. This also weakens the nation as there is not enough money to pay for "fleets and armies" and generally it is difficult for the government (Prince) to levy taxes, since most of the landlords get their payments in kind and commerce if heavily built on barter. Such countries may have considerable production although it is poorly dispersed about the economy, thus causing both surpluses and scarcity.

We have an interesting parallel to Hume's analysis from Sweden during the seventeenth century, when King Gustavo II and his Chancellor Axel Oxenstierna were prepared to assign whole regions to the nobility since they were fed up with all taxes paid in kind and instead wanted to rely on enforced customs duties and fees in foreign trade and in markets in the cities, which were paid in silver or copper coins (Stolpe 1982: 105–6). This is in fact some kind of swaps, if we use modern terminology; the King was prepared to give the nobility the ownership of important parts of the rural production in exchange for taxes and customs duties paid in cash in order to pay the liabilities of the Crown. As a matter of fact the principle has some similarity to a basis swap between a peripheral currency and USD.

On interest

Some words about Hume's attitude to *interest*. As we have said Hume lacks an anchor for his analysis; thus there is no equilibrium and he has no reference to labour value and/or land rent. Consequently he cannot assume a natural rate of growth. Although he recommends an increase of the money stock of 2 per cent per annum the arguments for this were more to see as psychological. Subsequently the interest rate on credits is a function of demand and supply;

> High interest arises from *three* circumstances: A great demand for borrowing; little riches to supply that demand; and great profits arising from commerce. And these circumstances are a clear proof of the small advance of commerce and industry, not of the scarcity of gold and silver.

(ibid.: 65)

Obviously we may develop some natural rate of interest implicit in the above quote but if so it cannot be assumed to have any general bearing on the economy over time. In fact he has an interesting distinction of the causes of the level of the interest rates, where he approaches Wicksell's distinction between market rate and natural rate (ibid.: 72–6). According to Hume an extensive commerce implies high competition and high growth thus diminishing both low interest rate and a lowering of profit rates, and a subsequent lowering of prices. This produces growth of consumption and growth of industry and although the lower profit rate there is a higher profit stemming from the high growth, which alters both demand and supply for borrowed capital thus lowering the market interest rate.

The other case is when commerce is low and concentrated to few actors which implies a high supply of credits while the demand of credits is restrained by the low activity in commerce.

Hume's argumentation on the matter is coloured by the specific historical circumstances and thus requires some interpretation to link his analysis to Wicksell's theoretical achievements but Hume's distinctions are viable and clearly possible to develop into the Wicksellian tradition of thought. What is important in Hume's arguments is the distinct dynamic feature of the market process.

Concluding words

In the end of Hume's *Essays* of money he closes up his analysis on the virtues of the monetary economy within a state:

> It appears, that the want of money can never injure any state within itself: For men and commodities are the real strength of any community. It is the simple manner of living which hurts the public, by confining the gold and silver to few hands, and preventing its universal diffusion and circulation.
>
> (ibid.: 59)

An aspect to remember when we now pass over to describe Adam Smith's approach to money is that Hume on one hand concentrates on the growth and the effects of this growth in manufacturing and commerce and on the other hand has a very dynamic attitude to this where he clearly separates short-run from long-run aspects. His analysis is void of any equilibrium in the Newtonian respect and furthermore he regards prices as set entirely by the forces of supply and demand and thus has no anchor in the sense of labour value or land rent.

With respect to metallism versus chartalism Hume advocates an international gold standard based on agreed conventions, metal purity and weight; for internal trade he seems to lean towards a mixture of metalism and chartalism, mainly because of lack of confidence both of bank money as well as treasury bills as money equivalents.

Adam Smith 1723–1790

In chapter IV of Book One Smith links the growth of trade to the division of labour implying that the supply of the individuals exceeds the needs, which was the basis for barter exchange. However the inefficiency of the barter made it profitable with a medium of exchange. This start is well known and goes back to Aristotle. The following argumentation of different character of mediums of exchange leading to a preference for metals and furthermore the official control of weight and quality in the form of coins is also going back to Aristotle.

Smith distinguishes two kinds of value of commodities "The one may be called 'value in use' and the other 'value in exchange'." The *real price* of commodities "is the toil and trouble of acquiring it" (Smith 1952: 12–13).

He furthermore notes carefully that money as a measure is varying and can never be an accurate value. However labour is the real value of the commodity and money price is only a nominal value:

> Labour alone, therefore, never varying in its own value, is alone the ultimate and real standard by which the value of all commodities can at all times be estimated and compared. It is their real price, money is their nominal price only.
>
> (ibid.: 14)

Some lines further on he explains: "The labourer is rich or poor, is well or ill rewarded, in proportion to the real, not to the nominal price of his labour." This is in fact a very interesting distinction.

Smith also claims that when selling a land estate the price should always be in account of a perpetual rent of the same value, which should be based on the real yield of the estate in corn or equivalents and not in money which undergoes variations over time irrespective of if it is gold, silver or some other metal.

> A rent therefore reserved in corn is liable only to variations in the quantity of labour which a certain quantity of corn can purchase. But a rent reserved in any other commodity is liable not only to the variations in the quantity of labour which any particular quantity of corn can purchase, but to the variations in the quantity of corn which can be purchased by any particular quantity of the commodity.
>
> … The money price of labour, as I shall endeavour to show hereafter, does not fluctuate from year to year with the money price of corn, but seems everywhere accommodated, not to the temporal or occasional, but the average or ordinary price of that necessary of life.
>
> (ibid.: 15)

He also shows that the price of silver seldom varies year to year thus it has approximately the same stability as the "ordinary" price of corn.

On foreign trade

With respect to international trade Smith takes much the same views as Hume. However Smith more explicitly discusses the mercantilist system and more specifically the ruling Act of Navigation from 1651, which implied that trade between Britain and her colonies must be transported on British ships. The Dutch shipping was however superior to the British, so the act was enlarged to cover even trade between European mainland and Britain. This caused much annoyance for British merchants, since it was combined with high fees and taxes, thus ways to circumvent the restrictions were continuously invented. Nevertheless the long duration of the act had created a specific structure within both industry and merchant companies and when Smith discusses the superiority of free trade he takes, very prudently, into account the necessity of gradual change not to create instantaneous difficulties for industry, merchants and employed (ibid.: 192–201).

Generally speaking there are only two reasons for laying some burdens on foreign import; "The first is, when some particular industry is necessary for the defence of the country", and the second case is

> to lay some burden upon the foreign for the encouragement of domestic industry is, when some tax is imposed at home upon produce of the latter. In this case it seems reasonable that an equal tax should be imposed upon the like produce of the former.
>
> (ibid.: 198)

He then links the use of gold or principally any metal for that matter to foreign trade given it is properly standardized coins in weight and purity, thus stabilizing its value.

On paper money and the real bill principle

Smith has a slightly more positive opinion than Hume in the sense that the circulation of paper money only needs a fraction of gold and silver. To cover the promissory payments since most paper notes continue in circulation, he mentions the relation 1/5. The remaining gold and silver could be sent abroad for profitable business. Smith separate then consumption purpose and investment purpose where the latter is on the whole beneficial for the country. Given one million pounds in gold and silver we thus have;

> the paper cannot go abroad; because at a distance from the banks which issue it, and from the country in which payment of it can be exacted by law, it will not be received in common payments. Gold and silver, therefore, to the amount of eight hundred thousand pounds will be sent abroad, and the channel of home circulation will remain filled with a million of paper, instead of the million of those metals which filled it before.
>
> (ibid.: 125)

At the same time however Smith requires one-to-one convertibility of paper into gold/silver and that means that if the £800,000 sent abroad for business purposes goes into consumption; "promotes prodigality, increases expense and consumption without increasing production, or establishing any permanent fund for supporting that expense, and is in every respect hurtful to the society" (ibid.: 125).

The convertibility of paper money is a key issue:

> The whole paper money of every kind which can easily circulate in any country never can exceed the value of the gold and silver of which it supplies the place, or which (the commerce being supposed the same) would circulate there if there was no paper money.
>
> (ibid.: 128)

Consequently a 20 shilling note must be identical to the amount of gold and silver necessary for the 20 shilling exchange. This attitude by Smith is however parallel to his laissez faire opinion with respect to banking. Thus:

> A banking company, which issues more paper money than can be employed in the circulation, of the country and which the excess is continually returning upon them for payment, ought to increase the quantity of gold and silver which they keep all times in their coffers, not only in proportion to this excessive increase of their circulation, but in a much greater proportion; their notes returning upon them much faster than in proportion to the excess of their quantity.
>
> (ibid.: 129)

This approach by Smith places him among those supporting the Real Bill Doctrine/Banking School, together with Tooke, Fullarton and Mill, opposing the bullionists, amongst whom we find Ricardo, partly also Thornton, and also effectively Wicksell although not participating in the British debate, which was intensive during the two first decades of the nineteenth century but had eruptions during most of the nineteenth century. David Hume could also be regarded as a kind of bullionist since he, although negative to bank money, did not see the circulating coins other than related to gold and silver as a basic relative measure; his "inflationist" suggestion also shows this.

The market

Smith regards the rent, the yield of the land estate as given in, what we may call, real terms, thus variations in market price of that yield will affect the *profit*, which is yield above the natural rent, and the labour costs either by carrying board and lodging of the quantity of hired labour or the remuneration of labour. The basic thought is that the rent is covering the basic needs of the landowner; the salary of the worker is covering the basic needs of the worker, which is the natural value of work. Thus we may have a natural price which "is, as it were, the central price, to which the prices of all commodities are continually gravitating" (ibid.: 24).

This discussion of the real price (value) of a commodity we can trace back to Aristotle but we do not find much of these discussions, either in those of the Salamanca School, or in the writings of Hume. Both Hume and the friars discussed the markets and they fully accepted the variations in prices which they linked to supply/demand conditions but they did not link this price to some natural price or fair price. The Salamanca scholars discussed moderate/natural profits on money exchange but that was a matter of moral and/or law. Hume saw the market exchange as augmented by the use of money and since he saw the increase of consumption with respect to a richer diversity of commodities as educating the mind of people and brought about a richer diversity of working possibilities, the moral value of the market was more in its development of minds and its increasing strength and stability of the society as a whole. Thus for Hume the real price in Smith's sense was constantly changing as the diversity of the market increased and he actually mentions that a consequence of shrinking money supply is unemployed resources caused by the limitation of circulation of goods and money in the markets.

Smith and Hume

The static opinion of Smith is in line with his rather rigid approach to the society.

> Civil government supposes a certain subordination. But as the necessity of civil government gradually grows up with the acquisition of valuable property, so principal causes which naturally introduce subordination gradually grow up with the growth of that valuable property.
>
> The causes or circumstances which naturally introduce subordination, or which naturally, and antecedent to any civil institution, give some men some superiority over the greater part of their brethren, seem to be four in number.
>
> (ibid.: 309)

He goes on and explains the four causes; (i) "the superiority of personal qualifications, of strength, beauty, and agility of body; of wisdom and virtue, of prudence, justice, fortitude, and moderation of mind"; (ii) "the superiority of age"; (iii) "the superiority of fortune"; (iv) "the superiority of birth" (ibid.: 309–10).

It seems as if Smith more or less reluctantly accepts and pursues the market economy but he is also keen to stress the stability of the market to keep the social structure.

Hume's attitude is the reverse with respect to the social implications of the market. He foresees the development of the monetary economy to have large social effects in "refining the minds of men" and increase the socialization as he discusses chapter II, "Of Refinements in the Arts" (ibid.: 24–42).

There are considerable differences between the analysis of Hume and Smith. Hume's analysis deals more with the dynamic characteristics of the market while Smith deals more with the static analysis of the market and the elements which affect the prices in a given moment. With respect to money Hume's discussion concerns mostly the problem of having a convertible currency in foreign trade via coins standardized with respect to weight and purity of the metal while Smith mostly looks for a medium of exchange which is stable and reflects reasonably well the value of corn. Since Smith regards the main component in the price, the long-run average, to be based on the amount of labour and corn is the basic commodity for the necessity of life one might say that Smith in fact advocates a sort of corn-standard both for internal and external trade, since he seems to implicitly assume a constancy of the production technology with respect to corn. Ricardo criticized in fact this static view, although he accepts the labour theory of prices.

Variations in the value of money are from Smith's perspective of more dissipative character, although a nuisance for both landowners and labour. However given the stability of rent and the average value of corn, the variations affect mainly the short-run profit for the landowner and the quantity and remuneration of labour.

For Hume variations in the money value is brought by variations in the supply/demand for money (coins) relative to supply and demand conditions of ordinary commodities. These variations affect both internal trade and external trade, particularly the latter. Hume's more long-term dynamic view makes him favour money (currency), which is stable thus the differences in commodity prices will then actually mirror the changes in efficiency in production structures of different sectors and countries. Such differences depend on both skill of labour and use of more efficient production methods, but they vary between sectors and countries. The consequence of such differences in efficiency will be capital flows both with respect to production sectors and countries.

The effects of changed money price on internal trade are mostly due to the volume and diversity of commodities brought to the market. He thus advocates a constant increase of the supply of money in order to raise the volume of trade. On the other hand he is very doubtful of paper credits supplied by banks (a sort of bank money). This is rather interesting in fact, and we thus find a path from Hume to the discussion of monetary policy in the middle of the ninteenth century.

It is of importance to note the differences between Hume's dynamic approach and Smith's more static approach and we also can see Hume's position similar to the School of Salamanca. Smith's analysis is from a theoretical perspective easier to develop within comparative static modelling and Smith emphasizes long-run equilibrium and thus that short-term variation will converge to such an equilibrium which is fully up to date with the scientific advances in physics developed by Newton.

The bullionist debate and real bills

From Hume's and Smith's somewhat primitive views on money in many aspects, the financial system became a key issue at the end of the eighteenth century when the Napoleonic wars upset the financial conditions in England, which fostered the development of a more sophisticated view on monetary matters. Furthermore London evolved to a hub in international banking; thus the financial/monetary analysis appeared to be most intensive among English economists. The bank panic of 1793 followed by the crisis of 1797 and the subsequent financial distress in England due to the wars provoked a discussion, the bullionist debate, of the monetary/financial system, which might be seen as the foundation for the monetary discussion today. The start of the theoretical debate which also was underlying the political debate came by Henry Thornton's path-breaking analysis in 1802: *An Enquiry into the Nature and Effects of the Paper Credit of Great Britain*. The main questions were the convertibility of paper money into gold and silver advocated by the bullionists, or paper currency based on the real bill doctrine as Smith advocated, implying issuing paper money which the anti-bullionists advocated implying that no importance was paid to the supply of gold guineas and banks were free to expand their affairs on the basis of their coverage with gold. Subsequent to this discussion was the question of financing the international trade.[9] One can say that the debate ended in 1826 when Ricardo's Ingot plan was published posthumously, which led to an initiation of a full central bank system, which was created by the Bank Charter Act when the Bank of England got the sole right to issue banknotes which were tied to the gold reserves.

To follow the debate in the original literature is a bit difficult, since it contains many political aspects, which implies that the participants, Ricardo, Fullarton, Thornton, Tooke, Bosanquet for instance, seldom took a clear position but were influenced by current political and economic events. Thus most of the participants held partly contradictory opinions during the period 1797–1826. The ultimate topic of the debate was England's financial position during and after the Napoleonic wars.

The two sides in the debate were the *bullionists*, later the Currency School, and the *anti-bullionists*, later the Banking School; however the positions were not really clear and shifted due to current problems and policy needs. Furthermore there were also many dimensions of the problem and for instance Thornton was regarded as an anti-bullionist even if he strongly rejected real bills; on the other hand he claimed cost-inflation as the regular type of inflation. As a member of the Bullion Committee 1810, he however supported the bullionist line; many argue that the reason was his critique of the lax issuing policy of Bank of England.

A superficial description of the two sides would be that the bullionists claimed that excess money supply caused inflation and that the total supply of paper money should be related to the defined gold reserves, bullions, which implied that the supply of paper money would be controlled by the Bank of England/ government.

The real bills doctrine claimed that paper money as Smith claimed should be one-to-one convertible in gold, but the gold supply should not be controlled by the Bank of England since it was self-regulated by business and excess supply would revert to the Bank of England with no effect on inflation, which, as said above, depended on other causes.

David Riccardo, a bullionist, claimed in a newspaper article (*Morning Chronicle*) that the issue of paper money from the Bank of England in a real bill regime would transfer the Bank of England to a gold mine and we would revive the days of inflow of gold from America.[10]

The bullionists claimed that inflation appeared when there was an excess of paper money, furthermore when the price of the bullion rose, paper money depreciated and the authorities should then decrease the outstanding stock of paper money.

The *anti-bullionists* claimed that inflation appeared from other causes and the issuing of more bank money was in fact a consequence of inflation. Inflation was a result of supply and demand conditions based on cost and technology conditions. Going back to Hume, although effectively a bullionist, we find that he attributed the dearness of commodities to such factors in conjunction with the degree of competition.

Many see the *bullionists* as a kind of reminiscence of mercantilism although Ricardo was or sooner became a bullionist; but having said that we should take into consideration that England was at war or suffering from the consequences, thus the positions of the two sides were modified due to national interests. Henry Thornton, who was one of the leading financial theorists was an anti-bullionist and opposed contraction of money as an anti-inflation policy, modified himself in 1810, in a parliamentary report on the bullion price to accept a certain contraction since he perceived the issue of bank money had become far too excessive.

In his theoretical work however Thornton argues in favour of an anti-bullionist position and is of the opinion that gold bullion mainly is a norm vis-à-vis international trade but the key issue in international trade is the balance of trade.

It is instructive to look at the two most important characters in the debate; Henry Thornton, whose work on paper credits, mentioned above, many regard as the first Keynesian view, and David Ricardo whose *Ingot Plan* (Bonar 1923) and *Proposals for an Economical and Secure Currency* (McCulloch 1888) became crucial for the development of the Bank of England into a fully fledged Central Bank of England.

David Ricardo 1772–1823

From the world of Hume and Smith to the one of Ricardo, about 30 years, there is an eternity. Ricardo was 17 years old when the French revolution started and his theoretical contributions were developed in the shadow and aftermath of the Napoleonic wars and the Vienna Conference. The financial difficulties of Britain were considerable and much of the public debate concerned how Britain should regain her strength in trade and finance. Furthermore Ricardo experienced a far more developed market economy in comparison with Hume and Smith. Although Ricardo became the "father" of free trade he so to say belonged to the *currency school* or *bullionists* in the monetary debate between 1797 and 1826. Although this is said to be a reminiscence of old mercantilist thoughts it has to be viewed with respect to the particular financial situation of Britain at the time.

Ricardo was affected by both Hume and Smith. The latter became the more important and in his writings Ricardo regularly relates Smith's analysis in *Wealth of Nations* but he has also studied Hume and we can trace this in his critics of Smith with respect to the constancy in the price of corn, where Ricardo relates to Malthus' writings on the nature of rent and the importation of corn and mentions that Hume was the first to appreciate these ideas. Ricardo is also well aware of the importance of technology changes; but not in the general sense as in Hume's more dynamic approach, but in more specific production view following the Aristotelian basis of the value of labour as being the main component of the market price.

> The produce of the earth – all that is derived from its surface by the united application of labour, machinery, and capital, is divided among three classes of the community; namely the proprietor of the land, the owner of the stock of capital necessary for its cultivation, and the labourers by whose industry it is cultivated.
>
> (Ricardo 1815: 1)

On these pillars Ricardo develops a theory of value which was of immense importance for Karl Marx and his labour theory. When we thus want to understand the difference in different approaches to money and its nature the approaches to what constitutes the value of a commodity is of vital importance.

Ricardo develops his theory of value in five propositions and two correlated problems about the character of what follows from the propositions and has to be explicitly addressed.

Five propositions

The first proposition says that the *exchange value* of a commodity depends on the quantity of labour necessary for its production *not the compensation* which is paid for that labour.

Starting in Adam Smith's distinction of the two meanings of value, *value in use* and *value in exchange*, Ricardo criticizes Adam Smith's static view of corn as the basic commodity and underlying the value of labour, thus Smith ends up in a sort of corn-standard underlying money value: "that is the comparative quantity of commodities which labour will produce, that determines their present or past relative value, and not the comparative quantities of commodities, which are given to the labourer in exchange for his labour" (ibid.: 19).

Thus he disconnects the actual remuneration of labour from the market price of the commodities and replaces it with comparative use.

The second proposition is that labour of different qualities is differently paid but this is no cause for variation in the value of the commodities. Ricardo assumes in fact that all changes in labour productivity, to use a modern concept, depend on reorganization of the production methods leaving the quality distribution among workers unchanged.

The third proposition is that not only the direct labour involved in a commodity affects its value but also the indirect labour involved in implements, tools and buildings. Given the second proposition the third proposition is more or less a corollary, and his arguments are principally a repetition of earlier arguments. There are, however, two passages which are essential for understanding Ricardo's view:

> Economy in the use of labour never fails to reduce the relative value of a commodity, whether saving be in the labour necessary to the manufacture of the commodity itself, or in that necessary to the formation of the capital, by the aid of which it is produced.
>
> (ibid.: 36)

As we see it repeats implicitly the constancy of quality distribution in the used labour force irrespective of the production organization.

The second quote deals with the real reason why the relative commodity value is independent of the price of labour, of a given quality:

> No alteration in the wages of labour could produce any alteration in the relative value of these commodities; for suppose them to rise, no greater quantity of labour would be required in any of these occupations, but it would be paid for a higher price, and the same reasons which should make the hunter and fisherman endeavour to raise the value of their game and fish, would cause the owner of the mine to raise the value of his gold.

Thus labour, or, more correctly, a unit of labour normalized with respect to quality differentials, is the basic unit of measurement irrespective of its price. We may think of an input–output system where we measure salaries to workers in a standard unit.

The fourth proposition is that the quantity of labour used in production of different commodities is modified by the use of machinery and durable capital. Also the fourth proposition is a consequence of the two first propositions and Ricardo's argumentation doesn't contain any particularly exciting passages. There is one sentence which we may think excited Marx: "There can be no rise in the value of labour without a fall of profits" (ibid.: 58).

In the fifth proposition Ricardo claims that although that value of commodities does not vary with the rise and fall of wages it has to be modified "by the unequal durability of capital and by the unequal rapidity with which it is returned to its employer" (ibid.: 65).

It is a rather natural modification to the discussion of the importance of changing production organizations by use of capital in the form of machinery.

Measure of value

After these five propositions Ricardo arrives to a discussion of a monetary system suitably adjusted to the basic principles of the market economy and not surprisingly his first problem is "On the invariable measure of value". He starts his analysis of this problem:

> When commodities varied in relative value, it would be desirable to have the means of ascertaining which of them fell and which rose in real value, and this could be effected only by comparing them one after another with some invariable standard measure of value, which should itself be subject to none of the fluctuations to which other commodities are exposed.
>
> (ibid.: 74)

Gold is, although it is reasonably stable, produced under the same conditions as any other commodity, thus it is not perfect as a standard mirroring the real labour standard. This is actually a rather interesting point in understanding Ricardo's attitude to gold standard.

He adds, also interestingly with respect to the discussions on metallism and chartalism, and furthermore from a methodological point of view, that:

> To facilitate, then, the object of this enquiry, although I fully allow that money made of gold is subject to most variations of other things, I shall suppose it to be invariable, and therefore all alterations in price to be occasioned by some alteration in the value of the commodity of which I may be speaking.
>
> (ibid.: 78)

Since the first problem was the constancy of measure the subsequent problem is logically his second problem; "*Different effects from the alteration in the value of money, the medium in which PRICE is always expressed, or from the alteration in the value of the commodities which money purchase*" (ibid.: 81, original emphasis).

With respect to rise in money wages it only causes fall in the value of money since all prices rise and so the proportions between wage income, profit and rent will be unchanged.

With respect to foreign trade we need to distinguish between price changes of the commodity as such and change in the foreign exchange value of the money.

Changes in the relative proportions of wage income, profit and rent are brought about by improvements in machinery and agriculture which may increase the parts going to profit and rent while the part going to labourers diminishes. This is a consequence of the earlier propositions.

Ricardo and the bullionist debate

In 1810 when Henry Thornton's parliamentary report on the price of bullion was published Ricardo started to engage himself in the general public debate on currency and inflation. England experienced high inflation and during the period 1800 to 1820 there were several serious bank crises. The general reason for the debacle was according to Ricardo the excessive emission of banknotes. He advocated a supply in conjunction with the price of bullion and consequently that paper money became convertible into gold. His opinion was strengthened by England's difficulties in foreign trade, as Ricardo meant, due to the high inflation and thus the high price of bullion. Suitable measure was a diminishing quantity of money with the subsequent consequence for demand and production, but seen in the perspectives of the competitiveness of trade the measure would be necessary. Ricardo rejected the market forces as determinants for the quantity of banknotes in circulation and was in favour of a Central Bank System consisting of two parts: the issuing of paper money and the control of money policy through convertibility into gold bullion.[11]

> This inconvenience [with respect to circulation of coins] is wholly got rid of, by the issue of paper money; for, in that case, there will be no additional demand for bullion; consequently its value will continue unaltered; and the new paper money, as well as the old, will conform to that value.
>
> ... In the next session of Parliament, the subject of currency is again to be discussed; and probably, a time will then be fixed for the resumption of cash payments, which will oblige the Bank to limit the quantity of their paper till it conforms to the value of bullion.
>
> (McCulloch 1888)

He developed his thoughts and from 1815 and particularly from 1819 when he took a place in House of Commons, Ricardo was a central figure in the official monetary discussion. In his Ingot Plan he took the first steps towards a central bank system in England.

Henry Thornton 1760–1815

Thornton, also known as philanthropist and for his fight against the slavery system, was in the beginning of the bullion debate on the anti-bullionist side, which is clear in his book from 1802.[12] In the parliamentary report from 1810 he however supported the convertibility of paper money into gold due to the instability of the English currency and the much too excessive supply of banknotes.

To say that he was a bullionist is to say too much. The very economic and financial position of Britain was precarious due to the wars and stabilizing measures was a necessity much due to the lax issuing policy of the Bank of England. In his theoretical approach he was closer to the anti-bullionists regarding the causes of inflation, but he realized also the effects of excess supply of money.

On circulation of money

Thornton (1802) criticizes Smith on his approach to money, i.e. his real bill approach, implying that the total nominal value of paper money of every kind can never exceed the value of gold. His criticism starts in the fact that paper money can appear in different forms – interest notes, exchequer bills, India bonds – thus he makes a distinction between a paper's *capability of circulation* and *forced circulation*.

With respect to a certain volume of paper *capable of circulation*, the actual circulation might be small or great and furthermore different kinds of papers have different degrees of rapidity of circulation, which is linked to the very character of the paper in question. That is the same nowadays when financial organizations use swaps or other derivatives to alter their financial positions in different modes. This also means that Thornton regarded the financial market as composed by different sectors more or less connected. The fundamental principle is that the capability of circulation mostly is due to business ventures and has a dual risk structure.

When we consider *forced circulation*, in Thornton's context, this is "law" money bound to its face value, irrespective of any intrinsic metal value, and thus a common medium of payment. This is forced into daily use and increases the relation of daily medium of payment in relation to the circulation of commodities.

Thornton discusses also the different modes of hoarding, which has some bearing on his position in the bullionist debate, and claims that guineas (gold) are hoarded in times of alarm, thus to some extent explaining the premium on bullion. But Thornton also gives examples of the opposite case of hoarding of banknotes. In 1793 there was a break out of bank panic. The parliament gave a loan of exchequer bills to mercantile companies giving them proper security for coming payments. This cure is not unusual in our times and recent events first USA and then Europe are quite parallel to what happened in England in the 1790s. Although the mode of action is rather obvious to us Thornton's analysis vis-à-vis his context is well worth to quote:

> The success of the remedy which the parliament administered, denotes what was the nature of the evil. A loan of exchequer bills was directed to be made to as many mercantile persons, giving proper security, as should apply. It is a fact, worthy of serious attention, that the failures abated greatly, and the mercantile credit began to be restored, not at the period when the exchequer bills were actually delivered, but a time antecedent to that æra. It also deserves notice, that though the failures had originated in an extraordinary demand for guineas, it was not any supply of gold which effected the cure. That fear of not being able to obtain guineas, which arose in the country, led in its consequences, to an extraordinary demand for bank notes in London; and the want of bank notes in London became after a time, the chief evil.
>
> (Thornton 1939 [1802]: 18)

Thus the demand for banknotes was a demand for liquid security in order to meet business commitments:

> It does not appear that the Bank of England notes, at the time were fewer than usual. It is certain, however, that the existing number became at the period of apprehension, insufficient for giving punctuality to the payments of the metropolis.
>
> (ibid.)

Thornton pays much attention to the variations in circulation of money, of all kinds, and he also regards the fact that different kinds of "money" may differ in the speed of circulation. In the related example the general unease led to a higher demand for liquid money which slowed down the circulation causing failures to meet business commitments. Increasing gold was useless since it was liquid bills which were wanted and the exchequer bills were as good for liquidity as banknotes.

This passage in Thornton is very interesting since he displays a clear understanding of the complex relations between long and short run. Smith and Ricardo both held the opinion that short-run movements, although a nuisance, were dissipative and that the economy would be restored in the long run. This understanding is natural since they both introduce the anchor of labour value, in Smith's case also land rent, into their analysis. Thornton has no such anchor in his analysis and thus the short-run events make up the long run; that is the short-run credit distress may change the whole path of the economy.

Thornton also describes in the case of increased demand for guineas (gold), due to distrust, a kind of *locking in* effect, which both causes a slower circulation of guineas and subsequently an even higher demand in order to meet payments *as well as* a higher demand for bank money. Thus with respect to the bullionist debate Thornton's analysis was far more sophisticated to be applied to a simple pro/con debate. Furthermore the inventiveness within commercial finance makes it virtually impossible to calculate the true volume of paper money;

> It may already have occurred, that if bank paper were abolished, a substitute for it would likely to be found, to a certain degree, in bills of exchange;… But further; if bills and bank notes were extinguished, other substitutes than gold would unquestionably be found.
>
> (ibid.: 464–5)

Credit defaults

However Thornton also addresses the problem of *credit defaults*. An abolishment of bank money above the total value of gold, Smith's real bills, would cause unnecessary systemic risks as the banking and commercial activities have to proceed smoothly:

Merely by the transfer of debts of one merchant to another, in the books of the banker, a large portion of what are termed cash payments is effected at this time without the use of any bank paper, and a much larger sum would be thus transferred if guineas were the only circulating medium of the country.

(ibid.: 464)

But he proceeds:

It might not be paper credit; but still it might be such credit as would spare, more or less the use of guineas. It might be credit of a worse kind, less accurately dealt out in proportion to the desert of different persons, and therefore, in some instances, at least, still more extended; it might be credit less contributing to punctuality of payments, and to the due fulfilments of engagements; less conducive to the interests of trade, and to the cheapening of articles; and it would, perhaps, also credit quite as liable to interruption on the occasion of any the sudden alarm or material change in the commercial prospects and circumstances of the country.

(ibid.: 465)

Gold and international trade

When it comes to the role of gold and its use as a means of payment, *real bills*, Thornton claims that:

no fund ever was or can be provided by the bank which shall be sufficient for such a purpose; and that gold coin is to be viewed chiefly as a standard by which all bills and paper money should have their value regulated as exactly as possible.

(ibid.: 470)

A gold reserve, mainly bullion, serves mainly two purposes; it can counteract the effects of a negative trade balance and it might be used in cases of financial unease which might cause bank panic.

It is hard to see that Thornton even advocates a gold standard in international affairs. Eventual relative price stability of gold may perfectly meet Thornton's arguments without enlarging the role of gold into a standard.

Naturally Thornton discusses England's international trade problems, where the low exchange rate was a main theme in the bullionist debate; he thus makes the following distinction which is productive:

The export trade to foreign countries is, generally speaking, one trade; the trade of importing from foreign countries is a second; the trade of sending out and bringing home bullion, in order to pay or receive the difference between the exports and imports, may be considered as a third. This third trade is carried on upon the same principles with any other branch of commerce, that is, it is entered into just so far as it is lucrative to be speculator in bullion, and no farther. The point, therefore, to be enquired into is clearly this, – whether the pressure arising from a scarcity of bank notes tends to render the importation of bullion a more profitable speculation.

(ibid.: 474–5)

In solving the question Thornton claims that the case of a negative trade balance in itself will force an increase in the gold inflow, as the standard case, but apart from that he examines "in what way the pressure arising from the suppression of bank notes will affect the quantity of goods which are in the way of trade either exported or imported" (ibid.: 29). The problem arises for example when we have an internal inflation but also a negative balanced external trade.

Monetary policy

To understand Thornton we must consider the rather strict division between manufacturers and merchants where the latter administered the trade flows based on the relative profitability. Thus a manipulation of banknotes would in the first instance "hit" the merchants although posterior effects to the manufacturers would appear.

Thornton mentions three effects:

i   A suppression of banknotes would thus in the first instance lower the prices at home due also to reduced sale and tempt the merchants to sell the goods abroad. However the reduced sale at home at lower prices together with the more inert market abroad will affect the financial position of the merchant which would demand longer credits from the manufacturers which leads to a recessionary development. This will in fact in Thornton's opinion lead to inflict such a pressure on the mercantile world as necessarily cause an intermission of manufacturing labour, is obviously the way to increase that exportable produce, by the excess of which, above the imported articles, gold is to be brought into the country (ibid.: 30).

ii   But the diminution of the manufacturers' price caused by the reduction of banknotes creates a temporary distress which will cause no corresponding fall in wages: "for the fall of price, and the distress, will be understood to be temporary, and the rate of wages, we know, is not so variable as the price of goods" (ibid.: 327). The effect will create liquidity distress and "much discouragement" of manufacturers, which hits the exporting power of the country.

iii Thornton states categorically "Thirdly, a great diminution of notes prevents much of that industry of the country which had been exerted from being so productive as it would otherwise be" (ibid.: 327). In adding this point Thornton shows a superior knowledge to industrial undertakings and investments compared with his contemporaries and similar to Hume in his argumentation.

His explanation starts from the risky character of real investments and sudden changes in credits and the volume of banknotes will introduce a further risk preventing the investor from an otherwise desired investment volume and settle with a minor volume.

> Every great and sudden check given to paper credit not only operates as a check to industry, but leads also to much of this application of it. Some diminution of the general property of the country must follow from this cause; and, of course, a deduction also from that part of it which forms the stock for exportation. It can hardly be necessary to repeat, that on the quantity of exported stock depends the quantity of gold from foreign countries.
>
> (ibid.: 328)

He then goes on explaining that a great and sudden reduction of the accustomed number of banknotes would most probably create such distress in the economy that foreigners would lose their general trust in English credit notes. Thornton is however keen to explain that such effects which we have related above are not some deterministic rules but depend on the general conditions.

Inflation and interests

Finally when it comes to inflation and interest (chapters X and XI), the Bank of England was under the *usury law* of a maximum lending rate of 5 per cent. Thornton takes a view which is consistent with his discussion on speed of circulation, namely that the circumstances of the lender might be such that his eagerness of an affair might dispose him of paying a substantial interest rate, which might lead to an augmented demand of credits: "The borrowers, in consequence of that artificial state of things which is produced by the law against usury, obtain their loans too cheap. That which they obtain too cheap they demand in too great quantity" (ibid.: 411).

Thornton is seemingly aiming at a Wicksellian type of analysis, although it is still implicit in his argumentation.

With respect to inflation Thornton admitted that increasing the quantity of paper money might augment the prices but he also enters Hume's argument that an increase in the money stock might stimulate the industriousness such that new sectors are introduced at the market. Thus on one hand the price augmentation appears in the intermediary period between the increase of the money stock and the ultimate effects on production, and on the other hand the more long-run effect due to the ultimate production effect caused by the money increase and the size of the increase, that is the long-term relation between money and the aggregate circulation of commodities will in principle anticipate a new stable relation. It should however be emphasized that Thornton regarded such a relation to be extremely difficult to measure due to, (i) variations in the speed of circulation, (ii) variations in the costs of commodities; he mentions bad harvests, affecting the demand supply conditions on the market, (iii) the multitude of kinds of money with different speed of circulation and affecting different sectors and groups in the society. Thus although Thornton in some sense agrees with Fisher on the partial relevance of the quantity theory he almost disregards it on the practical and theoretical difficulties to apply it. As we will claim later, the fact that $MV \equiv PY$ as an identity does not render it creditability as a theory based on different assumptions.

A short passage at the end of chapter X reveals Henry Thornton's qualities both as an economic and financial analyst and it also reveals what has been said earlier about the difference between Hume and Smith;

> Mr. Hume himself has remarked: "That want of money can never injure any state *within itself*; for that men and commodities are the real strength of any community." He might have added, that Want of money can never injure any state *in its transactions with foreign countries*, provided it sufficiently abounds with commodities which are in demand abroad, and which can afford to sell at a bullion price lower than that for which foreign articles of a similar kind can be afforded. The power of manufacturing at a cheap rate is far more valuable than any stock of bullion. Even at greatest quantity of gold which we can be supposed at any time to possess, bears but a small proportion to extraordinary expenditures in time of war, and affords a security which is extremely slender in comparison of that which we derive from commercial capital, the manufacturing skill, and other resources of the country.
>
> (ibid.: 424, original emphasis)

We have been fairly comprehensive on Henry Thornton, who nowadays is rather unknown, but with respect to Smith and also partly to Ricardo he combined a thorough practical knowledge as a banker and a good theoretical knowledge. He is almost fierce in his criticism of Adam Smith's doctrines of money and compared to Ricardo his analysis is less dogmatic and more open to the complexities and most of all it reveals an understanding of the dynamics of an economy away from the sterile dividing between long and short run as completely different categories.

The aftermath of the bullionist debate and the currency debate

Ricardo and Thornton were the two portal figures in the debate. Ricardo appeared late in the debate and his main contributions appeared after the death of Thornton. He got a considerable influence on the development of the Bank of England. Ricardo's opinion led to the Bank Charter Act 1844 where no bank except the Bank of England was allowed to issue new banknotes. However the Bank of England was also restricted to issue new banknotes since they must up to 100 per cent be backed by bullion, silver/gold. The convertibility to gold could be suspended by the government in times of extraordinary crises (Wicksell 1937 [1922]: 192–3).

The Bank Charter Act, based on the arguments of Ricardo and the Currency School, consequently institutionalized that the main cause of price inflation was due to the issuing of new banknotes.

Henry Thornton's lines of analysis were partly taken up by John Stewart Mill but most of all we see clear connections to Wicksell's monetary theory and later also to Keynes. While Ricardo and the currency school have a rather narrow perspective of money, as a pure medium of exchange, Henry Thornton's analysis aims at a broader perspective of money, including money as liquidity and security, which links money to a far more comprehensive economic analysis of the inherent dynamics of the economy.

Wicksell's short comment on the discussion between Tooke (anti-bullionist) and Ricardo is interesting: "Fullt övertygande var emellertid *Ricardos* framställning endast ifråga om sedlarnas förhållande till *guldet*, med andra ord deras disagio. Deras förhållande till *varorna*, alltså varuprisnivåns förändringar, är icke nödvändigtvis samma sak" (Wicksell 1937 (1922): 198, original emphasis) [However, *Ricardo* was only fully convincing with respect to the relation of bank notes to *gold*, i.e. their disagio (negative premium). Their relation to *commodities*, i.e. the changes of the commodity price level, is not necessarily the same thing] (author's translation).

Jean Baptiste Say 1767–1832

Almost contemporary to Ricardo was Jean Baptiste Say. His impressive work *A Treatise on Political Economy* was first published 1803 in the aftermath of the French revolution. It is written in the spirit of hope and trust in freedom and human inventiveness and power of innovation. Unfortunately Say is nowadays most well known for Say's law, which we all know that Keynes rejected, but Say is more interesting than that. First of all Say saw the economic progress as a part of the social process; in that aspect he resembles Hume a great deal. He saw the market as interlinked with human desires but these desires were successively created and enlarged as the market exchange penetrated the society. We have mentioned David Hume's discussion of the market as bringing access to new types of commodities enlarging the horizons of the consumers. His discussion on the effects of access to luxuries in civilizing the minds of people and thus causing a process towards peaceful existence and calm prosperity places Jean Baptiste Say on the same track as David Hume.[13]

At the same time Say is impressed by Smith's foundations of the market theory and Ricardo's logical analysis and thus tries to embed the philosophical reflexions of Hume into a more systematic analysis.

On money

With respect to money Say puts forward two important qualities;[14]

1   The general confidence, that money is a commodity acceptable to every body, inspires the assurance of being able, by one act of exchange only, to

procure the immediate object of desire, whatever it may be; whereas the possessor of any other commodity can never be sure that it will be acceptable to the possessor of that particular object of desire.

2   The capability of subdivision and precise apportionment to the amount of the intended purchase; which capability is a recommendation to all who have purchases to make; in other words, to every member of the community. Every one is, therefore, anxious to barter for money the product whereof he holds a superfluity, and which is commonly that he himself produces; because, in addition to the other quality, above stated, he feels sure of being able to buy with its value in that shape as small as large a portion of corresponding value, as he may require; and because he may buy, whenever, and wherever he pleases, such objects as he may desire to have in lieu of the product he has sold originally.

(Say 1834 [1803]: 222–3)

When discussing Hume and Thornton we mentioned that both of them see the dynamics of the monetary economy as a diffusion process. This is actually methodologically at variance with Smith and Ricardo who look upon the economy as basically an equilibrium system. A diffusion process can be delayed or even blocked while an equilibrium is a final state calculated from a set of assumptions.

Say's law

Typically for this is the famous Say's law, which Keynes attacks, and which is necessary for achieving equilibrium. In its classical formulation which Keynes discuss in *GT* chapter 4 pages 24–6, we have that aggregate supply can be written as a function of employment, $Z=\varphi(N)$, and the aggregate demand is also a function of employment, $D=f(N)$, which means that applying Say's law to all values of employment we thus have $\varphi(N)=f(N)\Rightarrow Z=D$.

To call this Say's law is a complete misapprehension of Say. Keynes might be excused since he adds "that applying Say's law to all values of employment" which hints that it is a classical interpretation of Say. So what did Say actually write?

It is worthwhile to remark, that a product is no sooner created, than it, from that instant, affords a market for other products to the full extent of its own value. When the producer has put the finishing hand to his product, he is most anxious to sell it immediately, lest its value should diminish in his hands. Nor is he less anxious to dispose of the money he may get for it; for the value of money is also perishable. But the only way of getting rid of money is in the purchase of some product or other. Thus, the mere circumstance of the creation of one product immediately opens a vent for other products.

(ibid.: 138–9)

The quote seems quite harmless but we might be disturbed about the two last sentences; these are however to be seen in the very context of Say's discussion. The uses of money augment the production and its variety. Furthermore money implies a quicker circulation of this augmented product which increases the production per se and thus the employment.

This actually raises a methodological question. The quotation attempts to describe a dynamic process, which might have unstable and stable states of equilibrium due to parameter assumptions. Obviously a slice of time gives an aggregate demand and supply with the resulting employment, which we might call a partial equilibrium; but what right do we have to define a general equilibrium model on such a dynamics? This is particularly important to ask when Say proceeds:

> The success of one branch of commerce supplies more ample means of purchase, and consequently opens the markets for the product of all the other branches; on the other hand, the stagnation of one channel of manufacture, or of commerce, is felt in all the rest.
>
> (ibid.: 139)

This is actually as far we can get from a general equilibrium model. First the description of the commodity space is completely different and second Say actually touches on the dimensionality problem of the commodity space, which Keynes dealt with and later also Maurice Allais.

Say discusses actually rather comprehensively reasons for limitation in supply in chapters XV–XVI. He mentions mismatch between supply and demand, insufficient technology, and execution of monopoly power, private or public and finally political and natural convulsions.

Prices

With respect to prices, Say distinguishes between *real* and *relative* prices. The real price is what we may call a supply price, subject to changes due to changes in production technology. The relative price is the market valuation; thus the supply price is 8 EUR but the market process implies that only 6 EUR is the maximum price for the product. When it comes to the market price relations and money prices he rejects more or less a global price vector on the same lines as Debreu:

> It is obvious therefore, that one cannot form an idea of the value of a commodity from its estimate in money price, except during a space and time, and within a space of territory, in which neither the denomination of the coin, nor the value of its material, has undergone any change; else the valuation will be merely nominal, and convey no fixed idea of value whatever.... In comparing values, the denomination is useful only inasmuch as it designates the quantity of pure metal contained in the sum specified. It may

serve to denote the quantity of the metal, but can never serve as an index of value at any distance of time or place.

(ibid.: 311)

Interest rate

Say is also quite interesting with respect to interest rate. He distinguishes between the charged interest rate on lent capital and profitability on industrial capital. Regarding the former he has a discussion which might be associated with the friars of Salamanca:

> The interest on capital lent, improperly called the interest of money, was formerly denominated usury, that is to say, rent for its use and enjoyment; which indeed, was the correct term; for interest is nothing more than the price, or rent, paid for the enjoyment of an object of value.

(ibid.: 347)

And he proceeds:

> The progressive advance of industry has taught us to view the loan of capital in a different light. In ordinary cases, it is no longer a resource in the hour of emergency, but an agent, an instrument, which may be turned to great benefit, as well of society, as of the individual.

(ibid.: 348)

Say divided the actual interest on lent capital in two parts: the actual bona fide interest and a premium of insurance to cover risk. In this discussion he also analyses the effects of regulations of the interest rate, which we saw that Thornton regarded as ineffective. Say takes a step further in writing;

> Thus the practise of usury has been uniformly revived, whenever it has been attempted to limit the rate of interest, or abolish it altogether. The severer the penalties, and the more rigid their exaction, the higher the interest of money was sure to rise; and this is what might naturally have been expected; for the greater the risk, the greater premium of insurance did it require to tempt the lender.

(ibid.: 349)

The variations in interest rate at free credit market varies with respect to supply and demand, "a rise in the rate of interest does not infallibly or universally denote that capital is growing scarcer; for possibly it may be a sign that its uses are multiplied" (ibid.: 353). Thus his distinction between interest on lent capital and profit on productive capital leads him rather close to the Wicksellian and also to the Keynesian analysis, particularly when we consider that he regards profit as residual and due to supply/demand conditions.

Consequently we find that although Say has, through his alleged law, played an important part as a sort of closure of the equilibrium bringing the ultimate axiom, there is actually nothing in Say's writing which makes him an equilibrium theoretician. Instead he seems rather to be forbearer of the Wicksellian/Keynesian analysis in his description of the dynamic forces of the economy.

Knut Wicksell and the two paths of thinking

As we have seen the dynamic analysis of Wicksell vis-à-vis market rate of interest and the natural interest on production capital is not appearing as a complete novelty.[15] Hume, Thornton and Say had clear thoughts in that direction although not elaborated into a systematic form. But we also see that while Smith and Ricardo together with the neoclassicists contemporary to Wicksell were discussing a rather static kind of economy built on an equilibrium thought, Hume, Thornton, Say and to some extent also Wicksell more attended to the dynamic patterns of the economy. There might exist local and temporal equilibrium but though the economy is a part of and interacts with the social structure no global equilibrium can be discussed.

Wicksell is interesting since he was a fairly good mathematician and well understood the marginal revolution leaned towards an analytical methodology reminding of equilibrium analysis. In discussing the market economy on the microscopic level he thus regarded the equilibrating forces as pretty strong. He compares the relative prices of a single good with a freely moving pendulum which after a perturbation converges to its stable locus (Wicksell 1937 [1922]: 222).

On the other hand he realizes the difference between the macroscopic level and the microscopic level in a *monetary economy*. He thus realizes that money as a medium of exchange was affected by the credit volume, international trade, economic and political crises which caused governmental misuse. Thus the stability of the macroscopic level is actually more complex than the microscopic level. He compares stability of the *general price level* with a ball on a plane which is in a temporary rest but unstable. A perturbation will then imply that the earlier position will not be resumed, but the new position will be equally unstable as the one before (ibid.: 222). This picture is in fact ingenious and if we compare with a Newtonian equilibrium this is analogue to the microscopic stability.

Wicksell starts from the two kinds of interest rate: bank rate, or we may also see it as interest rate on liquidity, and the interest rate on or profitability of production capital. Wicksell's discussion on the relative height of these rates is in fact rather similar to that of Thornton and Say. When the latter is higher borrowing is cheap and we are in an economic upturn thus investments will be undertaken which change the relative prices as well as the price level and thus also the conditions for the microscopic level. This process is irreversible.

When the former is higher than the latter we are in economic downturn with diminishing investments causing changing relative prices as well as changes in the price level and thus also irreversible changes for the microscopic level.

The rate of interest which he calls the *natural rate* is when the two rates coincide. It is obviously similar to a kind of equilibrium rate but for Wicksell's distinction between the stability on the microscopic level and the stability on the macroscopic level. Thus the two pictures of the stability conditions on the microscopic and macroscopic levels above are of a very deep-going character and place Wicksell outside the group of equilibrium theorists and as such a herald of the coming theoretical conflicts in the twentieth century.

Metallism and chartalism

In our initial quotes from von Mises and Iwai we started with a discussion between metallists and chartalists. Our little journey through time has given us no definitive answer pro/con. As long as we only regard money as a medium of exchange at a limited market there is no need for anything but white flat stones or material of that type. But when we involve international trade we need some kind of institutional structure granting the values. It is obvious that gold may do its duty in this respect but only after proper control of purity, weight and appropriate official stamps; thus we may ask if it is the gold or the stamp which means anything.

The bullionists demanding convertibility into gold were more up to a standard for relative money valuation than to valuation of commodities, according to Wicksell's comment on Ricardo, which is quoted above. The important thing for them is the central bank control. Von Mises is on this point rather unclear, but he advocates a systematic gold standard involving price relations of commodities, some kind of real bill system. To our understanding we would most certainly have severe problems with a changing dimensionality of the commodity space, which probably would cause deflationary tendencies. Furthermore it is hard to see that such a system would escape the innovativeness of the financial business and what would happen then is beyond the author's ability to foresee.

An interesting example of a discussion of different metal standards and its eventual political usefulness is when Sweden borrowed from Holland to fight a war against Denmark during late sixteenth century and pledged Älvsborg (Gothenburg) as a security. The down payments and the final amortization was a heavy burden for the Swedish kingdom and the Dutch wanted the payments in silver standard. At that time however Sweden had conquered a large part of the Baltic states and controlled the mouths of the major rivers which enabled Sweden to take tolls from the trade to western Europe, mostly Amsterdam, Brügge and Antwerp. The Swedish chancellor von Oxenstierna tried then to force the Balts to pay the toll in copper coins since Sweden almost had a copper monopoly in Europe, thus a copper standard. However since the Dutch controlled the silver supply and thus the other end of the transaction chain so to say, in setting the ultimate price of copper in silver and Swedish troops in Balticum were paid in copper coins thus the supply of copper coins in Balticum was high and the value of copper was shrinking so Oxenstierna's idea never had any success.

So von Mises' dream of an objective currency free from political manipulations, and he had also seen the MEFO-bills during the Third Reich, is understandable, but on the other hand the financial meltdown 2008 was the fruits of lack of control, so Iwai is also understandable.

3 Money, value and prices in neoclassical economic theory

Introduction

In macroeconomics we have three distinct theoretical perspectives: neoclassical theory, Keynesian theory and monetarist theory. These cornerstones are then completed with theoretical fragments which build on empirical observations. From a strict methodological perspective one may often wonder about the internal consistence of such a theory. As a matter of fact we may even question the need of internal consistence or rather we may question the need of internal consistency in the analysis with respect to the existence of several perspectives. In Chapter 12 of *General Theory* Keynes writes:

> There is no clear evidence from experience that the investment policy which is socially advantageous coincide with what is most profitable. It needs more intelligence to beat the forces of time and our ignorance of the future than to beat the gun.
>
> (1973 [1936]: 157)

Thus the three main perspectives mentioned above are of quite distinct character from a methodological point of view; the neoclassical theory, built on an a priori axiomatic structure, Keynesian theory with some kind of basic structure in the so-called IS-LM model, which is questioned and completed with assumptions that sometimes seem rather ad hoc, and the monetarist theory built on the famous identity $MV \equiv PY$ which, as seen in the previous chapter, Ricardo paid considerable attention to, while Thornton more or less dismissed it as a too-unstable relation with respect to measurement and causality of the contained variables.

The above description may give the impression that mainstream economics, which it is often called, is some kind of theoretical hotchpotch, which is true, but having said that we must admit that it may still have a theoretical importance. Let me explain with an example from astronomy and look at the development from a geocentric to a heliocentric approach. The heliocentric approach Copernicus suggested was actually worse than the ancient Ptolemaic geocentric approach, with respect to forecasting the position of the planets. In the Ptolemaic model there had to be included so-called epicycles, like the example in Figure

3.1, to increase the forecasting ability of the model, and around 32 such epicycles were needed to make decent forecasts possible. But since Copernicus assumed circular orbits and constant speed of the planets, he actually needed forty-eight such epicycles to have a reasonable forecasting ability which was still worse than the forecasts based on the Ptolemaic approach.[1]

Thus even if we have an erroneous basic theory we may still add complementary theoretical structures which are a bit ad hoc with respect to the basic theoretical foundation but still improve the practical work. When we discussed the bullionist debate, in the preceding chapter, during the beginning of the nineteenth century we saw that the participants changed their minds in relation to their basic theoretical standpoint due to the changing conditions for England's financial position, and they were all in responsible positions in the state and had to face crude necessity.

The problem is that such a hotchpotch may also cause damage, maybe not particularly in the celestial analysis during the fifteenth and sixteenth centuries, but in applying this sort of methodology in modern economic thinking, we may solve a problem locally and temporally but at the price of advocating policy measures which may cause long-run structural damage. Furthermore, with respect to the epicycles in the example above, some use of Occam's razor may also be of value to increase the transparency.

Thus it could be valuable to scrutinize theories with respect to both logical consistency and the appropriateness of the basic assumptions/axioms with respect to the real world.

In this chapter we will devote our attention to the neoclassical theory, and in the next chapter we will turn our attention to the Keynesian and monetarist

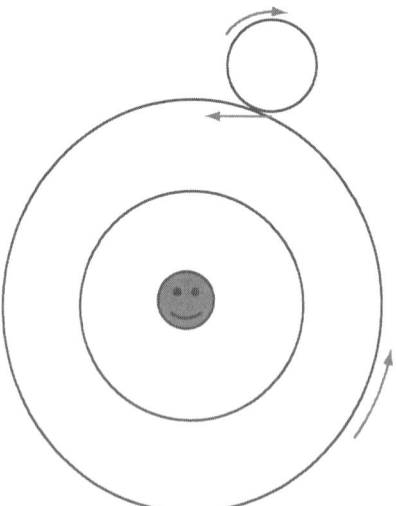

Figure 3.1 Epicycles of the planet orbits.

theories, with respect to basic assumptions/axioms and intrinsic consistency in the spirit of Wittgenstein's proposition 6.211 discussed in the introductory chapter and centred around the fact that we live in a monetary economy.

When we deal with the concept of money there are two kinds of questions which are of some importance: the first is whether there is any room at all for a concept like money in the theory, the second is whether the theoretical use of money is exhaustive with respect to the different dimensions embedded in the concept. We have already seen through our exposé of thoughts on money that the concept of money is multidimensional and we will in our discussions see different approaches to the macroscopic level and consider them in relation to their ability to handle different dimensions of the concept of money.

The difference between the three mentioned approaches is striking with respect to money. The neoclassical theory deals almost exclusively with the real economy and prices occur only as a theoretical index of *price relations*. The Keynesian theory in its analysis of real and monetary variables achieves the curious result that it can either be seen as a complement to the neoclassical model or as a complete disequilibrium model when we introduce the aspects of genuine uncertainty in which case the monetary matters more are seen as disturbances of the real sector as a cause of the inclusion of the concept of liquidity. Finally the monetarist theory based on the Quantity Theory of Money explains more or less the whole economic dynamics by the monetary developments but as far as we can see it neither has the neoclassical virtues nor the Keynesian ones but it does have the vices of both theories as prices in the neoclassical meaning are excluded as well as the Keynesian liquidity discussion. Thus from the view of the celestial example we discussed above the mainstream theory probably contains a quite impressive number of *epicycles*.

In our earlier exposé we have already met several dimensions contained in the concept of money.

The *medium of exchange* is of course the most explored dimension, starting already with Aristotle. However also Aristotle considered that the inter-temporal value of money following its use as medium of exchange implied that money became a *store of value* since the common acceptance didn't necessitate an immediate use of money.

Further dimensions included in the concept mainly by the friars of Salamanca and David Hume are money as a *base for contractual agreements*, a *basis of accounting* and thus a basis for the valuation of inter-temporal assets and liabilities. Convertibility should also be mentioned in relation to other kinds of money and monetary systems.

The *liquidity* aspect lingers of course in the background of money as a store of value but gets a more prominent place when Wicksell separates the bank interest rate from the natural interest rate, the latter indicating the growth of production. J.B. Say also touches on the character of the very concept (op. cit. 228). The risk concept was already, at least implicitly, imposed by David Ricardo and Henry Thornton although it seems if they never made a clear relation between liquidity and risk. It is during the twentieth century within the frames of the neoclassical theory that the relation between risk and liquidity was explored and explained.

The full development of the liquidity aspect, however, was completed by Keynes when he entered the concept of *uncertainty*.

The structure of the neoclassical theory

The neoclassical theory forms the most perfect and beautiful theoretical achievement in social sciences, in fact I would say all sciences. Its axiomatic foundation is a logically/mathematically consistent set of assumptions, which are pure mathematical concepts. The theory is centred on economic exchange and ends up in the General Equilibrium which is a Platonic creation of a society where the microscopic world is integrated such that we can achieve a global optimum both for each individual and for the macroscopic society.

At the same time however it is one of the mostly questioned theoretical approaches, and many economists as well as representatives from other social sciences claim that it is completely irrelevant for the modern world. Nevertheless it remains in the basic thinking of most economists and even if few work within the core of the theory, many researchers working with specific branches of economics make assumptions related to the basic neoclassical theory.

Many economists consider the neoclassical theory as the microeconomic foundation of the macroeconomic theory and thus it is important to look a bit more closely at it particularly with respect to its relation to money.

Looking at Wikipedia, neoclassical economics is boiled down to three basic pillars of analysis.

1   People have rational preferences among outcomes that can be identified and associated with a value.
2   Individuals maximize utility and firms maximize profits.
3   People act independently on the basis of full and relevant information.

These pillars cover reasonably well the implications of the axiomatic structure of the neoclassical economy, but as we will see the axiomatic structure contains implicitly other consequences which are more dissatisfactory and not clearly intrinsic to the above pillars. Leon Walras and Arrow and Debreu have given the neoclassical theory a precise structure but these structures are very restrictive. Mainstream economics seldom pays much attention to these restrictions but uses the theory in its mathematical form without much ado and includes implicit assumptions without bothering about the mathematical consistency. In reviewing the neoclassical theory, with respect to money, value and prices, we will start from the very basic axiomatic structure as it is chiselled out in the Arrow and Debreu form and particularly use the works of Gerard Debreu. We will also build upon the detailed analysis of the axiomatic basis in Eksted and Fusari, Chapter 2.

Exchange prices and indexes

As we have seen in our overview of the historical discussions on money, the market exchange was as such seen as a basic condition but the role of the demand side was seldom taken into a serious consideration as important for the price formation. Except for the Salamanca School and Hume the prices were built on the use of production factors, particularly labour. The roots of this approach go back to Aristotle although it was Smith and Ricardo who systematically developed the approach of comparative costs and its relevance for relative value of labour use. Ricardo also explicitly considered the different qualities of labour and made allowance for a kind of classification of labour quality and its effect on relative valuation of labourers' work, which indeed is a theoretical achievement.

When we arrive to the late nineteenth century and the marginal revolution recognized and integrated the demand side in the market exchange. This was developed on the basis of an axiomatic approach based on the utility theory.

Ricardo's alternative cost theory was easy to develop into marginal conditions of optimal use of production factors. Furthermore when the utility theory, which was developed by Jevons and Walras (independently) gave rise to marginal conditions for optimization of the consumer's total utility, given a budget restriction, the system for market exchange was closed and a path to General Equilibrium of the market economy could be traced.

Already Adam Smith gave clear hints of equilibrium even if they were vaguely expressed and used the metaphysical "invisible hand". In Ricardo's writings a detection of such a general equilibrium is possible to grasp intellectually and becomes a clear aim of the scientific efforts. We can say that the lessons from Newton seem to be incorporated in economic science by Smith and Ricardo, although we know that this was not evident to other contemporary analysts like Hume and Thornton. It is an irony that shortly afterwards physics was actually leaving the ordered world of Newton. In 1865 Rudolf Clausius stated the *second principle of thermodynamics* and introduced the concept of *entropy*.[2] He based his work on Carnot's earlier work on heat engines. The studies of the concept of entropy led the physicists to look upon the assumed universal development of increasing entropy, increased distribution of energy, as a sort of direction of time, thus time is irreversible. The implications for social sciences is that human actions of any kind in the physical space are irreversible in the precise sense that they cause an increase in entropy within some part of the physical space, not necessarily in the subsystem where the action actually takes place and this contradicts the existence of a global equilibrium.[3]

Anyway in economics Walras, Menger and Jevons discussed similar ideas and in different modes were the first who showed the existence of a general equilibrium in the form of analysing a system of excess demand functions. Thus Walras' Law says that in general equilibrium the sum of all excess demand functions must be zero. The principle builds on the fact that all markets have the usual property that if the excess demand is positive it will have an upward effect

on prices when we have the opposite in case of negative excess demand. Mathematically this implies for the following system:
    let:

$DP = H(Z)$; DP is a column-vector $p_1, \ldots, p_n$ and Z represents the n
excess demand functions $z_i = h_i(z_1, \ldots, z_n)$ (E.3.1)

Linearizing around equilibrium gives us:

$DP = HZ$ where H is the square-matrix $h_{11} - h_{nn}$ (E.3.2)

We will then have a stable equilibrium when the eigen-values of the H matrix have negative real parts. Using price elasticities we may say that this occurs when we have a dominant diagonal, that is, the diagonal of the own price elasticity dominates, so in a given row $e_{i1} \ldots e_{in}$ that is:

$|e_{ii}| > |e_{i1} + \ldots e_{ii-1} + e_{ii+1} + \ldots + e_{in}|$ the system has a stable equilibrium.   (E.3.3)

However Walras formulations leave room for doubts since the precise axiomatic conditions for general equilibrium are not clear.

  With respect to money the Walrasian approach is also unclear. In principle we can add a function h_{n+1} to the above H matrix and if the demand functions, representing the $1, \ldots, n$ markets, are in equilibrium the $(n+1)$th also have to be in equilibrium. We may then normalize the price of the $n+1$ commodity to 1 and use it as a *numeraire*; the problem is that any commodity will do as a numeraire and that is a problem also in relation to earlier discussions of the nature of money. The problem of cash balances is also a difficult problem within the Walrasian approach. Smith, Hume and also the friars of the Salamanca School basically repeating the Aristotelian view claimed that money, when looking at a closed market, should be empty of any intrinsic value not to interfere with the correct valuation of the commodities. On the other hand, Hume, Smith and Ricardo claimed that in international trade it would be an advantage if money actually had an intrinsic value, granted with respect to purity and weight, in order to have international commensurability or "convertibility". Thus money in Hume's and later also Ricardo's writings two partly contradictory roles are attached to money, namely the pure medium of exchange and the convertibility in international business relations.

  Hume has some trouble with this but solves it by a kind of bimetallism, gold in international business and silver/copper coins in ordinary business. He also discusses paper in the form of *bank money* but that from another point of view, which particularly Thornton analysed and aims at the analysis of Wicksell/Keynes. However money as a medium of exchange, according to Hume, is necessary for the growth of the market economy and, as we have seen, he explicitly considers asymmetric effects of positive and negative changes in the money supply. Thus he mostly attaches the "value" of money only to its necessity for *augmenting the market turnover*, a consideration which Thornton partly agreed to, as we have seen.

When we now look at the Walrasian analysis, we first can see that the very construction leaves room for any commodity to be a *numeraire.* Smith, as we have seen, had a somewhat complex argumentation that *corn* should be the basis of the money standard. His argument however was built on an analysis where he basically had a labour standard combined with the land rent, and *corn* was the basic commodity in the survival of the labourer and the owner, thus its price was thought to be stable in the long run and that all other prices would converge to a more or less stable price relation to *corn*, which Ricardo refuted but kept value of labour, as Aristotle did.

The Walrasian approach however lacks any connection to a social structure and thus one starts to wonder what he actually achieves when counting equations. There is no condition or presumption that the chosen *numeraire* should be more stable in its price movements and thus there is no "attractor" in the system. We know that a system like 3.1/3.2 is possible to solve but there are certain strict conditions to grant the convergence to equilibrium, not only decreasing marginal utility and Say's law. Thus from a mathematical point of view and in the spirit of Wittgenstein, the Walrasian achievement is doubtful. Yes, money may be a *numeraire* from one point of view but from another point of view it is still an ordinary commodity and the question is whether these aspects are consistent with each other.

An eventual intrinsic value of money in a temporal sense is in this sense very interesting. Aristotle was well aware of this aspect and thought it would interfere with money as a medium of exchange. Based on his thoughts Hume/Smith/Ricardo as well as the friars of Salamanca, from different perspectives yes, but they still claimed that money, as a medium of exchange, was more stable in its price movements than any other commodity. Hume attached it to the very fact, with respect to internal trade, that it was used as a medium exchange, while Smith and Ricardo saw an intrinsic value as stabilizing. Thornton saw gold/silver as a norm such that Guineas, £, s and p got their proper relations. The money value varied but it varied less. This is quite natural. If the commodity prices vary more or less independently of each other given a stationary defined value or we may also assume trends of different kinds we may expect a more inert average price, particularly if we have as a norm that the sum of price elasticities adds up to -1.

Thus, if we use any kind of commodity as a medium of exchange and disregard any intrinsic value we should expect that the value of the medium expressed in the rest of the commodities would be more stable in its variations. This is however not a result of intrinsic properties but of its actual use as a medium of exchange.

An interesting question is then of course if an intrinsic value of the medium of exchange will stabilize the variations even more? Jean Baptiste Say did not think so and we are apt to think the same, however at this stage this is only a valid statement for the question of a pure medium of exchange in a closed economy. So from this point of view we would be perfectly well off with flat white stones but inserting a real commodity as a medium of exchange is more doubtful since we then have two conflicting aspects, leading for example to Gresham's law.

Arrow and Debreu[4]

In the Arrow and Debreu approach the utility theory is replaced by a preference order and diminishing of marginal utility is replaced by the axiom of local non-satiation which concerns a basket of different commodities. Thus in a basket consisting of n commodities there is always a possibility to improve the total utility of the basket by increasing one of the n commodities. The Arrow and Debreu approach consequently concerns the ranking of baskets more than single commodities, although the axioms of choice build on binary comparisons.

There are six axioms which presuppose a definition of the concept of symmetry (Ekstedt and Fusari 2010: 50). The three first axioms concern the ordering of alternatives; these axioms have also become an almost universally recognized definition of rationality, at least in the sense that all analysts have to relate to it if they enter some kind of serious analysis of rationality. These axioms are about: (i) *completeness*, meaning that all commodities in a basket can be ordered; (ii) *reflexivity*, meaning that any commodity is identical to itself; (iii) *transitivity*, meaning that the ordering is consistent. Given the definition of *symmetry*, implying for instance that if commodity x is preferred to y, commodity y is not preferred to x.

They define a consistent ordering of commodities. However the axioms, (i)–(iii), and the definition of symmetry are in fact also the pure mathematical presumptions defining the concept of an *equivalence relation*. Equivalence relation – of what? Obviously if we are to transform the pure mathematical concepts into a theory of agents we must interpret the equivalence relation, called a preference relation, as a link between desires in the head of the agent and commodities existing in the outside world, such that these two "spaces" are *homeomorphic*, that is, they possess the same form; thus if prices are changed this implies by logical necessity a corresponding revision of the actions of the agents.

Furthermore identity, as in axiom (ii) is a dangerous concept in mathematics so consequently we have objections against the axiom of reflexivity. However we have three more axioms and they play the role of creating the commodity space to a Euclidian space which is extremely convenient in mathematics, a three-dimensional variant makes up the ordinary space we live in (at least piece-wise).

The last three axioms are; (iv) *continuity*, implying that all commodity axes are infinitely divisible, (v) *local non-satiation*, which is an interesting axiom, actually rather close to Say's law given a constant commodity space, (vi) *convexity*, implying that a consumer prefers a basket containing a combination of commodities to a basket containing one or only a few commodities.

The most crucial axiom among these latter three is the continuity axiom, not so much from the view that it excludes indivisibilities but from a rather complex point of view which has to do with the way commodities are defined and in relation to non-equilibrium analysis. To discuss continuity we need to have a space with constant dimensionality and this is granted by the equivalence relation but when we question the reflexivity axiom as well as additive aggregation the axiom of continuity will be at stake, but we will return to this.

The six axioms seen as a momentary description of a single agent ready to choose is relatively harmless, but when we come to aggregating the agents into some form of collective, we are in deep trouble in the sense that the axioms give us a very peculiar picture of the agents and the society/economy. This peculiarity is fully displayed in Arrow's paradox but unfortunately often disregarded.

Money and prices in the Arrow and Debreu analysis

The Arrow and Debreu analysis is an analysis of a barter economy. There is nothing in the axioms about money and the price vector appears in the form of an abstract index, which of course implies that we could have a Walrasian view and turn any commodity to a kind of money. However the index only appears in equilibrium which is unique and consequently we can call this index a price vector, but it has nothing to do with what we call money in daily business. The fundamental point is that in equilibrium all resources are exchanged so that we achieve the highest possible efficiency with respect to the preference structure for all agents as well as the aggregate of all agents. Thus the rather gloomy quote from Keynes which started this chapter does not cast its shadows on our minds if we stick to the neoclassical theory.

The Arrow and Debreu model can be completed with a Neumann and Gale model to include production and then we subsequently will have the maximum efficient use of productive resources implying that given the preferences and the initial endowments of the agents, we are in a Pareto optimum.[5]

This means that to use the neoclassical relative prices as some kind of rationale for money implies that we either think of an everlasting existing general equilibrium or that the price vector immediately adapts to new circumstances and that the money prices work smoothly in conjunction with the price vector and consequently we are immediately in a new equilibrium. Consequently the neoclassical model with respect to the general equilibrium has actually no room for money since anything will do as a medium of exchange and that is the only aspect. Nor does the neoclassical theory have anything to contribute when we deal with non-equilibrium situations. In such situations we have a multitude of price vectors and therefore money in the sense of the Walrasian $(n+1)$th commodity does not work, we are completely lost from a theoretical perspective, but still in everyday life money works, although we have a multitude of price vectors, so obviously money in its everyday meaning, whatever it is, seems to be rather practical.

Neoclassical theory and the problem of aggregation

We claimed that the neoclassical picture is probably OK as a momentary description of the exchange by an agent. If we then imagine that we are out of equilibrium it means that given some inertia of behaviour we may very well use standard micro-theoretical techniques for investigations of demand and supply. Thus although there are multiple price vectors the inertia implies that these can be expressed by representative commodities of certain physical characteristics.

The problem arrives when we aggregate the theoretically created agent into a collective. Thus when the optimal solutions of the agents are aggregated into a general equilibrium of the whole economy something happens or better expressed some features of the axioms which are not clearly seen at the microscopic level are fully displayed in the aggregation. The axioms define a Euclidian space where the commodities define the dimensions, which means that the agent is defined by the pair $(\lesssim_i, e_i)$, that is a preference ordering and a vector of initial endowments.[6] Thus when a price vector is given we can define the agents as commodity vectors. However within the axiomatic structure there is no way in which the agent can affect the price vector, which is the classical problem of the *invisible hand*, but that means that a simple vector sum of the agents will form the commodity basket of the whole economy. Since the commodity vectors of the agents are optimal with respect to the ruling price vector, we will at the same time reach an optimal basket for all the individual agents as well as the whole economy, which also fulfils the Pareto efficiency criterion. This type of aggregation is subsequently called *additive aggregation*, illustrated in Figure 3.2. It is worth noting that John von Neumann and Oscar Morgenstern (2004 [1944]: 21) in their discussions on measurability of expected utility arrive at the same kind of vector addition.

The general problem of this solution is that the agents actually do not choose. As we mentioned above the first three axioms concern an ordering structure and also from a mathematical point of view is a definition of an equivalence relation. That means that the preference orders, so to say inside the minds of the agents are equivalent to an ordering of the commodities. But that works quite OK when the agent stands in front of a counter in the shop but does it really work intertemporally or in relation to the choices of other people? The latter problem is present in Arrow's paradox. This is actually where the *axiom of reflexivity* enters into the discussion. We mentioned that this axiom is dealing with the identity of a commodity; a commodity is identical to itself. But is it really so? A commodity *as a physical item or process* is obviously identical to itself, but is a *commodity* identical to itself as a *commodity*? When we accept this axiom of reflexivity we also as a corollary get the independence of irrelevant alternatives, which can be expressed as:

> The binary choice between any two commodities in a basket is independent of the other commodities in that basket.

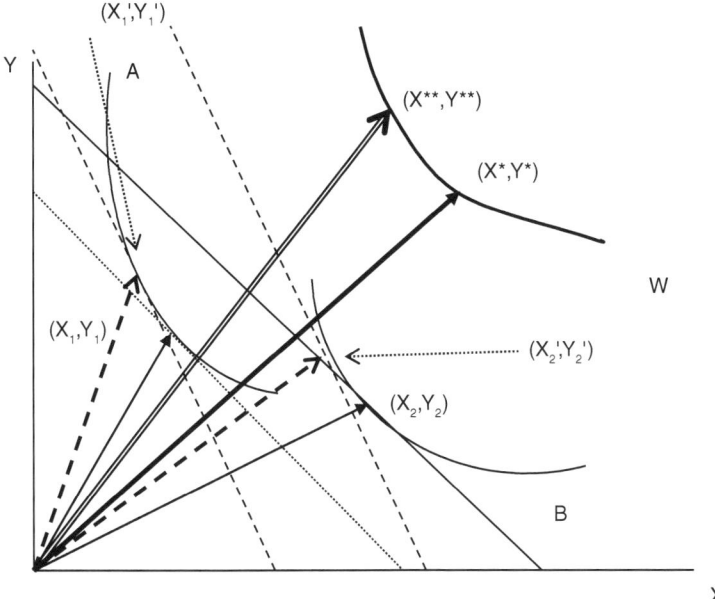

Figure 3.2 Additive aggregation.

The point is that a commodity contains a number of functions which in reality is demanded by the agent, thus the axiom of reflexivity tells us that the physical appearance of an item or a function is identical to its functions, which is next to nonsense. Consequently we may express this lacuna from an economic point of view, by saying that the identity of physical characteristics does not necessarily imply that the commodity is identical to itself in different spaces or different times. This leads to another apprehension of the concept *commodity*. The standard apprehension is convenient from a mathematical point of view, since the production sector produces the physical characteristics of a commodity, which means that if the preferences of the consumer only rank the precise physical characteristics irrespective of the context, then the existence proof of equilibrium is straightforward. But if we for example refer to modern consumption theory based on the *household production approach* by Gary Becker we see the weakness of the axiom with respect to the market behaviour of the individuals, the actor in Figure 3.2 is the one who controls the price vector whether it is an invisible hand or some deus ex machina.

The effect of the axiom of reflexivity in the very axiomatic structure is that since the production sector produces physical items or processes, an independent interpretation of these items/processes by the consumers with respect to their functions in a particular context would ruin the proof of the existence of general equilibrium. A rejection of the axiom would also imply a possibility of multiple price vectors. Another effect of a rejection would be that the interpretation of the *mathematical concept of equivalence relation* as a definition of human rationality would not be valid.[7]

Our discussions so far actually make us able to explain Arrow's paradox, which will have far reaching consequences for our discussions of money.

Arrow's paradox[8]

Arrow's voting paradox or more precisely *Arrow's Impossibility Theorem* has gained an undisputed rank as the leading theorem of the limited possibilities to achieve a Pareto optimum in a society built on democratic principles. It is also accepted in this role outside the traditional realms of economic science, particularly in political science as it takes a central role in the analysis of collective choice (Laver 1997; Downs 1957).

Arrow's paradox is built on the theoretical pillars of the economic theory, more specifically the neoclassical axiomatic structure and thus it is a paradox with respect to the neoclassical theory but it will not necessarily have something to say about the reality. In fact Arrow's paradox, although devastating from a neoclassical perspective, is less devastating to aggregate political actions in the real world.

The discussions in the aftermath of Arrow's Impossibility Theorem have unfortunately more concerned an assumed conflict between democracy and efficiency. Furthermore it has led to questions about and possibilities of the rationality of aggregate actions in a democracy. Arrow's paradox is instead to be regarded as a kind of question to the theory and its axiomatic structure, why a certain result shows up in relation to the reality. It is not a question about the reality which is what it is.

Technically speaking the paradox deals with the problem of additive aggregation, thus Arrow compares exchange equilibrium with a situation where the agents cast their votes for alternatives based on an individual ranking. That means that the paradox deals with the links between the microscopic and the macroscopic states, and is subsequently of importance relative to the concept of money, since money is on one hand seen as a pure medium of exchange, a medium which "is the oil which renders the motion of wheels more smooth and easy" to quote Hume (1770: 43), but it is also the most liquid asset as well as convertible in international affairs which affects the internal monetary system and thus the interest rates, distribution of credits and consumer prices. Consequently money is a strong link between the microscopic and the macroscopic world and if we are satisfied with additive aggregation like in the general equilibrium theory there are few things to bother about, but, if not, we certainly have a problem of *Money in Economic Theory*.

Arrow's voting paradox involves a particular axiomatic structure for the social welfare function on the aggregate level beside the axiomatic structure governing the behaviour of the agents and defining the features of the commodities.

The resulting paradox tells us that if the agents are able to rank alternatives and vote with respect to the social outcome according to the majority principle, this outcome will on one hand differ from the outcome of the market process and on the other hand since one of the used axioms of the social welfare function presupposes non-dictatorship the outcome of the voting process implies that this axiom is broken, and thus we consequently end up in a paradox.

The central point in Arrow's paradox is that he allows the agents to vote. However Arrow's paradox is developed within the frames of the neoclassical theory and deals with the aggregate level of the economy, thus the modelling of man at the exchange market and the subsequent commodity space is identical to the six axioms of the general equilibrium theory: completeness, reflexivity, transitivity, local non-satiation, continuity and convexity.[9]

In order to analyse the voting problem Arrow has to define an aggregate space, thus he imposes the following axioms defining the social welfare function:

- *Universality*: the social welfare function should be based on every agent's individual preference order.
- *Citizen sovereignty*: any individual agent could maintain the social welfare function as their own preference function.
- *Non-dictatorship*: the social welfare function should not satisfy an individual or a group of individuals irrespective of other agents' preference functions.
- *Correspondence between social and individual values*: if an individual preference is changed in a particular dimension the social welfare function must be changed in the same direction independently of other dimensions.

From a technical point of view we now have a commodity space for individual exchange and an aggregate space for the aggregate features of the social affairs. So we may ask whether or not individual actions/choices in the two spaces are consistent.

From a mathematical point of view the consistence will occur if we can link the two spaces point-wise, thus define an equivalence relation. With respect to the agents' behaviour we must define one type of behaviour in each space, for the ordinary exchange space we have the neoclassical general equilibrium analysis which can be aggregated but for the aggregate we now define a voting behaviour based on the majority principle. For the latter type of behaviour it is obvious that the individual wants the majority vote to ensure the best possible solution, thus given a form of rational behaviour the individual agents need to take other individuals' opinions into consideration and thus forming possible coalitions.

The well-known result of Arrow's voting paradox will then be as already indicated that the two behaviours will not coincide in their aggregate solutions, thus there is no equivalence relations between the space formed by neoclassical axiomatic structure and the space where the individuals are able to vote.

Why does this result appear? Let us scrutinize the two spaces.

The four axioms of the welfare function are clearly linked to Pareto optimum and the Pareto principle. Thus we are in a Pareto optimum when no agent can improve the result of the exchange without worsening the situation of another agent. We know that general equilibrium fulfils this optimality criterion. Thus if we look at the four axioms for the aggregate level we see that all of them can be derived from the six axioms for the barter economy.

The fundamental feature of Pareto optimality in general equilibrium is that it is achieved by additive aggregation. In Figure 3.2 we gave a simple illustration of the technique of vector aggregation of agents into a collective, which might be expressed as a Social Welfare Function; the commodities are represented by the axes and the agents by the two indifference curves respectively. The reader may quickly verify with a pencil and a ruler that the (X^*, Y^*) and (X^{**}, Y^{**}) baskets respectively define the longest distance from the origin for any feasible combination for the two agents given the indicated income and price relation. The reason for this is that the six axioms of the neoclassical theory define a measurable Euclidian space and then if all agents achieve their maximal points, adding the values of these points will give a maximum point for the aggregate basket which is constructed through an additive process, which is indicated for two price relations in the figure.

Thus the aggregate basket is in fact a simple vector sum of the individual baskets.

The *universality axiom* is clearly valid in Figure 3.2 since we have a simple vector addition. The *citizen sovereignty* is fulfilled since the aggregate basket contains the optimal point solutions for the agents. Hence we have that:

$$\sum_i \sum_j p_{ij} \cdot x_{ij} = P * \cdot X *$$

where agents $i = 1, \ldots, n$ and commodities $j = 1, \ldots, m$, and consequently:

$$\frac{1}{n} \cdot \sum_i \sum_j p_{ij} \cdot x_{ij} = \frac{1}{n} \cdot P * \cdot X * \text{ and } \frac{1}{m} \cdot \sum_i \sum_j p_{ij} \cdot x_{ij} = \frac{1}{m} \cdot P * \cdot X * \quad \text{(E.3.4)}$$

Thus there is an average consumer and an average preference function which can be attained by any of the agents and subsequently the universality axiom is fulfilled.

If the two first axioms are true in the sense of Figure 3.2, the third *axiom on non-dictatorship* has to be true. This is a simple consequence of our demonstration of the averages. (Interesting however since a single axiom in a particular axiomatic structure must not be explained by the other axioms in the structure.) This axiom is superfluous with regard to Figure 3.2 and the way we have constructed it, where we as a matter of fact already have incorporated the axioms in question. In the neoclassical general equilibrium we have also granted the Pareto optimality which means, given the preference structures of the agents, that a change in the price structure, *ceteris paribus*, leads to a new aggregate equilibrium but we will have redistributed effects. So, given the two indifference curves in Figure 3.2 we may construct a community indifference field with respect to changing price vectors but to each price relation is linked a unique distribution of resources.

Actually the last *axiom of correspondence between individual and social values* is also dependent on the first two axioms in our Figure 3.2, which is trivial according to what we have said above.

In fact, given the six axioms of the neoclassical general equilibrium theory none of the four axioms of the Social Welfare Function proposed by Arrow adds any new substance to the aggregate analysis. The four axioms are consistent with the six neoclassical axioms concerning the individual and the subsequent additive aggregation.[10]

Thus the aggregate space defined by four axioms is consistent with the space defined by the six neoclassical axioms and consequently we have an equivalence relation between the two spaces. *But then we impose the voting schemes and find that we cannot replicate the market outcome through a voting procedure and furthermore we find that any result from the voting process will violate the non-dictatorship axiom.*

Thus the introduction of voting agents breaks the axiomatic structure which is supposed to hold and the paradox obviously arises because of the imputed voting process. From the point of view of mathematics/logics it is thus very doubtful if we should see Arrow's paradox as a paradox. The imputed agent who votes doesn't belong to the collective of agents obeying the axioms. But voting is not a strange phenomenon in the real world so that means that we need to scrutinize the theoretical agent.

Thus if the agents of such a voting process are consistent with the agents defined by the axioms then we end up in a first rank logical paradox which might be rather ugly when we interpret it in relation to the reality. If not, we have implicitly defined a new type of agent which is not consistent with the axioms and then the paradox tells us that the two types of agents are different and that *additive aggregation* most probably doesn't hold for the new imputed type of agents. The result is fruitful since it sheds some light on the character of the theoretical agents of the neoclassical theory. Somehow concepts or axioms have a specific dimension which we overlook and that particular dimension is displayed in the paradox.

Thus Arrow's paradox occurs because the neoclassical agent defined by the six axioms is unable to vote and is thus contradictive to agents which possess this ability. Consequently the introduced agent who is able to vote destroys any possibility of additive aggregation.

In Figure 3.2 we see the principle of additive aggregation and that the agents are totally passive in this process. Thus the agents defined by the six axioms are totally isolated from any kind of social influence. The axiom most in charge of that feature is as we have seen the seemingly innocent *axiom of reflexivity*. The axiomatic structure leads to the result that we in equilibrium have a unique price vector and that the commodity basket as well as the income of the agents is measured with an (mathematical) index created by this price vector. In standard nomenclature this is the basis for the neoclassical money.

Whether Arrow's paradox has something to do with non-dictatorship or not is in this new context a nonsensical question. When we allow the agents to react on the aggregate result we have opened for a quite different analysis which is not possible to pursue within the realm of the six axioms. Thus if we, by a particular axiomatic structure, deny people to vote on the aggregate structures, in what other aspects can then this axiomatic structure be used to analyse other features of human behaviour and what are the precise frames for such an analysis? That is completely dependent on the inertia of behaviour and structures. Thus a global analysis is out of the question if we do not end up in a completely deterministic explanation of the human being.

The analytical result that the axiom of non-dictatorship is broken has received much attention and many efforts have been devoted to the assumed conflict between economic efficiency and democracy. What we have shown is that no such discussion is relevant from a strictly logical point of view. If the agents have the ability to analyse the relation of aggregate decisions with respect to their individual behaviour the whole question of economic efficiency on the individual level as well as on the aggregate level has to be analysed from an entirely different set of assumptions. Furthermore the concept of democracy in its everyday sense seems to have virtually nothing to do in an analysis dealing with the so-called "economic man" if we are to strictly keep to its axiomatic definition.

Consequently we have to interpret Arrow's paradox in a quite different relation namely that agents actually have the ability to consider and to form expectations of the aggregate result and let those considerations/expectations influence their actions. But then, if we do not put restrictive assumptions on these considerations/expectations, we leave the world of general equilibrium as a viable theoretical feature of the real world. This of course doesn't mean that we have to abandon the use of it as a theoretical tool but any attempt to rely on the general equilibrium as an empirical feature is bound to fail. In the analysis of money this interaction between the microscopic and the macroscopic world is of central importance and an analysis disregarding this is grossly erroneous and totally misses the gist of the monetary economy.

Money and cash balances

From our introductory comments on the Walrasian kind of money and our discussion on the price index in the Arrow and Debreu setting we understand that not only money as a medium of exchange in the neoclassical economy is problematic as is eventual holding of cash balances and the logical rationale for that. A reason which often is mentioned is that money diminishes the transactions costs which, alluding to Hume, money is the oil which makes the transactions go smoothly. At the same time the neoclassical theory has, with respect to both Adam Smith and Aristotle, the aspect of a store of value.

Let us look at both these aspects.

If we regard *transaction costs*, money obviously has a value separate from the residual equation in Walras' setting where it is defined identically to one, if exchange transactions appear asymmetrically over time. If we pass over to the Arrow and Debreu analysis we obviously have to define the transaction costs into some form of commodity or include it in the price of the particular commodities, but if we do so *ceteris paribus* vis-à-vis the axiomatic structure we are obviously at the same position as before. We have redefined the commodities or defined a new commodity dimension. Unfortunately such theoretical manipulations may create more problems than they solve. If we include the transactions costs in the definition of commodities they have to be uniform over time and space otherwise we have a multitude of markets in space and time and aggregation will indeed be problematic. If we choose to define transactions costs (or sooner the services which are behind the costs) as a commodity we are in worse trouble since we then define a dimension, which is not independent of other commodity dimensions.

Furthermore if we keep cash balance as a way of diminishing transaction costs the cash balance should appear in the utility function beside commodities and leisure and the price of the cash balance could be the forgone interest. But if so we will have two effects: first the utility of the cash balance increases with increased transaction costs and, second, we have to ask what happens if all prices and incomes are inflated at the same rate? In standard theory money is supposed to have homogeneity of degree zero implying that doubling all prices and incomes leaves the optimization problem as it has been before the doubling. But if we now let cash balances appear in the utility function it will certainly not be of homogeneity zero and thus we will have the result that its utility value increases with the degree of inflation.[11] Such a result is indeed strange and at variance with conventional macroeconomic wisdom.

Keynesians teach us that cash balances are linked to risk and uncertainty and we may accept that (at least the risk concept), but this also implies that money will have a value independent of other commodities and we run into the same kind of problems as when we introduced transaction costs.

Assume a market economy defined by the usual neoclassical axioms. This economy has an environment which is not affected by the market transactions but the opposite holds that the different state of art on the environment affects the market transactions. Rain – no rain, break down of computer systems or not given a time horizon. We certainly know that assuming complete knowledge of future development of the environment is impossible, so we introduce a concept of *risk* meaning that the states of the world, outside the market, affect the market. Given that the states of the environment are independent of the market transaction we understand that it is rational to assume some kind of probability distribution over the different possible states, relevant to a certain activity. In such a world we may introduce an insurance system for the agents, who have to devote some resources to buy an appropriate insurance service.

But given a smoothly working insurance system there should be no need for cash balances.

A difficult problem in relation to this example is if the perception of the risk structure varies. In that case we will have a definition *à la* Radner (1982) who completed Debreu's definition of an agent $(\lesssim_i, e_i)$, a preference function and a vector of endowments to $(\lesssim_i, e_i, \gamma_i)$ where γ_i is some kind of vector of information/

knowledge.[12] In Radner's setting we have a new type of risk which is internal to the agent and shows up as an uncertainty of the insurance needs. We also realize that such a situation could well explain the needs for a cash balance but as a matter of fact it is more serious than that. Since the individual perception of this risk will vary we will come to the situation that we will in fact have different price vectors in the economy in the beginning of the process and then we perfectly well understand the need for cash balances but at the same time we realize that we leave the neoclassical approach for some kind of what is called *false trading*, i.e. trading out of equilibrium. We may of course assume that if the environmental probabilities are constant the successive market results will result in a learning process and that in the long run the economy will converge to long-term equilibrium.[13]

Describing the problem in this way we may accept the neoclassical picture of the market economy and we are a bit lost again about money since we know that money indeed exists in the real world and plays a crucial role for economic stability and at least we may suspect that the requirement of an inert environment is not met. So obviously the above picture can be suspected not to be entirely true and there are as we will see more serious troubles with the nice future we have painted and basically these troubles are theoretically introduced by Arrow's paradox and our considerations with respect to that. The rejection of the axiom of reflexivity and the result of Arrow's paradox make us compelled to accept that people consider the aggregate behaviour of the society as well as other fellows' behaviour actually introduces a risk/uncertainty structure into the analysis which is not prevalent in the orthodox neoclassical axiomatic structure.

Let us compare the two economic subspaces, in Figure 2.4, where subspace A is agents created by the neoclassical axiomatic structure and subspace B is populated with the kind of voting agents Arrow introduced to get his paradox, with respect to their relation to each other and the environment.

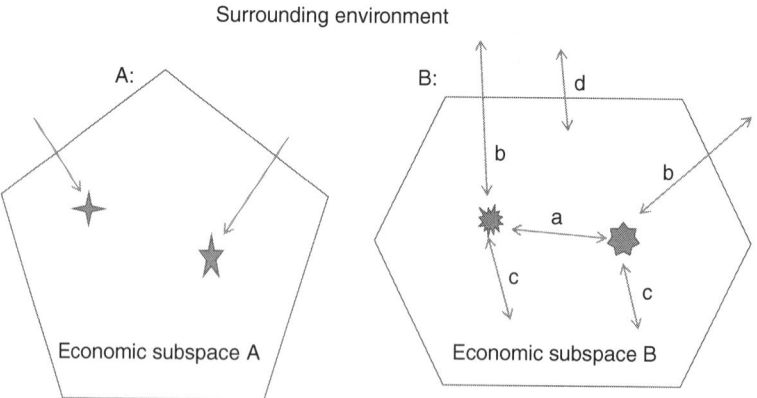

Figure 3.3 Relations between the agents and the environment.

In the A-space we see that agents are affected only by the environment outside the economic sphere which sets the risk structure with respect to choices. In the B-space the a-arrows represent interaction between agents, the b-arrows interactions between the agents and the environment, the c-arrows represent the interaction between the agents and the aggregate economic space and finally the d-arrows the interaction between the aggregate economic space and the environment. The neo-classical picture is limited to the A-space with an assumption that the surrounding environment is constant with respect to the probability structure of different events. The B-space is a result of our considerations of Arrow's paradox. This actually means that the agents and their behaviour belongs to the environment of each other, thus the agents induce a risk/uncertainty to each other. Furthermore if we add that the agents carry the ability of inventions and innovations we may see a seed to a dynamic process.

We can give a simplified example of a development of a B-type economic space, concerning a big company in Sweden and its development.[14]

This development is more or less the same for the greater part of the Swedish industry during these years. As we understand the development led to changed conditions for the Swedish government in its economic policy. It also led to changed relations between industry and the workforce and the labour market as a whole as well as changes in the internal relations on the labour market since we had a more pronounced heterogeneity and also to a more pronounced labour hoarding. Furthermore it resulted in changed conditions for Sweden's foreign economic relations. This example concerns a small open economy but we can find similar examples for bigger economies.

Subsequently we find that introduction of complex risk and uncertainty structures seems to be a rationale for using money and/or financial instruments near money as a store of value for insurance purposes.

Consequently we may say that the reason to find a rational for cash balances in the neoclassical theory is that concepts such as transactions cost, risk and uncertainty are impossible to handle within the axiomatic structure and almost certainly appear in states of out of equilibrium.

The neoclassical axiomatic structure is interesting in the sense that it provides some sort of general equilibrium which fulfils the Pareto optimum, but it is not sufficient for explaining economic behaviour outside economic equilibrium and it is indeed a matter of both philosophical and social considerations to compare the kind of result we will achieve in an analysis of an economic system

Table 3.1 Changing market structure

	Sweden		USA	
	1965	*1987*	*1965*	*1987*
Market share (%)	35	25	≈0	1.8
Share of production (%)	85	17	<2	25

populated with the voting guys in Arrow's paradox with a state of equilibrium where the axioms are fulfilled.

How can we avoid theoretical chaos?

The B-world in Figure 3.3 is really terrible from a theoretical perspective. A first glance indicates at best a kind of chaos analysis. A global model of such an economy must more or less describe the whole world in its complexity and such models are generally meaningless. Thus we have to mostly build our theoretical approaches on partial analyses under the assumption of at least some inertia. One question is how we deal with the theoretical construction of the agent, which is different from the neoclassical one; another question is that if we mostly have to deal with non-equilibrium approaches implying that we also have to formulate problems that are actually relevant in such a situation, we enter an undefined world relative to the earlier axiomatic structure.

We will start this discussion with analysing the individual predicaments and see in what way we can use the standard axioms, but in a modified form, and further what consequences this will have on an eventual aggregate analysis. After this we will discuss some interesting developments of the neoclassical model, which still keeps the flavour of the neoclassical world but is modified in the direction towards non-equilibrium analysis.

The neoclassical theory is an a priori theory. It is not supported by any empirical evidence.[15] It is based on an attempt to form some kind of deterministic system as the Newtonian equilibrium system. We know that Adam Smith was very impressed by Newton and he actually tried to impose Newton's way of thinking on economics. In a way this is explainable since he saw the land rent and the labour value as the two basic variables which, particularly land rent, should be seen as constants. Thus he did not entirely think of the invisible hand as the "deus ex machina" but had a dynamic attractor which formed a fixed equilibrium. This is by no means unique for Adam Smith but was expressed by Aristotle, even if he did not build any kind of systematic theory, David Ricardo, who developed Smith's analysis into a more rigorous system, and Marx, who draw different conclusions but worked with the same kind of systematic analysis. The *neoclassical analysis* was then only a perfection of the mathematical form of the classical analysis adding the demand side.

However we know that David Hume had a more critical attitude to Newton's closed system particularly when transposed into social sciences. Jean Baptiste Say also emphasized the inferences between the economic "system" and the surrounding social development. True that Say gave a general description of the diffusion process of money throughout the economy similar to that which Hume had described but this description was later squeezed into a deterministic rule that has been called *Say's law*, which indeed is a doubtful extension of Say's rather general diffusion process. It was however the law which Keynes attacked. It is therefore a bit ironic to realize that the *axiom of non-satiation*, although it is strictly mathematical, reveals Say's hypothesis to be more accurate for a constant dimensionality of the commodity space than the rule which Keynes attacked, but it is still insufficient in comparison with Say's discussion, which we later will discuss.[16]

When we interpret the neoclassical model as a choice model when the agent has made up his mind about a current limited commodity space it is probably a relevant interpretation, and that is the way Gerard Debreu actually interprets it. In chapter 2.2 "Dates and Locations of Theory of Value" he defines precisely the concepts of dates and locations and proceed in 2.3 "Goods":[17]

> Again, a good at a certain location and the same good at another location are *different* economic objects, and the specification of the location at which it will be available is essential. In the case now discussed a commodity is therefore defined by specification of all its physical characteristics, of its availability date, and of its availability location. As soon as one of these three factors changes, a *different* commodity results.
>
> (Debreu 1987 [1959]: 29–30, original emphasis)

Our earlier discussion on the neoclassical structure is parallel to Debreu's distinctions. If we thus stick to Debreu's distinctions we will, most probably, within the frames of an economy have a multitude of price vectors given a precise interval of time, and subsequently within a specified location we will, most probably, have a multitude of price vectors over a trajectory of time intervals.

Thus according to Debreu's specifications additive aggregation is extremely difficult not to say impossible. The difference between the standard use of the axioms and the precise definitions by Debreu is most probably one of the most important sources for disagreements over the neoclassical theory, particularly when it is applied on macroscopic problems.

Subjects and contexts

A reasonable view is that there is an inference between the economic subsystem and a surrounding social context. From such a point of view the neoclassical theory apart from its microscopic use, has nothing to tell us about aggregate matters save for an inclusion of additional assumptions which must be logically consistent and restrict the use of the theory to a very specific interval of time and space. In Ekstedt and Fusari (2010: 46) there is an example of a flea-market which can serve as a realistic use of the axiomatic structure as a mirror of some piece of the reality.

So what about the microscopic foundation for a macroscopic theory?

Let us first observe that money which is a troublesome object in the neoclassical theory when used in the standard everyday way is quite alright as a medium of exchange in multimarket economy with a multitude of price vectors. Since the use is, if we stick to Debreu's distinctions, local in space and time we don't need to bother with eventually contradictive price vectors.

As we mentioned the neoclassical theory is an a priori theory where the defined agents lack any social connection. Eventual stability in the system is created by assumptions on elasticities of demand and supply implicit in the preferences (ibid.: 190–1). But unfortunately one gets some rather nasty troubles with the implicit assumption of no false trading. Thus the stability of the market is completely outside the realm of the individual agents so the invisible hand has quite a job to do. If we then reject the axiomatic structure we obviously lose even the last straw of possible intrinsic stability.

Subsequently we have to search for another kind of agent who according to our discussion of Arrow's paradox is also able to vote. With respect to our findings in the scrutiny of the axioms and also with respect to Debreu's definition of commodities we may claim that choices are context dependent, but how about rationality?

First of all we see that implicit in our discussion of the commodity is the fact that a commodity is interpreted with respect to a perceived context. This means that it is actually possible to save the concept of human rationality by defining rationality with respect to the subject's contextual apprehension. We may even take one step more and say that almost all humans are almost always rational given a contextual apprehension. We use the word *almost* in case of pathological behaviour, which means inability to act consistently, to panic or suffer from grave mental distortions and such matters, which means that a rational behaviour is not necessarily to be regarded as particularly sound or good. This is written in the aftermath of the massacre on Utöja in Norway, 22 July 2011. The murderer Breivik was certainly rational in his planning and performance of the killings, although his writings exposed a perverted apprehension of his environment and of people.[18] In economic analysis the word rational has come to give rise to positive signals but that is only valid within the very precise axiomatic structure of the neoclassical theory where the agent is made into a machine or a rigid body.

As our philosophical foundation we may take David Hume's analysis in *Treatise of Human Nature*:

> Nothing is more usual in philosophy, and even in common life, than to talk of the combat of passion and reason, to give the preference to reason, and assert that men are only so far virtuous as they conform themselves to its dictates.... I shall endeavour to prove *first* that reason alone can never be a motive to any action of the will; and *secondly* that it can never oppose passion in the direction of the will.
>
> (2002 [1740]: 116–17, original emphasis)

So we can regard the neoclassical axioms as valid when the agent has made the contextual considerations and is ready to act, *and that is exactly according to Gerard Debreu and his precise definitions of the concept of commodity.*

Epistemic cycles

Since we have introduced the context of the agent and an assumption that, given the contextual apprehension, the agent is rational we may actually combine this into a concept which we call an *epistemic cycle*. This concept is originally introduced in physics, quantum physics, by Thomas Brody (1993). In Ekstedt and Fusari it was transposed into social science, particularly economics.

Definition of the concept "epistemic cycle": "An *epistemic cycle* is a set of purposes, contextual apprehensions, including perceived physical/social/cultural restrictions, which forms a base for action." Epistemic cycles are defined on any individual or aggregate level and are independent of how the aggregate decision is initiated; the only condition is that it is accepted by the individuals forming the aggregate (who by all means can be forced to accept it).

We may illustrate the concept as in Figure 3.4, which contains both a closed and a broken cycle. Observe that as a consequence of the fact that the preference relations are context dependent the purposes of the agents are also defined outside the economic realm similar to the kind of reasoning we have in the Household Production approach.

Thus a cycle is completed when the purposes are fulfilled. The agents are assumed to be rational with respect to their actions after the contextual considerations are done; thus we define rationality as *purposeful action* and imply that we keep the postulate that the agents are optimizing their behaviour. This is in fact a very important postulate since if we did not make it we must ask who is going to be the judge of the purposes and restrictions, set the norms of optimality and decide the correct apprehension of the environment.

When a cycle is closed, that is that the purposes are achieved, this is some form of affirmation for the agent that his judgements were right. Obviously this

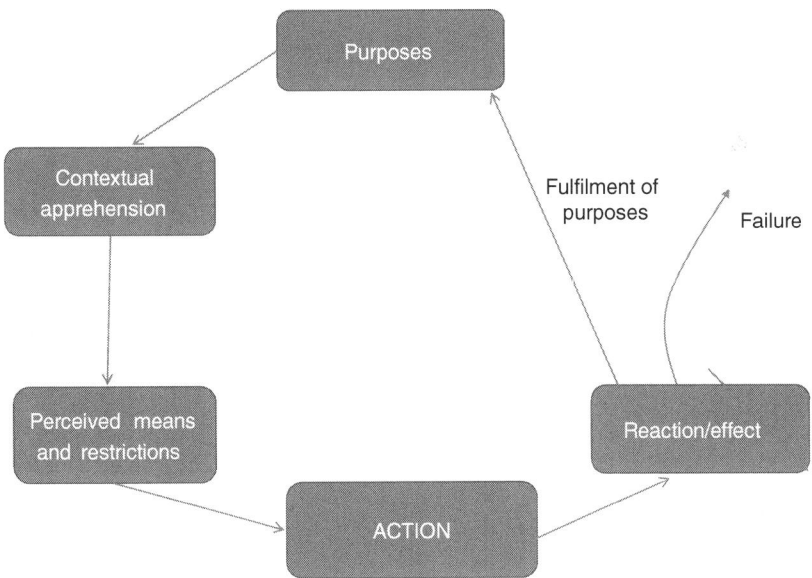

Figure 3.4 Epistemic cycle.

may not be true since the result may occur by coincidence in spite of bad judgements, but anyway the agent will probably interpret it in such a way that his/her judgements are cemented for at least a while and the phrase "what did I tell you?" is an reaction to inert behaviour in acting vis-à-vis purposes in relation to the contextual apprehension.

When a cycle is not closed this will give rise to changes either in purposes or in the contextual apprehension, thus we will have a dynamic impulse of similar kind as the *ex ante/ex post* reasoning.

The important thing with epistemic cycles is that we have a concept allowing us to discuss inert and dissipative behaviour and we may also extend the concept to aggregate organizations. However this makes the problem of aggregation acute again, so how do we deal with that given the concept of epistemic cycles? First of all we can dismiss the idea of a global rationality and optimality in the sense that an aggregate rationality is not contradictive to the containing individual agents' rationality; this also follows as we see from the discussion of Arrow's paradox. Thus an aggregate decision may well be optimal given the appropriate epistemic cycle which governs the decision of an eventual aggregate body, but the condition is of course that the individual agents contained in the aggregate are willing (or forced) to accept the aggregate decision. So there we have the voting agent with willingness to subordinate to a coalition. However since the epistemic cycles governing their "voting" behaviour with respect to aggregate matters are by definition different among the agents since they are *subjects*, we run into a rather deep logical problem which involves Russell's paradox. Given our definition of epistemic cycles we see that the agents in the neoclassical theory are so defined that if we look at two classes of agents, s_i and s_j, these belong to the aggregate class $S_i = [s_i, s_j]$, which also is a class of agents, Thus for the universal class S^* we find that the class $[s_1, \ldots, s_i, \ldots, s_j, \ldots, s_n] = [s_1, \ldots, S_i, \ldots, s_n]$, which implies that the universal class of agents is a class of agents. This follows from the axioms and means that they have the same form of purposes, and meet the same contextual structure and as we see from Figure 3.2 we make a simple vector aggregation. If we then transform the agents to epistemic cycles, which actually Debreu does in his definition of an agent $(\lesssim_i, e_i)$, we find that the epistemic cycles in the neoclassical theory belong to what is called *non-proper classes*; that is, the universal class belong to itself.

When we reject the axiom of reflexivity and thus additive aggregation we must define the rational agent according to the apprehended context. We might thus enlarge Debreu's definition of an agent to $(\lesssim_i, e_i, c_i)$, where c_i is the ith agent's contextual apprehension. We may also add that agents have not the same contextual apprehension, which follows from the fact that they belong to each other's context. Thus a sort of coalition as in the case of Arrow's paradox, some agents have to adjust to the coalition in relation to their individual purposes and thus if we look at the above non-proper class we find that; $[s_1, \ldots, s_i, \ldots, s_j, \ldots, s_n] \neq [s_1, \ldots, S_i, \ldots, s_n]$, and consequently that the universal class does not belong to itself, which means that it is a *proper class*.[19]

Anyway when we have rejected the additive aggregation we arrive at a theoretical structure where the individuals, represented by their respective epistemic cycles and also that following Arrow's paradox any collective decision can be represented by an epistemic cycle.

We can now formulate a theorem concerning the mereological structure.[20] Mereological Rule of Thumb (MRT):

> Assume a system A^* consisting of a finite number of subsystems, which are to be regarded as proper classes, $s_1 \ldots s_n$. If then we have a measure allowing us to define an optimizing rule both on A^* as well as $s_1 \ldots s_n$; optimization of the global system A^* must imply that at least one of the subsystems s_i must sub-optimize.
>
> If on the other hand all the subsystems, $s_1 \ldots s_n$ are optimized according to the same optimizing process the global system A^* must sub-optimize.
>
> (Ekstedt and Fusari 2010: 133)

Given MRT we realize that optimum is possible for organizations on any aggregate level independently of eventual optimum on any other level. That doesn't mean that the different aggregate decision levels of a system are independent of each other but this is more connected to the question whether the epistemic cycles will be closed or not.

Second, following the technique in Arrow's paradox, no epistemic cycle can be formed by an abstract organizational entity on any aggregate level but is formed by its individual members of the deciding body relative to its institutional and/or hierarchical form. That means that we do not accept any organizational metaphysics as of the ninteenth century bureaucratic philosophers like von Treitschke's "Welt Geist". The humans and the peculiarities in their relations form all kind of institutional decisions.

The third aspect implicit in the concept of epistemic cycles and the derived MRT is that the factor which is most important for the stability of the existence of epistemic cycles and decision entities on higher aggregate levels (if it is not stabilized with sheer repressive power), is the relation between the aggregate structures and its contained individual epistemic cycles. So what was a problem in the analysis of Arrow's paradox becomes now something very important for aggregate stability.

The concept of epistemic cycles is primarily a pure abstract concept, which must be seen as an analytical tool and it is thus an a priori concept. It cannot be observed empirically. The central feature is *action*, which we can observe. There is no way in which we can know of the motives and reasons of human actions but we can perhaps observe inertia of actions, which given general inertia of the environment in which the action takes place, may lead us to construct different kinds of models for the perceived causal structure. The latter is important as the inertia of environment also is a matter of apprehension. Well-situated and educated people have in general a high influence on their own lives and may look at a certain well-defined environment in time and space as inert, while poor and socially unsecure people may look at the same environment as highly unstable. The environment of an agent is formed by the physical, social, political and economic reality, thus the actions of other agents are as much a component in the environment as the possibility of having rain within the next hour. In fact it is to be claimed later that the agents themselves are the basic root of genuine economic uncertainty and this is completely outside the frames of the neoclassical theory.

Fundamental for the use of the concept epistemic cycle is that we focus on the agents' actions and the inertia of behaviour. Theoretically however we cannot derive any link from action to the purposes of the agents like we do according to the *correlate of revealed preferences* with respect to the axioms of the neoclassical theory, since we cannot say anything of the agents' apprehension of the context.

In the analysis of Arrow's paradox we pointed out that the agents have the ability to act on information of the aggregate results which means that some epistemic cycles of an agent may involve apprehensions of different aggregate levels depending on the actual purposes of the agent, thus the agent is actually defining the appropriate context which means that agents with the same purposes may apprehend different contexts and thus arrive at different conclusions with respect to actions on the aggregate levels.

Furthermore we have achieved to derive a logical rational for Wicksell's differentiation of stability on the microscopic level and stability on the macroscopic level.

The dimensionality problem and economic behaviour

Our analysis of the neoclassical axiomatic structure implies that we reject it in a universal sense and we also reject additive aggregation. The reason is that a general interpretation, in space and time, of the axiomatic structure leads to absurd descriptions of both individuals and commodities. One important feature is that we have to postulate constant dimensionality of the commodity space. In Chapter 2 on Jean Baptiste Say we mentioned Keynes', or more correct the neoclassical, misapprehension of Say's law, but in the current discussion we must admit that this misapprehension led Keynes to a very constructive path of thinking about the problem of dimensionality of the commodity space.

As we illustrated in Figure 2.3 we must interpret commodities as an axis of a commodity space. Therefore it is important to assume that the introduction of new commodities implies that they are substitutes for old ones. This is also the basic postulate in the Endogenous Growth Theory. Keynes writes in the foreword to the French edition of *General Theory*:

> I believe that economics everywhere up to recent times has been dominated, much more than has been understood, by the doctrines associated with the name of J-B Say. It is true that his "law of markets" has been long abandoned by most economists; but they have not extricated themselves from his

basic assumptions and particularly from his fallacy that demand is created by supply. Say was implicitly assuming that the economic system was always operating up to its full capacity, *so that a new activity was always in substitution for, and never in addition to, some other activity.* Nearly all subsequent economic theory has depended on, in the sense that it has required, this same assumption.

(1973 [1936]: xxxv, my emphasis)

It is obvious that the introduction of a new commodity forming a new commodity dimension is devastating for the uniqueness of the price vector. We can of course assume instantaneous adaptation but that does not help much since there are infinitely many price vectors which are possible after the introduction of the new dimension, which is illustrated in Figure 3.5.

As we see from Figure 3.5 there is no theoretically consistent measure between T0 and T1. True that we may adopt ad hoc measures but that requires rather comprehensive empirical information.

Technically speaking the *dimensionality problem* stems from a central theorem in mathematics by the Dutch mathematician Brouwer. It is called the Dimension Invariance Theorem and has the form:

R^n is homeomorphic to R^m if and only if $n=m$ [21]

There are three basic features involved in measurements: the purpose of measurement, the defined measure and the medium of measurement. With respect to Brower's theorem it is particularly the problem of *purpose* which we have to consider. We use prices as a measure between the market price of a commodity in relation to our relative desires and this should be unproblematic. But if we want this measure to be unique both with respect to different baskets at different places and times we have to specify the measure in the way we do in the neoclassical axioms. Thus if we drop the independence correlate and make the

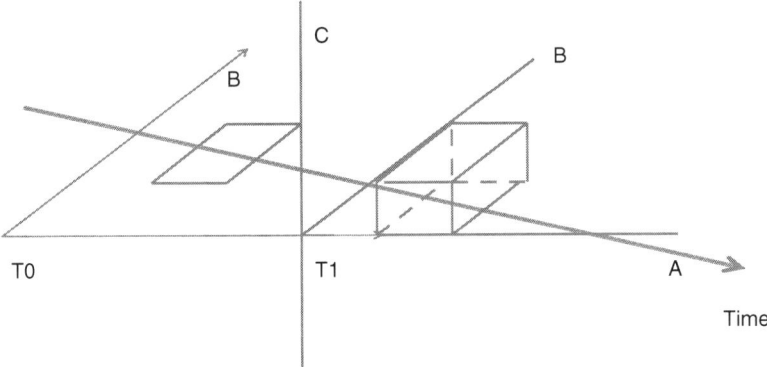

Figure 3.5 Changing dimensionality.

commodities context dependent we say that the desire for a commodity is different in different contexts and then we break the dimension invariance theorem and thus we lose the uniqueness of the measurement. However, this does not disqualify prices as measurements as such in a local and temporal sense, only the belief of uniqueness of price vectors and the existence of general equilibrium. With respect to the point made by Keynes the problem with Brouwer's theorem is even more evident when we discuss growth matters.[22]

These considerations however will be a release if we want to have a meaningful role for cash balances. When we have broken up the uniqueness of prices and got rid of the independence correlate we are now allowed to think of asymmetries in time and space and that is at least a good start for a reason to acquire a cash balance. However the rejection of the neoclassical axiom together with the dynamic dimensionality problem is a problem with respect to any assumptions of generic behaviour except for assumption of rationality in its general sense and optimizing behaviour which accounts for the three first axioms.

Axiom of local non-satiation

Say's law in its crude interpretation which Keynes rejected was in neoclassical theory replaced by the axiom of local non-satiation which is in fact closer to Say's original version which was more a description of the diffusion process of money in an economy. Say was actually discussing in the chapter where his alleged law appeared an economy of changing dimensionality of the commodity space, which also is close to Hume's discussion of how the money economy changes the social structures. Thus "Say's law" as interpreted in its original version is actually more a description of the interaction between innovations, the market process and the social structures. Some short-run interpretation of Say's law is not to be found in Say who discusses the growth process in relation to innovations as a trial and error process, where the important thing is that production of new commodities actually starts. Thus the productive ventures to increase the dimensionality of the commodity basket will change the consumption structure. Consequently Say advocates most of all that entrepreneurs meet as little state restriction as possible when starting new ventures. Affecting aggregate demand he is more doubtful to in the sense that it doesn't change the dimensionality of the commodity space (op. cit.: 139–44).

Interestingly Say criticizes Smith on the matter of the constancy of the commodity space as well as his attitude to commodities which was evolved into the axiom of reflexivity:

> The line of demarcation between necessaries and superfluities shifts with the fluctuating condition of the society. Strictly speaking mankind might exist upon roots and herbs, with a sheepskin for clothing, and a wigwam for lodging; yet, in the present state of the European society, we cannot look upon bread or butcher's meat, woollen-clothes or houses of masonry, as luxuries. [...]

Wherefore it is impossible exactly to define the boundary between the one and the other. Smith has fixed it a little in advance of Steuart; including the rank of necessaries, besides natural wants, such as the established rules of decency and propriety have made necessary in the lower classes of society. *But Smith was wrong in attempting to fix at all what must, in nature of things, be ever varying.*

(Say 1834 [1803]: 409, my emphasis)

However there is also another point to regard when it comes to the dimensionality problem and that is that commodities have to be seen as multidimensional complexes in themselves. That means that air transport as such is rather easily defined for me as a customer, but when it come to the total effect of air transport it is enormously complex. This has nothing to do with the trivial concepts of externalities but is intrinsic to the very nature of the commodity and its efficient working. Thus the growth of demand for air transport implies that new dimensions of commodities are added and that a large part of society is affected. Thus the very complexity of the individual commodity may create systems of support, control and sanctions. The institutional structure of a country is to a large extent affected by the current aggregate commodity basket.

Consequently the axiom of non-satiation is probably better to interpret in a social context than in an individual.

Thus we have discussed the dimensionality of the commodity space but the quote from Say enters our earlier discussion of commodities as multidimensional complexes. When we speak of the dimensionality of the commodity space we treat the commodities in the neoclassical way as dimensions of a Euclidian space but what Say discusses is the complexity of the commodity given its physical form, thus he implicitly rejects the axiom of reflexivity.

I have dwelt with Say's law quite extensively since it is of fundamental importance in relation to the axiomatic structure of the neoclassical theory and also because Keynes makes quite a point of rejecting it. However interpreting Say's law in the context of what Say actually has discussed gives a completely new meaning of the "law" and also has bearing on the use of money in a non-equilibrium process.

Axioms of convexity and continuity

The *axiom of convexity* has the economic meaning that consumers prefer balanced baskets to unbalanced, we avoid so-called corner solutions. If we look at the singular individual given an epistemic cycle it is not self-evident that this axiom holds but if we discuss macroscopic questions it is most probably reasonable to accept it.

From an individual point of view the axiom excludes addictive behaviour which indeed is missing an important part of society. Furthermore it is doubtful if the phenomenon of *fashion* can be contained within a convex space. In the Sociology Guide for students we read:[23]

What is the importance of fashion for social life and what role does it play in society? The question is important as we find people often victims of fashion. Fashion promises no utility; it makes no appeal to reason and being a fugitive and transitory deviation has little effect on the major trends of social change yet it has a strong hold over the people. Fashion satisfies two strong demands of social man – the demand for novelty and the demand for conformity.

The concept of fashion is interesting since it reveals a strong link from the macroscopic structure on the individual and if we shall talk about the *invisible hand* fashion seems sometimes to qualify for that position. In the Sociology Guide we also read: "Fashion is not an individual choice but is a group choice. So long as a particular choice remains confined to an individual it may better be called style and not fashion."

It is much the same thing with the *axiom of continuity*. It becomes indeed complex when we have modified the concept of commodities to be seen as multidimensional complexes and thus they are used and demanded for different purposes, dependent on the particular epistemic cycle. If we allude to the household production approach they serve as inputs, and are consequently dependent on a sort of technological development. This creates complementarities which may compromise the continuity axiom. Thus at the individual level it is doubtful if we can assume continuity but on the macroscopic level we can most probably accept it; we sort of sum over the epistemic cycles given temporal inertia.

Therefore, with respect to both these latter axioms it seems like the neoclassical approach applied to the microscopic level seems to fit some kind of average consumer. However, since we have ruled out additive aggregation we really do not know what such an average is.

We may illustrate this by adopting the characteristics model by Gorman (1956) and Lancaster (1966) which is close to the reasoning of Becker's household production model.

Given a random consumer we have:

$$\text{Max } U = z_1^\alpha \cdot z_2^\beta \tag{E.3.5}$$

subject to:

$$z_1 = a_{1_1} x_1 + a_{1_2} x_2$$

$$z_2 = a_{2_1} x_1 + a_{2_2} x_2$$

$$\sum_i p_i x_i = B$$

where z_1 and z_2 are so-called characteristics which are functions of the two commodities x_1 and x_2.[24] The usual assumptions in literature is that $z_i > 0$, $x_j > 0$ and $a_{ij} \leq 0$. Furthermore we must also add that the determinant of the characteristics matrix $|A| \neq 0$. In order to get the implicit prices of the characteristics we invert the matrix and express the budget restriction in characteristics and their implicit prices.

This gives us the transformed optimization problem:

$$\text{Max } U = z_1^\alpha \cdot z_2^\beta \tag{E.3.6}$$

$$\text{s.t. } [z_1(p_1 \cdot a_{2_2} - p_2 \cdot a_{2_1}) - z_2(p_2 \cdot a_{1_1} - p_1 \cdot a_{1_2})] = B \cdot |A|$$

We develop the corresponding Lagrange expression and receive the implicit demand function for the characteristics z_1 and z_2:

$$z_1 = \frac{B \cdot |A|}{\left(1 + \dfrac{\beta}{\alpha}\right) \cdot (p_1 \cdot a_{2_2} - p_2 \cdot a_{2_1})} \tag{E.3.7}$$

$$z_1 = \frac{B \cdot |A|}{\left(1 + \dfrac{\alpha}{\beta}\right) \cdot (p_2 \cdot a_{1_1} - p_1 \cdot a_{1_2})} \tag{E.3.8}$$

Thus we can see from the expressions E.3.7 and E.3.8 that the demand functions for the characteristics are more complex than in the usual demand functions and we see that we are going to get discontinuous shifts due to relative changes of p_1 and p_2, which will also imply discontinuous shift in demand for the commodities.

With respect to these considerations which concern the microscopic level Lars-Göran Larsson at the School of Economics in Gothenburg has presented an interesting approach (May 2010), where the consumer choice is described in probabilistic terms and transforms the consumer's behaviour subject to the budget restriction into a general continuous probability density function. Larsson finds that the general properties of demand, law of demand that is valid at both the individual and the aggregate level, holds and furthermore the demand functions are homogeneous of degree zero. It is also interesting to note that this approach implies that expected demand generally is found inside the budget set; thus the solution does not have to be on the budget line which gives the result that the adding up condition to the budget is not valid, and that will in fact be consistent with Becker's household production approach. From a macroeconomic point of view the approach implies that additive aggregation is not valid. The relation between the microstates and the macrostate will be quite complex. Let a microstate be either an individual or a group for which we can assume a probability distribution of price-quantity points. The aggregate probability density function is then formed by the sum of micro-probabilities for each macrostate; thus there will be no a priori resemblance between the macro-probability density function and the respective micro-functions. The macro-density function affects the market price of the singular product but that will be independent of the individual density functions so the simple addition of individual demand functions does not hold.

In fact this is an observed phenomenon. Lavoie and Liu (2007) have a very interesting discussion on this.[25] They found that positive pricing-to-market results in the literature could be a sign of product heterogeneity rather than evidence of imperfect competition. However pricing in a specific market may well depend on the form of the characteristics contained in the products rather than the demand for the product with respect to an average physical form (see also Warmdinger 2004).[26]

Developments of the neoclassical theory

There have been several rather interesting attempts to develop the neoclassical theory into different directions in the line of our above discussion. Two approaches both very interesting are the Temporary Equilibrium approach and the *equimarginal principle* by Maurice Allais. The former is well known and has received a lot of attention while the latter is unknown to many economists. In relation to the latter we will also mention a modification of Allais' approach by Jacque Drèze.

From our point of view it is particularly interesting if these developments in some sense incorporate money.

Temporary equilibrium theory

The end of the 1960s and beginning of the 1970s was a period when the ruling Keynesianism began to be heavily criticized, partly because both national economies as well as international economic relations had undergone substantial structural changes. This provoked a discussion about what was hidden in the rather abstract and general concepts of Keynesian models and ideas, and a more outspoken interest in the microeconomic foundation of the macroeconomic theory appeared. The neoclassical model became more or less the only alternative although a development along more structural lines in term of input–output modelling also gained some interest. However the latter was rather easily related to the neoclassical theory by the works of John von Neumann, Tjalling Koopmans and others.

Earlier we claimed that in analysing the neoclassical model we only care about conclusions concerning the macroscopic economy and regarding the microscopic world the neoclassical microeconomic methods are on the whole useful. Thus choosing the neoclassical theory as a microeconomic foundation for macroeconomic analysis is constructive per se and we will actually use some of those methods in analysing macroeconomic approaches. Unfortunately the simple and seemingly logical consistency of the neoclassical additive aggregation is often a too big temptation to resist. In the search for a microeconomic foundation the whole package was accepted; thus we had a long period when the neoclassical theory was regarded as the Theory.

However this required a development of the orthodox Arrow and Debreu theory. The above-mentioned work by von Neumann, Koopmans and others was one way, since it gave an explicit link between the multi-sector production side and the market exchange, but then we also had the embarrassing question of money and cash balances. To a great extent that problem triggered the development of the temporary equilibrium approach. Jean-Michel Grandmont, who was one of the leading theoreticians, starts the entry in the *Dictionary of Economics* by saying "The fact that trade and markets take place sequentially over time in actual economies is a trivial observation. It has nevertheless far-reaching implications" (Grandmont 2006: 1). Later in the same text he comments on the Walrasian equilibrium "But the coordination of the decisions of all traders is achieved at a single date through future markets. There is no sequence of *markets* over time, and no role for expectations, money, financial assets or stock markets" (ibid.: 1, original emphasis).

In relation to our concepts of epistemic cycles the temporary equilibrium theory is seemingly quite similar, although just only as we will see, and it is an important development of the neoclassical theory.[27]

It is easy to imagine a trajectory of general equilibria such that markets are cleared in each moment. The problem with such an approach is that there is no logical link between the successive equilibria, particularly not in correspondence with our critique of the axioms, so we will have some sort of random walk in the economic system. In the approach by Makarov and Rubinov (1977) based on the Neumann–Gale dynamics, they link the production side to an Arrow and Debreu barter economy, but the prices are set according to the production side and they stick to the classical labour theory, which thus is a sort of bridge between periods.

In the temporary equilibrium approach which basically deals with the barter economy, the connection between the periods is created by a constant space of outcome of the state space and a given probability distribution over the state space.

The main scope of the temporary equilibrium approach is to show that there exists a possible long-term optimal trajectory which fulfils the Pareto criteria, although agents might be mistaken in their short-run actions depending on insufficient information or expectation formation. This is in line with the thought that the Keynesian theory should describe the short-run aggregate behaviour while the neoclassical theory focuses on the long-run trajectory of the economy. The thought that the Keynesian theory should be a short-run approach while the neoclassical theory should be a long-run approach is however problematic since the short-run model implicitly accepts *false trading*. This is however a problem which the temporary equilibrium theory, is supposed to deal with.

The temporary equilibrium approach deals with sequential markets and it can be treated either in the form of price adjustments in each period or as temporary quantity rationing. In general it is postulated that prices move more quickly than quantities which means that we choose the first variant. Obviously it makes no big difference.

The agents form their expectations about the future in every period according to revealed information about the state of the environment and this makes it possible to analyse future contracts in successive periods. These contracts are at variance with the standard Arrow and Debreu theory which only allows such contracts once and for all, dependent on the fact that these models lack any time concept, save for Now–Future. We have thus in each period a temporal equilibrium also with respect to future contracts. Furthermore we also allow these contracts to be negotiated on the basis of inaccurate expectations and this means that the temporary equilibrium is in fact a kind of disequilibrium.

As we can see already this superficial description opens the field for questions of money of a more interesting character than in the ordinary Walrasian/Arrow and Debreu theory. The approach also allows at least for a rudimentary disequilibrium analysis. To a certain extent this approach is an integration of Keynesian theory and neoclassical theory since it actually allows for a kind of fluctuating trajectory, with temporary disequilibria, but may converge to some form of equilibrium path when the efficiency of information as well as the agents' ability to handle the information improve.

The agent decides with respect to the available information in the current period a plan for current as well as future actions according to perceived constraints. This means that the agent transfers money in the form of perpetuities to the following period based on the planned consumption and on the basis of current expectations of the next period. This implies however the possibility for mistakes either caused by erroneous information or by erroneous interpretation of information, but it is possible to attend to this in a later period since the agents may revise the use of the transferred perpetuities. Thus we in fact allow for false trading but the consequences of this may be corrected at later periods and the bad consequences are to some extent isolated to only one period, provided that the agent changes his behaviour based on better information. This latter postulate is based on the assumption that prices are carrying all essential information of past judgements of the agents. Thus false trading could, at least ideally, be detected and revised fairly quickly.

The central point to understand is the how the relation between current and future markets and the possibility to at least partly remedy false trading in a previous period is implemented theoretically. In our presentation we limit the analysis to two periods.

Basically we must see the agents' choice in period 0, in Figure 3.6 as between perishable commodities in period 0 and some form of "options" of future contracts to buy or deliver. These contracts are to be seen as perpetuities which are turned into money in period 1. This will imply that erroneous expectations may, given the outcome of period 1, on one hand imply a non-optimal distribution between consumption and future contracts in period 1 and on the other hand a non-optimal commodity basket in period 1. The introduction of perpetuities/money makes it in principle possible to analyse a changed monetary policy between period 0 and period 1, varying interest rates for instance.

Furthermore the choice in period 0 is affected by the expectations on period 1.

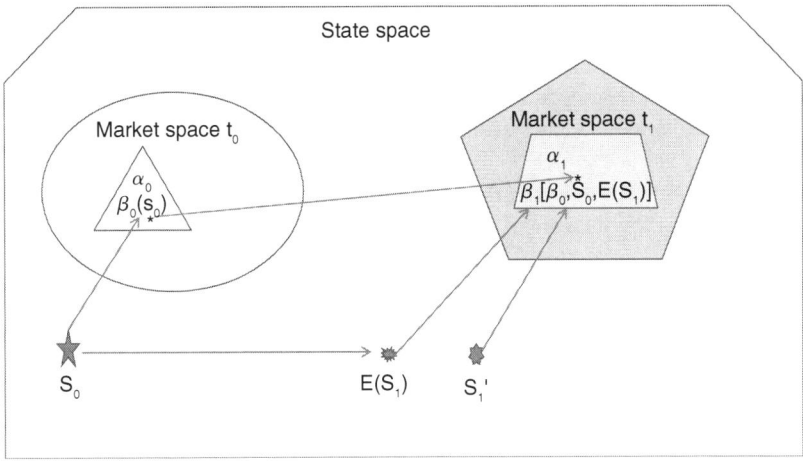

Figure 3.6 Temporary equilibrium theory.

The foundation of the approach is based on the possibility of the agent to have erroneous expectations. Such expectations are built on the existence of a state space which is *given and affects the agents' restrictions and expectation formation*. However the market actions will be of no consequence for the state space. We must also note that the possibility of erroneous expectations is, at least implicitly, symmetrically distributed among the agents. Thus given efficient learning we would most probably have a stable equilibrium trajectory.

The way of introducing money is interesting since money will actually have a value separated from zero, although this value is directly related to the choice between current trade and future contracts *and* the amount of erroneous expectations that create excess demand (of either sign) in period 1.

The state space is given, which means that all spaces of outcome of different variable dimensions, weather, computer breakdowns, car accidents, government actions which may be seen as exogenous, international conflicts and so on, are known and that we may attach a subjective probability distribution to each space of outcome of the different variables. The agent gets information of the state space denoted by S_i. The information defines a possible action space α_i where the agent chooses an action, which contains a combination of current actions and a "buying of perpetuities" (saving, investment) for the next period.

Thus based on a current signal S_0 the individual forms on one hand a plan for current action β_0 as well as expectations on the signal which will be received at t_1, $E(S_1)$. Thus the action in period t_1, $\beta_1[\beta_0, S_0, E(S_1)]$ will then be affected by the actions in period 0 devoting perpetuities to period 1 as well as the expectations S_1 for period 1 based on the signal S_0 in period 0.

The different spaces are assumed to be Euclidian spaces, hence measurable spaces imply that the state space can be uniquely ordered with respect to the probabilities of the contained dimension. Since the action space is built on the subjective probability distributions each individual agent fulfils the axioms of the neoclassical theory in this analysis. Of course, allowing for erroneous expectations and information this may be seen as invalidating the completeness axiom, but since we deal with different sequences we can say that the agents adapt to the current conditions in each period, and thus it is no big deal from a theoretical perspective. Consequently the agents optimize their actions in the standard way.

From Figure 3.6 we understand that there are two precise snags in the agents' actions and that is the interpretation and correctness of signal S_0 and second the expectation formation of signal S_1. Thus it may appear that $E(S_1)$ differs from actual S_1 a rather standard *ex ante/ex post* problem. This will cause two principle effects; on one hand the planned action in period 2, $\beta_1[\beta_0, S_0, E(S_1)]$ will be non-optimal, and on the other hand the transformation of perpetuities from period 0 to period 1 is also non-optimal. Consequently this will end up in a general state of excess demand in period 1 and subsequently a standard adaptation process to equilibrium. Since we discuss perpetuities/options we may relate it to the *arbitrage principle* on the spot markets in period 1. Principally that means that it is possible to achieve a state of equilibrium in period 1, which implies a different distribution of resources compared to the expected in period 0 but still is a base for further business. Furthermore the erroneous outcome will inform the agent of the "true" probability distribution so that the agent may correct the planning for the new future.[28] Thus, given that we assume unsystematic errors in the expectation among the agents, it is possible to have a process over time that displays "spot" states of equilibrium with varying distributions but the variations in distributions are diminishing and in the long run we will have a general equilibrium trajectory. Since the transfer of perpetuities is possible between successive periods we open for a kind of monetary policy which in principle can shorten the convergence period, although that implies a new set of assumptions of the character of the policy.

There is however a rather serious problem with this glossy picture; the *ex post* situation may lead to bankruptcy for the agent. This problem will be dealt with more extensively in Chapter 4 when we introduce *lexicographic preferences*. The existence of bankruptcy introduces however a problem in itself which may affect the transfer of perpetuities and require a modification of the optimization problem; in fact it will lead us to an analysis of the concept of liquidity. The temporary equilibrium theory is unable to deal with the problem of bankruptcy by its basic acceptance of the neoclassical axiomatic structure. Arrow and Hahn (1971: 119–22) discuss the possibility of a general insurance system which protects the level of demand for those agents who are bankrupt but that only concerns unplanned bankruptcies which are random. The introduction of such a system in the temporary equilibrium approach is possible given risk-averse agents, but we will still be left with the problem of demand for liquidity if not symmetrically spread.

Another problem of the same kind is the smoothness of the arbitrage and set of excess demand functions. Green (1973) claims:

Therefore, rather than place a priori restrictions on the model, we have chosen to consider the "perfect case", in the belief that generalizations including market technologies ... will produce, as a result of jointly maximizing behaviour, a pattern of available markets approximating the reality more closely.

This means that to grant a smoothly working arbitrage in period 2 the agents to a certain extent have to agree on their understanding of the reality. That means that they should at least agree on the space of outcome while they may differ on the subjective probability distributions.

Summing up the temporary equilibrium approach

The temporary equilibrium approach is indeed a valuable contribution since it attacks central weak points in the neoclassical model and introduces traditional Keynesian problems. The weakness of the approach lies, *pro primo* in the very same definition of the agents and commodities as in the traditional neoclassical theory and this allows for additive aggregation which is the ground for the possibility of arbitrage. *Pro secundo*, the strict division of the market space and the state space of the environment, implies that the sole link between these spaces is the agents' expectation formation. Furthermore the "true" probability distribution of the state space is, at least implicitly, assumed to be constant and, given preferences and probability structures in conjunction with a particular state of the environment, we will be able to uniquely define an optimal basket.

Pro tertio, the way money is treated may explain the existence of a positive price of money but it cannot explain liquidity holding. Grandmont (1982) is well aware of this. Thus the very central Keynesian problem is still unexplained in the temporary equilibrium approach since it requires introduction of uncertainty. Furthermore acceptance of liquidity holdings in the world of the temporary equilibrium approach creates both current disequilibrium and also a new type of uncertainty which is intrinsic to the market exchange.

The equimarginal principle

The temporary equilibrium approach indicates the difficulty in transforming the standard Arrow and Debreu theory into a dynamic theory. The main difficulty lies in the fact that it deals with the existence of general equilibrium not with the question of how it is attained. In order to at least indicate a dynamic movement we on one hand have to develop the aspect of quantity rationing into both a deficiency of the current production system but also a possibility of increased profits when the deficiencies are remedied. The temporary equilibrium approach opens a possibility of such considerations when we have the possibility of correcting erroneous behaviour in a later period. The problem is heavily dependent on the specific kind of risk concept, and partly also that it deals with a barter economy.

Many of the classical economists saw the market dynamics as a diffusion process. Since the general equilibrium in modern form was not conceived the discussion more concerned equilibrating processes of partial character. Such a process is the *equimarginal principle*, discussed by both Jevons and Menger and during the 1980s developed by Maurice Allais (1987). This approach is a kind of approach accepting some sort of general equilibrium as an ultimate state, more or less unattainable, but the important issues are the equilibrating forces which locally and temporally may improve the situation of the agent. Obviously, when using such an approach we have to accept *false trading*, which means trading at non-equilibrium prices and the existence of multiple price vectors. Hence the focus on the non-equilibrium dynamics or more correctly potential dynamics, make the approach in principle wide enough to be possible to handle some problems from the Keynesian world.

The fundamental point is that although it ultimately accepts the existence of a general equilibrium which in principle fulfils the Pareto efficiency criteria, it is used to discuss movements in the economy outside this equilibrium, based on the agents' search for local and temporal improvement of welfare in a certain commodity dimension given the welfare level achieved in the other dimensions. The equimarginal principle is with respect to consumption more or less a direct application of the *axiom of local non-satiation* in an out-of-equilibrium setting. Thus locally we may isolate areas of potential action where we may compare the actions with respect to their marginal welfare result respectively. Thus even in a situation where consumption of different commodity dimensions is built on complementarities there are still areas where the application of the principle might be possible.

Allais writes (1987: 298): "Consequently, situations of equilibrium and maximum efficiency are never reached, and what is really important is to determine the rules of the game which must be applied to come closer to them as rapidly as possible."

The equimarginal principle builds to a large extent on the classical theory of distribution of surpluses and we may also see it as a description of Hume's and Say's diffusion principle and it could be applied both to consumer search for improving welfare as well to producers' search for lucrative investments and markets. We know that perfect competition based on the six axioms of the general equilibrium will wash out any surpluses. In the real world we know that there is limited competition to a certain degree. The limitations in competition are however often temporal of more of less inertia due to technical progress, inventions of substitutes and similar factors, a model like the *product cycle model* gives a fairly good illustration of the dynamics.

The equimarginal principle starts from a very simple observation which is taught to first semester students virtually everywhere. We usually present the basic efficiency concept of economics as a so-called production possibility frontier as in Figure 3.7.

The economy is at the state X which is an under-capacity utilization situation and then we in principle have free resources in the sense that any advances towards the frontier is Pareto sanctioned.

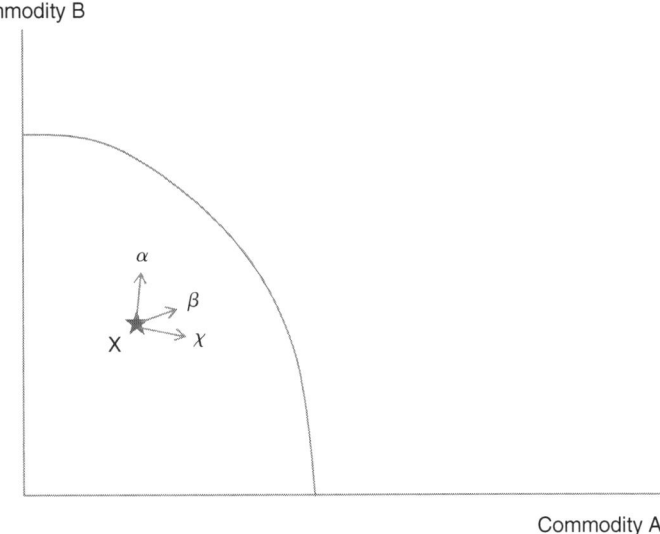

Commodity B

Commodity A

Figure 3.7 Production possibility frontier.

As it stands this analysis is more or less impossible within the neoclassical axiomatic structure, since it most certainly implies false trading; thus all the directions imply a positive change, but we are not on the resource boundary and hence we have different marginal conditions depending on the relative scarcity of the resources for the two sectors.

As Allais expresses it:

It shows in particular that the single price system condition is valid only at the margin and that, contrary to the prevailing view, maximum efficiency does not require that all units of one good be exchanged at the same price, nor that the prices used equate over-all supply and demand.

Consequently we must have a different theoretical underpinning for changes below optimal aggregate situations compared with the conditions necessary for general equilibrium.

We have already discussed such an underpinning and although we reject the neoclassical axiomatic structure per se, we do accept the axioms in a modified form. Thus for an agent in situation X in Figure 3.7 he may still act according to his perception of the local and temporal situation and thus make rational comparisons, and although we have entered a more complex commodity concept this also works for the precise agent locally and temporally although it has no bearing on a similar action in point Y.

Basic to the equimarginal principle is that it is built on marginal equivalences and marginal changes. Furthermore these marginal equivalences are not primarily built on binary comparisons in a global sense but on the existence of a particular structure which may be changed during the dynamic process; this implies that there is room for economic policy. Allais describes the fundamental scope of the model (1987: 690–1, original emphasis):

> This theory attaches much *more importance to the process which enables economy to approach situations of equilibrium and maximum efficiency than to these situations* per se, whose intrinsic interest for understanding how the economic world actually functions or as a basis for formulating economic policy is rather limited.... The basic concepts and propositions are presented in the framework of a very *general model which is free of any restrictive conditions, namely the model of the markets economy* (in contradiction to a "market economy").

Allais makes two important assumptions, which are pretty strong: first that all commodities enter all preference functions and second that the quantity of the commodities can vary continuously.

It is assumed that every basket of consumption can be projected on a one-dimensional preference index. Since we make no assumptions of convexity or derivability, a particular index number needs not be unique, which follows from the existence of several price vectors. Hence the individual preference functions may be aggregated into an *ordinal individual or social preference index*:

$$I_i = f_i(Y_i, X_i^1, \cdots, X_i^n) \tag{E.3.9}$$

We may particularly study the *Y*-commodity.

This means that Allais actually aggregates the "allowed" individual actions into a social index. *X* is positive or negative if it is consumption or a supplied service respectively.

It is important to realize that if we construct an index as E.3.9 starting from the *X* point in Figure 3.7 it will be different from the one started from *Y* irrespective of whether we work with individual or social indexes.

We may also define a production function. The production can be written:

$$f_j(Y_j, X_j^1, \cdots, X_j^n) \geq 0 \tag{E.3.10}$$

The arguments represent output and consumption respectively whether the quantities are positive or negative. Maximum efficiency implies:

$$f_j(Y_j, X_j^1, \cdots, X_j^n) = 0 \tag{E.3.11}$$

Allais allows for technical distinctions with respect to returns to scale or not, but we need not go into that here.

According to a standard input–output tableau we have:

$$\sum_i Y_i + \sum_j Y_j = Y_0; \quad \sum_i X_i^1 + \sum_j X_j^1 = X_0^1;$$

$$--- \sum_i X_i^n + \sum_j X_j^n = X_0^n;$$

(E.3.12)

where $Y_0, X_0^1, \ldots, X_0^n$ represents the available resources in the initial state H_1; in the input–output tableau it is the end use matrix.

Let now δH_1 be a modification of H_1 defined by variations $\delta Y_i, \delta X_i^1 \ldots \delta X_i^n$; $\delta Y_j, \delta X_j^1 \ldots \delta X_j^n$ the respective variations can be positive or negative.

Thus we have $H_2 = H_1 + \delta H_1$ subject to:

$$\sum_k \delta X_i^k = \sum_k \delta X_j^k$$

Let us now define a third state H_3 such that we make a modification in the commodity Y, $-\delta \rho_u$, such that the preference index I_i returns to the initial value H_1, if then $\delta \rho_u > 0$ the change δH_1 has implied a surplus, realizable and distributable.

It is a bit technical but still the meaning is rather simple. If in Figure 3.7 we had been on the efficiency frontier the modification $\delta \rho_u$ had obviously been zero. If we have a distributable surplus we have concavities in the production structure, thus increasing returns to scale. The only locus in an economy where we have a stable equilibrium is when we have no distributable surplus. Thus the existence of distributable surplus triggers dynamic modifications.

We can link this reasoning back to Figure 3.7 and the process of approaching the production possibility frontier. A central condition for this process to work, as Allais describes it, is the existence of economies of scale; thus when there are unemployed resources the production modifications imply no price changes in any of the markets (with different price vectors).

But the meaning of economies of scale is not so much with respect to different technologies and production sectors but to production below optimal capacity utilization which implies higher average costs and lower profit share like in Figure 3.8.

The Q^*/L^* curve represents the *ex ante* labour productivity when investment volume and technology were decided. In the short run, a part of the labour is fixed thus short-run variations around the optimal capacity production at (Q^*, L^*) given prices and wages implies lower labour productivity and thus lower profit share. The optimal capacity utilization does not need for the single company or sector to be at the production possibility curve on the aggregate level. That means that for the very firm/sector in Figure 3.8 the capacity limit may occur below the capacity limit for other sectors and thus that of the total economy. We will discuss this extensively in the next chapters but it actually means that a general equilibrium of the neoclassical form may occur well below the production possibility curve in Figure 3.7 if we stick to the working of the equimarginal principle. Hence we may modify Figure 3.7 to that seen in Figure 3.9.

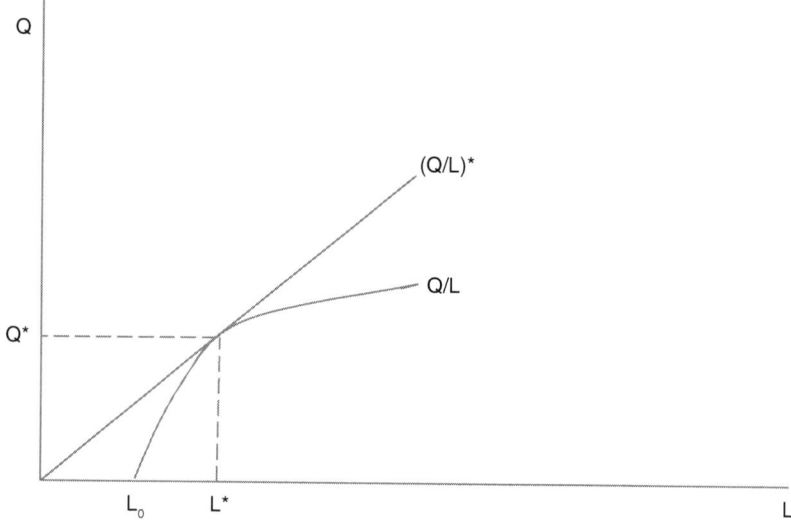

Figure 3.8 Ex ante productivity in relation to short-run variations.

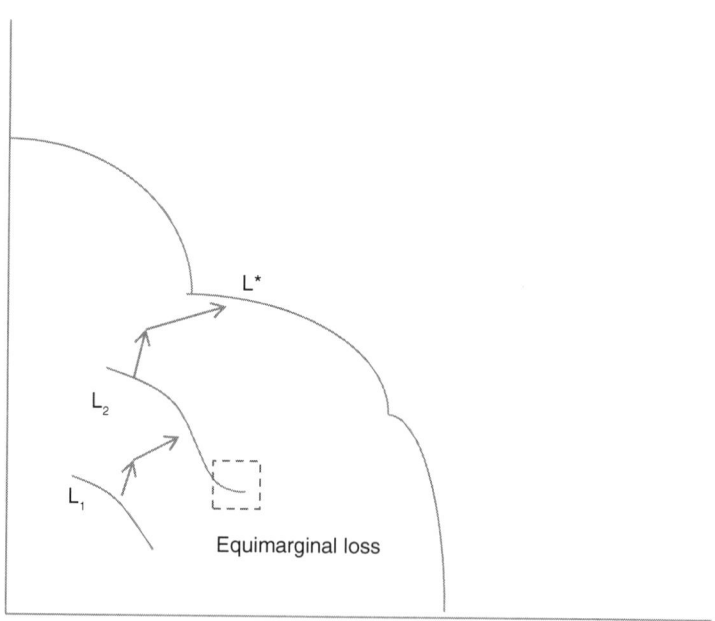

Figure 3.9 Approximation process and local convexity.

The L^* represents the locus of a general equilibrium, which not necessarily needs to be globally convex since the equimarginal process implying a multitude of possible distributions also may affect the character of the equilibrium. When the economy somehow has reached a point of maximum efficiency, that is there are no distributable surpluses which can be realizable, the standard conditions of convexity and differentiability must hold. The form of the locus in Figure 3.9 actually fulfils the conditions except in certain points which are nowhere dense, thus there is no neighbourhood to such a point where the conditions are fulfilled. These points are usually seen as points of bifurcation, with respect to technology or consumption patterns. However there is no reason to believe that the equimarginal process ever converges to a point of maximum efficiency. Allais (1987: 707, original emphasis) writes:

> Consequently, when maximum efficiency obtains, most operators are in a situation of local convexity and marginal decreasing returns. However, this condition cannot be interpreted as a meaning that all fields of choice and production are convex everywhere, *this is a hypothesis being totally contradicted by observed data.*

The equimarginal principle is interesting in the sense that it shows a stringent way of analysing out-of-equilibrium situations. As we see we do not need to question rationality of choice although we limit the choice space for the agents and thus we have a multitude of price vectors. Furthermore Allais differentiates between a potential surplus and a realizable equimarginal change. The existence of a distributable surplus implies in principle that there is an inconsistency in the exchange of goods. This might appear in the form of capacity limitations in the production sector but realizable equimarginal change implies that the distributable surplus exists in under-optimization in the production sector, and subsequently there are local concavities as shown in Figure 3.9.

The question of money is not discussed, but since Allais accepts multiple prices and also that potential surplus is not necessary realizable it is rather easy to enter cash balances into the analysis. The weakness however is that although Allais imposes aggregate indexes he in strict sense never leaves the microscopic level, thus money as a medium of exchange gets a more realistic role but other features of money are outside his analysis.

Drèze's contribution

There are other efforts of describing the state of under capacity utilization and eventual remedies. Drèze (1985) keeps the standard neoclassical axioms and attains a second best analysis. A second best situation appears when we impose new restrictions to an optimization problem. Drèze starts from the very existence of an economy in a second best situation, with the existence of taxes, monopoly power, incomplete markets and so on. That opens for a Keynesian policy and Drèze analyses a rudimentary Keynesian policy where the economy is divided in a private and a public sector and based on cost–benefit reasoning similar to that which we may apply to Figure 3.7 he then derives a Keynesian multiplier in the interior of the choice space. Since we have a public sector production which is demanded we can activate this multiplier by manipulating the prices of the public sector commodities. Although this approach is less general since it restricts the analysis to a standard neoclassical realm, it still is interesting since the second best situation implies that price manipulations can be used.

Comments on Allais and Drèze

An observation we may make is that actually describing in mathematical terms what is going on in the real economy is a huge problem, when we seek a microscopic underpinning to the macroscopic analysis. It seems to be far simpler to handle the macroscopic concepts relatively independent from the microscopic structure. Still we know that the macroscopic concepts are fundamentally dependent on the very structure both in a macroscopic and microscopic sense, but traditionally we are used to looking at the macroscopic structure as created by the microscopic entities, but if we look at Arrow's paradox and also remembering Wicksell's distinction between stability on the macroscopic level from the stability on the microscopic we have most probably a strong influence of the macroscopic level on the microscopic. Thus as we have seen in these modifications of the neoclassical dynamics by Allais and Drèze they only discuss the microscopic structure and the aggregate is in fact remote since we on one hand have a sort of aggregate index but we do not really know if an alleged general equilibrium interpreted as all sectors are producing at their optimal capacity utilization coincide with the production possibility frontier as illustrated in Figures 3.7 and 3.9. This problem is brought in to the analysis via Figure 3.8 and poses a problem which actually requires, as we will see in the next chapter, some considerations of the concept of inflation.

None of the discussed approaches, neither Allais' nor Drèze's, even mentions money. Both approaches, Allais' explicitly and Drèze's implicitly, discuss a multitude of price vectors but money is still outside the approaches, save for a rather passive medium of exchange. This might be seen as a bit curious since when we discuss states of non-equilibrium and the existence of a multitude of price vectors, money hoarding and cash reserves are not a remote thought. But when we reflect a bit we find that imputing money in the analysis would have required the inclusion of a more complex apparatus as uncertainty, liquidity and also as we have pointed out a model for the interaction between the microscopic and the macroscopic levels.

Allais' and Drèze's analysis is nevertheless fruitful. It can be used to define a microeconomic foundation for an economy which is logically consistent and may work in a dynamic with changing dimensionality of the commodity space. The very concept of general equilibrium can be replaced by locally and temporally equilibrating forces. Allais' equimarginal gives an excellent rationale for the existence of a multiplier process and Allais decouples the microscopic and macroscopic levels quite effectively as the consequence of his analysis is that additive aggregation technique is virtually impossible. It also shows the uncertainty of a welfare index based on prices and he actually is forced to lean on real capacity indexes or employment indexes.

Summing up the neoclassical theory and its modifications

It is fairly clear from our analysis that the inability of the neoclassical theory to treat money in a way which mirrors in a fairly adequate way the everyday use in a monetary economy depends on its strict axiomatic structure in defining agents and commodities. Modifications to include money in the neoclassical analysis fetches to a certain degree the most rudimentary characteristics of money mentioned by Aristotle, the medium of exchange and subsequently its value over time as such a medium. Other aspects as liquidity and the valuation aspect in accounting is left outside the analysis since those aspects do not exist in the neoclassical setting provided that the axioms hold. Furthermore the Keynesian concept of uncertainty is completely outside the neoclassical setting.

We have discussed several problems of the neoclassical theory; the additive aggregation problem, the dimensionality problem both with respect to the single commodity as the commodity basket as a whole. These problems are in fact disqualifying the use of the neoclassical theory at the aggregate level and saying that it could be used as a microscopic underpinning is thus a contradiction in terms since we then accept its deficient treatment of aggregation and the dimensionality problem.

4 Money, value and prices in the Keynesian and monetarist theories

From the microscopic level to the macroscopic level

The preceding chapter left us in some unrest. Rejecting the axiomatic structure of the neoclassical model, and subsequently additive aggregation, implies that using the neoclassical theory as a micro-foundation for the macroeconomic level is indeed problematic. The need for such a microscopic foundation is evident although it is not clear what questions need to be asked. To impute a theory based on a priori axioms seems more to lead to a metaphysic analysis than to a basis for studies of the physical reality. However we also looked at systematic approaches to overcome the weaknesses of the neoclassical economy and particularly Allais' approach seems to be fruitful. This approach is by no means new and we can trace it back to Hume and Say; it describes a kind of diffusion process in non-equilibrium economies. Allais kept the links to Pareto optimality and Pareto criteria in a local sense concerning local convexities. He developed a paradoxical example, Allais' paradox (Allais 1953), concerning expected utility and he shows that the choice is two-dimensional, expected value and degree of certainty, thus based on that he at least implicitly considers a more complex commodity space for decisions for future markets.

From a technical point of view however Allais does not advise us with respect to the relevance of the behavioural content of the axiomatic structure and how we shall cope with that. Our introduction of the concept of epistemic cycles however makes us able to modify the axioms in such a way that we can use them in an out-of-equilibrium analysis. Doing that however forces us to change the commodity concept, reject additive aggregation and to accept that the macroscopic level to a large extent evolves independently of the microscopic level and that the one way causality from the microscopic to the macroscopic level has to be replaced with causal interdependence. This is as we have seen at the end of Chapter 2 clearly in line with Knut Wicksell.

With respect to money, we have shown the difficulty even to discuss the most rudimentary characteristics of money we meet in the real world within the neoclassical setting since the whole money concept is an anomaly in the neoclassical theory. Saving and investment are linked a priori, since we may introduce an interest rate, given some time-preference and then we will have an optimal solution between present and future consumption.

Keynes' criticism, which gave rise to much of the modern form of macroeconomic theory, attacked the macroeconomic consequences of the neoclassical theory. He contemplated the microeconomic foundation and his criticism of Say's law was sensible, not with respect to what Say actually discussed, but its interpretation by neoclassical theoreticians, which raised the problem of dimensionality of the commodity space.

Our discussion of the temporary equilibrium model also focused on the problem of risk and the agents' apprehension of risk. We saw that as long as the state space is constant and that the agents do not interfere in their market behaviour we will probably converge to a long-run general equilibrium. Keynes introduced the concept of uncertainty which had of course a huge effect on the concept of expectations. In *General Theory* chapter 12 he discusses the long-term expectations and came to the conclusion that investments in inert capital which is expected to yield profits during a substantial future period but which today is just a cost and of no current worth, are based on expectations which in their turn are based on some historical experiences but mostly on current conditions, both with respect to the market and also with respect to the current sentiment of the investor. Thus when we speak of long-run matters these are always basically grounded on the current situation and the state of confidence of the investor, as well as are short-run decisions.[1]

This very idea is a basic problem of the general mainstream economic theory and the subsequent attitude towards risk and uncertainty, which we will discuss in later chapters, particularly Chapter 6. In neoclassical theory the only relevant aspect of money is its use as a medium of exchange and as a medium of measurement. However we are then dealing with relative prices of the equilibrium price vector unique for that particular equilibrium and thus money in the daily sense is irrelevant. The process of establishing a unique market price vector at a certain moment may occur on the financial market and such markets as overseas transport but not on ordinary consumer markets. Prices and quantities change but more like the equimarginal principle which leads to a basically out of equilibrium dynamics.

With respect to future markets the neoclassical theory, given its axiomatic structure, is not particularly interesting since the future price vectors are fixed *given* interest rate and the risk structure, *which is given*. Thus the interest rate must be set by the *invisible hand* as well, thus the individual can be represented in analogy with Debreu's definition of the agent, concerning current exchange, as $(\lesssim_i, e_i)$. We can of course add different perceptions of the risk structure in accordance with Radner (1982) but that will imply other difficulties which we partly discussed in relation to the temporary equilibrium theory $(\lesssim_i, e_i, \tau_i)$.

However we are not left in total despair since our discussion at the end of the preceding chapter particularly on the equimarginal principle and also our discussion of the content and character of the neoclassical axioms with the subsequent modifications have provided us with some useful concepts for the macroscopic analysis. True that we never can claim a global relevance of our theoretical conclusions of the same kind as the neoclassical general equilibrium analysis but given some inertia we should be able to have some reasonable results, which holds locally and temporally.

However none of the extensions of the neoclassical analysis provide us with any clue how to analyse money. During the latest decades more or less starting with the Black and Scholes model, economists have more systematically analysed the concepts of risk and uncertainty and the developments of Black and Scholes as the Heston model (Heston 1993) has turned the risk/uncertainty concept into a kind of measuring the *aggregate perception of uncertainty* by systematic analysis of the volatility structure, but this is a completely different attitude compared to the neoclassical theory. We suppose that given precise instruments the agents optimize their behaviour with respect to apprehended yield and volatility. This can certainly be brought in accordance with the neoclassical theory given the correlate of revealed preference, but we drop that and in principle follow Keynes (1973 [1936]: 154) where he claims:

> For most of these persons are, in fact, largely concerned, not with making superior long-term forecasts of the probable yield of an investment over its life, but with foreseeing changes in the conventional basis of valuation a short time ahead of the general public.

Thus analysing short-run changes in volatility may yield better prices in trading financial instruments and an approach like the Heston model have few a priori assumptions in analysing the development of the volatility structure. It is however still based on historical data even if it is including the market data of yesterday when we make a numerical evaluation overnight to be used next trading day.[2] We will however come back to such considerations later in Chapter 6.

In our historical exposé we noticed that virtually all the economists/philosophers from Aristotle to Wicksell mainly saw money as a medium of exchange, to some degree they also attached store of value as a characteristic of money and when we came to Wicksell demand for liquidity was at least implicit in his analysis. The latter aspect grew in importance from just a short mentioning in Aristotle to an almost equally important quality as being a medium of exchange when we come to Ricardo and later on. This evolution is of course due to the development of the market economy as well as growing aggregate structures. The friars of Salamanca and David Hume saw mainly the problem of foreign trade as the principal aggregate sector, and Hume as well as Say explicitly mention money as principally unimportant in internal trade save for the medium of exchange. Hume incidentally mentions bank money, although reluctantly as a doubtful way of increasing the circulation of money, and the reason for that is that although it is simple for business it induces a new element of risk/uncertainty in the market exchange. From Ricardo and his Ingot Plan concerning the reorganization of the Bank of England and the organization of money printing this aspect is fully accepted, but has to be controlled. Ricardo's interventions followed the economic and financial turbulence after the Napoleonic wars when we had major crises concerning the aggregate level in England and its finances.

What we aim at is the fundamental role of aggregate levels in the analysis of the monetary economy. As we saw from our discussion of David Hume he in fact mentions this aspect in an example from some backward countries/regions in Europe where some of the taxes have to be paid in kind, thus preventing economic growth depending on inadequate organization of aggregate structures. We also mentioned the example from Sweden during the seventeenth century when the state gave away land in exchange for the possibility to impose taxes and fees paid in money. The fundamental reason for the state's attachment to the monetary economy is of course the vast character of commitments of the state compared with the individual and thus the state administration could be more efficient at considerably lower costs so when Jesus Christ is asked about a Roman coin and what to do with that he answered by asking whose picture was on the coin and when they said "the Emperor" Christ recommended to give what belonged to the Emperor to the Emperor and that what belongs to God to God, he was certainly right in the sense that money is an aggregate phenomenon and closely linked to political and economic power.

One could say that an efficient monetary system is the very condition for efficient aggregate structures and the friars of Salamanca were probably right when they claimed that the three pillars constituting a nation was a legal system, military defence and the existence of a monetary system. On the other hand the formal aggregate structures are a basic foundation for the capital/financial markets and their efficiency. Thus reducing money to just a medium of exchange is indeed a bit doubtful.

The complexity of the macroscopic structure

Our discussion of Arrow's paradox and epistemic cycles implies that on one hand it is actually meaningful and even necessary to look for a microeconomic foundation for the macroeconomic analysis, and on the other hand people are affected in their behaviour by events and processes at the aggregate level in their individual choices. Furthermore their behaviour affects the conditions for the aggregate level. Thus the very aggregation is a very complex matter involving interdependencies between the levels and among the agents of each level and furthermore the interactions and complexities are varying in the society. It is impossible to think of a set of macroeconomic relations independent of underlying levels. Thus macroeconomic theory cannot exist as a system of its own in some macroeconomic heaven, while the poor agents toil in their grey microeconomic reality. However these discussions also imply that money will become a crucial concept, since we must on one hand have a link between the microscopic state and the macroscopic state, but on the other hand this link will be obscured since we cannot any longer use an additive aggregation technique since the agents are not influenced only by other agents but also by the macroscopic outcome. Still however when we use money as a means of accounting we may very well *perform* additive aggregation.

Thus although we theoretically reject additive aggregation with respect to barter, we actually can, and we do, perform additive aggregation with the help of money, irrespective of whether we are in a general equilibrium or not.

This means that the agents in dealing with money on one hand have a relation to the real commodity situation and a partly different relation to money, depending on the specific money features of liquidity and use in current and future accounting. Thus when we add money contracts concerning future deliveries the situation is even more complicated, particularly when we add uncertainty as a key concept. In a modern democracy all links between individuals and the different aggregate levels are in the form of money contracts and money flows, evidently these contracts often are in the form of laws, based on the right of the aggregate organization to execute different forms of compulsion, and that also concern the state's supervision of the relations between agents based on property rights. However such contracts with respect to future values can never be defined in a real sense but their values only exists at the very moment of the transaction and the value in between is by necessity based on expectations of the states and their development of the real economy. We remember that the friars of Salamanca carefully separated prices in space and time when a contract was signed from prices when and where the contract was actually executed.

Going back to our discussions of the neoclassical theory and its modifications we understand the necessity of strict assumptions concerning the state space and its probability structure was necessary in order to grant any form of general equilibrium or convergence to an equilibrium trajectory.

Thus the relations between the individuals and the aggregate organizations are quite complex when we think of several aggregate levels but these different aggregate levels also have relations which finally affect the individual. In Chapter 3, Figure 3.3 illustrates schematically such relations and when we think of the inherent dynamics of such a simplified system concerning financial and real flows as well as different forms of commitments and we realize when we consider the necessity of systems of decision and control, of implementation and information that the analysis will be vastly more complex even in such a schematic picture of reality. In Figure 3.3 we illustrate the problem of the simple state space with the complex risk/uncertainty structure in an out-of-equilibrium situation, we may also add Table 3.1 illustrating an inter-temporal development of the environment of a company.

With respect to Figure 3.3 it is important to realize that the relations between the agents *A* and *B* are mostly in the form of exchange of money for commodities, while the rest are more complex. The links between the individuals and aggregate levels are exclusively monetary and the "commodities" that the individual receives in exchange are usually not linked to commodities as such, which implies a system of control and sanctions.

The fact that the aggregate structures are fundamentally dependent on an efficient monetary system is of utmost importance when we analyse the monetary economy.

In modern society the aggregate level is vastly more complex than in Figure 4.1. When we discussed epistemic cycles we saw the aggregate levels as some form of organizational sequence similar to the Russian *matryoshka* dolls and accepting human as a *subject* forces us to allow for almost infinite possible ways

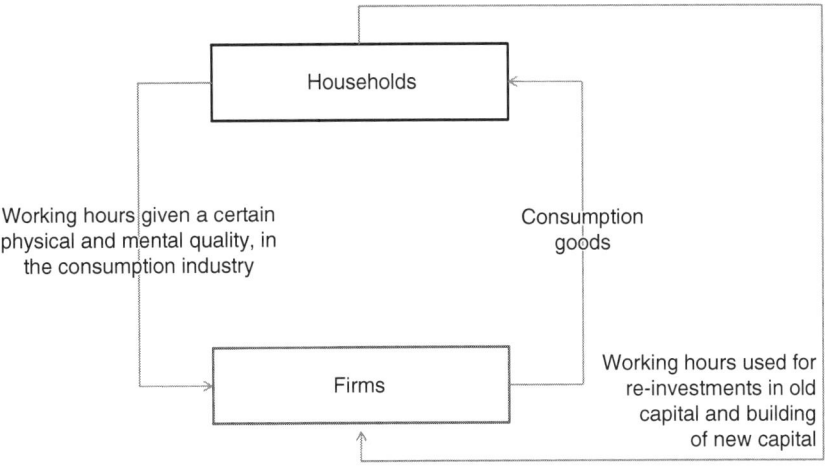

Figure 4.1 Circular flows in a barter economy.

of aggregation. On one hand we have aggregate levels in the form of implicit structures, for example, norms and behavioural patterns, fashion to mention some and on the other we have the more explicit structures as the state, of course, with its regional and local substructures but also different kinds of privately organized superstructures. This complexity obviously affects the financial flows on the aggregate level above the individual and obscures ownership, control and responsibility of liabilities and assets.

On basic courses in economics we often start with a flow chart of the economy. The first variant often illustrates a kind of Robinson Crusoe economy as in Figure 4.1.

Although we may use money in such a barter economy as some kind of medium of exchange, it is basically redundant as in the axiomatic structure of the neoclassical economy.

We may however develop the flow chart of Figure 4.1 into illustrating the monetary economy as in Figure 4.2. The solid arrows represent real flows while the dotted ones represent flows of money and/or financial liabilities and assets.

What is apparent in Figure 4.2 is the overwhelming complexity of the financial flows. When we think of the three classical features of money, medium of exchange, medium of measurement and liquidity, we can understand that in the monetary economy, money as a medium of exchange is of a rather moderate importance. This also makes Wicksell's distinction between the microscopic and macroscopic stability understandable.

The medium of measurement/valuation and the aspect of liquidity will in fact be central to the monetary system. An example of this, which we will come back

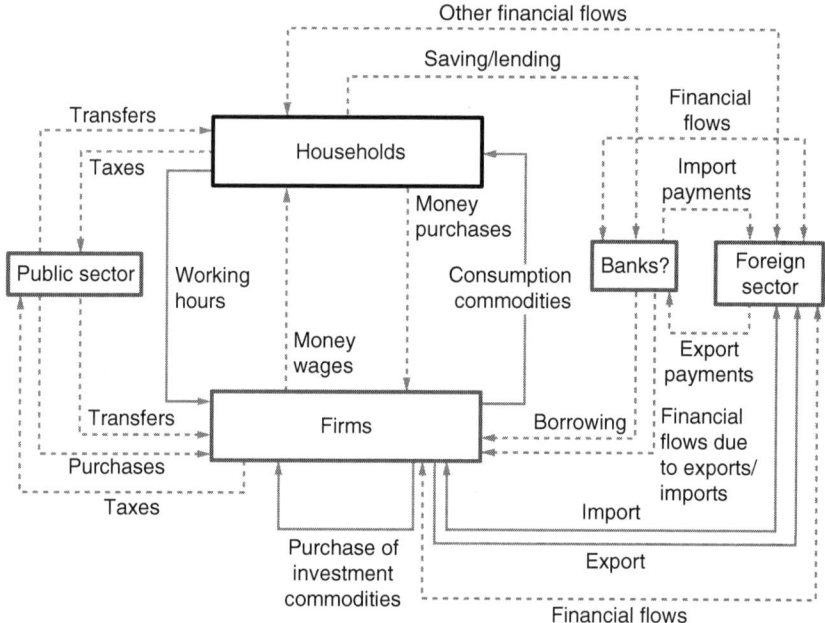

Figure 4.2 Flows in a simplified monetary economy.

to, is the necessity of liquid resources in order to defend a certain valuation of real/financial assets and liabilities.

Fundamental is however that Figure 4.1 cannot be seen as a picture of the *real flows* which is a fundamental skeleton, where the money flows are just passive duals to the respective real flows, and this picture is just modified in Figure 4.2, to account for the modern circular flow, in such a way that the monetary flows are still a sort of passive dual system.

Thus it is not a strange thought that the monetary flows per se affect the real flows considerably.

An example is that in most OECD countries the financial cross-border flows caused by the real export/import flows are around 5 per cent of the total financial flows; thus if we look at the exchange rate the pure financial flows are both quicker and more important in the short run. Hence a standard assumption of neutrality of money has more or less no sense in a fully fledged monetary economy. The neutrality of money is implicit in the neoclassical general equilibrium theory, if money at all should be needed, our discussion of the axiomatic structure and subsequently Arrow's paradox and the dimensionality problem, both with respect to the single commodity as well as the entire commodity basket, implies that the assumption of neutrality of money is doubtful. To restrict the neutrality only to the long run implies that our reasoning implicitly is similar to that of the temporary equilibrium theory and some effects of actions are limited to only be valid for one period. It is hard to see any convincing realism in such an assumption.

From Figures 4.1 and 4.2, the latter describing a monetary economy seems to be a completely different organism living a different life compared to that of the former. Still however the working of the real skeleton as it appears in Figure 4.1 is the fundamental aim and requirement of the monetary apparatus. If that is forgotten we are on a dangerous path because we do not eat money. Thus the complex monetary apparatus only partly illustrated in Figure 4.2 still does not bring any other type of *real* welfare to the circulation of goods and services, which may be the same as in Figure 4.1, *except for security for the future*.

It is probably so, that the complex money flows of Figure 4.2 forms a more efficient technology for means of savings to turn into productive investments, but that is still expressible in Figure 4.1. But adding the features to money of liquidity and current and future accounting measure vis-à-vis money contracts add something which cannot be expressed in a simple circular flow like in a Robinson Crusoe economy.

This is the very point which makes Wicksell's distinction between the microscopic and the macroscopic stability regimes with respect to prices and price level really intriguing. Thus allowing trading out of equilibrium, which Wicksell does when the market rate of interest is different from the profit rate on production capital, implies that effects of inflation/deflation will have redistributive and reallocation effects in the economy. But if we add to this aspect the other features of money plus the very advanced monetary apparatus, only partly illustrated in Figure 4.2, we realize that the stability problem becomes a very complex problem to cope with from a theoretical point of view.

We have mentioned the word anonymity, even the barter economy has difficulties keeping the consistency of pricing when the flea market expands in space and time, and in the theoretical barter economy the risks concern the factors of environment which affect the consumer choice, not the market in itself.

When we rejected the axiom of reflexivity and also draw the proper consequences underlying Arrow's paradox we questioned the consistency of the very foundation of the theoretical barter economy. Thus the existence of aggregate structures created at difference with additive aggregation induce also a source of uncertainty in the very forming of coalitions based on affecting the aggregate result, also increase the social effects of anonymity, which is augmented in the monetary economy and become more complex in its character. This drives us from a state of simple risk analysis of a constant state space into a world of genuine uncertainty, where the multitude of epistemic cycles becomes the fundamental source of uncertainty. This is in fact the first step towards a theoretical approach for the monetary economy. However once this step has been taken we must also introduce the three earlier mentioned features of money and consider them in this new theoretical environment.

As long as we emphasize only money as a medium of exchange nothing really happens to our analysis of a barter economy, particularly when we keep the neoclassical theory as some form of a microeconomic foundation. But when the money, medium of valuation and liquidity something happens because those features might be at variance with money as just a medium of exchange.

We have earlier quoted Arrow and Hahn on the necessity of realizing that contracts are made in money in order to develop a "serious theory of money". This quote is meaningless if we look upon money as some kind of "atomistic" concept where the different characteristics unite to a whole. To understand the quote we must realize the complexity of money and the monetary economy and the possibility of contradictions between the inherent features in money.

Keynes and Keynesian macroeconomics

Our intention to discuss Keynesian macroeconomics is somewhat difficult: the question "what did Keynes really say?" is an often implicit part of a title of a research paper. We can nowadays admit that Keynesian economics did not necessarily have particularly much to do with Keynes' discussions in *General Theory*, *Treatise on Money* and *Treatise on Probability*.

We have already emphasized three problems with which Keynes was particularly occupied: *uncertainty*, *expectations* and *liquidity*. As we see all these three features have to do with the problem of future and the disposition of monetary resources in a sensible way relevant to each and all the inherent features.

First of all we need to understand the difference between *uncertainty* and *risk*. In our discussions of the temporary equilibrium theory we saw the heavy dependency of the whole theory on the constancy of the state space and the assumption that all necessary market information was implicit in the price vector and the excess demand function. Thus the relation between the agents only appeared through the resulting price vector. Furthermore a piece of information of the current state, irrespective of if it was right or wrong, induced one and only one set of expectations which was the ground for actions. The expectation might be wrong in the sense of either faulty information or erroneous apprehension of the probability distribution of the state space and we consequently had redistributions but in the long run we would have a learning process which made the apprehension of the probability structure to converge and if defective information was randomly spread among the agents we would have a long-run equilibrium trajectory with some fluctuations.

Consequently we can say that temporary equilibrium theory has nothing to do with the concept of *uncertainty*. How should we then enter the concept of uncertainty into a systematic theoretical approach? We leave this question to Chapter 6 but note that Keynes' notion of uncertainty is often deliberately neutralized by assumptions of randomness of shocks and similar matters which is far from the uncertainty concept; Keynes' use of words like *confidence* and *degree of rational belief* makes the complexity of the concept of uncertainty even more accentuated, since it not only refers to a set of states of the environment but also to the attitude/mood of the agent.

However we have to limit our analysis of uncertainty so we link it to expectations and liquidity, which indeed is wide enough, since liquidity might affect the degree of uncertainty and as well induce long-run "sagacity" of the current money disposal but it might also induce prodigality.

Keynes introduced a kind of model reasoning in *General Theory*, but his model reasoning was partial and limited to the fundamental questions he raised. The *Keynesian* modelling started with John Hicks' paper in *Econometrica*, 1937, "Mr Keynes and the Classics", and was completely different from Keynes' fundamental discussions, which also Hicks admitted in his 1980/81 article in the *Journal of Post Keynesian Economics*.

So we will discuss Keynesian theory as it has developed through Keynesian modelling and we will not care particularly about its eventual links to Keynes, other than occasionally.

Keynesian economics during the 1950s and the 1960s was as dominating in economic analysis as ever the neoclassical theory before. In the beginning of the 1970s some of its influence was broken among the interested public, earlier among the economists. This was partly due to the breakdown of the Bretton Woods system and partly as a consequence of the oil crises, but there were other factors which we will come back to. Anyway, in a Swedish morning paper in the early 1970s there was an obituary notice at the editorial page announcing that now John Maynard Keynes' economic ideas were dead. Nowadays we may have to admit that it was an exaggerated statement, but also that a lot of economic approaches are half dead, even Keynesian, and limp around in the brushwood trying to get hold of the complex economic reality.

Keynes discusses in *General Theory* (1936) concepts like consumption, investment, liquidity and rate of interest, but he does not present any regular model, although he singles out some precise model formulations for some central variables. With respect to money he leans on his comprehensive analysis in *A Treatise of Money* (1930) but the models he uses in that book are hardly consistent with his structure of thoughts and used concepts in *General Theory* although his thoughts are. So Keynes never formulated a Keynesian model. True that Keynes accepted Hicks' initial paper of the later called IS-LM model, but it is doubtful if Keynes really penetrated Hicks' formulations in depth.

Hicks' interpretation of the classical model

Hicks' model, "a little apparatus" as he calls it in his paper, has been developed by Alvin Hansen and later Paul Samuelson in his textbook (Samuelson 1948) into a synthesis of neoclassical and Keynesian theories, so let us go through the birth of the model in Hicks' famous paper from 1937.

Hicks started to develop a simple illustration of the classical theory and then follow his presentation of Keynes' ideas along those principles.

In his discussion of the classical theory he divides the economy into two production sectors, investment goods and consumer goods. Respective prices are set according to the marginal productivity of labour in relation to the wage level, which is the same for both the sectors. There might be technological differences between the two sectors but labour is assumed to be homogeneous; thus the generated income in the two sectors is respectively:

$$Y^I = w \cdot I \cdot \frac{dN_I}{dI}$$

$$Y^c = w \cdot C \cdot \frac{dN_C}{dC},$$

(E.4.1)

and consequently the total income is:

$$Y = Y^I + Y^C$$

(E.4.2)

He uses the Cambridge Quantity Equation $M = k \cdot Y$ and claims that it is invertible thus:

$$Y = \frac{M}{k},$$

given k.

Demand for investment goods, is dependent on the rate of interest $Y^I = K(i)$ and equal to saving, $Y^I = S(i, Y)$. Subsequently we can express the classical model as:

a $M = k \cdot Y$
b $Y^I = K(i)$
c $Y^I = S(i, Y)$

(E.4.3)

Since the total income, Y, is uniquely determined by the quantity equation both i and Y will be determined and this will consequently determine the employed labour in the two sectors respectively.

The classical system as it is presented by Hicks is now complete. From a strict technical point of view the system E.4.3 is a bit curious, since Y is completely determined by E.4.3.a, the two other functions E.4.3.b and E.4.3.c are obviously an identity, thus saving is by necessity equal to investments, measured in money terms although it is in line with the standard neoclassical theory, and that actually induces a complication when we link it to his assumptions about the two production sectors which he introduces. Thus an increase in inducements to invest will increase interest rates and thus the saving and consequently we will have a switch in the employment from consumption to investment industry. However Hicks claims that if the elasticity of supply in the investment production is greater than it is in the consumption production, we will thus have an increase in the total employment and the opposite if the investment supply has a lower elasticity than in the consumption production. It is a bit hard to understand what Hicks means when he writes elasticity of supply. Since he discusses the effects on total employment it seems that he keeps the money supply constant as well as the wage level. In such a case the result depends on one hand on the assumption of different technologies in the two sectors and on the other on the assumption of homogeneous labour. Thus if we look at a Cobb-Douglas production function for a given capital stock, $Q = k_0 \cdot L^\beta$ we have:

$$\frac{\delta L}{\delta Q} = \frac{1}{\beta \cdot k_0} \cdot Q^{\frac{1-\beta}{\beta}}$$

which can be written as:

$$\frac{\delta L}{\delta Q} = \frac{1}{\beta} \cdot \frac{L}{Q}$$

thus the higher capital intensity the lower effect on labour. Hence we have that the high capital share in the investment sector relative to the consumption sector gives a reduction in total employment and vice versa. We will thus have a mixture of price and quantitative effects which Hicks entirely overlooks in his discussion although in Hicks (1980/81) he is aware of it.

A rise in the supply of money will raise the total income and consequently the employment, since both demand for investment goods and consumption goods will rise. The effect on employment depends on the relative factor proportions in conjunction with the spending behaviour. What is remarkable about the model is that it seems that labour supply is perfectly elastic and consumption is obviously a residual to the saving, furthermore the total income is uniquely determined by the money supply in conjunction with the technology parameters and thus independent of the saving-investment behaviour. Consequently it seems that equilibrium in the commodity market does not imply equilibrium at the labour market, or at least an equilibrium dependent on technical matters.

In the discussion of the critical points of the classical model Hicks discusses mainly three points: (i) there are variations in M during the trade cycle induced by variations in *bank money*, (ii) variations in cash balances during the trade cycle which affects the money circulation, k (iii) the demand for money depends on interest rate.

Hicks' version of the Keynesian model

Hicks actually has two Keynesian models, one which he calls Mr. Keynes' special theory, and consequently one which he calls Mr. Keynes' general theory. We begin with the former.

The classical system of equations in E.4.3 is compared with a corresponding system with three equations catching Keynes' ideas:

a $M = L(i)$
b $Y' = K(i)$ (E.4.4)
c $Y' = S(Y)$

These differ from the classical equations in two ways. On the one hand, the demand for money is conceived as depending upon the rate of interest (Liquidity Preference). On the other hand, any possible influence of the rate of interest on the amount saved out of a given income is neglected. Although it means that the third equation becomes the multiplier equation, which performs such queer tricks, nevertheless this second amendment is a mere simplification, and ultimately insignificant.* [the footnote is omitted] It is the liquidity preference doctrine which is vital.

(Hicks 1937: 152)

The insignificance of the second amendment is received by inserting the Cambridge Quantity Equation instead of E.4.4.a which consequently means that we transform E.4.4 to the classical version E.4.3 since "it is impossible to increase investment without increasing the willingness to save" Hicks (1937: 152n.). To claim that the equation E.4.4.c is insignificant based on the replacement of E.4.4.a with an equation from the seemingly completely different system E.4.3 seems from a mathematical point of view a bit adventurous, nevertheless it gives a gist of Hicks' analysis. Anyway the Keynesian *special theory* has made consumption the primary variable and shows that an increase in consumption does not affect the interest rate:

For it is now the rate of interest, not income, which is determined by the quantity of money. The rate of interest set against the schedule of the marginal efficiency of capital the value for investment; that determines income by the multiplier. Then the volume of employment (at given wage rates) is determined by the value of investment and of income which is not saved but spent upon consumption goods.

It is this system of equations which yields the startling conclusion, that an increase in the inducement to invest, or in the propensity to consume, will not tend to raise the rate of interest, but only increase employment.

(ibid.: 152)

What Hicks call Keynes' general theory is then the completion of the money demand function with the transactions motive so E.4.4.a is replaced by:

$$M=L(Y, i) \tag{E.4.4.a$'$}$$

This modification is closer to orthodox theories and Hicks is then able to classify Keynes' theory as a theory for Economics of Depression. The arguments go through a fairly standard IS-LM diagram completed with Keynes' discussion in chapter 15 on "Incentives to Liquidity" (Keynes 1973 [1936]: 194 ff.) where he claims that there is a minimum rate of interest where there are no incentives to keep resources other than liquid ones. We thus will have an LM-curve like in Figure 4.3 expressing that if the IS-curve intersects the LM-curve in the horizontal part under which the interest rate is unlikely to go, the

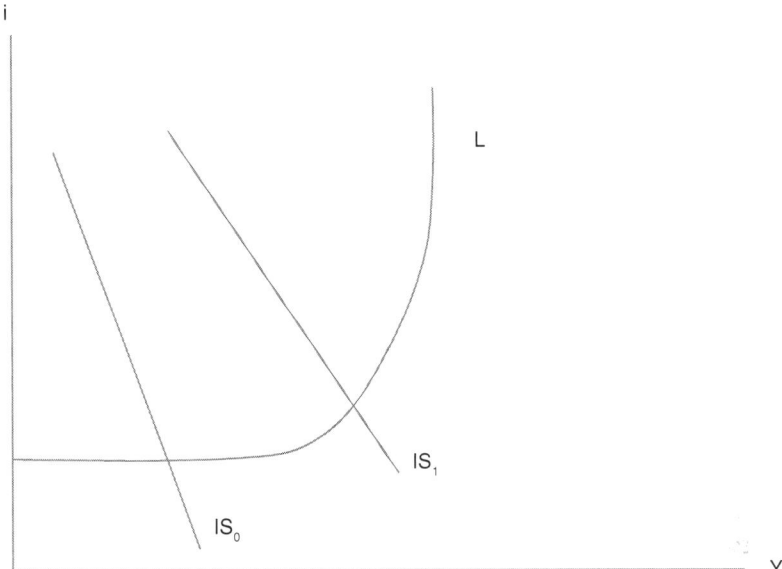

Figure 4.3 Hicks' interpretation of the economics of depression.

vertical part is the maximum income which can be achieved at a given money supply.

Hence the intersection between IS_1 and the L-curve lies in an interval where an increased inducement to invest will increase both income and the rate of interest, which is in line with the classical model. The intersection between IS_0 and the L-curve however lies in an interval where an increased inducement to invest or an increased propensity to consume will increase income but will not affect the rate of interest rate, and this is the case of a depression economy.

Later Hicks relaxes the constancy of the money supply and we will have the case where there is an increase in investment in conjunction with an increased money supply. This is similar to the Wicksellian analysis where the monetary authorities keep the rate of interest below Wicksell's *natural rate*, "When generalised in this way, Mr. Keynes' theory begins to look very like Wicksell's; this is of course hardly surprising" (ibid.: 158).[3]

Hicks maintains that Keynes' contribution can mainly be characterized as "sort of Slump Economy" and thus rather partial (ibid.: 158):

> But even if it may claim to be a slight extension of Mr. Keynes' similar skeleton, it remains a terribly rough and ready sort of affair. In particular, the concept of "Income" is worked monstrously hard; most of our curves are not really determinate unless something is said about the distribution of Income as well as its magnitude. Indeed, what they express is something

like a relation between the price system and the system of interest rates; and you cannot get into that curve.

Hicks' reaction is interesting since he boils down the General Theory "to a rather tiny set of equations". His description of the classical theory is in one way correct but his treatment of employment in his two sectors model is indeed curious and might be excused by the dismissal of the prices but if so it has to be contrasted to the last quote above and furthermore we leave the labour market in disequilibrium. We could criticize Hicks' article rather hard in many aspects but that is pointless since Hicks admitted many of his mistakes and misapprehensions in Hicks (1980–81), particularly the omission of uncertainty. Nevertheless Hicks' article in 1937 set the standard interpretation and the "Keynesian" model was developed particularly by Alvin Hansen (1949) and Paul Samuelson cemented the "synthesis" of neoclassical and Keynesian thoughts in his famous textbook *Economics* that most economists of the author's generation are brought up with.

Consequently it was a bit strange in the 1970s when the debate started among economic researchers about the microeconomic foundation of macroeconomics; Robert Lucas was one of the leading names. Lucas (1972) developed the concept of *rational expectations*, to be used for macroscopic analysis. The concept stemmed from Muth (1961) who used it for short-run expectations for well-defined commodity markets on the microscopic level.

Generally it seems that it was forgotten that the neoclassical synthesis, IS-LM, was a macroscopic theory for which neoclassical theory was an appropriate foundation completed with the money side of the economy. As Paul Krugman claims on his homepage, the IS-LM might be seen as an enlarged neoclassical model.[4] Furthermore the concept of rational expectation was shown, as in Radner (1982), to be rather obscure in its use on general macroscopic problems and most of the elements in it could be traced back to Keynes' beauty contest.[5]

The debate sooner concerned the developed political practice around the IS-LM model containing the questions about the Phillips curve and we will later see that this was a constructive approach but it hardly belonged to the Keynesian theory expressed in IS-LM, particularly if we regard Hicks' problem with technological differences between production sectors which already appeared in his illustration of the classical model.

Keynesianism and the neoclassical synthesis

The *Keynesian theory* as it appears in the IS-LM model, deals with interest, money and to some extent liquidity but where are the prices? Thus Hicks' question in the last quote above about the relation between prices and interest is relevant, particularly since Keynes was aware of the problem of changing dimensionality of the commodity space. In principle the model worked as illustrated in Figure 4.4 with respect to national income and the price level. Nothing happens to the prices until we have full capacity utilization. An increase in demand in full capacity utilization adds nothing to the real national income but only to the price level, it is said nothing in the model of the relative prices. Thus we have a rather comfortable world from an economic policy point of view. We have no, or a small, end-mean conflict between unemployment and inflation, since we either have unemployment or inflation. Policy considerations are mostly about making precise diagnosis of where we are in the business cycle, and making fine adjustments of the implementation of the used means. Those things are pretty difficult but nevertheless it is a good deal compared to how we perceive the economic reality nowadays.

Thus the model illustrated in Figure 4.4 concerns variations in capacity utilization at a more or less stationary optimal capacity in the economy where the optimal capacity coincides with the social desirable level of unemployment, which is zero, save for some insignificant level of *friction* unemployment.

So fixing the aggregate demand curve to the locus AD_2 will take us to the best of worlds. The long-run aspects are clearly outside the model as the investments, although having an impact on aggregate demand, are practically inessential for the total capacity and the technological state of art. A simple textbook formulation of the IS-LM (omitting public and foreign sectors) can be written:

IS
$$C = a + b \cdot Y$$
$$I = I_0 - c \cdot R$$
$$Y = C + I$$

LM
$$M^d = L_0 + \mu \cdot Y - \rho \cdot R$$
$$M^s = M_0$$

(E.4.5)

Price level

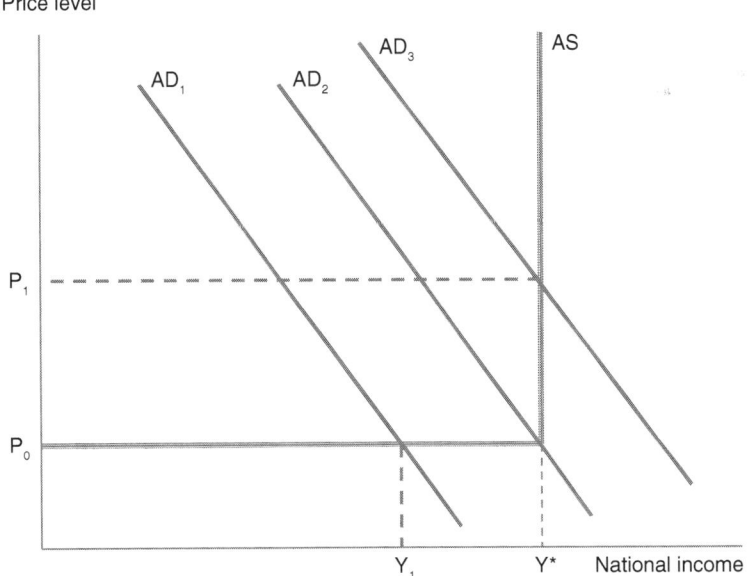

Figure 4.4 The original IS-LM model.

Hicks writes that Keynes has "monstrously" overworked the concept of income, so apart from a state of depression Keynes' approach according to Hicks did not add much to the economic understanding. Given Hicks' apprehension of Keynes' approach this is quite understandable. The multiplier effect was known and analysed already in the 1920s and Keynes' fuzz about Say's law was indeed questionable since the dimensionality problem is not at all self-evident in Keynes' text except from the foreword to the French edition which we have quoted. According to Say's writings the multiplier process seems to be a very relevant description of what Say actually discusses and the derived income multiplier in a system like E.4.5 is indeed dependent on a theoretical underpinning as Say's law. In fact when we read Say it is clear that he never advocated the entire income to be spent immediately but, as far as we can understand advocated a principle in concordance with how Keynes describes *marginal propensity to consume* (1973 [1936]: 96) which basically underpins the income multiplier. Thus Hicks' comment on Keynes' overestimation of the role of income is actually understandable given Hicks' apprehension of Keynes.

That means that it is easy to interpret E.4.5 as a part of the general equilibrium theory since we obviously have an equilibrium solution. Adding the reasoning of what appears in temporary equilibrium theory implies that we well can think of fluctuating short-run equilibrium; but this converges to some long-run general equilibrium trajectory.

Our illustration in Figure 4.4 as well as E.4.5 suggests however that we have a theoretical infinity of states of equilibrium depending on the exogenous variables, and that is in fact a crucial point. To understand this we can quote Keynes (ibid.: 242n.), where he writes:[6]

> I had, however, overlooked the fact that in any given society there is, on this definition, a *different* natural rate of interest for each hypothetical level of employment. And, similarly, for every rate of interest there is a level of employment for which that rate is the "natural" rate, in the sense that the system will be in equilibrium with that rate of interest and that level of employment.

Here it is clear that what Keynes means with equilibrium is something completely different from the neoclassical general equilibrium, and also different from Hicks' sketch of an equilibrium model which requires perfectly elastic labour supply to obtain equilibrium.

We can describe equilibrium as a state where counteracting forces are in balance. If I hold a book outside my window at the second floor I attach a counteracting force to the gravitation but if I drop the book the gravitation sets the book in motion until another counteracting force is arranged, for instance an awning at the first floor; otherwise the ground has to be seen as the ultimate general equilibrium. Still the ground exists irrespective of how many levels of awnings there are, but may be that has more to do with the physical general equilibrium in $0°K$, than what we mean by general equilibrium in economics.

Keynes actually dismisses the whole existence of general equilibrium when he claims that the economy is intrinsically unstable; however that does not mean that equilibrium as such does not exist or is uninteresting from a theoretical point of view, it only means that Keynes changes the normative focus to what is politically and socially desirable, furthermore his famous expression "in the long run we are all dead" must be seen as relating to a basic condition for a constantly changing society. Thus a convergence process *à la* temporary equilibrium theory takes time and if the constancy of the state space can be questioned then in fact even rather short periods of recessions may change future prospects for people. That means that the realism of our eventual model representations are dependent on inert structures but this inertia is only temporary and the short-run events may well change the conditions for further inertia as well as future inertia.

If we use the concept of epistemic cycles we can say that on the microscopic level a certain behaviour and its consequences may well be *almost* reversible in many cases, however this aggregated to the macroscopic level leads to the conclusion that the macroscopic development is *almost never* reversible, which follows from the mereological rule of thumb. Keynes' rejection of the stability of the market economy can never be explained by scrutinizing a so-called Keynesian model which in fact is centred round some kind of equilibrium concept. Hume describes this rather well when he emphasizes the interaction between the market process and the social structure.

Keynes discusses a world where the economic and social conditions are in constant change and thus what might have been a general equilibrium last year is not so this year, but given a particular structure of production and a given capital stock it is sensible to think of a locus which can be regarded as the optimal capacity utilization in the medium term, Y^*, where the capital stock and the technology can be regarded as given. Formulated in this way the marginal efficiency of capital in this locus could be regarded as the natural rate of interest. This seems also to be in line with Wicksell's stability discussion. However around Y^*, there are variations in the employment depending on the demand, which is seen as partly exogenous, which sets the optimal yield on capital given the capital stock, technology and employment. This is elementary but for these short-run variations, linked to demand, could obviously be interesting to affect by authorities by means of affecting the exogenous part of demand. The nasty question then pops up whether the policy authorities have such good understanding of the factual situation that their measures will improve the aggregate situation for the individuals with respect to the ruling social and political ends and thus is superior to the individual search for improvements of the current situation at the microscopic level. This question is often interpreted in the light of the theoretical conflict between Keynesianism and the neoclassical theory and we may also add Marxist thinking. It is thus interesting to note that the only theoretical approach in which this question can never pop up is an orthodox neoclassical approach since we then by the axiomatic structure have made the problem impossible. As soon as we add the problem of Arrow's paradox and the impertinent agents who claim their right to vote, the question becomes relevant and our derived "mereological rule of thumb" in Chapter 3 spells out the problem.

Thus the conflict between those who claim that macroscopic problems are better solved by the individuals themselves and those who claim the necessity of aggregate measures to solve a macroscopic problem is necessarily not a question between Keynesians and neoclassicists, in fact from a orthodox theoretical point of view the neoclassical economist has problems to explain why the conflict even can exist. Keynesians should however always ask themselves about the relevance of such a question.

That means that the neoclassical synthesize cements modelling of the link between the microscopic world and the macroscopic world which did not exist in Keynes analysis vis-á-vis uncertainty, liquidity and decisions about the future.

Thus in the model E.4.5 the *Keynesian influence* is to be searched in the stability of the exogenous variables, particularly the relation between saving as a residual to consumption and the investments which is partly exogenously determined, and it is exactly here that money enters as a vital factor in the analysis.

Keynes' approach to stability applied to IS-LM

The development of the IS-LM model implies an exogenous recognition of money in the form of liquidity as well as a substitute to physical capital in the form of a financial instrument called *bond*. The market interest rate is attached to and affects the demand for liquidity but is ultimately interpreted as the bond rate which links the public outlays to both the actual money supply and investments. We thus close the policy model at the macroscopic level.

This closure is actually closer to the Wicksellian analysis of discrepancies between the market rate and the natural rate of interest than to Keynes' concept of marginal efficiency of capital, which he defines:

> More precisely, I define the marginal efficiency of capital as being equal to that rate of discount which would make the present value of the series of annuities given by the returns expected from the capital-asset during its life just equal to its supply price.
>
> (ibid.: 135)

The spirit of this quote is clearly based on a rather standard microscopic analysis, and so interpreted we have a rather natural interpretation of investment as a market process converging towards the ruling market rate as an alternative cost.

However this definition is to be understood in concordance with:

> Only at the conclusion of Book IV will it be possible to take a comprehensive view of the factors determining the rate of investment in their actual complexity. I would, however, ask the reader to note at once that neither the knowledge of an asset's prospective yield nor the knowledge of the marginal

efficiency of the asset enables us to deduce either the rate of interest or the present value of the asset. We must ascertain the rate of interest from some other source, and only then can we value the asset by "capitalising" its prospective yield.

(ibid.: 137)

So let us go to the end of Book IV and see what he writes. The essence of his discussion is to be found in pp. 249–54.

The above is a summary of the General Theory. But the actual phenomena of the economic system are also coloured by certain special characteristics of the propensity to consume, the schedule of the marginal efficiency of capital and the rate of interest, about which we can safely generalise from experience, *but which are not logically necessary*.

(ibid.: 249, my emphasis)

Thus, due to sufficient inertia, the generalizations of the different central variables and their relations can be brought into a system of endogenous and exogenous variables where the exogenous are not logically necessary but *given* these variables the system *can be solved* by logical necessity. Thus some empirical experiences cannot be turned into a logical system but are merely expressing possibilities and that raises the question of the eventual stability of the economic system. Thus the fact that we may achieve one or the other equilibrium is really not the ultimate point and we come to the same problem as we mentioned when discussing the general equilibrium; we may well assume, in following Debreu's definition of commodities, that the economy in each moment of time is in equilibrium but that the successive states of equilibrium have, from an axiomatic point of view, no relation between each other. Thus we have to search for the stability creating forces outside the model, and the stability is due to social forces.

Hence we will have stability problems of three levels: the first level of stability problems concerns the relations between the endogenous variables and their intrinsic dynamics, for example in the form of a multiplier/accelerator model. The second level concerns the stability of the exogenous variables. If in a model like E.4.5 the exogenous investments I_0, vary violently or between rather narrow limits, the stability of the exogenous variables is central to the stability of the model, linking the exogenous part of investments to expectations. We saw in our analysis of the temporary equilibrium theory that it was necessary (Green 1973), to assume "a pattern of markets approximating the reality more closely". The third level of stability concerns the social and political stability, which we will comment on in Chapter 8, but with respect to Keynes it might be relevant to remind of his "Economic Consequences of the Peace": "The events of the coming year will not be shaped by the deliberate acts of statesmen, but the hidden currents, flowing continually beneath the surface of the political history, of which no one can predict the outcome" (Keynes 1920: 278). Consequently even if we regard models like E.4.5 as short-run models we must have an idea how the sequences of "short run" are linked and what kind of stabilizing forces might be present.

In his discussion of stability in the end of chapter 18 in *General Theory*, Keynes discusses only those forces under what we called levels one and two. He mentions four main features important to stability (pp. 250–54): (i) the income multiplier must be greater than one but not very large, (ii) changes in the prospective yield of capital will cause relatively proportionate changes in investment, (iii) changes in employment will cause relatively proportionate changes in money-wages, (iv) the fourth condition can be linked to an often claimed hypothesis in the financial market "Mean Reversion Hypothesis", which Keynes describes "as a tendency of a fluctuation to reverse itself in due course".

The four conditions were relatively commonly accepted but the economic development during the 1970s and 1980s implied that probably all four must be questioned and nowadays both policy makers and business people are careful not to depend too much on some rather general assumptions of stability; furthermore money and financial assets and liabilities play a key issue in this, which implies that even if we assume the agents' behaviour towards real factors, as such, to be inert the development on the monetary and financial markets most probably increases the variability of the financial conditions for the agents.

Cash balances, inflation and uncertainty

In the end of 1960s and the beginning of the 1970s there was a development of increasing shares of financial capital in relation to the total capital in the industry, and an increased demand for assets with high liquidity. A loose interpretation is then to consider it similar to cash balances. We know that the financial profits for producing companies are quite considerable, but still we look upon the financial assets of the producing industry as a kind of "insurance" of the inert production capital.[7]

The very introduction of cash balances in the IS-LM model, both the constant L_0 as well as the parameter ρ, is a bit curious and rather tricky to explain. Obviously we can always determine them by some econometric manipulations, but that is hardly an explanation since it gives us some form of average behaviour over time or over a cross-section of agents.

Save for the public sector outlays and the foreign sector, which are extremely important of course, the model E.4.5 contains fundamental variables which somehow ought to include some relations to L_0 and ρ. Hicks was fully aware of these shortcomings in his article *IS-LM: An Explanation* (Hicks 1980/81) and confessed that the cash balances are unexplained without the concept of uncertainty. But still, if we introduce uncertainty, where does it come from? Is it enough to relate it to a state space as we do in temporary equilibrium theory and then assume insufficient knowledge of probability distributions or even lack of knowledge of some dimensions of the state space? Furthermore Hicks discusses in the article the usual problem of fixed prices and wages and if we have such rigidities and/or others we understand that if we are victims of uncertainty this will affect us in a more or less severe way. Assuming perfectly homogeneous production factors and perfectly flexible prices and wages are of course an efficient solution to the problems although it may imply some other theoretical inconveniences. Thus if we use the neoclassical theory as a microeconomic underpinning we solve the theoretical problems within the IS-LM model but of course then the whole IS-LM model is superfluous. Another variant is to recognize that we have some short-term inertia but in a long run the neoclassical theory will rule. If so we will end up in the problem of false trading and also in interesting speculations of whether we will be dead or alive in the long run.

However a basic problem lurking under the IS-LM model, the uncertainty concept and liquidity/cash balances is the rather trivial theoretical treatment of *inflation*.

We may see liquidity as some kind of insurance against uncertainty but to be a meaningful approach the liquidity must been seen firmly linked to real purchasing power of money and this is obviously the key issue about the value of money, and financial contracts in nominal terms. We have seen from the historical exposé and our consideration concerning the neoclassical theory that money as a *medium of exchange* does not need and should not have an intrinsic value.

But the concept of liquidity is different and this implies that the traditional features which are intrinsic to money may, with respect to their interrelations be partially contradictory, and the factor which creates this potential contradiction is actually inflation.

Thus with respect to the concept of money the central issue is inflation and its causes.

If we stick to the neoclassical axiomatic structure inflation cannot be a problem. In equilibrium we will have an index which we will call a price vector and which measures the relative prices. Inflation is thus a rather obscure concept since such an index may be based on whatever base, it does not matter from a theoretical point of view if we choose 100 or 10 000 as our basis.[8] Thus when we claim neutrality of money the mere numerical size of the relative prices is completely insignificant. In such a theoretical context the only cause of inflation is via the quantity identity: $M \cdot V \equiv P \cdot Y$.[9] We remember from our discussions about the bullionist debate that the so-called currency school claimed that the only cause for inflation is the increasing of the proportion of bank money to gold.

However given the considerations on neutrality of money it is hard to understand all the fuzz about central banks, monetary policy and even the quantity identity as such when we stick to the neoclassical axioms. It might perhaps be relevant given that the economy is loaded with public sectors, sectors with poor competition and natural monopolies and general market failures, but if so there will also be other analytical consequences so we do not need to brood over general equilibrium.

Consequently from a strict analytical point of view a neoclassical approach has little or nothing to tell about inflation.

Therefore we must turn to Keynes and Keynesians. We remember from Hicks that he claimed that Keynes grossly overrated the role of income and that he overlooked prices and interest rates. But what Hicks overlooked was that although Keynes did not discuss the price formation as such he actually has a most interesting discussion of prices in relation to the quantity identity in chapter 21, "Theory of Prices" (1973 [1936]).

He introduces some assumptions or sooner propositions, which enables him to enunciate or more correctly evaluate approaches built on the Quantity Identity (ibid.: 296):

1   Effective demand will not change in exact proportion to the quantity of money.
2   Since resources are not homogenous, there will be diminishing, and not constant, returns as employment gradually increases.
3   Since resources are not interchangeable, some commodities will reach a condition of inelastic supply whilst there are still unemployed resources available for the production of other commodities.
4   The wage unit will tend to rise, before full employment has been reached.
5   The remunerations of the factors entering into marginal cost will not all change in the same proportion.

If we now look at the Keynesian theory built on the IS-LM model we can see that none of the five points from Keynes are regarded. The IS-LM model deals with the macroscopic level as one sector composed from a sort of additive aggregation or an enlarged average where in principle multiplied averages coincide with the aggregate values. In Figure 4.4 the inflation occurs in such a way that we might call it *demand inflation*. As the concept stands, one gets the impression of an overall increase in demand relatively symmetric to all sectors fuelled by an increase in the money stock. In an open economy we can understand it when we have a strong foreign demand which raises prices and wages but even in such case the aggregate demand is probably asymmetric and will cause reallocations among sectors.

If we think of demand inflation in a closed economy as adding all microscopic sectors which are all working in a reign with increasing average costs, hence above average cost minimum, relating to a standard textbook cost-diagram for a firm, we obviously get a combination of demand and cost elements, like the Phillips-curve shape, and then it is a good chance that technology differences will create asymmetric effects which are of course interesting to analyse. But the start of the inflation must come from the demand side, but where does that demand come from? Is it the money supply? Hicks' analysis of the classical model in "Mr. Keynes and the Classics" allowed for two sectors with different technology and that leads to an undetermined unemployment although Hicks does not seems to observe it. Consequently that kind of sector difference may have analogous effects on prices or at least combined effects depending on eventual differences in the flexibility of price and quantity adjustments. However if we look at only one aggregate sector without allowing for structural differences in technology we enter into a rather futile debate of differences in rigidities in prices and wages, assuming homogeneous labour and capital makes obviously such a debate completely nonsense since the inflation is then reduced to a symmetric mark up of prices and wages. Why should the inflation have anything to do with employment in an aggregate IS-LM model and why should we care about it? If it is troublesome to keep record of the price changes reduce the money supply for heaven's sake. That is what Hicks says when he lets employment be uniquely determined by the money supply. If the relation is a bit obscure then we can keep the supply in the upper interval of uncertainty if we are most worried about unemployment and in the lower end of the uncertainty interval if we are most worried about inflation.

Thus we indicate the principles for economic policy in Figure 4.4 such that we might achieve by aggregate measures a balanced situation with no inflation and no unemployment. It seems rather difficult to catch such a picture of the economy of the real world.

Both Henry Thornton and Jean Baptiste Say were of the opinion that inflation was a kind phenomenon of friction in the real economy; thus the inflation they saw was a kind of cost inflation combined with structural differences and foreign trade. The only opposition to that at those times came from the currency school which meant that inflation was created by money supply.

If we look at Wicksell the only way to understand his distinction between stability on the microscopic and macroscopic levels is to see changes of the price level as asymmetric and then we must add a kind of *cost inflation* concept in conjunction with a structural analysis. But such an analysis requires quite a different theoretical apparatus from the IS-LM model both in its crude form and more elaborated forms and then the five points by Keynes quoted above becomes of utmost interest because we then approach a much more elaborated microscopic foundation than the neoclassical approach can ever present to us. The striking difference is perhaps the assumption of non-homogeneity of production factors and the asymmetric growth of supply and demand with respect to different commodities implying that an aggregate underutilization of resources is also asymmetric which makes a recovery more like a search process like Allais' equimarginal principle, where he distinguishes between potential and feasible distributable surpluses.

The very point however with respect to inflation is that it may well occur at the same time as we have underutilized resources, as Keynes claimed in point four. Thus the problem of stagflation was actually discussed by Keynes rather explicitly while in the IS-LM model it is very hard to detect and it is remarkable that in Hicks' text we find traces of it in his curious discussion of the classical model with respect to two production sectors, investment and consumption goods, with different technical conditions, but that is only implicit in the technical elaboration of his assumptions.

When we continue our story of the more intricate elaboration of aggregate supply with respect to the inflation problem it is important to remember Keynes' five points. They also cast some light over the policy recommendations based on IS-LM during the 1950s and 1960s since Keynes' points imply on one hand that inflation and unemployment are asymmetric phenomena in the economy and consequently anti-unemployment and anti-inflation policy have to be asymmetric in its effects.

The IS-LM model as a policy tool and its alleged death

The first oil crises during the beginning of 1970s with a follow-up at the end of the decennium, was an important reminder of the weakness of the Keynesian approach, or more appropriately the IS-LM use as a policy tool, so the obituary notice of Keynes' theory in the Swedish morning paper was very alert, although it somewhat missed the theoretical point. The problem of the early 1970s was linked to the inability of the demand policy but had more to do with the presumptions of the IS-LM model with respect to its use which in principle does not say anything about the model as such. The first oil crises coincided with the breakdown of the Bretton Woods system, and this was a complete change of the conditions for economic activities and international trade. For the industry it implied a different attitude to international affairs and the need of currency protection as well as an orientation towards new production technologies with respect to a more flexible use of different energy sources as well as energy saving. The aggregate effect became similar to a negative income effect; fighting inflation implied further pressure on aggregate demand and not fighting inflation implied raising real prices and loss of international competitiveness, leading to much the same real effects as the opposite policy. Furthermore the structural composition of the industry affected the consequences of the oil crises.

In the 1970s and onwards the IS-LM model was replaced by the so-called Mundell-Fleming model, developed in the 1960s, saying that the internal interest rate was perfectly elastic with respect to the international rate for most countries which were substantially dependent on international trade. Import and export became functions of inflation and exchange rate. It is said that the Mundell-Fleming model is supposed to show that fiscal policy is relatively inefficient to monetary policy and that may be true sometimes, but to claim that as a general rule requires rather strict assumptions with respect to different elasticities of export and import as well as a general assumption that the financial relations between the currencies is a reflection of the real flows. The Mundell-Fleming model emphasizes the international sector to a higher extent than the traditional IS-LM but with respect to money and financial flows it is as rudimentary as the IS-LM and the concept of inflation is still poorly developed although it is linked to the exchange rate and thus leans heavily on Purchasing Power Parity (PPP) which means that the problems in the IS-LM model are more or less the same in the Mundell-Fleming model, save for the problem of capital flows but that is more or less endogenous as a consequence of the PPP approach. Hence our discussions concerning the IS-LM model concern the Mundell-Fleming model as well.

From a methodological point of view we may ask ourselves if there is real benefit in manipulating the IS-LM model with respect to policy analysis, since the model is explicitly short run, when the two most important variables from a policy point of view, *uncertainty* and *expectations*, are left out of the model. It becomes a simple deterministic model of which the basic theoretical foundation is similar to Allais' equimarginal principle and its modification by Jacque Drèze. The aspects Mundell-Fleming added imply that fiscal policy alters the interest rate and subsequently the exchange rate, thus altering the distribution while it has a negative short-run effect on the production volume, which makes the policy contrary to the Pareto criteria, given the importance of the export sector. The problem is that from a long-run structural point of view the monetary policy which is in line with the Pareto criteria in the short run from the point of view of currency stability may punish the internal production sectors and from another point of view may lead to higher risk premiums at the international financial market if not anti-inflation is drastically imposed. The word *drastically* indicates that the agents on the financial market do not react on current inflation but on the expected inflation. Thus an anti-inflation policy should not fight current inflation, which is already anticipated by the market, but the *expected inflation*, which causes are indeed unclear; sometimes expectation depends on structural features which are commonly accepted but sometimes they are built on rather loose reasoning.

The greenhouse effect during the 1950s and 1960s

To understand the development of the economy as well as the theoretical reorientation during the 1970s and 1980s it is important to understand the economic features during the 1950s and 1960s.

The happy times of the IS-LM model were the 1950s and the 1960s. The reasons for this are of course many, but one line of explanation which has a reasonable support (Lundberg *et al.* 1975, Boltho 1982, Ekstedt and Westberg 1991, and Eichengreen 1995), puts the emphasis on a combination of the effects of the war, high demand and low capacity, and the currency stability created by the Bretton Woods agreement, all this combined with low energy prices, particularly oil prices. Thus we had a rather monotonic positive development of the production capacity and the aggregate optimal capacity utilization in the industry approached the social desirable level of employment. Eichengreen calls it a sort of greenhouse effect which maybe is a good characterization of the aftermath of the Second World War in an economic growth sense and Eric Hobsbawm (1994: 6) says:

> An Age of Catastrophe from 1914 to the aftermath of the Second World War was followed by some twenty-five or thirty years of extraordinary economic growth and social transformation, which probably changed human society more profoundly than any other period of comparably brevity. In retrospect it can be seen as a sort of Golden Age, and was so seen almost

immediately it had come to an end in the early 1970s. The last part of the century was a new era of decomposition, uncertainty and crises.

Thus the aggregate supply curve was not that far from the one pictured in Figure 4.4. An aggregate supply curve like this which illustrates the principle message of models like E.3.5 normally goes with assumptions of homogeneous factors of production, particularly labour, which indeed is a strong opinion, in the neoclassical approach at the microscopic level we make this assumption.[10]

However if we think of the specific conditions in the aftermath of the Second World War and the so-called greenhouse effect we had a period in Europe and the US with increasing demand in virtually all sectors, and new commodities were introduced as well as investments in the welfare sector. At the same time we had at least in Western Europe a relative shortage of labour and particularly it is important to mention the low participation rate of women. Such a situation will most probably create an aggregate supply curve which seems to be similar to that of Figure 4.4 although labour is not to be assumed as homogeneous, although it might have been less heterogeneous than today, but the growth of economy both with respect to volume as well as the dimensionality of the commodity space made it easy for people to find adequate jobs.

For a politician of the hardened twenty-first century economy this seems probably a dream-like situation with no, or at least small, direct end-mean conflicts between unemployment and inflation and a business cycle policy that often was rather successful.

However this "war-effect" ended, and the Swedish economist Eric Lundberg (1975) claimed that it ended during the middle and late part of the 1960s. Then the OECD countries entered a new era with a higher degree of competition in virtually all areas. Thus investments became more risky and technology growth linked to increased competitiveness became more important than capacity expansion. The breakdown of the Bretton Woods system aggravated these effects. The 1950s and 1960s had resulted in a high growth of international trade which meant that as long as the growth of international trade was high the economy worked more or less as described in Figure 4.4, but underneath that development we also had a development implying that companies developed new relations to companies in other nations; we got a development like the one in Table 3.1 but this was not symmetric to all companies. Thus we got a development of a gradual complexification of trade and financial flows as in Figure 4.2. As said, as long as the growth of international trade was high it so to say hid this development and made it look like all standard assumptions of the IS-LM model were prevalent, but as Figure 4.5 shows the mentioned causes in conjunction with the first oil crises made the growth of international trade decline in the beginning of the 1970s.

Thus instead of the nice aggregate supply curve of Figure 4.4 we got the more problematic one in Figure 4.6.

It is interesting to consider the shift of the aggregate supply curve from Figures 4.4 to 4.6. Let us then treat the reality in the 1950s and 1960s as similar

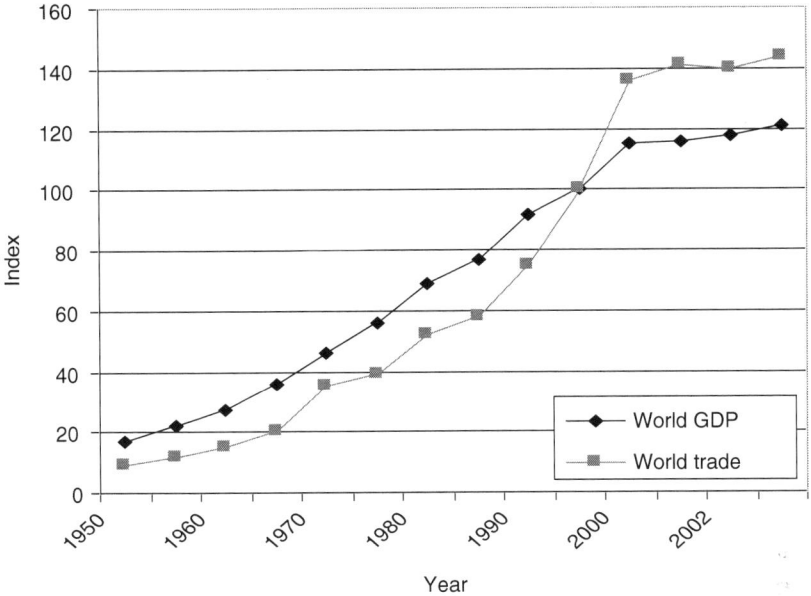

Figure 4.5 Growth of world trade and world GDP (source: IMF).

Note
1995 = 100.

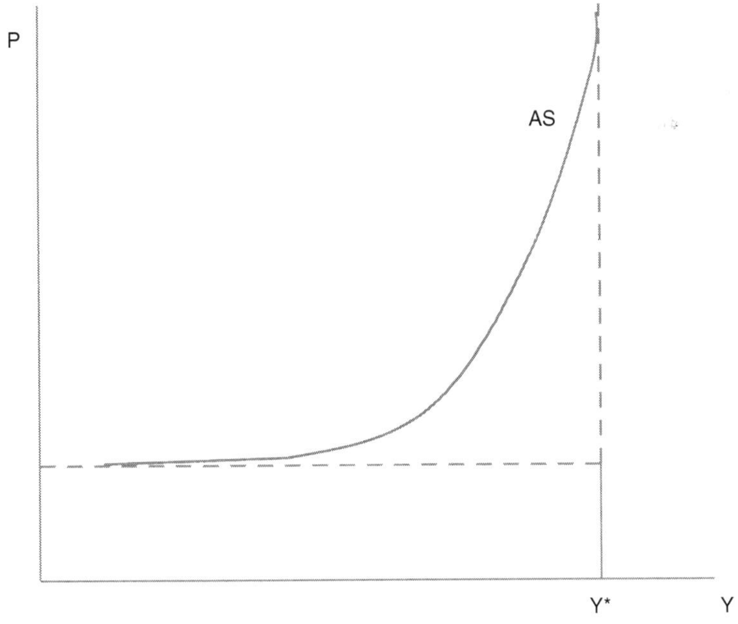

Figure 4.6 Modified aggregate supply curve.

to the theoretically ideal curve. We may then ask how it comes that the situation in Figure 4.6 developed rather quickly.

In fact the curve in Figure 4.6, which is the basis for a Phillips curve, was discussed already in the 1940s, and the problem of structural inertia was well known. Hence the development of the causes of the existence of a supply curve like the one in Figure 4.6 had gone on for a substantial period but it was hidden by the high growth of trade.

Thus when the growth of trade slowed down due to a rather complex set of factors the aggregate supply curve as in Figure 4.6 appeared and set new conditions for economic policy. The changed situation appeared to be violent since some sectors were heavily invested in a long-run over-capacity situation, thus the 1970s started already before the oil crises with structural reallocations. In Ekstedt and Westberg (1991: 36–9) it is illustrated by successive eight year periods from 1963 to 1986 created by successively adding two years at the end period while taking away the two first years in the period. Their enquiry concerned only the competitive goods producing sectors, their results are highly illustrative of the structural change.[11]

The demand and supply of labour was more differentiated due to the higher degree of competitive investments in new technology, apart from the fact that we got a downward pressure on the aggregate demand. Thus the problem of so-called permanent unemployment rather commonly perceived during the late 1970s seemed to be a new feature at least with respect to the ruling Keynesian tradition and then the problem has been aggravated to the level it has today when it in many Western European countries is a threat to social stability, particularly with the feature that young people have to struggle longer times before they are established and can maintain family and children. The danger of this development cannot become overestimated and we find Hobsbawm's characterization of "an era of disintegration, uncertainty and crises" well chosen.

The reason why we have dealt with this development 30–50 years ago is partly due to its effects on economic theory and partly to the fact that it shows the problem of the complexity of an economic development which can be interpreted in many ways and give rise to almost contradictory theoretical approaches.

There are many reasons for a principal shape of the aggregate supply curve as in Figure 4.6, for instance different factors of risk and uncertainty, most of all technological uncertainty, composition of the industry in a country, physical rigidities created by technological factors, combined with heterogeneous labour force; several such factors are discussed in Ekstedt and Fusari (2010) as well as in Ekstedt and Westberg (1991).

The crises start when the aggregate production capacity relatively well can meet the aggregate demand. Then the industry will meet a new situation of risk and uncertainty and more and more sectors meet higher market risks as well as technological risks; thus investments will more be attached to different kinds of competitive investments rather than capacity increasing investments, which restrain investments and most probably increase the financial capital in relation to the total capital.[12]

Thus at the macro-level we may expect an aggregate supply curve like the one in Figure 4.6 telling us that when more and more sectors reach their optimal capacity utilization as the national income increases, we subsequently will have a more and more pronounced cost-inflationary pressure.

It is rather obvious that the causes of inflation in Figure 4.6 are more complex than in Figure 4.4. Figure 4.4 works as if we in a boom have excess demand in every sector while in Figure 4.6 at some level of national income some sectors are booming, some are at their optimal capacity level and some are under their optimal capacity level, thus there is an obvious problem of aggregation, which also implies that macroeconomic policy both becomes difficult and also questionable. While in the first case an inflation measure will fairly well express the situation for most sectors, the second case will be difficult since any average will hide severe asymmetries; economic policy in the first case will be relatively similar in its effects on most sectors, while in the latter case the effects might be vastly asymmetric. The reason for such asymmetries is that inflation in the second case mirrors the relative capacity limits in different sectors. We do not need to go into the causes for this here. However from a strict theoretical point of view there is no inflation in the monetarist sense so the money supply needs to be decreased but we may well have some kind of demand inflation in some sectors causing over optimal capacity utilization. Similarly unemployment becomes difficult to classify. One type is permanent unemployment which we will discuss more later on but there is also unemployment depending on insufficient demand which might appear although we are in or near a general boom since some sectors may have a slump in their demand, due to their specific international demand structure. This shows that after the 1970s the economy has developed in increasingly more complex patterns.

Keynes' discussion on stability of exogenous factors

It is of some value to relate the described development to Keynes' discussion of the stability of exogenous factors (1973 [1936]: 249–54). First it seems reasonable to assume that the stability of the marginal propensity to consume has probably not changed in a significant way.[13] Second, the change of prospective yield of capital has changed in the sense that the economy has developed into a different risk and uncertainty regime. Third, Keynes claimed that changes in employment and money income were relatively proportional; this condition was indeed a broken not to say lost sense in the new economic context. Fourth, the "mean reversion" hypothesis with respect to investments and yield of capital is hard to interpret in the two regimes, before and after the 1970s. Generally a greater share of the total capital in industry consists of financial capital nowadays than during the 1950s and 1960s. Furthermore investment as a share of GDP is lower today than during the 1950s and 1960s in the OECD countries; however in the world economy it is not so. Thus in some sense the condition of "mean reversion" still holds but particularly under the transformation process between the two regimes, the 1950s and 1960s compared with the situation today which started in the 1970s, it was problematic to interpret.

Going back to Keynes' third aspect, the relation between unemployment and money income, we find it problematic in Western Europe and USA since on one hand the permanent unemployment has risen, and on the other hand that the growth of production capital has slowed down, and that means that the distribution of income has both changed its structure as well as it has become more uneven among both individuals and sectors, however the principle as such still works with respect to the business cycle, to a variable extent.

After Keynes' discussion of the four factors necessary for stability he discusses their relevance and comes to a conclusion which is at variance with the experiences during the 1950s and 1960s but which is quite similar to our experiences in Western Europe and the USA during the last two decades. We will implicitly discuss his considerations with respect to investments and the yield of capital. Anyway he arrives at the following conclusion:

> Thus our four conditions together are adequate to explain the outstanding features of our actual experience; – namely, that we oscillate, avoiding the gravest extremes of fluctuation in employment and in prices in both directions, round an intermediate position appreciably below full employment and appreciably above the minimum employment a decline below which would endanger life.
>
> (op. cit.: 250–1)

Factors one and three deal with primary real behaviour, while factors two and to a certain degree four contain financial matters. We will later develop Keynes' discussion in a slightly more technical way and add his five points affecting inflation.

The aggregate supply curve of Figure 4.4 was however developed in the analysis of the Phillips curve. The Phillips curve, according to standard discussions, is supposed to contain two kinds of inflation; on one hand *demand inflation* which is expressed through movements along the curve, and on the other the above discussed *cost inflation*, which is expressed by the distance from origin.

However, the Phillips curve, illustrating the relation between inflation and unemployment, does not necessarily express a direct logical relation between these two variables, but can be seen as dependent on structural discrepancies as we have discussed above and which Keynes described in his five assumptions earlier quoted.

Supply side economics

In the beginning of the 1970s the supply side of the economy gained more attention. As we have described the development above it was of course high time for a changed focus. We had no war effect on demand and capacity left, the Bretton Woods era was ended and we were facing the first oil crisis. Those factors in one sentence are indeed scary for most economic policy makers. The world entered a fundamentally different environment of uncertainty.

The problem of aggregate economic policy is dependent on asymmetries and required a more comprehensive analysis than before with respect to the microscopic level and its structural composition and there was subsequently a more pronounced interest of these questions during the 1970s and 1980s. Unfortunately this legitimate search for a *microeconomic underpinning of the macroeconomy* was to a large extent interpreted in such a way that the neoclassical analysis gained an increased role in analysing the aggregate behaviour of the economy. From the description of the development after the Second World War it follows that this has nothing to do with some general equilibrium modelling but with a structural reshaping of the economies adding new sources of risk and uncertainty.

The Phillips curve and the problem of aggregate supply

Among the theoreticians the discussions of the Phillips curve increased since it seemed that inflation and unemployment could very well coexist. In relation to Figures 4.4 and 4.6 this is a result of a more pronounced distance between average optimal capacity utilization, given the capital stock, and a production level where there is a socially desirable level of employment. This also became to a high degree dependent on the increase and structure of international demand. Thus it is the consequence of a change from an aggregate supply curve (which is a very extreme case) illustrated in Figure 4.4 to a supply curve in Figure 4.6. Such a development has not much to do with short-run factors but more with the structural composition of the economy.

Assume that in Figure 4.7, Y_1^* represents the socially desirable employment level, while Y_2 and Y_3 in their intersection with P^* represent respective NAIRU points.

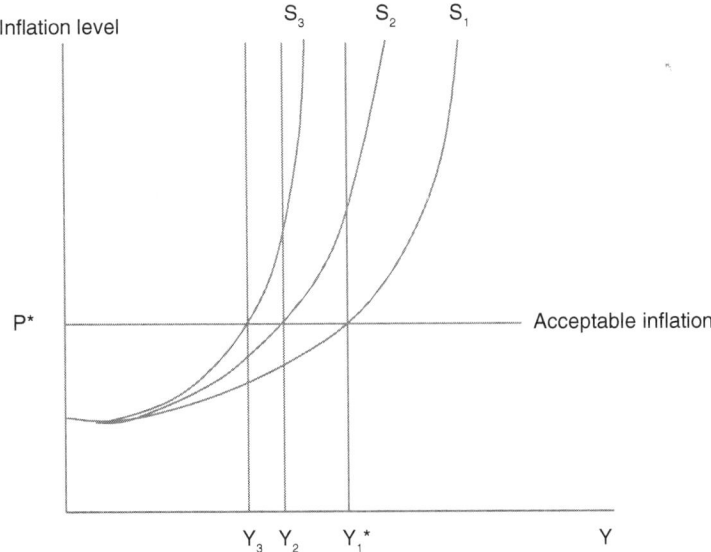

Figure 4.7 Inflation and unemployment.

During the 1950s and 1960s we had a "greenhouse effect" to quote Eichengreen (1995), promoting capacity increase through capital investments leading to increasing returns to scale and also investments in education and health, infrastructure and social welfare. Thus we had a development both creating increased inertia of the production sector as well as changing the preference structure of the population. In the author's home country, Sweden, a small open economy, this development was perhaps earlier and more pronounced than in many other countries but that was merely a matter of time and degree.

The "greenhouse" era ended and was replaced by an economic environment characterized not only by the factors already mentioned, which increased the market risk for companies, but also by increased competition from new countries, in those times belonging to the third world.

All this implied a higher risk on inert production capital and we also had a development of higher dependence on external trade. Since Sweden is a small industrialized country it was perhaps in the lead of this development and therefore we have some nice examples from Sweden. In Table 3.1 we illustrated the development for a big Swedish firm, and the changed risk structure. This development was rather common for many goods producing companies in Europe in particular and to some extent also in the US, even if it was not as pronounced as in Europe, as a consequence of the difference in size of the home markets. It affected the risk structure in both the real dimension and the monetary dimension, the latter in a rather intricate manner.

After the end of Bretton Woods, countries in Europe tried to stabilize the currencies by different kinds of agreements or by relating their currency to appropriate currency baskets. This naturally promoted the importance of inflationary policy.[14]

Under these circumstances it is natural that the aggregate supply curve and its development becomes the top issue of the economic analysis. The inclusion of these problems in a macroscopic model indeed requires a proper microscopic foundation. The main weakness of the ruling Keynesian theory was, as already said, the rather rude concept inflation.

If, in periods like the first and the second oil crisis during the 1970s, we have a general rise in prices because the most important energy source has become relatively more expensive, is this then to be compared with the inflation we experience during the boom in a business cycle, basically dependent on structural matters in conjunction with asymmetric demand pressure? Is inflation depending on generally decreasing terms of trade comparable to inflation caused by excessive wage increases or money printing?

The revival of neoclassical analysis was to some extent a bit of fresh air in this situation since it entered an analytical tool to analyse the effect of relative price changes into the macroeconomic discussion, but as a whole it in fact blurred the understanding of the microscopic structures by focusing on irrelevant matters emanating from the axiomatic structure.

The problem however was whether the problem illustrated by the Phillips curve was a short-run phenomenon or a long-run one; if the latter structural matters of the economy become important and also the risk/uncertainty structure. If it is a short-run phenomenon, we may expect that it in some sense has to do with the business cycle.

Many economists refers to the short-run Phillips curve as a circular form over the business cycle and the reasons for the variations are the variations in capacity utilization and subsequently the labour productivity (Ekstedt and Westberg 1991). With respect to the variations of labour productivity these are also dependent on the heterogeneity of the labour force and by all means also on the production capital.

A schematic figure like the one in 4.8 is of course blurred by different cyclical behaviour in different sectors. Furthermore a functional relation as the Phillips curve and its development is of course useful since it provokes questions, but can we really regard it as a theory? Our discussion suggests that the Phillips curve is a mixture of short/medium-run cyclical factors and long-run structural factors. In the short run we may isolate a point which we may call NAIRU, which seems to indicate that employment and inflation varies round a locus of average optimal capacity utilization, which implies that "long-run" Phillips curve is vertical if the NAIRU point is assumed to be constant. Such an assumption should imply that NAIRU is independent of the structural development of the economy, which is doubtful.

The real importance of a microscopic foundation for macroscopic analysis is that we investigate changes in the economic structure as a consequence of changes in the relative prices, and structural changes in the demand and production.

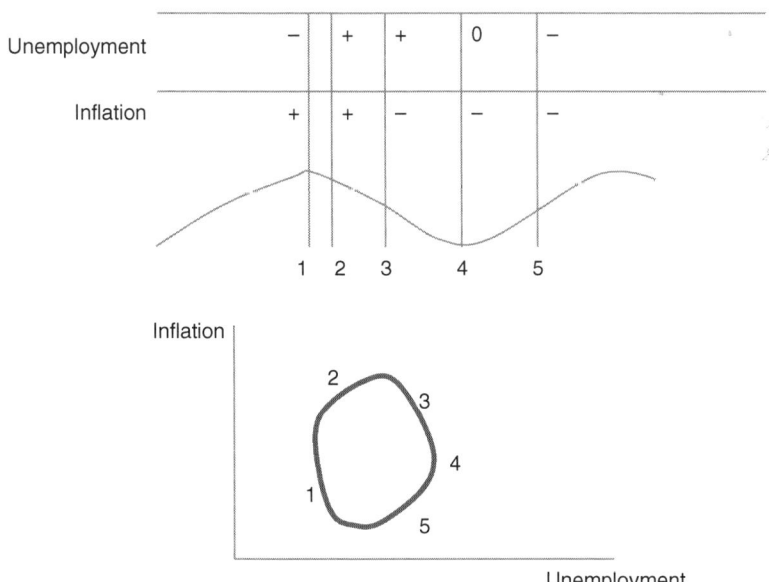

Figure 4.8 Phillips curve and its circular shape.

However, this also indicates the weakness of the neoclassical theory as the specific microscopic foundation.

Okun's law and expectations

Many different explanations of the inaccuracy of the macroeconomic theory to explain the problem with the Phillips curve and the coexistence of inflation and unemployment has been given. On one hand we have the so-called Okun's law from the beginning of the 1960s, which tells us that unemployment is related to output such that a decrease in unemployment corresponds to a rise in output, and furthermore that variations in unemployment, or we should rather say employment level, affects also productivity in the production sector. The "law" is hardly surprising with respect to traditional theory and should be apparent in a proper treatment of the production possibility curve in relation to short- and long-run growth. Okun's law mainly concerns the variations around NAIRU and it could partly be illustrated by adding a curve for the labour productivity to Figure 4.8. Figure 4.9 gives a schematic illustration of the variations in the labour productivity during a business cycle. It should also be noted that the profit share in industry reasonably well follows the labour productivity curve.[15]

Okun's law is very much attached to the circular form of the short-run Phillips curve, given a certain level of NAIRU, and links variations of labour productivity to levels of capacity utilization. Thus inflation is primarily a cyclical phenomenon around an optimal capacity utilization. The unemployment, which occurs as the difference between optimal capacity utilization and the social desirable employment level, was however dismissed as some form of *natural unemployment*.

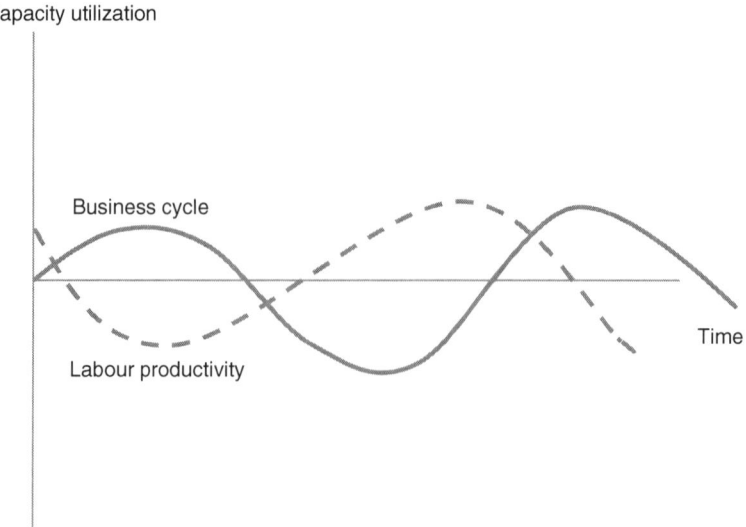

Figure 4.9 Okun's law.

However if we look at Figure 4.6 and assume that the appropriate NAIRU is Y_2, the enhanced inflation cannot be explained by variations like we illustrate in Figure 4.6 but requires other explanations given the assumption that NAIRU is at Y_2. Milton Friedman suggested a solution by introducing inflation expectations. A rise in inflation triggers expectations of even higher inflation. To some extent there is empirical evidence for the realism of such an approach. The inflation at the end of 1970s and the beginning of the 1980s was certainly a problem in many countries and was aggravated by the agents as they both in private and public sectors tended to link contracts of different kinds to future inflation by indexing payments and wages. In Sweden, 1982, the then minister of finance started a virtual crusade against the indexations in the Swedish economy.[16]

Nevertheless also this approach was insufficient to explain the rather complex structure of the relation between inflation and unemployment.

If we look at the changes in unemployment and inflation in Sweden between the second quarter 2005 and the third quarter 2011, we enumerate the quarters 1–25, in Figure 4.10.

From a sort of "Gestalt-theoretical" perspective we find, apart from the seasonal variations which are mainly caused by students reported as unemployed during summer, that changes in inflation and changes in unemployment live their own lives. Apart from late 2008 and 2009, probably because of the financial crises, there are no clear signs of business cycle patterns common to both

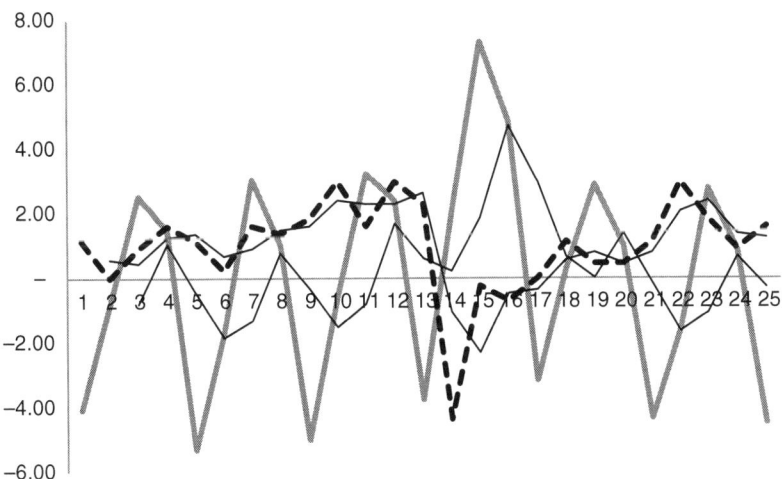

Figure 4.10 Quarterly changes in inflation and unemployment in Sweden, 2005–2011 (source: Swedish Bureau of Statistics).

Notes
Solid lines: changes in unemployment and its linear trend. Dotted line: changes in inflation and the linear trend. Thin lines: moving average three and two-quarters respectively.

inflation and unemployment, although the financial crises are obvious. It is hard to see any trend in either series. Important to note is that Sweden has a substantial amount of unemployed in training and education, paid by tax money, but these are outside what is shown in the figure, which only regard so-called *open unemployment*.

Supply side policy

The policy implemented to cope with the supply problems appeared to differ between countries. The US policy under Ronald Reagan followed in principle a neoclassical pattern in focusing on the incentives to work. There were two main lines of reasoning: (i) taxing people leads to diminish the incentives to work and consequently tax cuts would be a stimuli to increase the aggregate supply at a given rate of inflation, (ii) traditional fiscal policy increasing demand would have a tendency to raise both prices as well as salaries but also to induce unemployed people looking for adequate jobs to take jobs which were suboptimal with respect to their individual qualifications, leading to an aggregate suboptimal productivity growth. Such a theory implicitly defines unemployment as frictional or search unemployment, thus in concordance with the neoclassical theory. The first line of reasoning led to tax cuts and the second line led to diminishing outlays for unemployment and other social policy. Unfortunately this policy was implemented at the same time as there was an even larger increase in military spending, the so-called Star-War technology. Thus the social cuts were replaced by military spending.

We may of course comment on the realism of the theory as such but ironically this policy had the same effects as ordinary demand stimulation in traditional Keynesian policy. The reason is of course the difference in time between implementation and effect, and furthermore that both kind of policies use exactly the same medium of execution, namely money and on an aggregate level. Both policies are effectuated through manipulating the money flows between the state and the individuals and the money is unmarked whether it is a result of supply policy considerations or demand policy considerations. Thus the experiences indicated that such a policy has to be supported by other means in order to be successful.

In Sweden a policy focusing on aggregate supply was discussed in the 1950s and resulted in a more long-run policy to alter the industrial structure in promoting high growth sectors at the expense of slow growth sectors by stimulating labour to change occupation. The policy called the Rehn-Meidner policy was rather successful with respect to its goals but it also resulted in a concentration in production sectors which implied a considerable inertia to the Swedish economy which turned to be rather problematic from the 1970s and onwards.

The Swedish experience indicated on one hand that affecting the aggregate supply curve requires political means which affect the industry structure and on the other hand that directly favouring a certain kind of structure may result in higher inertia of the production system to adapt to a new environment and thus create future problems.

Let us go back to Figures 4.4 and 4.6 and the concept of NAIRU, which may define the optimal aggregate capacity utilization. Obviously such locus is not an eternally given law, which seems to be the case when using expressions such as *natural rate of unemployment* but more realistically we can assume such a point temporally inert, since it is mostly dependent on structural composition of the economy. It fits rather well into Keynes' analysis and our quotation above from the conclusion of his stability analysis. From that point of view it is rather diffi-cult to understand the claims of some economists that this concept of NAIRU should add anything new, except that they gave it an almost normative status.

Anyway when we have such a point as NAIRU we have to raise questions on the dynamic patterns around this point. Rejecting the neoclassical theory as a relevant microscopic foundation of the economy we have to start with the acceptance of the fact that the production sector looks at the demand as exoge-nously given and thus the profit, *ex post*, is seen as a residual, which by all means could be in line with the IS-LM model where usually both investments and consumption functions contain exogenously given variables, not to mention export and public consumption.

Thus the basis for the claim that the market economy cannot create full employment in the sense that the optimal capacity utilization coincides with the desired income necessary to reach the socially desired employment level, is that the demand which the firms face is to a large extent to be seen as exogenous and thus the profit can be regarded as a residual; thus the economy is open in a theo-retical sense irrespective of whether we consider foreign trade or not. The neo-classical theory, as well as the Marxist, does not have these problems since both the variants of the classical theory discuss a closed economy from a theoretical point of view.

The closeness of economic theory in its neoclassical or Marxist setting is depending on the specific features of the definitions of an agent and its sub-sequent definition of the commodity and the commodity space. Furthermore the generic explicit or sometimes implicit assumption of homogeneous production factors, which simplifies the mathematics greatly, is indeed devastating in ana-lysing the economic processes in the reality.

Let us look at an elementary flow chart of the economy as in Figure 4.1.

Let us make the usual assumption that technology and capital stock is given, which may induce us to believe that there exists a point of optimal capacity utili-zation. Around this point we may have a more or less stable dynamic pattern but if so Say's law or an income multiplier is in fact indispensable for stable dynam-ics. If such a point of optimal capacity utilization exists it implies that if optimal employment is far from the socially desired we may face social unease which may be economically devastating for other reasons, thus there is nothing particu-larly unnatural that the society maintains a policy for shifting NAIRU towards higher employment. We must also consider that nowadays the increasing unevenness of income distribution to a large extent depends on permanent unemployment, and the unevenness per se may increase the permanent unemployment through a kind of "social heritage". What is meant here is that the judgement of an economic policy should be done on the basis of its social sustainability not eventual states of equilibrium which are not even properly defined.

A further problem is how money comes into the picture of these movements around the point of optimal capacity utilization. The income multiplier suggests that eventual changes in cash holdings smoothly adjust to the business cycle which means that it is in some sense proportional to the income. But that implies that we get some theoretical problems of explaining the cycle itself and particularly why we should intervene politically.

Another way is of course to assume constant cash holding in nominal terms but then we can hardly manage without Pigou's famous "real balance effect"; but on the other hand that makes it a bit difficult to explain what happens to the nominal stock of liabilities and their relative size to cash holding. Thus the introduction of money into the standard IS-LM is fruitful with respect to policy instruments but it also requires a whole set of additional assumptions in order to keep other features of the monetary economy outside the model. Suggestions like the "real balance effect" are an attempt to close the model and make it independent of exogenous factors, and it is in the tradition of a Newtonian equilibrium approach. With respect to the real balance effect it is typical that the desired effect on the creditors is counteracted by the effect on the debtors. The basic problem is that real items measured in somehow fixed prices are not making the monetary value in fixed prices of the real item real but it is still a monetary valuation. We may use it as a proxy of a real price but only given inert structures.

Furthermore, de-connecting saving and investments and passing over to Figure 4.2 implies that the basic measure of a decrease in consumption only sends a measure that people consume less with no bearing on eventual future consumption needs. This is the reason why the multiplier effect, the axiom of local non-satiation, or Say's law in a general meaning has to be assumed; but we still do not get a proper message for the single agents in the form of precise price signals since we have a multitude of price vectors as well as technical and structural uncertainty. This problem is also aggravated when a high proportion of demand and supply concerns markets which are outside the borders of where it is reasonable to assume that the multiplier effect works. Obviously we have a worldwide multiplier effect but that is indeed complex and difficult to judge particularly with respect to the time dimension and it is also affected by the features of the internal supply and demand structures.

If we go back to Allais' equimarginal principle which we discussed in Chapter 3 the question is not whether it is a relevant theory or not, it probably is, but what causes the principle to work. That is, the uncertainty of the structures of future consumer demand and supply makes investments in inert capital problematic, and this uncertainty does not only relate to real matters but also to uncertainty of the monetary flows. This must be the very start of the microeconomic foundation.

Looking superficially at macroeconomic equilibrium models like IS-LM they seem different from the neoclassical approach but scrutinizing the different concepts in the models makes it difficult to actually see any essential difference if we do not pay specific attention to the exogenous factors causing uncertainty. As said above, Paul Krugman regards the IS-LM model as an enlarged general equilibrium model with an inclusion of a bond market and we cannot see that Krugman's claim is irrelevant given standard interpretations.

However when we actually look at the use of the IS-LM reasoning, or later developments, as a policy tool there is particularly one interesting point and that is the implicit distinction between an actual equilibrium and a politically desirable one. We have discussed the business cycle as a movement around the optimal level of capacity utilization and then we leave the assumption that this level should be of long-term relevance. That means that such a level is more inert than the short-run movements but still it can be discussed in terms of what is desirable or non-desirable and thus give rise to policies which are supposed to affect more inert variables. Thus employment has also several causes which must not be blurred.

If we assume the general equilibrium theory as a viable microeconomic foundation such a distinction is irrelevant since we then only have to keep policy out of the market economy in order to reach full employment. However, if we accept the criticism of Chapter 2 of the neoclassical theory such a distinction between actual equilibrium and a politically desirable equilibrium is not only relevant but most probably necessary since the market economy is basically unstable and this is also an explanation of Keynes' analysis of the natural rate of interest as being uniquely attached to a specific level of employment.

From a technical point of view we then have to watch for the relative inertia of variables. In economics we make such distinctions to a certain degree, we may define long run as the period length when all variables are flexible; this is however a cheerful picture. For a single company or even a single production sector such a definition might be relevant but looking at an entire national economy such a discussion must be pursued in structural terms.

When we transform economic reasoning into mathematical models it is of importance that we beside the functions of the model also define in what economic space they make sense. From our exposé of historical economists and our discussion of the main current theoretical approaches we can see that theoretical concepts as well as model formulations are affected by current problems of the reality. A good example is the concept NAIRU which occurs around optimal capacity utilization. Obviously it is unrealistic that it appears at the same time for all sectors but given some margins there may exist such an aggregate space, its relative inertia depends on several factors, where structural factors, as technology and inertia of capital, are most important, and has to be subject to empirical enquiries. Anyway, given such a space, we may define a locus for the economy representing the optimal capacity utilization. If so it seems reasonable to expect that the dynamic patterns of the different sides of this locus are different. When we look at Figures 4.4 and 4.6 we of course can make some comparative static observations and these are of course of importance but that should also trigger us to try to analyse the dynamic properties of different states of equilibrium.

In such an analysis the aggregation of the economy takes the form of an averaging of the behaviour, which is rather tricky since a policy directed towards the average behaviour will then have asymmetric effects, acceptable or unacceptable, and thus structural consequences.

Complementarities in production and labour hoarding

A generic property of modern western economies is the occurrence of labour hoarding. This is partly due to increased heterogeneity of labour and partly due to increased complementarities between the physical and organizational capital and labour.[17] The implications are that we will have a relation between labour and output as in Figure 3.9. We develop it a bit in Figure 4.11.

The L_0 points for the respective curves represent the amount of labour not dependent on the short-run variations of the production volume. $L*$ is the optimal capacity utilization producing $Q*$, which also minimizes costs. Thus at the time of implementation of the capital investment we more or less invest in an organization. Obviously the inertia of capital as well as organization varies among different industries and sectors and the two short-run functions F_1 and F_2 illustrate two different firms where the latter exhibits a higher degree of inertia with respect to variations in the demand of the product. The reason why we emphasize this rather evident illustration is that we at the same time look at the demand as exogenously given, thus profits are a residual to the industry in question.

There are then two important features.

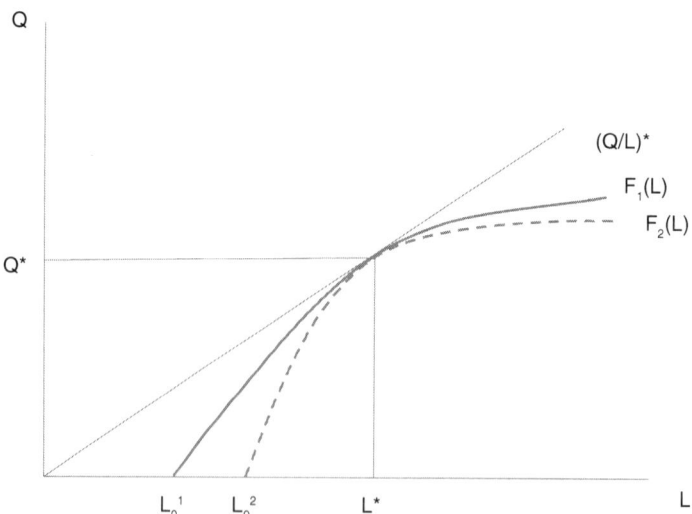

Figure 4.11 Complementarities in production.

With respect to labour productivity this is monotonically increasing but convex, which means that:

$$z_L = h(L) \text{ such that } h' > 0 \text{ and } h'' < 0 \qquad \text{(E.4.6)}$$

That means that labour productivity will vary with the demand around Q^*, and this is actually in line with our discussions above of the Phillips curve, NAIRU and its circular form.

The second important feature is the variations of the *profit share*. Normally we discuss the profit rate which to some extent covariates with the profit share but not entirely so. The profit rate in fact is important with respect to the liquidity of the firm. Thus if it is adequate to think of an aggregate economy displaying the features of Figure 4.11 it will also be reasonable to have some kind of a pattern for the variations of the relative liquidity stress in the economy.

The assumptions of such an aggregate short-run behaviour are not unreasonable but nonetheless of significant effects.

Allais' analysis of the equimarginal principle implies that while the economy is out of the maximal efficiency locus the local production frontier could not be assumed to be globally convex and thus there existed concavities where firms produced increasing returns to scale, and that feature we also find in Figure 4.11, thus in principle we have a space for traditional Keynesian stimulation to the left of L^*.

Hence if we may look at the aggregate of the economy into a production function like the one in Figure 4.11 we may impute some kind of probability function with increasing aggregate income where more and more industries/sectors reach optimal capacity utilization; thus the existence of concavities becomes more and more rare and at some aggregate income the Phillips relation will appear, which is at the right of L^* in the figure.

From a pure real point of view Figure 4.11 would thus explain our discussions above on the Phillips curve and related matters. However, when we consider the variations in productivity and the profit share due to variations in demand we must also consider that the production variations might also have financial repercussions and that might also affect the real dynamics.

Consequently we introduce a new kind of factor which has to be entered into the optimization problem namely liquidity, hence the variations in the profit and particularly the profit share are fundamental for the financial position of a company. As a matter of fact I think this is the singularly most important problem for any producing company with a relatively substantial capital stock. Activities like R&D, commercial publicity and design development are of utmost importance but also induce an aggravated risk since these activities are more or less independent of the short-run production activities.

Given a pattern like in Figure 4.11 we might have a situation where the profit rate, which also depends on other factors than the short-run variations in demand, may still be sufficient but the profit share which focuses more on the relative financial position, can deteriorate. In Ekstedt and Fusari (2010), the impact on the profit share was derived. Given prices and wages they arrived at the following conclusion concerning an output to labour curve as in Figure 3.8 (Ekstedt and Fusari 2010: 226–7, original emphasis):

i   A higher variability of gross profit rate with respect to short run variations in the production volume.
ii   With respect to the gross profit share the difference with the standard case of fully flexible labour is even more striking. GPS [Gross Profit Share] will decrease both with respect to decreases as well as increases in the production volume. Thus there will be a higher variability of the liquidity position of the firms, *but worse is that GPS reaches its maximum only at the optimal capacity utilization.*

When we look at the curves in Figure 4.11, and imagine the aggregate output to labour curve to have a similar form, we arrive at a rather standard macroeconomic analysis of real economy with concepts like the short- and long-run Phillips curves present as well as a locus which might be called NAIRU. However when we introduce not only profits but also a measure, profit share, of the variations in the financial positions of the average industry, the real analysis will be more complicated. The reason is of course that we are discussing disequilibrium where the profit actually has to be seen as a residual, since the demand for the product is exogenous to the firm although we may have expectations. It is well worth noticing that the way the neoclassical theory discusses the concept of risk, as we described in our discussion of temporary equilibrium theory, actually closes the economy in the long run and thus we have a long-run endogenous system, although short-run mistakes, but in the long run we may see labour income and profit endogenously determined. Not so in our analysis, where the ultimate consequences of entering the profit share into the analysis is that we will have some kind of long-run optimization of the investments based on expectations but *ex post* when the capital stock and the production organization is in place the short-run considerations of the development of financial position will be at the top of the CEO's agenda.

A clear sign of this is the rapid increase of the factoring business as well as the invoice discounting. In the former case discounts of 10–15 per cent are rather normal but may in specific cases be higher. Ordinary business payment terms are regularly 30 days but in international trade 60–90 days are normal and 120 days not unusual. These periods have to be covered and small- and medium-sized firms pay considerable amounts for this; thus when the profit share decreases there will be a direct effect on the liquidity position.

The really ugly point in the analysis of Figure 4.11 is that the maximum profit share only appears in the optimal capacity utilization given prices and wages. Consequently we may ask what to do with our initial assumption of prices and wages.

Thus it is of interest to consider the question of flexibility of prices and wages. Let us assume that Figure 4.11 represents an aggregate production function. We may then ask how the prices and wages must vary to compensate the variations in the labour productivity in order to keep the profit share constant. Let the function represent the profit share:

$$g(\cdot) = \frac{P \cdot Q}{W \cdot L} - 1 \Rightarrow g(\cdot) = z \cdot \frac{P}{W} - 1 \tag{E.4.7}$$

Constant profit share implies thus:

$$\delta g = 0 \Rightarrow g_z' \cdot \delta z + g_P' \cdot \delta P + g_w' \cdot \delta W = 0 \tag{E.4.8}$$

Implying:

$$\frac{\delta z}{z} = -\frac{\delta P}{P} + \frac{\delta W}{W} \tag{E.4.9}$$

Thus if we look at the curves in Figure 4.11 we find that an increase in labour from L_0^1 to L^* will imply that the sum of the relative price decrease and relative wage increase must be equal to the relative productivity increase while an increase in labour from L^* and upwards implies that the sum of the relative price increase and relative wage decrease is equal to the relative decrease in productivity.

Ekstedt and Westberg (1991: 53–62) studied the dynamics more closely in a closed model where they separated consumer demand and investment demand with respect to elasticities of wages and profits respectively. In the case where the consumption elasticity is greater than the investment elasticity they found that at a production below the optimal capacity utilization there exist stable states of equilibrium, thus similar to a Keynesian unemployment equilibrium. However when the investment elasticity is greater than the consumption elasticity we get a saddle point where the economy is unstable in the price dimension.

The result is interesting and in line with Drèze's analysis, which we discussed at the end of Chapter 3. If the consumer elasticity with respect to wages dominates we have a standard Keynesian stable unemployment equilibrium. Affecting consumption through state policy may have positive effects. The other case when investment elasticities with respect to prices are larger is probably more unusual when we are in an under-capacity situation, but still it is interesting. The instability in the price dimension implies that if, by some reason, prices are perturbed it will start a dynamic process, either depressing investments further if prices deteriorate further or if prices rise a dynamic process of increasing investments. The stability in the wage dimension suggests that perturbation of wages has no or little effect. Thus a classical policy of wage reductions will have no effect on the production

The corresponding cases when production is above the optimal capacity utilization is that in the case that the consumption elasticity is greater than the investment elasticity the system has a saddle point and is unstable in the wage dimension. In the opposite relation between elasticities we have a saddle point with instability in the price dimension.

From our point of view with a particular interest in inflation this case is of highest interest. First of all we have no stable equilibrium as in the opposite case, but two saddle points dependent on the relative size of the elasticities. In this case it is difficult to tell which of the elasticities is the more important. It might well be that investments are more elastic with respect to prices than consumption is with respect to wages, but the opposite may also be true. In reality it seems natural to think that this relation also varies between sectors. However it tells us that if prices are allowed to rise it will trigger a dynamic process of rising investments.

Of course the basic model is unrealistic, it does not allow for inertia of the investment process, it is closed but nevertheless when we just look at Figure 4.11 and imagine a situation of over-optimal capacity optimization at a ruling high permanent unemployment. Why should we immediately kill the tendencies of inflation? The more curious it becomes when we add that economic growth often is led by new types of commodity dimensions which relay needs to meet a high aggregate demand to be properly introduced at the market.

Every politician in Europe today is shouting for growth as a prayer to God, at the same time they are nervously watching every tendency to inflation in order not to upset the financial market and kill by different means any tendency to growth. We will in the next chapter discuss this question more but growth always means tendencies to inflation because we cannot really measure inflation when we change dimensionality of the consumption basket as well as change technologies. Hume's suggestion of a rise in the money stock in order to secure the enthusiasm of the entrepreneurs is probably one of the more constructive suggestions for economic policy at least for an economy of his times.

So far the conclusions with respect to E.4.9 and Figure 4.11 are rather straightforward from a technical point of view, but the problem with respect to price and wage flexibility is that the aggregation is not an additive one as in general equilibrium theory, although we may create an aggregate demand function; this must not be confused with a neoclassical aggregation. It is an *additive aggregation in money terms* but not in real terms, alluding to Allais' equimarginal principle. The aggregate optimal capacity utilization may contain sectors which are in a state of a convex production space while other sectors are still in a concave production space. This is also aggravated by the heterogeneities of labour which may cause positive excess demand for certain groups of labour while for other groups there might be excess supply; thus although we have permanent unemployment there is a mismatch between demand and supply of labour.

However from a policy point of view the important thing is the monetary effects of an aggregate curve as in Figures 4.6 and 4.7, measured in monetary terms. The structural rigidities make prices and wages inert and the relative inertia of wages and prices are subject to structural conditions which may vary in the longer run thus confusing statistical studies. However as long as the optimal capacity utilization of the economy is in the neighbourhood of the income sufficient to obtain the socially desirable employment level there will be no major end-mean conflict between price stability and full employment. If it is not so any kind of short-run demand policy to increase employment above the level of the aggregate optimal capacity utilization leads to an inflationary pressure, although we still have unemployment. This inflation which is a sort of mixture between demand inflation and cost inflation due to structural features of the economy will then have some intricate combined financial and real effects which we will discuss in Chapter 5.[18]

Dynamic macroeconomic consequences of production complementarities

In a dynamic sense the firms invest in new technologies and we may consider two types of industries; goods producing and service producing. Traditionally it is often maintained that service production is more labour intensive. Thus the picture in Figure 3.8 is easy to understand with respect to capital intensive industry. This might be right to a certain degree if we regard just physical capital but when we look upon the need of organizing the service production in order to have an efficient supply of services we on one hand need physical capital with respect to communication, transportation and organization and on the other the responsibility of each individual of the labour force tends to increase which often implies higher demands on personal characteristics as well as increased rigidities of labour.

Thus the form of the curves in Figure 4.11 is a consequence partly of technical characteristics and partly heterogeneities in the labour force and when we consider the dynamics of the competitive industry we are apt to describe it as in Figure 4.12.

Let us start from the curve $Q_1(L)$ and the optimal labour force L^* giving rise to the optimal production Q_1^*. The labour volume not dependent in the short run on production variations becomes then L_0^1. Let us imagine a technical change such that the optimal production at L^* increases to Q_2^* and the new short-run production function increases to $Q_2(L)$. However another consequence of the technical change will be that the labour, not dependent in the short run of variations in production, will rise to L_0^2, and consequently the variations in productivity and profit share will increase and subsequently the demand for liquid assets for "insurance" purposes will rise.

Thus the technical development also increases the risk for the industry. It is therefore not unrealistic that we instead have a more moderate increase of production as a consequence of the technical change to production optimum Q_3^* and the short-run production function $Q_3(L)$. Consequently the technical change leads to an increase in production that is true but equally true is that it leads to a decrease in the optimal labour force. Whether the redundant labour force remains in unemployment or not is partly a structural problem, the diversity of sectors and companies in the economy plays an important part in the creation of permanent

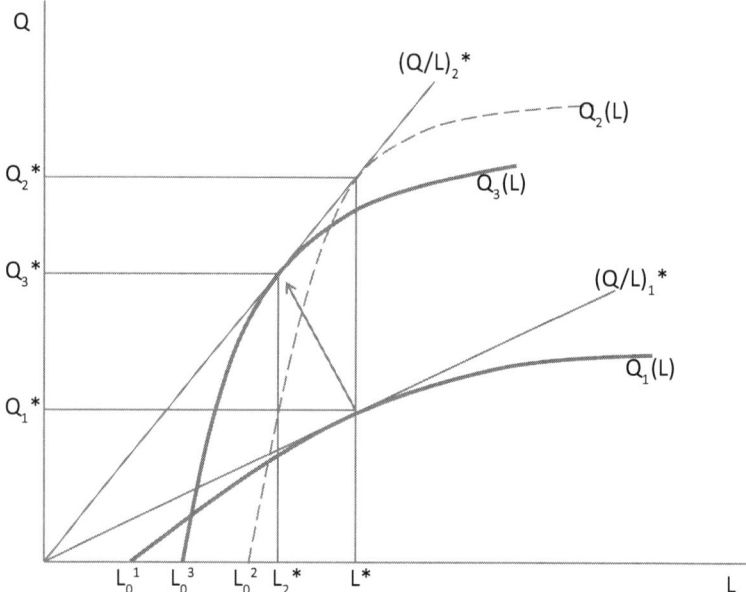

Figure 4.12 Dynamic consequences of production complementarities.

unemployment. Partly it is also a problem of the risk and uncertainty of international real and monetary factors, which we will discuss more in Chapter 5.

If this kind of development is generic to a considerable part of the industry
we will actually have a conflict between employment and the technological
development, which is not necessary a priori, but mostly due to sector concentration and small diversity of the production sector combined with heterogeneity of
labour and similar causes.

There is an old debate whether or not technological changes cause job losses
or not, see for example Humphrey (1982). This question cannot be based on
purely aggregate reasoning but is dependent on the structural composition of the
economy. In the case of the single firm it is obvious that technical growth may
cause replacement of capital for labour. Whether or not this increases the unemployment is more uncertain since that depends on the surrounding production
structure. Definitively it is so that in an economy like Sweden very dependent on
exports, sensitive to inflation and the sectors outside the export sector is a big
public sector, which must be balanced and a relatively small private sector, has a
rather narrow window of labour demand and thus we might well believe that
technical innovation is at least partly at variance with job creation. For a big
economy like the US it is probably different.

Thus we do not regard it possible to answer a priori on the question whether
technological change causes job losses other than *it depends*.

Anyway a development like the one depicted in Figure 4.12 and its implication of still larger variation in the profit share will most probably result in a rather common need for increased financial protection of the inert production capital, both physical and organizational, and thus an increased relation of financial capital to total capital. The problem with this is that such financial capital is basically to be kept in rather liquid assets thus in fact partly withdraws from the real flows of the economy other than possibly short-run credits. *In this environment the role of inflation will be changed.*

The monetarist challenge

We started in Chapter 3 with the neoclassical model and our view was that additive aggregation was not consistent, given a proper description of the human agents as subjects. Our discussion in this chapter so far has led to the opinion that a microeconomic foundation is indispensable. When entering the monetarist approach into our exposé we really go further on in the other direction, that is, we abstract to a higher level, in discussing the effect which the medium of exchange/measurement will have on real production in determining both long-term and short-term growth. The foundation of the approach is the quantity equation completed with an assumption that cash balances on the whole are in constant relation to the incomes. That gives us:

$$M^d \cdot V = P \cdot Y \tag{E.4.10}$$

Thus given equilibrium and money supply controlled exogenously we will have:

$$M = \frac{P \cdot Y}{V} \tag{E.4.11}$$

Where M is money stock, V is velocity of money circulation, P is price level and Y is real production.

Assuming V to be constant gives us the principle equation:

$$M = \alpha \cdot P \cdot Y , \tag{E.4.12}$$

implying that we can affect the nominal GDP by manipulating the stock of money. Given then for instance Figure 4.12 we may think that below optimal capacity utilization we might affect real GDP, since there are free resources, and consequently above optimal capacity utilization we affect only prices. Friedman also suggests, and that is similar to David Hume in fact, that the money supply should have a steady increase thus allowing a growth of the economy.

Historically the quantity theory goes back to Aristotles, friars of Salamanca and David Hume, although these analysts were mostly concerned with metal coins. We remember from our discussion on Aristotle that he emphasized the legal aspect, which also the Salamanca friars and Hume did. Furthermore if we look at Hume he wrote about an expanding monetary economy and praised the social effects. His feelings on paper money were rather doubtful in the meaning of lack of control and temptations to fraud. Given the specific context, Hume's and his predecessors' considerations with respect to money were quite natural. Increasing the medium of exchange affected the growth of economy and if there was excess supply of the medium it affected prices, the value of the medium was not intrinsic but in relation to the availability of other commodities.

Although no economist denies that the excess supply of the medium of exchange will affect the price level it is interesting that the most clear examples we have are taken from rather extreme situations such as the inflow of gold to Spain during the sixteenth and seventeenth centuries, the inflow of gold from the west in the US during the ninteenth century, the super inflation in Germany in the early 1920s and the specific situation with MEFO-bills in Germany during the 1930s.[19] Empirical evidences from more balanced times are more difficult to interpret. Already Thornton and Say were aware of the fact that cost inflation stemming from different causes was a more usual cause for inflation than excess supply of money. Thornton gave as we saw in Chapter 2 a good reason for this, in his distinction between potential and enforced circulation, where the former concerned bank money which was exchanged with respect to business opportunities and covered by securities.

Our first reaction to such a formulation as the quantity equation from a more formal perspective is of course the distinction between nominal and real variables. In a widely used textbook for the first year studies in economics, *Macroeconomics* by Gregory Mankiw (2003: 107, my italics) we can read:

> Real GDP is the quantity of goods and services produced in a given year and the capital stock is the quantity of machines and structures available at a given time. The real wage is the quantity of output a worker earns for each hour of work, and the real interest rate is the quantity of output a person earns in the future by lending one unit of output today. *All variables measured in physical units, such as quantities and relative prices, are called **real variables***.
>
> In this chapter we examined **nominal variables** – variables expressed in terms of money. The economy has many nominal variables, such as the price level, the inflation rate, and the dollar wage a person earns.

We need to remember that this is written for very basic educational levels, so we may allow for some theoretical shortcuts. Nevertheless the quote is interesting because we actually do not measure anything in the economy on the aggregate level other than through nominal prices. The real variables are derived through mathematical and statistical manipulations which have to be a part of a theory. Another small problem which appears in the quote is actually the examples of nominal variables, price level and inflation rate, because they are part of the process to transform nominal priced variables to real variables.

Whether or not these are purely nominal of course depends upon the constancy of relative prices and the dimensionality of the commodity space, if this cannot be assured we plunge into a brushwood of statistical and mathematical/logical principles of measuring inflation, which we will come back to, but the basic difficulty here is that all the factors in the quantity theory are on the most aggregated level which is possible in an economy, furthermore it is based on an identity with all the problems that will imply from a logical/analytical point of view.

$$M \cdot V \equiv P \cdot Y \qquad \text{(E.4.13)}$$

We have earlier in our discussions about the neoclassical axiomatic structure wrestled with an identity, the axiom of reflexivity. In that case we separated the identity of a commodity as a physical item or process from the commodity as a commodity which is open to different use for different or even the same consumer. Thus the physical item or process is not necessarily equivalent to the apprehended functions of the commodity in question. Consequently we have to treat a commodity as a multidimensional complex.

The problem with the expression E.4.13 is in principle the opposite. The identity as such is tautologically true, and this is the deceptive point in monetary analysis.

We have quoted Wicksell and his critical attitude to the quantity theory but he continues:

> Meanwhile it is far easier to criticise the Quantity Theory than to replace it by a better and more correct one. Up to the present every attempt in this direction has come to grief; or rather, scarcely a single serious attempt has been made, apart from the Cost of Production Theory, which to-day, except in orthodox Marxist circles, can no longer reckon on any direct supporters.
>
> (1936: 43)

This was written in 1898 and unfortunately it is still true.

The clue to this problem lies in the fact that for any reasonably practical definition of money, a medium of exchange and an accounting unit, the quantity theory is based on the identity E.4.13. That means that irrespective of if we treat the variables more or less as constants or if we define them as complex structures the identity still holds. Wicksell is fully aware of this and writes:

> Both the strength and the weakness of the Quantity Theory are now adequately revealed. It consists of more than a mere "*truism*", i.e. a truth which is self-evident but barren; it consists of more than the rule that the sum of quantities purchased, each multiplied by its respective price, must be equal to the amount of money paid for them. The Theory provides a real explanation of its subject matter, and in a manner that is logically incontestable; but only on assumptions that unfortunately have little relation to practise, and in some respects none whatever.
>
> (op. cit.: 41)

The very weakness of the monetary theory, which by all means is shared by the standard macroeconomic theory, is that the variables are at such a level that may host considerable structural complexes and still seemingly be consistent. If we compare with the general equilibrium theory the exciting feature of this is that a multidimensional space may be projected on a one-dimensional index, called the price vector, the whole axiomatic apparatus serves this scope. This gives us an exact microscopic underpinning of the macroscopic variables and consequently if we assume the neoclassical axiomatic structure to be valid also the quantity identity of E.4.13 will resume its status as an uncomplicated identity. The problem then will be to explain the need of monetary policy since variations in the economy are difficult to explain and at the same time reject the existence of *false trading*.

From a statistical point of view we can suspect that the identical character of the quantity relation affects the definition of the variables to make them measurable. We have all these different money definitions M0–M3 and MZM. It is interesting to note that in the end the 1960s M3 (M2 plus long-term deposits), was regarded as widest money concept although Henry Thornton already in 1802 discussed treasury bills as equivalents of money, thus something like MZM. We will come back to this problem in Chapter 7, but in a world of securitization to get the balance sheet proper, swaps and other derivatives, it is tricky to find a measurable money concept.

The variables in the expression E.4.13 are aggregated complexes, even M, money, and consequently the problem of this identity is whether or not it is observable or even meaningful as a basis for logical analysis. We know from as early as Henry Thornton's analysis that banks were entitled to create money at the same time that the enforced circulation only concerned gold and silver money and the circulation of the bank money was variable.

Thus all the variables build on assumptions, as Wicksell says, and the meaningfulness of the variables depends more on the assumptions and their independence of each other than on observed empirical inertia. Thus we may well agree with the identity as such but if the variables are subject to internal interdependencies and relate to structural patterns, real and financial, they may in practice be impossible to base an inter-temporal theory on, and the extremely high level of aggregation suggests these suspicions.

It is important that we recognize the technical difference between the two types of identities, the axiom of reflexivity and quantity theory. The axiom of reflexivity alludes to a real physical item or process, and it claims that the apprehensions of the consumers are the same both spatially and eventually also inter-temporally, which is in fact a rather severe restriction on the reality and may be questioned as we have done in Chapter 2.

The quantity identity, however, only tells us that if we look at a barter economy and have a controlled volume of the medium of exchange, this medium will have a velocity of circulation, as well as we have a price vector and commodities. Consequently the quantity identity does not restrict the reality but may hold under many kinds of assumptions.

In fact the quantity theory in economics is the very quintessence of the central problem in economic theory; how do we arrive from the microscopic structures to the macroscopic aggregates? The title of this book *Money in Economic Theory* is in the deepest sense alluding that any theory of money and/or monetary matters cannot be seen as independent of the economic theory in which it is embedded.

Let us also state that in the case when the neoclassical axiomatic structure is assumed to be valid, the expression E.4.13 *is also valid as an identity*.

That is if we think a trajectory of successive states of general equilibrium an identity like the one in E.4.13 holds. However if the states of general equilibrium are not identical the identity of the quantity relation will still hold, but either the composition of the variables will differ and/or the very definition of the variables will change.

Furthermore if we think of a trajectory between two states of general equilibrium through a state of non-equilibrium the variables of the resulting quantity expression will be undecidable since we are in a state of non-unique price vectors as a consequence of false trading. Thus the only case we can imagine from a logical perspective, when we discuss a trajectory of mutually different states of equilibrium, is when no trading occurs between the states. This implies that any kind of manipulation with the quantity expression is not only unnecessary but also erroneous since we are manipulating an identity defined by the various states of equilibrium. So the quantity equation is built on an assumption that the variables P and Y are homogeneous variables on the aggregate level, that is that the relation between Y_1 and Y_2, $Y_2 > Y_1$ and given any number ε there exists a number φ such that $(Y_2 + \varepsilon) > (1 + \varphi)Y_1$ and the same hold for P, given that the concept money is the measure of P. With respect to measuring inflation means that the condition is not met inter-temporally if we redistribute the relations of the commodity basket and it certainly does not hold if we have changes in the dimensionality of the aggregate commodity basket.

That means that the only case when the quantity theory *is adequate* from a theoretical perspective is when we are in a persistent general equilibrium but then it is next to meaningless, since the price vector is just equivalent to a mathematical index. However the quantity theory could only *be relevant* as a theory when we are out of equilibrium but to our understanding the difficulties really begin, since this is the also base for uncertainty of the aggregation process itself.

Where is money and where are the prices in monetary economics?

When we discussed the classical Keynesian economics as expressed in the IS-LM model we started to ask where the prices came in. We have obviously some form of money in the model which has a particular role to play in the form of liquidity, and varying desires for it. When we come to the monetary theory our concern of the prices is still not satisfied but even worse we have actually lost the contact with a reasonable concept of money too.

Our discussions in this chapter shows that there are perfectly legitimate reason for households as well as firms to hold liquidity for precautionary and speculative reasons, the latter reason in a wide meaning. We have also argued that inflationary pressure, both cost inflation as well as demand inflation might go on in a structurally complex economy. This means in the first instance that we could have an implicit conflict between money as a medium of exchange and money as a store of value. Second the aggregate measure of inflation could well be composed by inflation caused by different factors which by no means are related to some excess supply of money.

The monetary theory actually sterilizes the concept of money when cash balances are supposed to be constant as well as the velocity of money. Already Henry Thornton discussed the velocity of money as problematic when banks could create money, in the modern economy, which we will touch on in Chapter 7, the velocity is on one hand virtually impossible to measure, but given the quantity identity we have:

$$V = \frac{P \cdot Y}{M}$$

so why bother when the variables P, Y and M give us more than enough trouble to define.

Thus the only case when the quantity theory should work proper is when it is founded on general equilibrium theory and its axiomatic structure but then the quantity theory is also redundant. In the case where economic policy is needed that is when we are out of equilibrium or stumbling between different states of local and temporal states of equilibrium the very intrinsic content of the variables in the quantity theory is actually changing.

5 Concluding comments on the nature of money in economic theory

Some lessons from history

Meaning of concepts

As we have seen in our historical exposé in Chapter 2 and the discussions of the neoclassical and macroeconomic theoretical approaches, economics contains seemingly vastly different schools of thinking. With respect to money we have also seen that the different approaches have difficulties with the concept, in some cases even in explaining its very existence. Concepts derived from money-like inflation are sometimes irrelevant in the meaning that it is just a kind of renumeration of its face value but sometimes of fundamental interest to the real analysis. Such discrepancies should indeed affect the definition and use of measures of inflation, and in the historical exposé we saw that the origins of inflation were intensively discussed. As long as there was a relatively simple monetary economy based on metal coins and the industrial structures were frugal, the supply of coins or precious metals was the main cause of inflation. Thus the quantity identity was more or less established by the friars of Salamanca in the sixteenth century.

Henry Thornton's analysis is in this respect very illuminating, himself a banker in a fairly advanced economy, as he realized the enormous potential of bank money and he also realized the potential of bank money in affecting the circulation. We paid attention to his distinction of *capability of circulation* and *enforced circulation* which is basically forgotten in economic theory of today. Roughly we can say that during the times of Thornton the former concept related to business sectors and contained agreements where the *bank money* transactions, bills, securities and similar financial items, created an aggregate balance between assets and liabilities, which augmented the total supply of means of payment way beyond the crude money, or *law money*.

The latter concept of enforced circulation concerns law money, and is the very basic medium of exchange. A transaction involving law money ended in time as the physical transaction was concluded. Henry Thornton's *anti-bullionist* side stemmed from the fact that he saw bank money as a business matter which was subject to responsibilities and risks which induced a sort of automatic regulator. Thus bank money affected a different group of agents in comparison with the law money; the former affected business while the latter affected the consumers. His distinction is extremely interesting and relevant to our own time.

Our historical exposé gave us also an impression that none of the great economists we discussed in Chapter 2 were discussing an abstract theoretical model. Even Ricardo who was most eager to form abstract principles, took part in the very policy discussions and was in fact a member of parliament. His position in the debate during the early nineteenth century was changing according to the changed structure of Britain's economic situation which affected his theoretical positions. We also saw that analysts such as Hume, Thornton and Say paid more attention to the interrelation between the economic and social structure than did Smith and Ricardo who were more eager to form some abstract principles for economic thinking.

In Chapter 3 we claimed that humans are to be seen as subjects and thus local and temporal final causes. This implies that humans actually have the ability to create and recreate local and temporal axiomatic structures and this is the very meaning of the concept of epistemic cycles. Whether or not the created axiomatic structure is dissipative or inert is a different question. As we saw from our analysis of Arrow's paradox this will have huge influence on the ability and character of economic abstractions with respect to generality and inertia.

A concept like inflation which is a key concept of the monetary economy is most probably sensitive to the particularities of the social and economic structure we actually discuss. In Chapter 4 we made a short overview of the development in Europe and the USA during the aftermath of the Second World War and came to the conclusion that the particular structural components during the 1950s and 1960s implicitly also were the roots of the end of the development.

In a world of structural change we may allude to Wicksell and say that on the microscopic levels we may find parts of high inertia and stabilizing forces, while on the macrostructure we seldom find either the inertia or the stabilizing forces, thus to form theories as the quantitative theory on the highest possible level of generalization and abstraction is a bit doubtful.

Structure of theory

In our historical exposé we met a couple of basically different approaches to the monetary economy. Hume, Thornton and Say looked upon the money economy as an entirely different organism compared with the barter economy. While the former had deep-going effects on the social, institutional and political development and change the foundation for circulation of production factors and commodities in the barter economy had little or very slow effects of that kind. Both Hume and Say explicitly saw the money circulation in a society as a diffusion process and that was the basic reason for Say's discussion which later by equilibrium theorists was interpreted as Say's law. However when thinking about such a diffusion process we can understand that in the societies of the eighteenth and nineteenth centuries it gave rise to social changes as we have observed during the last 50 years in Africa, Asia and Latin America. However when societies become more and more transformed to a "monetized" society we will have other structures and also money will have a changed role. In a sense the difference is the same as in epidemiology when we make a distinction between an epidemic and an endemic situation. Thus patterns of analysis are vastly different in the endemic situation compared with the epidemic.[1]

This means that the development of economic theory during *secula seculorum*, or at least since Aristotle, is due to completely other conditions compared to physics for instance. The physical reality is a slowly changing system, and theories built on observations made 300 years ago are still valuable. Thus the Newtonian system is still as correct as it was when developed by Newton, but better scientific equipment and the detection of new processes as Cournot's and Clausius' entropy principle have made the Newtonian version of the natural laws a special case, even if most of our daily lives are governed by little else.

Physics is however completely different from economic science. While the physical conditions in the universe are practically unchanged save for some changes in the constellations of stars the economic and social systems have gone through a tremendous development, which means that although the Aristotelian economic and money concepts still are interesting the economic and social context of these concepts call for an analysis where a general equilibrium is not of a primary theoretical interest.

The different approaches we have discussed, neoclassical, Keynesian, monetarist, are sometimes hard to separate. Sometimes they are more or less complementary, sometimes they imply different perspectives, but in principle they can be brought into concordance with each other given appropriate assumptions. It can be claimed that although the Keynesian approach introduces money in its analysis it has lost prices as a central variable, and with respect to the neoclassical approach it is almost the opposite case.

Thus when Hicks introduced a kind of synthesis, developed by Samuelson and others, it appeared as a necessity in order to find a bridge between the microscopic and the macroscopic levels. Consequently the IS-LM interpretation leaves us with a possibility to get around the focus of general equilibrium, at least in the short run. We have also discussed developments more specifically within the neoclassical tradition, as the temporary equilibrium theory and Allais' equimarginal principle that links closer the *ex ante/ex post* concepts of the Stockholm School to the IS-LM model as a part of the microscopic underpinning.

With respect to the axiomatic structure of the neoclassical theory in Chapter 2 we practically kept all the axioms with respect to their economic interpretations but modified them in such a way that they work in economic non-equilibrium dynamics and that also implies that we leave the focus on general equilibrium and only use equilibrium in a partial and temporal meaning in dynamic patterns. However the axioms in their new interpretation do not form an axiomatic structure in a mathematical sense.

The fundamental argument for rethinking the basic structure of economic theory is to a large extent the changing dimensionality of the commodity baskets and new technology caused by innovations and social changes, which gives rise to out-of-equilibrium processes as for example described by Allais. Such an approach has support from early economic analysts as the friars of Salamanca, David Hume and Jean Baptiste Say. These are different from Smith and Ricardo in the sense that they pay attention to the social dynamics within the workings of a *monetary* market economy, while Smith and Ricardo, in an attempt to make a scientifically appropriate theory which builds on "real" barter, tries to build a similar economic theory as the physical theory created by Newton and this was more or less achieved within the Arrow and Debreu setting. To understand the difference between Smith and Hume it is well worth reading Hume (1770: 24–43) in his chapter "Of Refinements in the Arts", to see an almost devoted appreciation of the *money market economy* for enlarging the possibilities for individuals' education and refinement in bringing new dimensions of needs which cultivate the minds and increase the freedom of life, and this is also basic to understand the interaction between social and economic structures. When we look at neoclassical growth theories, such as Solow's growth theory and endogenous growth theory (Solow 1971), these are closed and thus can never catch such processes as changing dimensionality of the social commodity basket. This follows from the closed axiomatic structure. Consequently the growth process is a conjunction between social change and technological, in the broadest meaning, innovations.

With respect to money he writes (Hume 1770: 59):

> Here then we may learn the fallacy of the remark, often to be met with in historians, and even in common conversation, that any particular state is weak, though fertile, populous, and well cultivated, merely because it wants money. It appears, that the want of money can never injure any state within itself: For men and commodities are the real strength of any community. It is the simple manner of living that hurts the public, by confining the gold and silver to few hands, and preventing its universal diffusion and circulation.

Here Hume touches on a most fundamental principle of the monetary economy, very elementary but still a complete departure from the barter economy, namely the money economy as a *diffusion process*. This diffusion process is also what underlies Jean Baptiste Say's analysis which has been known as Say's law, not in its neoclassical interpretation but as a social process. Agents' industriousness and entrepreneurial creativity imply a potential increase both in volume and in the dimensionality of the commodity space but it requires money to be spent on the productive process which feeds the consumption and further investments. Such diffusion means that money has a role not only as a medium of exchange but also as a medium of venture.

The basis for the general equilibrium process is the static commodity space where we seek an optimal solution as in a flea market in a park, where the customers also brought the junk and are entitled to buy commodities for the value they brought, thus the money prices are just a mirror of the relative price vector which is implicit to the ultimate result of the barter. In Hume's and Say's analysis the very existence of money, free from connotations to real items, open for a diffusion process where "industry and refinements of all kinds incorporate it with the whole state, however small its quantity may be: They digest it into every vein, so to speak; and make it enter into every transaction and contract" (ibid.: 59).

Thus it is impossible to see the monetary economy in a static sense but we have always to incorporate it into wider social dynamics, and perhaps the worst effect of the modern so-called "main-stream economic theory" with its obsession with low inflation and constancy of prices is that it brings us back to the mercantilist form of thinking. The market economy surely is a competitive economy but it is not closed as in the neoclassical economy but open to constant changes and innovations which makes it an open space in the time dimension. The openness is in fact contradictive to a general equilibrium in both temporal and spatial terms.

We have anticipated that the fundamental features of money can be seen as a medium of exchange, value preserving linked to liquidity and a medium of accounting. Our discussions particularly in Chapter 4 left us with a clear suspicion that these features are not consistent with each other. Under certain conditions the three features might even appear as contradictory to each other. Let us therefore start with some considerations on money, inflation and liquidity.

Some important features of liquidity

We have already discussed the motives for acquiring liquid assets. It is affected by hopes and fears about the future. In Chapter 4 we described a process inducing companies to keep a higher share of their total capital as financial/liquid capital as a reaction to variations in their financial position when there are substantial variations in profit rate. This example shows that standard assumptions of homogeneity and substitutability blur the whole problem. The tradition to solve a closed model implies often that in modelling the profit rates are based on standard theoretical marginal conditions, save for market imperfections. It is therefore of importance that putty-clay analysis and/or *ex ante/ex post* analysis is taken *ad notam* in modelling. Probably a marginal analysis may be employed during the investment planning but after investments are implemented we are in the stage of economic and financial survival problems where profit has to be seen as a residual.

Thus acquiring liquidity and the motives for that is not an independent matter but related to the actual structure and functioning of the economy and this *also* holds for the risk/uncertainty structure per se.[2]

However the central role of liquidity stems from a particular feature of liquidity, namely the emphasis on immediate payment. Lacking liquidity, including possible fund raising, may lead to deep-going structural changes. The problem of bankruptcy centres on the concept of liquidity. In everyday discussions bankruptcy is seen as a failure of a production concept, or an innovation and similar things, and that is of course partly true, but our discussion of the effects of complementarities in production and labour hoarding illustrated in Figures 4.11 and 4.12 shows a more complex situation.

Lexicographic preferences

In theoretical analysis of preferences there is one concept which we may use to explain the character of liquidity, although it was developed for other kinds of analysis; *lexicographic preferences*.

Lexicographic preference orderings are seen as a bit troublesome and in Arrow and Hahn the concept is discussed but only as a case of degeneracy.[3] We may define lexicographic preferences in the following way:

> Assume two baskets X and Y, containing the commodities A, B. A *lexicographic ordering* exists if the following holds: let X contain the quantity α_1 and Y α_2 of commodity A. Then lexicographic ordering implies that if $\alpha_1 > \alpha_2$ then $Y < X$ irrespective of the amount of commodity B in the respective baskets.

Generally speaking this concept can be used in many contexts. We may express a lexicographic preference for Burgundy wines with respect to Côtes du Rhone wines or baroque music to romantic music. It only means that we don't substitute the commodities depending on price differences. We may also use the concept when we discuss certain public goods as a condition for certain actions of the individual. In analysis of externalities we can also use the concept as limiting supply/demand; thus we will get a kind of constrained Pareto optimum. In the case of the wine example the individual basket is void of one type of wine but seen from a market point of view this is insignificant, although the individual agent breaks the convexity axiom since the tastes generally vary. We can just treat it as an individual corner solution which is for the market as a whole rather easy to handle provided that the lexicographically preferred commodity behaves in a nice continuous manner and has no side effects.[4]

Anyway the concept is also useful with respect to liquidity (money or other means of media of exchange). Let us look at Figure 5.1. Let the quantity A^* represent a quantity of the commodity A under which the survival of the agent, in some meaning, is threatened. That will normally imply that the indifference curves to the left of A^* do not exist and furthermore that the intersection of the line with the indifference curves depicts a point where the willingness of the agent to pay in principle approaches infinity. We can think of many such commodities; water, food, medicines and so on. The very aspect which turns the lexicographic preference into a serious theoretical problem is the very character of the commodity and the fact that it has vast effects on the agent's life prospects and/or behaviour.[5] These things were discussed by the friars of Salamanca as well as both St Thomas and Aristotle when they emphasized the need for an

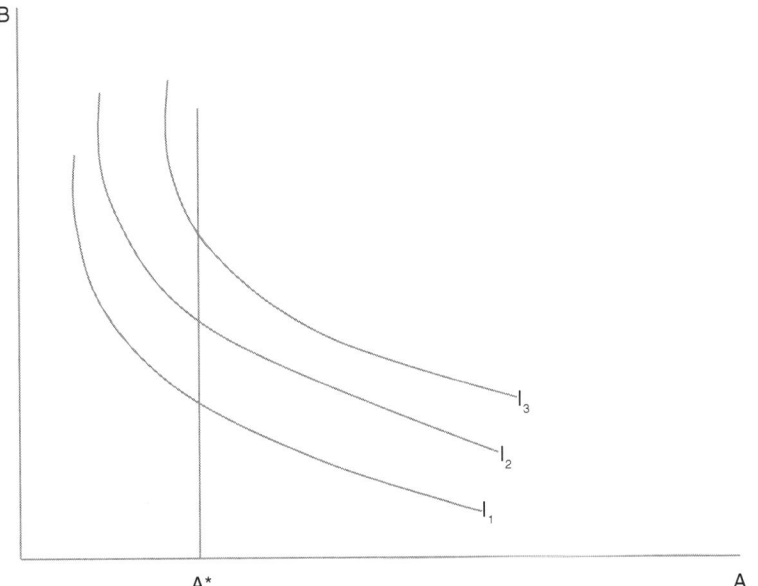

B

I_3

I_2

I_1

A*

A

Figure 5.1 Lexicographic preferences.

individual ethics based on the gospel when handling money exchange and the credit market.

Looking at Figure 5.1 in the light of our earlier discussions we can see that to the right of the line at A^* we have a non-directed space with respect to the existence of solutions and there also exists prices $0<p_i<\infty$. At $A=A^*$, $p_a\to\infty$ and thus $B\to0$ given a limited budget but more than that given complementary restrictions, defined in the lexicographic relation, the space is directed to the left of the line at A^*.

The fundamental meaning with respect to money is that we have to decide theoretically whether liquidity is a dimension different from income/wealth or not, or more specifically if lack of liquidity may change the value of income or wealth.

At a quantity A^* in Figure 5.1 there is no unique price of commodity A, thus we will face changes in the relative prices which may both have real income and income distribution effects. This is particularly important when the income distribution is such that some agents cannot set up a cash balance as a consequence of lexicographic preferences related to other commodities. Thus in an n-dimensional commodity space there may exist several points, as A^*, attached to different commodities which in "normal" times make cash balances for one agent less important than for another agent. In such a situation *liquidity stress* of a more fundamental character may seriously affect agents.

Another problem with the occurrence of the point A^* is the effect on wealth. The situation can be such that we may save the situation by liquidating some non-liquid wealth at the price of changing our medium/long-term economic position.[6] Such a problem cannot even occur with respect to the neoclassical axiomatic structure. But if this situation can occur in real life we have to deal with it theoretically.

Of course such an analysis breaks all kinds of continuity and convexity axioms. But more than that, we may say that the indifference curves, locally and temporally, illustrate a reasonable way of locally representing the choice situation of the individual. The intersection points between the curves and the vertical line then represent a fundamental change in the behaviour of the individual. The individual well to the right of the A^* quantity is exercising a predictable fine tuned behaviour but at A^* and leftwards the behaviour becomes totally unpredictable and impossible to represent by the axiomatic underlying the indifference curves. Thus the area to the left of the line A^* is not defined.

The consequence of these considerations is that liquidity is a restriction on the agents partly independent of income and wealth restrictions, but from an optimization point of view that also implies that cash balances are attached to the volatility of prices, temporal variations in consumption, unexpected or not, or other types of commitments. However the situation is more complicated since we now have a rational reason for acquiring cash balances/liquidity this will also have macroscopic effects in tightening the market exchange which may have consecutive effects on the microscopic effects.

So adding a cash balance in the goal function requires indeed a more complicated analysis than just the technical problems of optimization. Lexicographic preferences do not explain uncertainty as such but have more to do with effects and possible leverage effects of uncertainty.

The *lexicographic preference approach* helps us to understand the urgent nature of liquidity but it tells us nothing about its relation to money, since it is clearly linked to the real variables in the economy; thus it does not necessarily have anything to do with money per se. Consequently we must link liquidity to the inter-temporal valuation of money, which leads us into a dynamic analysis of the nature of inflation.

Measuring inflation

Prices as measures

In our analysis in Chapter 3 we already touched on the problem with prices as measures. In neoclassical theory, given a particular general equilibrium the clearing price vector is in a mathematical sense a measure; it only concerns the particular equilibrium in question, nothing else. If we then regard an out-of-equilibrium situation where we have multiple price vectors the difficulty to find an appropriate measure is evident.

With respect to measures there are three questions: What shall be measured? What is used as a measure? What is the medium of measurement?

These questions are in fact rather tricky to answer for a market economy and already Jean Baptiste Say promptly rejects the existence of a general measure

Money or specie has with more plausibility, but in reality with no better ground of truth, been pronounced to be a *measure* of value. Value may be estimated in the way of price; but it can not be measured, that is to say, compared with a known and invariable measure of intensity, for no such measure has yet been discovered.

(1834 [1803]: 246, my emphasis)

When we for instance measure the temperature we do not measure *our appre-hended* coldness but it is an objective scale starting from a defined norm given a certain atmospheric pressure. Our apprehension of coldness and heat is then cali-brated with this objective scale. (Say does not take this example but measuring length, which is analogue.) We have different scales, the Celsius scale, setting the difference between the freezing and boiling point of water from 0 to 100 degrees, the corresponding points in the Farenheit scale are 32 and 212. The point is that we can convert one scale to another relatively easily. However in the neoclassical theory the axiomatic structure grants a priori that the objective price vector measures the subjective preferences in one and only one locus and that is general equilibrium. Thus what to do with price vectors in non-equilibrium is indeed a logical problem and Say is of course perfectly right in the quote above.

The answer to the above questions is actually rather important for our attitude to measuring inflation. If we doubt prices as a measure how do we then treat the concept of inflation?

The theoretical basis for measurement of inflation

Measuring inflation is rather tricky, as there is no unique price vector, meaning that the price relation among commodities is stable. If there had been a unique price vector we could have joined the monetarist theory and the quantity equa-tion had worked as a policy tool and inflation had then been dependent only on the stock of money, M, and the velocity, V. Unfortunately this is valid only in general equilibrium and theorizing on inflation in a non-equilibrium economy is indeed demanding; it is a mixture of economic theory and statistical methods which in themselves are only loosely connected to economic theory.

The contributions to the theory of inflation measurement are rather confusing. First we have the heritage from neoclassical microeconomic theory of price dependence of demand, but also of the character of the market structure. In non-equilibrium both these factors are prevalent in varying degrees over time. When it comes to demand we can expect changes to be asymmetric, while market structures are a bit more inert. Then we have the cost structures and most of all variations in primary products which affect prices of production in different sectors of production in an asymmetric way. According to the equilibrium theory we assume a high degree of substitutability. That is however highly questionable particularly in the short run, as we discussed in Chapter 4, which then implies that inflation has sometimes considerable real income effects.

Second we have heterogeneities in the factor market capable of creating excess demand and shortage in demand for different qualities of labour and capital at the same time.

Third, although aggregate demand inflation per se is hard to imagine in a closed economy, demand inflation is certainly possible in an economy open to foreign trade, and furthermore it is possible in a closed economy if we have structural asymmetries of the locus of optimal capacity utilization as well as asymmetric changes in demand.

Consequently we see that apart from inflation created by excess supply of money, the causes are created on the microscopic levels and thus treating inflation as a pure aggregate problem may lead to unwanted effects at the microscopic level, and we must realize that microscopic effects are basic for the macroscopic development and should also be so in the theoretical analysis.

Subsequently we talk about demand inflation and cost inflation as causes, in a non-equilibrium situation. The problem with aggregating the microscopic explanations is that the structural patterns often make a nested problem which makes it difficult to isolate the causes of inflation. Our discussion in Chapter 3 on optimal capacity utilization in relation to permanent unemployment shows that "inflation pressure" probably varies among different production sectors due to technological differences as well as the heterogeneity of the labour force. This means that an inflation policy will have asymmetric effects not only on the consumers but also, in principle at least, on the aggregate structural composition.

We discussed the Phillips curve and the appearance of inflation in different stages of the business cycle. If these patterns are rather stable to a high degree due to a nested effect of cost- and demand pressure, why should an eventual inflation be a macroeconomic problem if that the economy is relatively stable? Furthermore if we have optimal capacity utilization much below a socially desirable employment level, a tight anti-inflation regime will force the economy into a more or less permanent deflationary state.

However with respect to inflation measures the heterogeneity of the economy makes it difficult to tell the meaning of a fixed price comparison of different periods. Perhaps we may say that it is an approximate measure of the turnover of commodities, although as such it is a poor basis for growth measures. In the short run however a measure of the total turnover of commodities is valuable since, given a relatively high inertia in the short run, the turnover is linked to employment and aggregate income and similar variables important for general economic policy. Over longer periods the structural composition becomes more important and thus makes the inflation measure more complex. Unfortunately periods of relatively constant structural composition seem to become shorter and shorter due to increased pace in capital turnover due to technological changes and increased global competition.

The two inflation measures we normally use are the Laspeyre index and the Paasche index, and different kinds of methods for linking these. Laspeyre is used as a short-run measure and when time goes on it is converged by an averaging technique to a long-run Paasche index. From a strict theoretical point of view however the Laspeyre index is the only acceptable one due to the structural changes and the increased dimensionality of the commodity space.

We here agree with Jean Baptiste Say that there are no long-term measures based on money prices, particularly not with respect to economic growth.

Inflation and growth

In real exchange it is easy to understand relative price changes. A farmer and a shoemaker may exchange their products but the relative prices will most probably be affected by the quantity and quality of the harvest, the supply of leather and so on. In a monetary economy it is a bit more complicated and depends on how we actually think about the dynamic process.

A Solowian model for example implies that, given a convergence to "golden rule", technical change increases the productivity of labour such that every hour of work can be remunerated with more commodities. We can also apply an endogenous growth model including a learning/education process which explains the efficiency growth.

The problem with these models is that they give an impression that economic growth is a quantitative process with possible qualitative improvements, cars are safer and houses are better from an environmental point of view.

In our analysis of the neoclassical model in Chapter 3 we emphasized the problem of the dimensionality of the commodity space. We divided that into two sub-problems actually. On one hand the rejection of the reflexivity axiom implied that commodities have to be seen as multiple complexes. Thus although the commodity as a physical item is given its precise use is contextually determined. On the other hand we might think of the total commodity space where the commodities as physical items (or processes) form the different dimensions.

The latter aspect was, as we earlier quoted, noticed by Keynes, who used it in his criticism of the neoclassical use of Say's law.[7]

As a matter of fact these dimensionality problems form from a mathematical point of view a rather nasty problem when we analyse value of money and money as a medium of measurement.

We discussed in Chapter 3 *Brouwer's dimensionality theorem*. It says that in order to have an homeomorphic correspondence between two spaces they have to be of the same dimension. Homeomorphic implies also that we will have reversibility between the two spaces. This is an important theorem in mathematics and it is of extreme interest in economics when we translate the economic reality into mathematical variables and perform a mathematical analysis.

This theorem will be of importance in many aspects of money, prices and equilibrium but let us first look at it with respect to inflation indexing.

Figure 3.2 is an illustration of additive aggregation and how preferences can be aggregated into a social preference relation, thus for a given equilibrium we have a relative price index such that the value of the aggregate basket may add up whatever base we prefer. Now if we change the endowment distribution we achieve a different general equilibrium which is not comparable in its distributional consequences with the first one but with respect to the price vector and the aggregate commodity basket we can perform the same operation. Thus, relative to different price vectors we will have differences in the optimal quantities of different commodities but we may still have the same total index. If we instead think of some kind of Solowian growth we have an enlarged physical production which does not necessarily affect the price vector and if it does we have to realize distributional consequences of the growth but applying the above reasoning we do not need to change the basis for the indexation. So if we set one labour hour to one dollar, we get more for the labour hour after the growth has taken place, due to efficiency increase, which is underlying endogenous growth theory.

This reasoning fits rather well into the opinion of the Currency School during the bullionist debate and implicitly we can see that inflation is created by an excess supply of money. It also fits into Ricardo's reasoning since he also bases his analysis on the *value of labour*.

It is also in line with the Laspeyre indexation principle, to start with a historical commodity basket and see the price evolution in nominal and real terms.

However we have many price indexation principles and the so to say contrary principle to Laspeyre's is the Paasche principle, which starts from the current commodity basket and we then compute its values backwards. Given a Solowian equilibrium growth trajectory these two principles should give the same result, but they usually don't – why?

There are mainly three reasons. (i) The quality of the commodities are changed: this can in principle be accounted for through quality indexing; if this was the only reason why Paasche and Laspeyre indexes differ, the difference between them would be a sort of quality index. (ii) Production technology is asymmetric which implies that price changes of commodities also would be asymmetric implying asymmetric demand changes due to different price and income elasticities. (iii) The dimensionality of the commodity space is changing.

Keynes mentions in his discussion of price indexes, in *Treatise of Money*, that if we want a real long-term index for the millenniums back to Sumeres we could probably not use anything but the price of corn, but that might exclude some important features in the economic evolution.

The first two reasons apply even to constant dimensional commodity spaces. But from an indexing perspective it is relatively simple to cope with in the neoclassical approach. The second reason would not cause any trouble if we assume gross substitutability of demand for commodities and production factors. If we impose different kinds of rigidities we would have both a kind of demand inflation as well as structural unemployment. We may also spend some time to discuss which are more flexible, prices or wages.

The third reason why the Paasche and Laspeyre principles might differ is of quite a different theoretical quality. We can illustrate the technical difficulty as in Figure 5.2.

The commodity combinations α_1 and α_2 respectively are denoted with a star. The dotted lines are only included to ease the dimensional imagination. If we compare the location of the star in the two diagrams it is exactly the same with

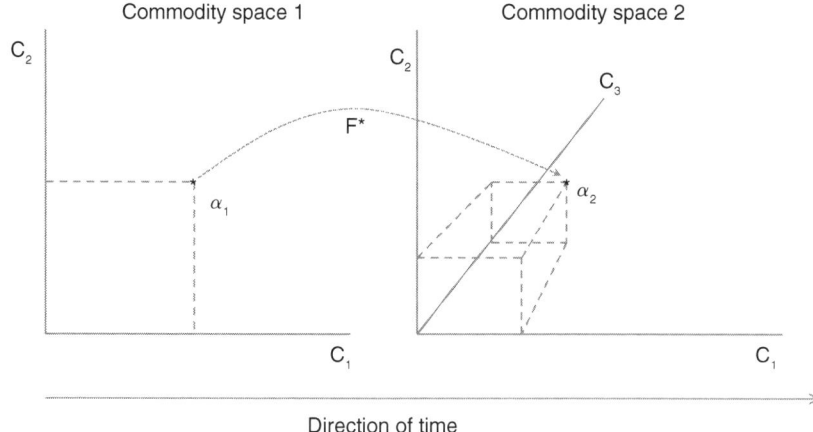

Figure 5.2 Growth of dimensions.

respect to the axis C_1 and C_2 if we disregard the indication of the third commodity dimension C_3, but as it is we have a three-dimensional box of the suggested kind.

The arrow indicates a temporal correspondence F^* between α_1 and α_2. What this correspondence tells us, if anything, is that the total consumption outlays (P_i–prices) in Space 1 is $P_1C_1 + P_2C_2$ while in Space 2 it is $P_1C_1 + P_2C_2 + P_3C_3$. Let us first say that from a technical point of view the correspondence can mean anything from a simple exogenous inclusion of P_3C_3 to a complex theory of innovations and diffusion of money. Given any kind of such a correspondence it is hard to think of any reversible relationship, in line with revealed preference correlate, without rather drastic assumptions.

The illustrated problem is essentially fundamental to the discussion of the quantity identity and also with respect to prices as a measure. Let us be influenced by the monetarist thinking: $MV = PY$. Assume constant M and V. An introduction of a new commodity dimension will imply that PY is constant thus the demand of "old" commodity dimensions must either proportionally or asymmetrically shrink in order to let the new commodity into the market, implying a deflationary effect for the dimensions C_1 and C_2.

Mathematically the correspondence F^* cannot be reversible, thus there exists no mathematical possibility that the Laspeyre and the Pasche indices can give equivalent results of the past inflation, irrespective of any statistical bridging of short- and long-run measuring. Of course we may make reasonable assumptions but then of course it is a question of how many "reasonable assumptions" scientific reasoning can manage without being inconsistent.

Anyway if we look at Figure 5.1 from the point of view of Ricardo and the Currency School where we first claim that inflation depends on excess supply of bank money and second that the supply of money shall be strictly related to gold bullion with some kind of intrinsic value, we end up in some problems. A comparative static view indicates that there will be a revaluation where the relative prices of (C_1, C_2) will change to (C_1, C_2, C_3) given the aggregate value which is related to the value of gold bullion; this will occur for the producers of C_1 and C_2 as a deflationary process and future contracts in the nominal price level of Space 1 will be very problematic. To cope with this problem we have actually to support Hume in his recommendation to increase the money supply every year to keep up the spirit of the entrepreneurs. How much the money supply should increase is of course hard to say anything about.

In fact a stubborn anti-inflationary policy without regarding the discussed complexities will appear similar to the policy under the mercantilist era when the key thing was to keep and enlarge the national wealth measured in precious metals, but we switch the latter to keep and enlarge the acquired wealth by the individuals, but we will come back to this.

If we go back to Figures 4.11 and 4.12 the expansion of aggregate demand above would cause a combination of demand and cost inflation. On the other hand if we go on killing any tendency of inflation and run into the long-run development illustrated in Figure 4.12, who can then tell which consequences there will be for the economy in question? Introduction of a new commodity dimension is equally tricky. Entering a new concept on the market requires at least one thing and that is a rather high general growth of demand. If that is lacking there will be rather thin times for entrepreneurs.

The two principles Laspeyre and Paasche must therefore be compared with respect to such dynamics sooner than with the traditional growth aspects of Solow and the endogenous growth theory and in doing so it is hard to see any theoretical defence for the Paasche principle in a society with a changing commodity space. It might be convenient from a political point of view but it adds nothing theoretically to a continuous updating of the commodity basket in using the Laspeyre principle.

We have so far only discussed the change of the dimensionality of the space of, let us call it the physical apprehension of commodities. The commodity complexity with respect to intrinsic characteristics is a problem of finding representative commodities in price comparisons. We earlier referred to Lavoie and Liu (2007) and Warmdinger (2004) and the problem of using commodities of an average physical definition and here we also have a process which is more or less constantly evolving in the market which makes the commodity spaces rather incommensurable over time.

Inflation and its real and monetary effects

When comparing neoclassical theory, Keynesian theories and monetarist theory we find inflation only in the two latter ones. The reason is of course that the latter two theories explicitly acknowledge the existence of money. However the Keynesian inflation is basically what we call demand inflation, while the monetarist inflation is due to excess supply of money. We have earlier accepted the identity $M \cdot V \equiv P \cdot Y$ so therefore we accept the monetarist explanation that excess supply might have positive effects on inflation, which is also historically well founded. The fundamental problem however is that linking the monetarist explanation to some kind of general equilibrium setting makes the identity meaningless to develop into a theory, but on the other hand, using it in an out-of-equilibrium condition creates problems to define the contained concepts.

If we look at the quantity identity the exact content of the variables are not particularly clear as we discussed in Chapter 4. Apart from that however comes the problem about what inflation means vis-à-vis the real economy in which money is supposed to be a medium of measure.

Inflation as a mere proportional mark-up is trivial, which is the only kind of inflation we have in neoclassical equilibrium. Inflation must therefore have real effects which are to be measured against other real effects. Inflation concerns the value of money. From Aristotle we know that the very fact that money is a medium of exchange endows money, irrespective of any intrinsic value, an intertemporal asset which might be accumulated for later use.

In this context we can understand that even a proportional mark-up can be annoying in an out-of-equilibrium setting and in fact have both allocation as well as distribution effects. Thus the claim of the Currency School and the monetarists is legitimate to some extent particularly with respect to a money system built on specific coins, or by all means paper bills in Adam Smith's real bill meaning, or generally speaking law money. When we have a fully fledged financial system where the banks may produce near substitutes which are at least almost as good as law money, what does the quantity identity then mean and what do we mean with inflation on the aggregate level when we are not able to define the velocity of circulation not to mention the quantity of money?

When we on the other side look at the effects of inflation we realize that money works irrespective of any price vector, and thus it works quite well in an out-of-equilibrium situation and a multitude of price vectors, so if the prices in money terms are a measure they can hardly be a measure of the relative prices other than locally and temporally. J.B. Say takes an example with a comparison between two houses where one house cost 4000 dollars and the other 2000 dollars so we can say that the former costs twice as much. However adding some calculations of how many loafs of bread either of the houses costs is not a relevant comparison (1834: 247).

Consequently we are stuck with the feeling that inflation has to do with what we call the *purchasing power of money*, whatever that might be.

There are then three areas where the effects can be problematic: production, saving and liquidity effects.

We may assume a proportional mark-up of prices for example if I have saved 10 SEK and all prices and wages are raised to the double by some public action, the inflation then will cause me a loss, and consequently the effects are usually not proportional in time among agents, but affects allocation and distribution. It is obvious that such a policy is doubtful and we have seen this in Germany in the early 1920s and in the 1930s when the Nazi government introduced the MEFO-bills, but also in other countries on the brink of collapse. This type of event is not unusual and in fact Hume touches on this problem (1770: 43) and it was also the basic reason during the Napoleonic wars why Henry Thornton turned into a temporal bullionist.

But what happens when say 30 per cent of the commodities rise in price, due to shortage of some important mineral by, let us say 9 per cent, which gives an overall increase of the inflation of 3 per cent; is then a general anti-inflation policy legitimate in order to save the purchasing power of money saved? What about innovations and structural changes to diminish the dependence of this mineral or innovations to substitute the commodities in question? These processes take time but most probably there will be a period of structural changes. A general anti-inflation policy in that case would actually destroy the signalling system of the market since the policy per se would most probably incur asymmetric effects on the economy.

The example shows that the causes of inflation affect the very interpretation of the inflation concept. When we, as in the real world, have a multitude of price movements depending on many things from excess supply of bank money, cost inflation combined with demand inflation as we have illustrated in Figures 4.11 and 4.12, to changes in the dimensionality of the commodity space, and then by the eventual composition of the norm basket for measuring inflation, can we really then say that there has been an inflation? Can we then assume a certain percentage which will trigger the anti-inflationary policy button and are we sure that the percentage is constant over time?

Thus from the perspective of money as a measure of purchasing power we seriously doubt that the concept and measurements of inflation are enough defined and understood with respect to asymmetric effects to allow for any fixed rules, since the application of such rules may have different effects at different time periods, and most of all that the policy per se may have severe effects on growth and thus aggravate the inflation problem successively.

However if we turn to financial assets, liquid as well as more long-run bonds, the apprehension of inflation is quite different and that also includes expectations of inflation. We above emphasized that inflation due to asymmetric cost increases implies as such that it triggers market behaviour such that the effects of the cost increase will after some time most probably be diminished. An imposed anti-inflation policy will then most probably be counter-productive. Thus real effects are generally relatively microscopic and particular.

This is not the case when we pass over to money and financial assets. The effects of inflation on financial assets are general and cannot be meticulously analysed with respect to allocation of capital and such matters. Since the financial assets often are used as insurance against uncertainty and thus affect the liquidity the time aspect which is perfectly legitimate to analyse in the real case is not even important.

If I have a one year financial asset of 100 GBP and demand a minimum of 3 per cent real interest and the inflation is 1.5 per cent interest I pay around 95.7

GBP. If I then happen to hear a rumour, reasonably well founded, that inflation is supposed to increase to 3 per cent so the market price would be around 94.3 GBP, I certainly do not wait to act until an extra enquiry set up by the government has confirmed the figures. I act immediately, true figures or not, because I believe that all the other agents are acting in the same way.

If we look at a standard textbook written by Mankiw he discusses two main types of inflation: expected and unexpected (2003: 98–9). The costs of expected inflation are seen as trivial. The more sinister type of inflation is the unexpected one of which the main costs are: (i) deformation of the credit market, particularly long-term credit conditions, (ii) problems for agents who have their incomes in fixed nominal contracts, for example pensioners, (iii) the economy is hurt by high variable inflation in more general terms since it creates uncertainty.

In principle we agree with Mankiw but the problem is that *pro primo* we don't know the current causes of inflation and there are a number of reasons why inflation figures are actually wrong or misinterpreted and *pro secundo* irrespective of causes or eventual misinterpretations the agents must act on the market since eventual losses are not a function of inflation per se but are caused by the actions of other agents.

This adds up to the fact that whether it is inflation which causes problems or the fact that inflation might occur that causes actions which are negative for the economy, is not possible to say in many cases in the current situation.

Consequently we understand that the real and monetary effects, which have real effects over time, with respect to inflation are different and partly contradictory and that is to our meaning a key problem in understanding the role of money.

The fundamental intrinsic feature of money

If we link our discussions above on the specific problems of growth to our discussions in Chapter 4 on the variations of demand around some kind of optimal capacity utilization and the subsequently derived need of liquid reserves we can see conflicting views on anti-inflation policy. Alluding to Amoroso's expression it looks like the "the dead city rules the living city" and to a large extent it is true, since the demand for security is growing with the volume of wealth, as we quoted from Smith, "so the principle causes which naturally introduce subordination gradually grows up with the growth of that valuable property" (Smith 1952[1776]).

Thus a conflict between what is, what has been and what is to be.

This conflict is indeed articulated in the monetary economy in comparison with the barter economy and consequently the theory of economic barter displays no history, and no future, which is actually a central intrinsic feature of money and the monetary economy.

The neoclassical economy is in its mathematical form a beauty from an aesthetic point of view, but not only that, its axiomatic clarity makes it possible to scrutinize with respect to the social relevance and led to that we needed to reject the axiom of reflexivity in the theory of barter.

The mathematical foundation with respect to models for the monetary model is not that clear, in fact it is pretty diffuse. We have however earlier expressed some concern that both monetary and real variables are expressed in money. If we want to discuss the logical role of money in an economy and we face that we cannot actually measure real matters but in money where we are stuck with non-uniqueness of price vectors, doubtful measures of inflation and so on we are indeed in some theoretical mess. However we may investigate if there is some logical difference between money and real matters.

Pecunia non olet was Emperor Vespasian's answer to criticism when he imposed a fee for visiting public toilets in Rome, *rem acu tetigit* we may comment; probably his expression hits the very core of money.[8] As we discussed above there is a difference between real and financial effects of inflation. This does not depend on the peculiarities of the concept of inflation but on the very difference between real and financial items.

We have in our discussions found that neoclassical theory, Keynesian theory and monetarist theory all have problems to define money and to give it an independent role from the real economy. The two flow charts in Figures 4.1 and 4.2 display that money plays a role beside being a medium of exchange of real commodities. Furthermore our discussion on liquidity relation to permanent unemployment and the optimal capacity utilization in Chapter 4, illustrated in Figure 4.11 makes us suspect that money in fact not only has an independent role beside being the medium of exchange but also a role, sometimes at least, at variance with this. So let us start by stating the difference between money and commodities theoretically and develop the suggestion in Ekstedt and Fusari (2010: 233, original emphasis), who wrote "*Thus accepting the theoretical difference between fiat money, as belonging to non-proper classes, and ordinary commodities belonging to proper classes, is a necessary condition to construct a true theory of money.*"

We have already in Chapter 3 touched on the principles which are problematic in the difference between money and commodities. What is problematic about the neoclassical axiomatic structure is that it transforms the commodity space to a Euclidian space. This is excellent with respect to mathematical analysis but it has some nasty by-products, namely that agents are seen as defined by the commodity space and the mythological invisible hand.

The neoclassical axiomatic structure can be seen as a trivial description of the very choice situation when the agents' contextual judgements are completed. This is also implicit in Debreu's notion of commodities. We may also see it as a description of the actual working of the market and then ending up in difficulties in conjunction with Arrow's paradox, and the introduction of epistemic cycles.

Introducing the concept of epistemic cycles saves the concept of rationality in the neoclassical sense but then it has to be completed with the agent's contextual apprehension. This leads us to the proposition which we call *the mereological rule of thumb*. Proving this we have to lean on Russell's paradox (Russell 1992 [1903]: 512–16 §485–9), which contains the extremely productive distinction between proper and non-proper classes, which we may use to describe money in the deepest logical sense.

We remind of the fact that for proper classes the universal class does not belong to itself while for non-proper classes the universal class belongs to itself. Properly expressed (Weisstein 1999):

Let R be the set of all sets which are not members of themselves. Then R is neither a member of itself nor not a member of itself. Symbolically, let $R = \{x: x \notin x\}$. Then $R \notin R$ if $R \notin R$.

Let us start again with the neoclassical axiomatic structure; it transforms the optimization and aggregation problem to a Euclidian space where the commodities are transformed to the dimensions spanning the space, see Figure 3.2. This implies that commodities are transformed to real numbers and as such belonging to non-proper classes. When we on one hand in rejecting the axiom of reflexivity, claim that the commodities are multidimensional items, and on the other hand introduce epistemic cycles where the agents' choices are dependent on contextual apprehensions we obviously make the interpretation of commodities as numbers very limited and also dependent on a particular epistemic cycle, which means that we in principle allow for disjoint Euclidian spaces.[9] Furthermore these spaces are subject to varying spatial and temporal inertia.

This means that the epistemic cycles do not belong to non-proper classes, and neither do commodities.

Thus elements from the classes of kitchen stoves, bananas, frying pans, ice cream and cocoa, make me able to make an aggregate of different actions using the different physical classes, in the form of a tasty dessert. However the *physical universal class* of the classes of frying pans, bananas, kitchen stoves and ice cream, does not belong to itself as a class of the same character as its subclasses. But the *sum of money* paid for the different elements in the respective classes adds to the global sum which belongs to itself as a sum of money which is paid to procure the different items necessary to make the dessert.

So we earlier mentioned that we reject additive aggregation of real commodities but now we can add that we do not reject additive aggregation of *money values*.

This is also the reason why it seems so natural to measure inflation with the Laspeyre index in the shorter run given a commodity basket and earlier we have touched on the difficulties in the longer run. All this is facilitated by using standard commodities.

Consequently, if we look back on Figure 5.1 we are allowed to interpret the "GDP" of the two commodity spaces in the same way so we actually *allow* the correspondence F^* to be homeomorphic. If we look at this technique with respect to marginal steps, for instance monthly calculations, the problem we raise is futile, but looking at long-run developments there are rather deep-going changes in the economic structure. If we are practical persons however the best forecast, with respect to the success rate, is probably that the weather will be the same tomorrow as today.

Thus the failure in explaining money in economic theory emanates not necessarily from a bad understanding of money but from a theory concerning the real economy which transforms real commodities and assets to *exactly the same mathematical structure* as money.

This is particularly obvious when we link our discussion to economic growth. In many politically active groups of young people it is common to criticize economic growth per se. But actually growth, measured in its most trivial sense as GDP increase, is necessary when we scrutinize our discussions with respect to Figure 5.1. Economic growth is and can only be measured in money terms but it needs a defined commodity basket. Consequently when we measure inflation in a Laspeyre way without changing the commodity basket we so to say measure growth in the current economic structure and the current allocation of the capital stock. Hence when we have a structural change in demand we will probably get a flow from the old demand structure, implying local excess supply, to a new demand structure, implying local excess demand due to shortness of capacity. We will thus have a stagflation phenomenon. Interpreting this with respect to the ordinary Phillips curve it will appear as a displacement outwards from the origin. If we in this situation apply a rather sinister anti-inflation policy, decreasing demand, it will probably uphold the transformation of the capital stock to anticipate the new demand structure, which thus requires a new commodity basket as a basis for the inflation measurements and in that basket we may revive the economic growth. Hence the need for changing the norm basket probably appears in some form of structural crises but then the political answer with respect to choice of policy will become essential.

This is also the very reason why Wicksell can distinguish between stability conditions on the microscopic and macroscopic levels, although he indicates another causality. As he expresses it the aggregate the price levels is perturbed, which sets up a series of actions moving the economy to a new structure which will converge to a new equilibrium that is equally unstable. Our reasoning starts from the real actions by innovators and entrepreneurs which gradually switch the basis for price comparisons but it is not until the successive changes trigger some kind of structural crises that we might detect the need for a new basis for price comparisons. But then we also need to consider a different demand and probably also production structure.

On the microscopic level the direct link between the consumers' dealings with money and their physical needs of commodities stabilizes the prices and the general use of money while on the macroscopic levels we have *nothing but money*. Thus the microscopic use of money is normally stabilized by the social structures; thus a phenomenon such as inflation can of course be triggered by raising cost structures and extraordinary events as catastrophes; but for instance such a concept as demand inflation, should in normal cases not lead to some persistent price rise threatening the economic stability. If we look back in history on heavy inflation periods we mostly find that states have intervened in different ways which have led to excess state borrowing and as Thornton also adds *enforced circulation* of money. The reasons for this are sometimes highly understandable; it could be a way to avoid structural crises but sometimes the reasons are more ulterior not to say anti-social.

State and inflation

The accounting aspect as well as the liquidity aspect both suggest that money has some intrinsic value. The measuring aspect per se doesn't require a value. If we want to go from Jena to Heidelberg or measure the length of the radius of dangerous radiation, we measure the length with a kind of measuring rod, but whatever used, the medium of measurement is independent of the usage and the purpose of measuring.

However we have come to the conclusion that the commonly accepted measuring rod in market exchange also provides the measuring rod with a value for the future which is implicit in the word liquidity and our earlier analysis implies that it is fundamental to the agents as an insurance against value revaluations of real assets and uncertainty of the future. We also know that the state has the power to manipulate this money value with respect to aggregate goals which might be at variance with many individuals' interests. What is prudent monetary policy is sometimes difficult to say. It is interesting to look at particularly Europe during the latest two decades when we have had a significant anti-inflation policy which has been, at least partly, instrumental to a substantial permanent unemployment which currently is leading to some social unease, which if aggravated, is actually threatening the monetary system system per se. At the same time however this anti-inflation policy has not been able to save Europe from one of the worst financial crises after the Second World War, so apparently from historical experience monetary prudence saving us from inflation seems to be independent from monetary prudence saving us from financial crises.

A mathematical view of measures in non-equilibrium

Jean Baptiste Say is very firm in his rejection of the interpretation of money and money prices as measured in a general meaning and his arguments start from the fact that he regards an out-of-equilibrium economy, although he did not use this concept. He thus accepted a multitude of price vectors and he also actually discusses liquidity:

> A man that has any other commodity, jewels, for instance, to offer in exchange for the necessaries or luxuries he may have occation for, cannot get those necessaries or luxuries by the process of exchange, until he has found a consumer for his jewels; nor can he even be sure, that such a consumer will be able to give him in return, the very identical article he may want: whereas, a man, with money in his pocket, is quite certain, that it will be acceptable to the person of whom he would by any thing.
>
> (1834: 228)

In the same line as we discussed in the former part of this chapter we may formulate a rejection of money as a general measure on more mathematical grounds.

Accepting the reasoning along the principle of epistemic cycles makes us suspect that in conjunction with Russell's paradox this will affect the existence and character of measures. When separating optimization on aggregate levels different from each other as well as from the optimization process of the individuals, it seems natural to accept that different individuals will react differently to an aggregate decision even if they accept it because they prioritize other aggregate goals higher. But that also implies that for example some kind of efficiency measure on a specific level of aggregation will not necessarily be relevant for other aggregate levels or for individuals. Thus claiming that we increase efficiency on a certain aggregate level by imposing a certain policy will of course fall under the correlate the *mereological rule of thumb*.

However again we have to go back to the very basic mathematical principles in order to have a basis for our methodological approach to measures in economics. In order to measure something, there must be some kind of topology. Measuring temperature for example requires that we know of the pressure of the environment. Thus for an egg boiled for five minutes in London we must add a good ten minutes in Bogota, due to the altitude, to have the same degree of density of the egg. Thus measuring requires a reason, an object to measure, furthermore a definition of a measure, and an environment where the measure is stable, the topology and a medium of measurement.

With respect to money, we again see its double nature. When it is used as a measure of real commodities it is only a medium of local and temporal measurement, but what about its quality as liquidity? Can money measure itself? Let us take an ordinary bond of some years to maturity when we bid a money price of that, the bond is defined in nominal value. What is the underlying value of this bond? We can answer quickly that it is the maximum of an expected future premature price discounted to present value and the present value of the bond at maturity. Which discount rate should we then use? We might answer the maximum of the ruling interest rates and any other discount rate we decide as most relevant for the implicit future of the bond. Thus the underlying value of the bond is defined by the expected future price. So we pay a current price for an expected future price, while in buying real commodities we pay a price for an item which we expect to be of some real utility. Naturally we can use the trick of backward valuation of future real consumption as is done originally by Markowitz (1959), but that implies of course a prevailing equilibrium or a deterministic equilibrium trajectory, and excludes uncertainty. Thus non-equilibrium adding uncertainty and our defined concept of epistemic cycles are devastating for the existence of a topology.

The most general form of topology can be defined in the following way:

Let X be a set with a collection of subsets T, we then define a topology if the subsets in T obey the following properties:

1   The universal set X and the empty set $\varnothing$ are subsets of X.
2   Whenever sets A and B are in T so is $A\backslash B$.
3   Whenever two or more sets are in T so is their union.

A topology means that we define a space where we can apply some kind of measure. The three properties of a general topology imply that any subset of the universal set should be defined in the same way as the universal set of the subsets. Already the first feature of the definition is broken for proper sets, so according to that we will not be able to define a global measure for proper sets, and consequently when we identify the real entities as belonging to proper sets and money as belonging to non-proper sets we run into a contradiction concerning a general index. Thus for a defined epistemic cycle it may exist a measure but not for two contradictive sets unless the subjects agree to a certain measure, but that is only valid for a restricted space–time. This is as a matter of fact what Arrow's paradox deals with.

Hence the introduction of epistemic cycles implies that it is virtually impossible to define a theoretical measure which works in the same way on all aggregate levels.

Furthermore with the help the *mereological rule of thumb* we can say that locally and temporally there might be a topology for the respective epistemic cycles. That means that it is hard to find a common topology among individuals but at some kind of negotiated (via elections for example) aggregate level there might exist a consistent topology temporally and locally. However this means that there might sooner or later come to conflicts of interests which depend on what we might call an asymmetric growth.

Some further comments on equilibrium

From our discussions in Chapters 2 and 3 we have found that the concept of equilibrium constantly pops up in some form, thus we need to say a bit more about it from a principle point of view.

Equilibrium is a key concept in all sciences but in different senses. Natural sciences as a rule dismiss general equilibrium apart from the one in maximum entropy, which is a rather unpleasant state. Newtonian physics, which is a special case, has a form of a general equilibrium, important but nevertheless approximate in terms of a more general theory. Normally they deal with states of temporary equilibrium or what we may call stability in non-equilibrium. Nicolis and Prigogine (1977: 3, original emphasis) write:

> Then, nonequilibrium thermodynamics leads us to formulate a sufficient condition for the stability of the thermodynamic branch. If this condition is not satisfied the thermodynamic branch may become unstable, and the system may evolve toward a new structure involving *coherent behaviour*.

None of the social sciences, except economics, have a concept which might be called "general equilibrium", but discuss locally and temporally stable spaces, which may occur with respect to particular social characteristics which are inert but in a longer run they are dissipative structures. In logical and mathematical models general equilibrium does occur but that is due to the restrictions of the parameter structure and as such the equilibrium has no particular relations to the real world, since those models neither express causality nor time dependence.

In fact we do not meet the very particular form of general equilibrium we described in Chapter 2 other than in economics. As we saw from our discussions in Chapter 3 of the IS-LM model it might be seen as an extension of the neoclassical model but then we need to have a clear link from the macroscopic concept of liquidity to the microscopic concept and then we come into difficulties. The basic difference is that the neoclassical microscopic setting is built on *choice* while the macroscopic setting of IS-LM involves *necessity* when we define the different exogenous variables, thus we increase the restriction space and particularly when we allow for asymmetric information and a multitude of price vectors we approach a complexity which by itself may provoke new structures.

Equilibrium as a norm

Central to economic general equilibrium is that it is normative. It is seen as a state of art where the economy attains its highest efficiency. Thus when we derive the necessary and sufficient conditions, these are mandatory in achieving the maximal efficiency. However when we look back at Wittgenstein's proposition 6.211, and Figure 1.1 in Chapter 1, the mathematically formed conditions in a science have to be interpreted in the real world, and the problem is that all kinds of mathematical/logical axioms are universal with respect to a particular structure, which means that a set of axioms forms an entire world which we are either inside or outside. Thus conclusions within the axiomatically formed universe have little or no relevance outside this universe. Thus there are no approximate axioms, either they hold or not; furthermore adding conditions might jeopardize the whole axiomatic structure if no appropriate caution is taken. That means that an axiomatic structure is precise and closed with respect to interpretations while the single axioms outside the structure may be interpreted more loosely.

We therefore may still use partially those axioms as for example behavioural approximates, but then in a dynamic and partial way in the analysis of non-equilibrium.

It is also interesting to note that the fundamental normative criterion in the neoclassical equilibrium analysis, the efficiency criterion, Pareto optimum, which indeed is demanding, may also in fact be used outside an eventual general equilibrium but then of course in a modified form. Accepting the idea put forward in Arrow's paradox that agents not only affect each other in their actions but also that agents react on the aggregate results transforms the Pareto principle to a general sociological idea where the economic interpretation is just a part. Thus the Pareto optimality and principle has not necessarily anything to do with the market economy per se, although that has been the general idea, which also Pareto embraced.[10] It is a sociological principle which can be interpreted in several ways, not only linked to economics, and the very definition of the kind of efficiency which relates to general equilibrium is just a particular interpretation.

From a theoretical point of view that implies that we may use the Pareto concept deliberated from its connotations to neoclassical equilibrium theory, even if there most probably will be difficulties in defining it, but that is another matter.

During time the conditions for general equilibrium have come to represent a rational behaviour of the agents and the particular approach to the concept of commodities. In our analysis in Chapter 2 we showed the inappropriateness of those interpretations which are rejected by a proper interpretation of Arrow's paradox and also by Debreu's very definition of commodities, when the axioms of choice appear as a part of an axiomatic structure. The three axioms of choice are within the precise axiomatic structure to be interpreted as an *equivalence relation* which has a mathematical interpretation which seems to be extremely unpleasant for a basically social science (Ekstedt and Fusari 2010: 50–1). At the same time we accept the axioms of choice as a part of the concept *epistemic cycles*. But in the latter case they appear given a contextual apprehension which opens for a non-equilibrium analysis.

Thus although we may well use neoclassical techniques and concepts in order to describe individual behaviour and we may also accept both rationality and optimization behaviour given a defined level of the society, as well as we may even use the equilibrium concept partially, we do not use it in a normative way, with respect to judgements vis-à-vis the welfare and efficiency status of the economy which follows from our rejection of additive aggregation in real terms of optima. However our discussion on macroscopic analysis in Chapter 3 obviously used some kind of additive aggregation, particularly our discussions of Figure 3.2 and forward.

This is a tricky part of the analysis. If we stick to the general equilibrium meaning of inflation it is just some multiplicity of the price index, which means that the index could be renumerated, but that is not valid in non-equilibrium. Given that we have multiple price vectors both for commodities and for production factors we must think of inflation as an average and as such a change in inflation will have distributional effects. Furthermore if we enter the problem of liquidity inflation will also have effects on the risk and uncertainty structures.

Thus our aggregation in money terms will hide real effects which are of utmost importance on the microscopic and subsequently on the development of the macroscopic level.

One may ask why this kind of normative state of equilibrium is adopted within economic theory. When we compare the two early economic analysts David Hume and Adam Smith we see that such a kind of equilibrium is non-existent in Hume's analysis and he also sees an ever ongoing interaction between the social and economic development thus changing the conditions for both the social and economic structures, although he also describes equilibrating processes like Allais' equimarginal principle. When he discusses the effects of restrictions on the money supply he mentions its negative impact on expectations and the progress of the development of the market economy which will have social effects.[11] Smith however looks at a more closed society. Both with respect to the price mechanism which was centred round the labour value and the land rent and the fact that the norm was expressed in real terms, not in money prices with respect to corn which is built on the necessity of keeping labour productive which grants the land rent to the proprietor, he actually ranks the land rent before the remuneration of labour. Smith's analysis was taken over with modifications by Ricardo and Marx, but still also the latter analysts kept Smith's closed analysis where social changes are of no importance but as disturbing phenomena.

When we mix Keynesian, and neoclassical theoretical elements into some macroeconomic systematic thinking, it is thus a mixture between a fundamentally closed model and a fundamentally open one where the stability of the exogenous elements are decisive. The openness which we discuss here has less to do with the existence of foreign trade, although that of course plays a role, than with the earlier discussed dimensionality problem and thus with the changing structure of epistemic cycles.

This is from a philosophical point of view significant. The neoclassical world as well as the writings of Adam Smith is based on *reason* in the rationalistic sense, which is completely different from Hume's attitude that reason is the humble servant of the subject's will and passions. This explains why the neoclassical theory is well suited to explain the choice mechanisms of the subject but once the contextual considerations are done the theory is not suited at all to explain the changes of the contextual structures. That's why Debreu's definition of commodities is so important to understand. Money as a concept enters actually right into the rift between the neoclassical closeness and the Keynesian openness. In fact money as something more than a medium of exchange is fully explained by the openness of the economic system, in the form of innovations, changing social, economic and political structures, changing apprehensions of the individuals and thus revisions of behaviour and so on. The described openness implies that the neoclassical division in a market space and a state space has to be replaced with a joint space where there are interrelations between what we might define as a state space and the market space, and consequently the price system loses its role as the unique information system of the market space, save for local and temporal subspaces.

We can see the rift between the neoclassical theory and a Keynesian approach in the treatment of unemployment, where the so-called Keynesian unemployment is hard to explain in a neoclassical framework other than as a consequence of erroneous expectations and/or inappropriate inertia in price and wage formation; such phenomena as permanent unemployment are almost non-existent in equilibrium thinking, are considered as an individual choice or a result of institutional obstacles. Such eventual institutional obstacles are not a part of the theoretical picture of the economy and are thus seen more or less as anomalies.[12] A fundamental reason for this rift is that when we open the economic theory in the way we have done we almost automatically reject additive aggregation and then we get the treacherous effect we have discussed above that although money prices are possible to aggregate in an additive way the real commodities are not.

The fact that the production structure adapts to the current social reality both implies that companies must define the optimum technology according to the current structure but that has to be met by a demand also defined by the current social reality. It implies that playing around with theoretical solutions implying flexible wages and prices as well as using the employment rate as a financial moderator threatens other social structures, which might lead to social unease, thus threatening the very base for both the monetary system and the economic growth.

We said above that the neoclassical theory has no history and no future, which means that also *now* is a mystery. That has induced ideological interpretations to question any kind of institutional structures, save for those protecting private property. Institutional structures in general are a way of directing the agents' behaviour, thus diminishing the uncertainty of the future. Even a pure general equilibrium setting could actually be interpreted such that Kant's ethical imperative is implicit in the setting and that is indeed demanding (Ekstedt and Fusari 2010: 108–13). However *Debreu's definition of commodities* which means that we analyse the choice given the contextual consideration does not contradict any institutional system, not even the centralized soviet system.

True is that institutional structures may have negative effects and also that such structures, if imposed by public authorities, are efficient during some periods but they may also decline into obsolescence by changing economic and social environment. These are empirical developments which are not a part of the axiomatic system and thus economic theory is not able to handle them properly within the axiomatic structure. This is particularly evident if we take into account the theoretical conclusions we must draw from Arrow's paradox.

Institutional and ethical structures may surely exist and must exist within the neoclassical theory setting the frames but given that perfect flexibility is a necessity for the economy to work and thus the condition for the relevance of the normative imperatives. Consequently it is interesting to note the pattern that any kind of institutional restriction on economic behaviour is classified as a second best situation, while the laissez faire solution is the first best.[13] This results among other things in the fact that a tax system as *lump-sum* taxes is regarded as an *efficient* tax system, without any considerations of the social effects. This is perhaps one of the most obvious proofs the fact of that the neoclassical approach lacks any form of history and thus no future.

Our discussions on Arrow's paradox led us to comment upon the alleged conflict between efficiency and democracy and/or voting democracy in relation to some alleged market democracy. Our analysis shows that all such speculative theories are based on poor understanding of the meaning of the paradox. When we start from a non-equilibrium perspective implying that an organization of different levels of aggregation may optimize their action without any restriction of optimality of other aggregate levels, we will find that social desirability of action is far more complex than the simple additive aggregation of optima in the neoclassical theory.

Obviously public policy is of shifting character and quality and some public measures may well have negative effects on the economy both on aggregate and individual levels and may in both the medium and the long run lead to increases in unemployment, reduction in real wages and profits or have other negative effects, but this cannot be calculated on the basis of a priori defined equilibrium models.

Equilibrium, measure and inertia

Virtually all meaningful dynamic models rest on the concept of equilibrium which also makes it meaningful to work with comparative static models to scrutinize the parameter structures of an inert system. Inertia of a system has to do with the measurability and the consistency of the measure in time and space. Inertia as a concept which is contradictory to the economic concept of general equilibrium, which depends on the fact that every state of general equilibrium so to say defines its own measure and a change of state of equilibrium also implies a new measure. This means that when we pass over to a non-equilibrium economy in the sense of rejecting additive aggregation in the neoclassical sense we must also assume that the economy is not totally unstable but displays both local and temporal inertia where it is possible to apply consistent measures. This is however a bit tricky when we consider money as a medium of measurement. Since we have rejected the uniqueness of price vectors we have to pass over our analysis to accepting an average price, even when we regard a physically well defined commodity, and that is where the concept of inertia comes in. We mentioned earlier the so-called *mean reversal hypothesis* in financial analysis meaning that given a portfolio reasonably well chosen to represent different sectors of the economy we may rather safely assume that the variations of the portfolio follow the variations of the economy and if the value of the portfolio is perturbed by some shock, it will after a certain time return to its mean. That means that we regard the structure which the portfolio represents as inert.

If we now apply this reasoning to a macroscopic model, we build the model on behavioural parameters and in principle we have a set of parameters on the demand side and another set on the supply side. If parameters on the demand side are perturbed we in the short run may expect that if the cause of the perturbation vanishes the parameters return to a neighbourhood of the values before the perturbation. This depends on that we rather generally might expect the set of parameters on the supply side to be inert. If however the parameter set on the supply side is perturbed we are generally not supposed to assume a similar outcome even if the cause of the perturbation vanishes. The reason is of course the general inertia of production capital in relation to the distribution of human capital and its intimate relation to uncertainty due to the social process. Thus in the economy the inertia is most probably asymmetric between the supply side and the demand side and this is of course the principle background to Figures 4.11 and 4.12. This is basically also the reason why Wicksell can distinguish between stability on the microscopic level and macroscopic level, since the natural interest rate concerns the return on capital.

This is actually the essence of Keynes' discussion on the stability of the contextual structure when he claims that the economy, although not fulfilling the neoclassical form of full employment, was not entirely unstable (Keynes 1973 [1936]: 249–54).

Dynamics and irreversibility

In social sciences, as we mentioned in Chapter 2, we have the very disturbing fact that humans are subjects and not objects. The meaning of this is that humans have to be regarded as final causes, i.e. humans are able to start a causal chain without any apparent reference to a particular context. We may explain individual action with reference to some alleged socialization process but that is often based on rather weak grounds. Thus we may see ourselves as if we are living in an ongoing gigantic full-scale universal social experiment where it is hard to separate whether we are *objects* in the empirical investigation or *observers* of the very investigation or *acting subjects*. All we have is very narrow observations of what is actually happening both in time and space.

Hume's attitude is that there is an intimate relationship between the development of the market economy and the development of the social structure is therefore a reasonable attitude. To develop an economic theory as an independent subsystem of the social system requires in fact rather strong assumptions concerning the social inertia. In our earlier discussions on epistemic cycles we showed a reasonable modification of economic theorizing implying that we can actually use standard economic concepts for inert social and economic states. The consequence however is that we break the additive aggregation link between the microscopic level and the macroscopic level and thus we also lose the unique role of prices as a measurement. The ambiguity of the interpretation of whether the diagrams in Figures 4.2 and 4.3 show sustainability or non-sustainability are due to assuming additive or non-additive aggregation.

The present situation (December 2011) of the euro zone when one member country claims its national sovereignty to handle its affairs, while at the same time it is both dependent on and inflicting problems on fellow countries, i.e. a clash between two aggregate levels, is a good example of the globalization, which in fact is a consequence of the money economy.

All this boils down to the fact that the states of equilibrium are at most partial and temporal. Thus we cannot use any *a priori axiomatic* structure, particularly not of a normative character, but as we have claimed above we may still use the practical content of the mathematical principles involved in the axioms and turn our investigations into descriptions and enquiries of eventual stability in non-equilibrium systems which are inert.

Let us however go back to Chapter 1 and our discussion on Wittgenstein's proposition 6.211 and Figure 1.1 which serves as an illustration of the proposition. We have discussed the problem of translating reality into mathematical models but there is a concept we have so far not brought into our discussions on economic theory and that is the concept of *reversibility*. To our knowledge the Norwegian economist Ragnar Frisch introduced the concepts of *putty-clay*.[14] It means that for investments we can make revisions in technology, capacity and so on as long we have not transformed the plans into physical entities. After that transformation earlier optimization of technology, capacity and so on is very restricted. First this implies that changes in the environment resulting in demand variations give rise to variations in cash flows and profit. This is the basic reason for treating profit of physical capital as a residual. Second, the concept of putty-clay most naturally links to the *ex ante/ex post* analysis of the Stockholm School, contemporary to Frisch. The concept of putty-clay is mostly used in different kinds of investment analysis in microeconomic theory but ought to be more contemplated in macroeconomic theory.

Anyway the putty-clay concept, as well as the *ex ante/ex post* analysis, gives rise to a distinction between flow and stock equilibria in real terms, and by that also revaluations of physical stocks.

However the reversibility problem is larger than illustrated by the putty-clay approach, it concerns all economic actions, both with respect to changing valuations of stocks as well as agents failing in fulfilment of their purposes. This means that we might theoretically assume converging processes as Allais' equimarginal principle, which is not unreasonable to assume, but irreversibility of actions gives rise to a fundamental source of instability in the process. The basic problem is that individual actions may give rise to effects on fellow individuals or groups of individuals whose consequential re-actions actually change the aggregate structure. Thus an action might well be regarded as reversible on the microscopic level but once it has aggregate effects these are not reversible. However this problem is particularly important for the money economy. Given a barter economy as long as the individuals stick to the social norms, an exchange operation gives rise to a change in the temporal welfare but over time it will not affect the aggregate structure. In the money economy we may think of real investments based on partly own resources and partly borrowed ones; bankruptcy will then affect the aggregate liquidity of the group involved and then also to a higher or lesser degree the whole credit system.

We may also draw a methodological conclusion, namely that the irreversibility of the physical and social reality is in sharp contrast to the reversibility of mathematical/logical models. As we have mentioned the neoclassical axiomatic structure gives rise to the *correlate of revealed preferences*, which means that derived functions have inverses, and thus are reversible. This is most clearly expressed in the problem of saving and investments. We also saw in Hicks' analysis of the IS-LM that Hicks boldly assumes that the quantitative equation is fully invertible so that the national income is uniquely defined within the equation and this also implied that the investment function is invertible. In solving an ordinary IS-LM system we make a whole series of mathematical transformations which are based on the existence of invertible functions in all relevant intervals, most of all the calculations of the multiplier process.

Thus in both neoclassical and Keynesian models monetary and real entities are treated exactly in the same way in the modelling. If we solve the textbook IS-LM model in E.4.5, with respect to interest rate, we get:

$$R = \frac{(1-b) \cdot (M_0 - L_0) - \mu \cdot (a + I_0)}{(1-b) + c} \tag{E.5.1}$$

Thus we have an equilibrium which in principle, apart from the simplified linear structure, is calculated on the same premises as a neoclassical equilibrium. Implicitly we assume continuity, convexity and differentiability of all functions; if exogenous variables are defined, equations are invertible. The difference to the neoclassical theory is that we have to assume some exogenous variables which are non-existent in the neoclassical theory such as liquidity preference, L_0, and expectation dependent investments, I_0.

Paul Samuelson's classification of dynamic systems

As we claimed in Chapter 2 the neoclassical general equilibrium theory is lacking time but at the same time approaches like Allais' and the temporary equilibrium theory, completed with Drèze's approach make attempts to develop a dynamics in a Keynesian direction.

The IS-LM on the other hand is as we see above rather close to a neoclassical approach. Samuelson lays in fact a theoretical foundation in his discussion of dynamic approaches to a synthesis of the two seemingly converging thoughts.

Paul Samuelson makes a categorization of different dynamic models, which also is a sort of manual for using comparative static modelling: it is instructive to start with his total categorization (Samuelson 1947: 315–17). This classification is in general terms the ruling classification in current economic research: (i) static and stationary, (ii) static and historical, (iii) dynamical and causal, (iv) dynamical and historical, (v) stochastic and non-historical, (vi) stochastic and historical.

Type (i) is a normal analysis of a particular structure, for example an ordinary general equilibrium model, an input–output model and similar. The analysis is not dynamic but gives a current picture which may be used as a basis for dynamic considerations. Type (ii) is best described as a comparative static model, where we analyse the features of different states of equilibrium, as in the IS-LM model. The technique is not dynamic since the road between the equilibrium states is not analysed but two different structures are analysed and their implicit dynamics.

In these model types all the real dynamics take place outside the logical analysis within the imagination of the theoreticians. As such the analysis is basic to structural understanding.

From our point of view (iii) and (iv) are the most interesting. We can see that the fundamental dividing line is between causal and historical dynamic processes. It is perhaps more proper to denominate the causal system a *deterministic system* since it is doubtful whether Hume's causality concept can be applied to such a system.[15] A dynamical and historical system does not preclude causality in Hume's meaning.

The causal/deterministic process is an initial value problem. Thus the determination of the initial structure and values of the economic variables resolves the future process.

By a historical process Samuelson means a dynamic process, determined by also non-economic factors. The non-economic factors at, let us say, t^1 can be a state of art of confidence, expectations, structure of restrictions and similar.

Formally logical time models state that all variations of the state of the world depends on the conditions settled at t^0 and time distance between t and t^0, irrespective if the models are stochastic or not.

$$x = f[(t - t^0); \bar{x}(t^0)] \tag{E.5.2}$$

Such a model has in general, an inverse. This is of course very suitable, since it allows us to analyse parameters and search for optimal trajectories.

This kind of model, which has an inverse, implies that time is in principle reversible. Thus any logical time model describes a dynamic process of the economy which suggests that we may calculate the whole trajectory from the knowledge of two different time states. A Solowian model is such an example.

In contrast to logical time models we may analyse historical time models, which are described by Samulson as:

$$x = g[t; \ t^0; x(t^0)] \tag{E.5.3}$$

This means that X is dependent on the conditions at t^0 but it is also dependent on the respective conditions in each period through which the trajectory passes. The IS-LM model actually fits well into the historical time models in Samuelson's classification, although it is mostly a comparative static model, but it may be completed into an accelerator model. The dynamics of the economy so to say restart from every point of time with the imputation of the particular state of art at that point of time and this is actually what happens when we specify the two exogenous variables L_0 and I_0 to represent the current liquidity preference and the current state of expectations. Thus from a theoretical and methodological point of view the IS-LM model, in different variants, is indeed an extension of the neoclassical model, also if we add liquidity preference and expectations as exogenous variables. For example we can use a variant of the IS-LM model in the case where we have a locus of optimal capacity utilization which is separate from the socially desirable national income level, but then we must strictly separate inflation and unemployment variations due to other factors than variations in the aggregate capacity utilization. A policy of affecting the locus of optimal capacity utilization must then most probably be defined under the restriction of short-run balance in the IS-LM sense.

Historical time in Samuelson's meaning provokes once more questions of the probabilities of the state space, which concerns the learning process of the agents but now with respect to the money economy.[16] Our claim that the individual agent is to be seen as a subject, thus a final cause theoretically enlarges the state space to include the agents themselves. Hence we cannot claim independence between the state space and the market place. Even if we imagine that it was possible for the agents to get the full information of the probabilities of the different states of the so to say objective state space, we would have false trading and since the purposes and the epistemic cycles of the agents are hidden it is doubtful if we could have a convergence to a long-run equilibrium trajectory; to make that possible we probably need institutional restrictions on agents' behaviour. Thus we may suspect that any learning process will be insufficient which in itself adds to the uncertainty. To this we may add the question of whether all agents know, and even need to know for their own actions, the dimensionality of the state space.

Summing up all such kinds of methodological questions can be dealt with by different assumptions but in mirroring the reality they form a gigantic truncation problem which seldom can be cured by adding a bunch of new equations and concepts thus complicating the model. The most intriguing problem from a methodological point of view is that all variables in both neoclassical and Keynesian models are measured in money terms. In the case of neoclassical equilibrium analysis the measure only holds uniquely with respect to a particular equilibrium while in the Keynesian case of an IS-LM model we have a real side and a money side and both sides are measured in money terms but actions on the money side affect the real side both in nominal and real terms and the eventual switch between one and the other hinges on the probability that we can precisely define the elements of the quantity equation of money either in its classical form or in its Cambridge form.

Social space–time

Luigi Amoroso wrote in his essay on Vilfred Pareto that "the dead city ruled the living" and Keynes wrote "the importance of money essentially flows from being a link between the present and the future" which Arrow and Hahn completed by writing "to which we may add that it [money] is important also because it is a link between the past and the present". Samuelson's historical time is indeed an improvement with respect to the market exchange in a non-equilibrium economy, a process like Allais' equimarginal principle or the temporary equilibrium theory are good examples of the *historical time* in Samuelson's version. Still however it is a kind of physical analysis where the space which undergoes dynamic changes is in a way deformed. If we look at a simple example of Einstein-Minkovsky's time concept as in Figure 5.3 we can think of a projection, which is dotted, of the rectangle ABCDA drawn on a time slice t_0 at the time slice t_1. However since we add a time dimension the rectangle A'B'C'D'A" as a consequence of the moving space will be distorted in respect to the environment.

In economics we actually have a kind of distortion function, namely the time preference expressed as an interest rate, and if we think of different possessions, purposes and restriction an agent does not have only one time preference but a whole set of time preferences with respect to different parts of the life both in space and time.

Thus when we add the quotes from Amoroso, Keynes and Arrow and Hahn even the historical time concept is insufficient as describing the social space–time.

Time according to
some kind of norm

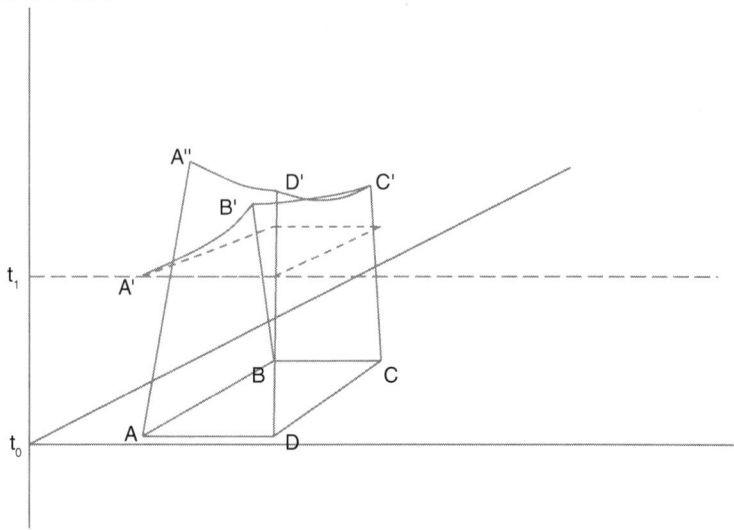

Figure 5.3 Space–time in Einstein-Minkowsky meaning.

The key element in a social space–time is the fact that humans are to be regarded as subjects and at the same time they are social creatures. The role of institutions, explicit or implicit, is to restrict the individual behaviour thus hopefully diminishing the uncertainty of the future. Hence the fundamental uncertainty of the agents is induced by the agents themselves.

Say's law once again

How do we create growth in the real meaning that we diminish the permanent unemployment and get a society reasonably sustainable in social and environmental meaning. Let us immediately say that the market process in itself is just a sort of machine as a planned socialist economy. Keynes is right and we have showed that the glossy neoclassical picture of the reality is an analytical dead end. But the question is if we must leave it there with a market economy fundamentally unstable and just hope for the best.

History as well as our analysis of Arrow's paradox shows us that a pure laissez faire is bound to fail. We need collective actions as well as control of the individual actions but it is important to remember that also the collective bodies are built on individuals. Ekstedt and Fusari (2010) emphasized the necessity of recognizing the ethical dimension and the attitude that the market replaces systematic ethical norms in the society is devastating for the long-run stability.[17]

But still, how do we get a growth which may help us to solve the permanent employment?

There is obviously no clear answer but we may try to paint a picture of the evolvement of the society where we may see signs of possible strategies and for this we must go back to David Hume's and Jean Baptiste Say's views of the society. We may claim that these are a bit too optimistic but if man is generically a crook and a nasty devil there is not much to do other than having a good glass of wine before Ragnarök breaks loose.

Anyway we look a bit more at Say.

There are mainly three pieces to link together before we reach Say's deepest meaning of his law. The first is about the fact that the economic system is an integrated part of the social system. Thus the social development, which is to a high degree augmented by the monetary system, creates new commodity dimensions all the time. Thus inventions as ideas contemplated by the lonely genius reach the market under two conditions: first there must be a social need for the new product. Ekstedt and Fusari (2010: 180) take examples from Heron whose inventions became viable during the late ninteenth century since the cattle breeding technology required a cow-watering machine and the industry required a steam turbine. Someone also has to detect the need and appreciate the invention properly as the British engineer who developed Heron's automatic cow-watering machine and de Laval in Sweden who developed the steam turbine for marketing. Thus a social need for a certain kind of product needs somebody to be detected and that is the role of the innovator, the entrepreneur. The consumer demand is important but the consumer demand does not detect new commodity dimensions.

Second there must exist financial capital which is ready to be invested in real ventures. There is much talk today about risk capital and by that is meant capital prepared to be invested in real ventures. The economies of western countries has a growing permanent unemployment, the structure is such that many young people do not get access to the labour market, which is devastating in the long run. Financial capital is used to make money on smart financial products sold to make money of funds for prospective pensioners. Money is invested to get favours on financial fellow agents. Money is invested in bonds financing deficits to pay some minimum to those who are permanently unemployed, to try to avoid social unease, to save financial agents from the consequences of their latest financial invention. Real production shrinks to fewer and fewer dimensions following mergers and acquisitions to reduce the real risk by monopolization/oligopolization thus streamlining products into standards. Investments in real production outside the "allowed" paths are seen as too risky and this opinion is supported by economists who already at the first lessons in macroeconomics tell that investment in real production is the most risky form of investment. Almost at the same time however we tell the students that there is no profit in the world from an aggregate perspective except that which is produced to give utility for the individual and welfare to the society. We have separated the microscopic and the microscopic level in Chapter 2 and given this we may wonder how the rather ugly real social development must go before we realize that investments in real production from a macroscopic point of view is the only safe use of saved money. We come back to this in the end of Chapter 7.

Third, the dead city rules the living; these producers who have succeeded try to protect their economic influence and power by fighting new ventures. Who likes competition? Certainly not the single producer or those workers who have a good job; this is perhaps one of the fundamental points why the competitive model does not work and is basically unstable. The normal outcome of criminal economic structures is a local and temporal monopoly. It is in this way financial power together with need for liquidity can be used in protecting an old structure from competition. The state/society has to guard the market from illicit use of financial power. When we look at the romantic neoclassical approach where everybody obeys the orders of the invisible hand, whoever that may be, we can see that there is no recognition of search for power in its different forms and the protection of power in one dimension is to acquire power in another. We must also be aware that although the workers are the weaker part, their unions are mighty powers which through rigid rules and principles may stop developing ventures and also new ways of organization which might be of interest for the future.

It is said that the market economy is a necessary condition for the democratic society but it is equally well the other way around; the democratic society, one man – one vote, is a necessary condition for a functioning market economy. But all parts must realize that an economy sliding backwards with respect to diversification and innovativeness in the long run is a threat also to the political freedom.

Given these three types of considerations we look at Say.

Basically regarding consumption it causes money to diffuse into many directions, worthy as well as less worthy.

Thus we can say that keeping up demand is necessary. But demand does not create growth. The society changes through social interaction which creates new possibilities, but it is the ones who detect these possibilities, who develop it into business, and create the growth.

Thus production does not create its own demand but hopefully the entrepreneur detects new demand worthwhile to exploit; the market must work freely and the financial system must prioritize the production needs. Say is quite clear of the fact that stimulation of demand in itself does not create growth. Thus from this point of view the Keynesianism has overemphasized the demand policy. Keynes' analysis appeared in a depression and Hicks has a point that part of Keynes' analysis is dictated by the particular context. The simple Keynesian model betrays us in the sense that the multiplier appears as a kind of machine. We have an ever ongoing process of structural change and in recessions this structural change so to say takes its negative toll but the reason why we might have stable Keynesian equilibrium in recession is not only a general lack of demand but also that it takes time for new sectors to establish and this might cause prolonged deficits and also that we get a shrinking dimensionality of the production system. Thus economic policy with idle general stimuli of consumption is quite problematic in the long run and a policy directed to areas of investments which support the development of private production seems more in line with Say's attitude, and he actually discusses as an example investments in infrastructure in terms of that the social value exceeds the costs; "probably, in most cases, the benefits they afford to the community far exceed the charges" (1834: 447). But he discusses other areas as education, health care in the same line as Gary Becker (1964) in *Human Capital*.

Consequently we may see Say's law in conjunction with economic policy of what Hume advocates and what sometimes is called a mild inflationary policy together with support of the entrepreneurial activities.

Figure 4.12 shows an ugly development it depicts and to this we can add the almost perverse scarcity of inflation. To worry about the increase of inflation of the last quarter to 3.4 per cent when 3.1 per cent was expected is a bit strange when we think about the theoretical weakness of measuring inflation that we have discussed. We fight inflation which logically must come if employment rises over the average optimum capacity utilization but which we know very little about in practice.

In such a world Say's law as discussed by Say is relevant. The entrepreneurs must be given a margin of demand. If we measure 3.4 per cent inflation but 2 per cent is due to companies working above their average capacity utilization and furthermore that new products are growing but are outside the norm basket of commodities, real inflation is just in a longer run when things have settled and capacities have increased, perhaps 1.4 per cent. This also leaves room for public expenditures. Any real growth will end up in new demands on the public sector. There are services which are unsuitable for private production and this varies over time. The neoclassical dream of integrating the public sector is emanating out of a rationalistic dream as unrealistic as the invisible hand; but from this to claim that the public sector represents a benevolent fairy as sometimes is claimed by the Marxists is also a rationalistic dream. The public sector is also organized by the same kind of people that populate the private sector. Institutions, control systems and public support of general welfare will always be necessary but the character will be subject to structural changes as the entire commodity basket.

Anyway we may say that to kill inflation to any price is also killing the economy.

6   Uncertainty, money and liquidity

Risk and uncertainty

Both in neoclassical and Keynesian economics the concept of risk has a prominent place within the analysis in the sense that we have a conceptualized structure of thought. Not so the concept of uncertainty; it is often discussed but its complex structure, or perhaps we should say non-existent structure, make the concept difficult to use in a consistent analysis.

In modelling uncertainty is often treated synonymously with exogenous shocks and we then investigate the short- and eventual long-run effects. Given a model, this mode of analytical procedure is fully acceptable but it implies that the existence of uncertainty does not affect the structure of the model, which sometimes is a rather limiting postulate and that is where the problems begins.

One obvious reason for this analytical bias towards risk in economic science is the rather strict mathematical/logical mode of risk analysis which makes it difficult to impute a concept of such lax character as uncertainty but uncertainty pops up when scrutinizing different theoretical approaches. In the discussion on Arrow's paradox the fundamental result of rejecting additive aggregation in fact deprived us of the possibilities to make a consistent risk analysis on the macroscopic level. On microscopic levels it is still possible given appropriate definitions of the problem. Similar in an analysis like the one leading to Allais' paradox, the expected utility approach is invalidated with respect to the uniqueness of the optimum which follows the two-dimensional character of the risk analysis. On one hand we have the very probabilities as such which are possible to analyse in terms of risk but on the other hand we have dimension following from the character of the probability distribution, which may be measured in terms of volatility or by the entropy measure. True that we may assume risk aversion to get around the paradox but that is normally only reasonable with respect to the microscopic level.

Modern financial analysis focuses on the problem which Allais raised in the way that assumptions concerning distributions and volatilities are dropped and mathematical models, developed on the principles of Black and Scholes, as the Heston model, are used which can be used give an impression of the current status of volatility among the agents on a well-defined market based on the immediate history of market actions. Not that any model can give any information whatsoever of the current status but such kinds of models seem to improve the analysis. We will come back to this but as we can understand such models completely drop standard economic modelling and are directed towards detecting behaviour among the agents which can be seen as a proxy for *apprehended* uncertainty. Their eventual success obviously depends on the existence of inertia of behaviour, which most probably varies.

We may provisionally define uncertainty as the situation when the space of outcome is not known, or, a more favourable case, when it is known but there is no concordance about the subjective probability distribution; this is like playing roulette – you know the space of outcome but if you at the same time know that the owner has a name for manipulating his wheels you cannot say anything about the probability distribution. On the other hand you may take the assumption that the owner wants to maximize profit and then it's a good policy to look at the bulk of the other player's bets. Unfortunately the owner may take such policy into consideration and you end up in Keynes' famous beauty contest, so perhaps you had better not go there after all (Keynes 1973 [1936]: 156).

The effects of uncertainty, whether they stem from the more easy case of Allais' paradox or from the more extreme cases as the occurrence of black swans, as Keynes discussed in his *Treatise on Probability* (op. cit.: 222 ff.), are the dual effects on the real and financial sectors which might ultimately lead to redistributions of real as well as financial capital in the direction of higher concentration. This will also have dynamic consequences for the credit market which are crucial for the stability of the financial system; unfortunately the stability might go in either direction.

A first look at uncertainty

Uncertainty is from a theoretical perspective an awkward concept. It is without limits and its dimensionality is unknown so replacing it with a risk concept is a huge improvement from an analytical and technical point of view, but it is a substantial modification of the reality, sometimes reasonable, sometimes not. Chaos is used to describe uncertainty but that is incorrect; in many aspects it is well ordered, the physical chaos for example is indeed unpleasant, but nevertheless well ordered in the sense that energy has reached its maximal entropy. From this point of view the neoclassical theory is very interesting, depending on how we formulate the problem. The axiomatic construction of the neoclassical theory on one hand implies that the agents are completely atomistic and furthermore they possess a sort of individual veto. The consequences of this are fully apparent in Arrow's paradox; the agents cannot vote. The expression in Scandinavian language "Polsk riksdag" and German "Polnischer reichtag" refers to the historical Polish parliament where the nobility possessed individual veto, which resulted in the situation that the important political process took place on the road to the parliament when traps to take hostages, physical violence and killing were normal means to arrange a sufficient foundation for a certain decision. In

Scandinavia the concept "Polsk riksdag" is equivalent to political chaos and that is the consequence of creating agents according to the neoclassical axioms. The reason why the neoclassical theory seems to be well ordered is that it is fully obeying the *invisible hand*, which decides the price vector. How this can be linked to democracy is a mystery from a theoretical point of view. That a well-functioning market economy is an important feature in a democracy is almost self-evident but to mix a market economy in the common way we think of it with the kind of economy created by the neoclassical axioms is indeed mysterious thinking.

Ekstedt and Fusari (2010: 109) claimed however that we may formulate the neoclassical theory differently in the sense that all individuals maximize their utility given their respective endowment vector and also given the utility function of everybody else:

$$\text{Max } U_i(x_1, \ldots, x_n) \tag{E.6.1}$$

Subject to $e_i \leq e^*_i$ and $U^* = \max(U_1, \ldots, U_{i-1}, U_{i+1}, \ldots, U_n)$.

This will in fact show great similarities with Kant's ethical imperative on which we may apply Nash's analysis and when the number of agents appears very large the number of individual solutions is ultimately reduced to one.[1] Thus already the neoclassical barter economy becomes polluted with uncertainty through Arrow's and Allais' paradoxes.

However when we enter money it becomes worse. The principal point of view regarding money concerns our distinction between monetary and real matters in the preceding chapter and our conclusion that money belongs to non-proper classes while real matters belong to proper classes: this distinction was based on one hand of the rejection of the axiom of reflexivity, which rejects reversibility, exhibited through revealed preference correlate. On the other it was based on the analysis of Arrow's paradox and its correlate the mereological rule of thumb.

Furthermore if we look at the flow-chart in Figure 4.2 and its complex monetary superstructure and thereby also add the particulars of the concept of liquidity which we treated as a lexicographic preference, we may wonder if this monetary superstructure in itself might add new dimensions to uncertainty which might affect the real side of the economy. We have mentioned that money/liquidity/financial assets as some form of insurance with respect to inert production structures but this insurance is also vulnerable since it is not carrying any intrinsic value. The discussion of metallism and chartalism can in fact be boiled down to the very problem of the insurance of the insurance. We remember from Thornton that he regarded gold guineas as less liquid than paper money because of their intrinsic value, particularly with respect to foreign trade. This implies that the very concept of liquidity must not be confused as valuable assets for long-term saving/protection. Confusing these two aspects may lead us into a still sharper conflict intrinsic to money where Gresham's law affects the very supply of the medium of exchange.[2]

Money as we experience it in our daily lives is on one hand superfluous in a world without uncertainty but when it comes into use it adds other dimensions of uncertainty.

An interesting economist is Ludwig von Mises, who was a forceful defender of the free market, not perhaps altogether laissez faire but indeed doubtful of public interference. He used the interesting concept *praxeology*, which is said to have been introduced by the French philosopher Bourdeau in the late nineteenth century. It means the deductive study of rational action, which from our point of view is an appropriate concept. Anyway von Mises discarded such things as complete future markets and full knowledge of the future and accepted uncertainty as a necessary ingredient in human affairs.

He writes (2007 [1949]: 105):

> But however that may be, or appear to the mind of a perfect intelligence, the fact remains that to acting man the future is hidden. If a man knew the future, he would not have to choose and would not act. He would be an automaton, reacting to stimuli without any will of his own.

This quote is in concordance with our analysis of the shortcomings of the neoclassical theory, in which the developed risk analysis is built around its axiomatic structure and therefore it keeps the perception of man as an automaton.

When we read von Mises further on the same page he says:

> Natural science does not render the future predictable. It makes it possible to foretell the results to be obtained by definitive actions. But it leaves unpredictable two spheres: that of insufficiently known natural phenomena and that of human acts of choice. Our ignorance with regard to these two spheres taints all human actions with uncertainty. Apodictic certainty is only within the orbit of the deductive system of aprioristic theory. The most that can be attained with regard to reality is probability.

Von Neumann and Morgenstern discuss along the same line as von Mises when they make the distinction between the "Robinson Crusoe" economy and the social barter economy. They note the complex interaction between agents and that "it is certainly no maximum problem, but a peculiar and disconcerting mixture of several conflicting maximum problems" (von Neumann and Morgenstern 2004 [1944]: 11), but they also make an interesting comment on the socialization of this, sometimes chaotic, process:

> Every participant can determine the variables which describe his own actions but not those of the others. Nevertheless those "alien" variables cannot, from his point of view be described by statistical assumptions. This is because the others are guided, just as he himself, by rational principles – whatever that may mean – and no *modus operandi* can be correct which

does not attempt to understand those principles and the interactions of the conflicting interests of all participants.

(ibid.: 11, original emphasis)

The comment is important since it spells out a fundamental difference between the risk analysis in the relation between a constant state space and a market space on one hand and the risks and eventual uncertainties rising from the acting of fellow agents. Furthermore the analysis by von Neumann and Morgenstern deals only with microscopic relations developed in game-theoretical terms while we add a macroscopic level which links to the microscopic levels and thus adds another space of uncertainty, since we have rejected additive aggregation.

The idea of a state space

In order to display the different aspects of the concept of uncertainty we will in principle analyse the two aspects which von Mises mentions, the physical world and human actions. With respect to the physical space we start to follow the neo-classical theory and divide the world into a state space and a market space as in Figure 6.1

The outcomes of the state space will affect the market action but in the simplest formulation there is no reverse influence. We will assume that under certain conditions we can attach a subjective probability distribution over the state space and achieve the concept of *expected utility*, which then is analysed, particularly with respect to Allais' paradox.

In the next step we complicate the state space and assume it consists of multiple dimensions which each have separate probability distributions. This leads ultimately to the *copula* which is a function projecting the *n*-dimensional

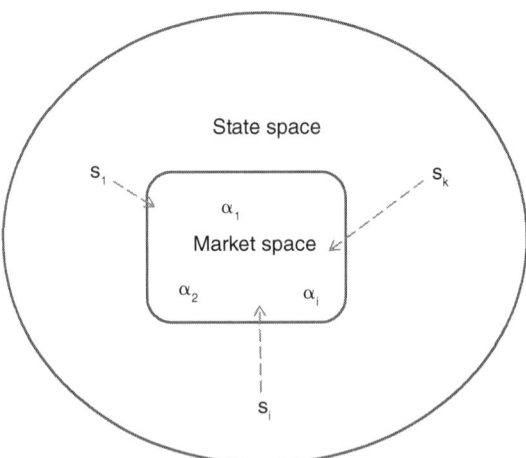

Figure 6.1 State space and the market space.

probability space on a one-dimensional line. This concept has been important in the financial analysis and we discuss in this chapter more the theoretical character of the concept and in Chapter 7 we discuss it vis-à-vis pricing of financial assets and liabilities.

The two first steps, given certain conditions, keep us within the risk world but the third step which is the introduction of so-called *probability ensembles* bring us to the border of uncertainty when we decouple the specific outcomes from the average outcome in the sense that we will have discontinuities in the probability distributions.

The analysis of the state space is important since specific microscopic problems often are such that the most elementary analysis with respect to expected utility will in fact be quite sufficient; when we however perform a macroscopic analysis the complexities of the state space are often more similar to the probability ensemble approach.

The fourth step is the final step into the uncertain region and it concerns von Mises' second problem: the acting human subject. It is obvious that assumptions of human nature and similar is a contradiction in terms when we use the concept subject. However there is no reason for total despair since humans also are social creatures. We will come back to our concept of epistemic cycles in this analysis.

Expected utility and the state space

In basic neoclassical theory the concept of risk has a particular construction with respect to expected utility. In Debreu and Arrow and Hahn we see the economic reality as divided between the endogenous market variables and the exogenous state of the surrounding world. The very definition of *Homo Œconomicus* as an optimizing creature with the preference space as defined by the precise axiomatic structure implies that the human reactions to exogenous events are transformed to rational market behaviour and thus it may affect the reactions towards prices and by that also the distribution of endowments, thus the reality is seen as divided into two spaces: one we may call the market space which consists of individuals defined by Debreu as $(\lesssim_i, e_i)$, the other space is the state space which defines the environment that is exogenous, $S=(s_1, \ldots, s_n)$. The state space affects the market decisions but is not affected by the market decisions. This means that if there is a change in a state variable and we could use Debreu's example rain/no rain, this will affect the price vector and thus also the distribution of endowments. Furthermore it will also affect the aggregate optimum, which is a consequence of the additive aggregation technique. If we think of a sort of temporary equilibrium approach, we are left with a rather ugly perspective of a totally unstable dynamics of the economy; this may however be removed by assumptions on constancy of the state space and reversibility of the market process, given a stable preference structure. The latter assumption serves as an attractor of the same character as the land rent in Smith's analysis.

We then introduce a concept, *expected utility*, $E(U_i)$, such that the welfare of the ith agent depends on the particular outcome of the state space. Since we assume all agents, at the relevant market space, to experience the same state space we can link a particular state s_i to a particular market outcome, a_i. When we look at Figure 6.1 it is important to note that the different states $s_1, \ldots, s_n$ are mutually exclusive with respect to the market space so we must understand a state s_i as a particular disposition of the entire state space. To each of these states we can attach a market action, a_i, providing a certain utility, U_i, and a subjective probability $\mathcal{P}_i$, such that $\sum_i \mathcal{P}_i \to 1$, subsequently a state s_k leads to a market action $a_k \Rightarrow U_k$, and the expected utility $EU_k = \mathcal{P}_k(U_k)$. If we assume the probability distribution to be continuous and the market actions mutually exclusive we will have a unique ranking of expected utilities according to a specific state.

This makes it possible to integrate the state probabilities into the optimization process, thus given a continuous probability distribution over the state space we may elaborate the neoclassical axiomatic structure to hold also for the expected utility.[3] For this to be a feasible solution to the problem there are however still some problems to be dealt with, particularly if we carry on our analysis in a sort of temporary equilibrium approach. Adam Smith actually touched on such an analysis, where price variations converged to relatively stable orbits around a point of attraction, set by the land rent:

> The occasional and temporary fluctuations in the market price of any commodity fall chiefly upon those parts of its price which resolve themselves into wages and profit. That part which resolves itself into rent is less affected by them. A rent certain in money is not in the least affected by them either in its rate or in its value. A rent which consists either in a certain proportion or in a certain quantity of the rude produce; is no doubt affected in its yearly value by all the occasional and temporary fluctuations in the market price by that rude produce; but it is seldom affected by them in its yearly rate.
>
> (1952 [1776]: 25)

Smith's society was a socially ordered society where people may experience uncertainty but this was not to affect the *land rent* which became the anchor of the price system.[4] So from an economic point of view the market process was dependent in the short run by the uncertainties of the physical world but in the long run dependence was rather small, not to say none whatsoever.

That implied that apart from fortunes and misfortunes following the occurrence of mostly natural phenomena there was a constant price norm. Thus the variations due to circumstantial variations could be systematically observed and led to estimations of the probabilities of their occurrence. Furthermore since the social structure was stable the price variations did not change anything substantial in the structure and the price variations did not have any lasting effects, the fundamental economic structure was treated as it was reversible.

The relation between the two spaces is a bit special, thus given a specific dimension of the state space; rain/no rain, computer crash/no computer crash and similar kinds of events will *ceteris paribus* give rise to different market solutions; so if there is a permanent change in the state space this will affect the market space in a permanent way and subsequently change the price vector and the distribution of endowments. However if the change of the state space is temporary and reversible, there will be a temporary effect on the price vectors and the market behaviour. If all agents apprehend the same probability distribution and make the same forecasts there will be no problems but if not all agents perceive the same probability function or make erroneous forecasts depending on misinterpreted signals, we will have a market solution where some agents are better off and some worse off. So entering the decision problem for the next upcoming period we will have a different distribution of endowments. So how do we find a kind of attractor for this kind of problem?

Furthermore to have a kind of convergent temporary equilibrium approach the market solution must also be reversible, the market solutions so to say last for the current period but are of no consequence for the succeeding periods. Thus the very basic condition for the expected utility approach is the assumption of reversibility, and the further assumption of *no false trading*.

Another assumption which must be taken is that the market solutions neither affect the state variables nor their probability distribution. Thus we think of the state space consisting of different dimensions of which we have a certain probability distribution. Whether or not these dimensions are independent of each other is a matter of assumed degree of complexity. With a bold assumption of inertia we may treat them as independent, but save from an incalculable complexity, there is no reason why we should not be able to cope with partial dependence.

A third problem which is more serious, is that if we have a change from A to B in the state space this will affect temporally the distribution of endowments but a reverse change of the state space must then have a reverse effect on the distribution of endowments thus eventual gains and losses are limited to the very period of the changed price vector. This may induce us to think of changed investment patterns as a consequence of the changed distribution but this will play no role for the reversible process, thus there is no connection between two successive periods in the sense that the changes in distribution will "spill over" to the following periods.

We remember from our discussion of the temporary equilibrium theory that the fundamental question was: which conditions were necessary if we should have a converging process?

First we must point out that this is a different problem compared with Smith's which concerned only the price stability; here we also care about the distribution of endowments where Smith just kept the land rent given.

The key to this is the assumption of the constancy of the state space of which the agents may learn, but the learning has to be related to the effects on the market space; thus given the set of states $S = \{s_1, \ldots, s_n\}$ and a probability $\mathcal{P}_i(s_i)$ such that $\sum_i \mathcal{P}_i \to 1$, and furthermore that $\mathcal{P}_i(s_i) \Rightarrow a_i$, where a_i is the market solution caused by the particular state s_i, will be a necessary condition for a learning process.

Obviously we here have the problem of false trading and in temporary equilibrium theory it raises the problem of bankruptcy, which Green (1973) suggested a solution to, in that the variance of the agents' beliefs must not be big, and we furthermore add an assumption that the agents are erroneous in their expectations in a random way, then there ought to be a good chance that we will have a convergent process over time. But we have an extremely strong assumption under this and that is that not only the state space is reversible but also the market solutions. This is why bankruptcy is such a problem to deal with and Maurice Allais gives an implicit answer to this problem when presenting his famous paradox, which implies that we must add risk aversion (Allais 1953).

As we mentioned above we still follow the tradition from Smith to impute an anchor in the market analysis. In the neoclassical theory the price stability is created by the constancy of distribution which is the norm. So, if we assume all agents to know the probability distribution over the state space, which is constant, and act according to the expected utility we will have convergence to an equilibrium trajectory, within a limited variance, provided that we rule out behaviour which increases the risk for bankruptcy; this is provided for with the assumption of risk aversion, that is, given two alternatives with the same mean the agent chooses the one with the smallest variance.

The latter condition is obviously an answer to Allais' paradox, and implies that we regard the choice as two-dimensional, but we rule out one line of action by an assumption. Whether this is relevant with respect to choices in reality is a different matter which is outside our scope to discuss.

In the basic approach all agents are aware of the space of outcomes for the state space as well as the subjective probability distributions, which also are the objective ones.[5]

A natural development is therefore when the agents agree about the space of outcome but disagree on the subjective probability distribution. We may then ask if the market outcome can converge to some common view about the relevant state space.

A first condition is of course that the space of outcomes is constant and further that the "objective" probability distribution also is constant. In such a dynamic process the market price vectors will serve as a signal system both with respect to current consumption and to arrangements concerning the future. We don't need to bother about whether we have states of general or temporal equilibrium, but there are equilibrating processes going on at the market in terms of equimarginal processes. Given this the market actions are performed with respect to the agents' economic resource structures as well as the information structure. We thus leave Debreu's notation (1982) of an agent $(\lesssim_i, e_i)$ for Radner's (1982) $(\lesssim_i, e_i, \gamma_i)$ where γ_i is an information vector. We disregard the fact that in a dynamic analysis we ought to specify the commodities both with respect to time and space since we just discuss the matter loosely. Furthermore Radner shows that with a setting like his there does not exist rational expectation equilibrium for more than the first period if the information vectors are different, but we still might discuss equilibrating processes by learning and general information of different kinds. That means if we look at a sequence of states of temporary equilibrium, we will have different distributions in different states of temporary equilibrium due to differences in information, but given that we may assume that those who lose will change their behaviour. It is not unreasonable that in a longer run there will be a converging process with respect to a common view of the subjective probability distribution. Such a converging process will of course be dependent on the speed of information and the homogeneity of the market but it will also be dependent on the misinterpretations about majority positions as in Keynes' "beauty contest". This is also actually the implications of Radner's analysis when he analyses his definition of agents in a rational expectation perspective. The reason is that the obtained temporary equilibrium is to be seen as false trading. That means that the efficiency of the learning process is dependent on information outside the market information. This is of course implicated in Radner's formulation but it is important to stress its importance.

The temporary equilibrium approach imputes the possibility of asymmetric information of the state space and Roy Radner modifies Debreu's definition, thus the resulting equilibrium is dependent not only of preferences and initial physical endowments but also of information/knowledge. Such a modification will of course make expectations problematic and an approach like *rational expectation* will have little value in a dynamic process. However this can be remedied with what we earlier said about the market prices as an information system. In the temporary equilibrium theory the agents are allowed to have erroneous information which affects the market solution in the subsequent period but the market result triggers revisions in expectations and judgements of the available information. Thus we can have a process where the erroneous information affects the distribution but since the state space is held constant we will converge to a stable equilibrium trajectory in the long run. Central however is the fact that the market actors are fairly in agreement with each other about the subjective probability distribution as Green pointed out.

Expected utility and Allais' paradox

Expected utility in its original form is composed of three characteristics: a particular event in the state space, a probability distribution and utility values related to the different events in the state space. This means that when we perform a binary comparison of two alternatives we are affected both by the utility value as such but also by the character of the probability distribution. In modern financial analysis the expected value is certainly important but the variance is equally important, distributions with *fat tails* are indeed to be analysed differently from those with *thin tails*. When we are analysing exogenous/natural phenomena there is usually not a strong call for going further in the analysis than mean and variance, but when the analysis involves agents' behaviour we need higher moments.

The utility values relative the different events are ordered such that $\alpha_1 \le \alpha_2$. Consequently we may have a complete ordering for a certain probability distribution of the expected utilities $P_i^n(\alpha_i)$, but the agent must pay attention also to the character of the distribution so in fact we have a two-dimensional optimization problem.

This problem was analysed by Maurice Allais in his so-called Allais' paradox. It is really not a paradox except with respect to an oversimplified picture of the concept of expected utility. Allais' main purpose was to show that the correlate of independence of irrelevant alternatives does not hold with respect to the expected utility hypothesis. Thus an introduction of a third alternative may alter a binary comparison.

Allais' paradox (whether or not it is a paradox), is interesting since it takes its fundamental stance in differences in the degree of disorder, or what a physicist should call differences in entropy, which affects the choice.[6] Allais' result implicitly shows that in maximizing expected utility the rational agents must consider the degree of uncertainty understood as the degree of dispersion in the distribution, in conjunction with the value of the outcome. As long as we just consider single probability values Allais' result may seem a bit paradoxical but realizing that the introduction of a new alternative changes the space of outcome and thus the probability distribution, there is nothing paradoxical in the result.

Let us take a small example to establish the role of entropy which is a more general concept than variance and thus has a wider use.

Let us assume that we have a varying alternative X and some alternatives with certain outcomes A, B and C.

Let us look at two cases, in Figure 6.1. The entropy of the two distributions is calculated from the formula:

$$H(X) = -\sum_{X} p(X) \cdot \ln[p(X)] \tag{E.6.2}$$

where X is the respective outcomes and p the probability of the specific outcome. In case 1 for probability distribution 1 the entropy H_1^1 is 0.611 and for probability distribution 2 the entropy H_2^1 is 0.816, corresponding for case 2 is $H_1^2 = 0.325$ and $H_2^2 = 0.546$. Thus we observe that the degree of disorder in general is higher for case 1 than for case 2, due to the higher probability of the then unknown alternative X. Thus although X is unknown there is a high probability that it will appear.

Table 6.1 Outcomes and probabilities in Cases 1 and 2

Outcome	Probable distribution 1		Probable distribution 2	
Case	1		2	
X	0.7	0.64	0.9	0.84
A	0.3	0	0.1	0
B	0	0.3	0	0.1
C	0	0.06	0	0.06

Notes
We set A=100, B=250 and C=20.

Table 6.2 Expected utilities

Case 1			Case 2		
X	$E_1(U)$	$E_2(U)$	X	$E_1(U)$	$E_2(U)$
700	520	524	200	190	194
750	555<	556	250	235<	236
800	590>	588	300	280>	278

We can see here that in the marked interval we will have a switch in order, exact calculations give us 770 for Case 1, and for Case 2 the switch takes place at a lower value of *X*, 270.

The argument for the switch is of course the increasing value of the variable factor *X*. Furthermore in Case 2 the general weight of the variable factor is more pronounced than for Case 1; this is also clear from the differences in entropy between the distributions and the cases. The general certainty of the importance of the variable factor is considerably higher in Case 2; thus expectations on its value will have a higher significance. Hence we have not only to consider the distribution per se but also the degree of entropy of different distributions.

Since at least the 1960s these considerations are not particularly sensational when there has been a common knowledge that the expected value has to be completed with some value of risk measuring the relative degree of volatility, which is as a measure similar to entropy.

So when we discuss expected utility we in fact deal with a two-dimensional problem, the relative uncertainty and the expected value of outcomes. The practical theoretical solution to get a unique optimum is to assume risk aversion, but this assumption is probably only relevant when we analyse strictly exogenous events. When dealing with events where we have interactions of agents' behaviour it is even hard to see the meaning of the very concept risk aversion.

With respect to financial matters the neoclassical approach has led to a picture of risk in relation to asset portfolios is divided between the systemic risk which relates to all events outside the market space and is independent of the unsystemic risk, where the latter is manageable by diversification.

The complex state space – the copula

However we have so far discussed only one probability distribution for the entire state space, which seems to be a bit curious. We may look at the state space as consisting of classes or dimensions of events, where we may attach different probability distributions or the different dimensions. This actually introduces a vastly more complex problem into the analysis. The different distributions may represent different dimensions of events which all affect the expected utility, but in different ways. An example is buying a house which is affected by the developments of interest rates, transportation costs, transportation facilities, local housing market and so on. We may attach a univariate probability distribution to each of the dimensions but the joint result of the analysis is quite complex. This leads us to a multidimensional analysis, which might be possible to handle on the individual level where still the choice problems are relatively simple, but it is certainly more complex at the macroscopic level, where the problem of *joint probabilities* are more frequent.

Historical time in Samuelson's meaning leads to some very interesting conclusions about the probabilities of the state space, which concerns the learning process of the agents.[7] Implicit in Samuelson's discussion is that as time passes by, new events occur which change the conditions for decision making. A logical time model, similar to a Solowian growth model is in principle reversible and also invertible, while the historical time model is not necessarily reversible (depending on which assumptions are taken), and that makes us wonder about the character of the state space. Obviously to be a meaningful contribution it must somehow mean that the new state has a different character from the earlier one introduced. The way we treated the state space above was similar to order the states along a one-dimensional line and attached some kind of probability distribution. Such a representation of the problem seems to be a bit over-simplified; when I want to take a walk and choose what clothes to wear, I might consider three dimensions – wind, precipitation and temperature. These dimensions are sometimes connected but sometimes not. For each state space we have a joint probability composed of three dimensions which are partly nested and partly independent.

This example indicates that a state S_i is probably a vector of outcomes of different dimensions so if we look at a time sequence we can describe it as in Figure 6.2.

If we systematize this problem as in Figure 6.2 we look at a particular state S_i in state space as depending on simultaneous occurrence of events in different dimensions. The different columns represent dimensions such as rain, wind, computer breakdowns, political crises, nuclear accidents or whatever we may consider important dimensions in a certain moment. The rows indicate the events with respect to these different dimensions; thus for some dimensions we may think of dichotomous events and for some, like air humidity an almost continuous distribution.

Three slices of time are indicated and with respect to this we may postulate that the probability matrix always is the same; this is in fact what is done in the temporary equilibrium theory and technically this means that all events are reversible so when we come to the end of a time slice somebody tidies up the disorder and puts things as they have been. Obviously we may take another view, namely that some events are irreversible and some seem to be almost reversible; in this case the state space will change over time and thus also the probability distributions.

For each dimension, $j=1 \ldots \varphi$ of the space S there exists a set of states E^j_i, $i=1 \ldots i$ such that:

$$\sum_i P(E^j_i) \to 1$$

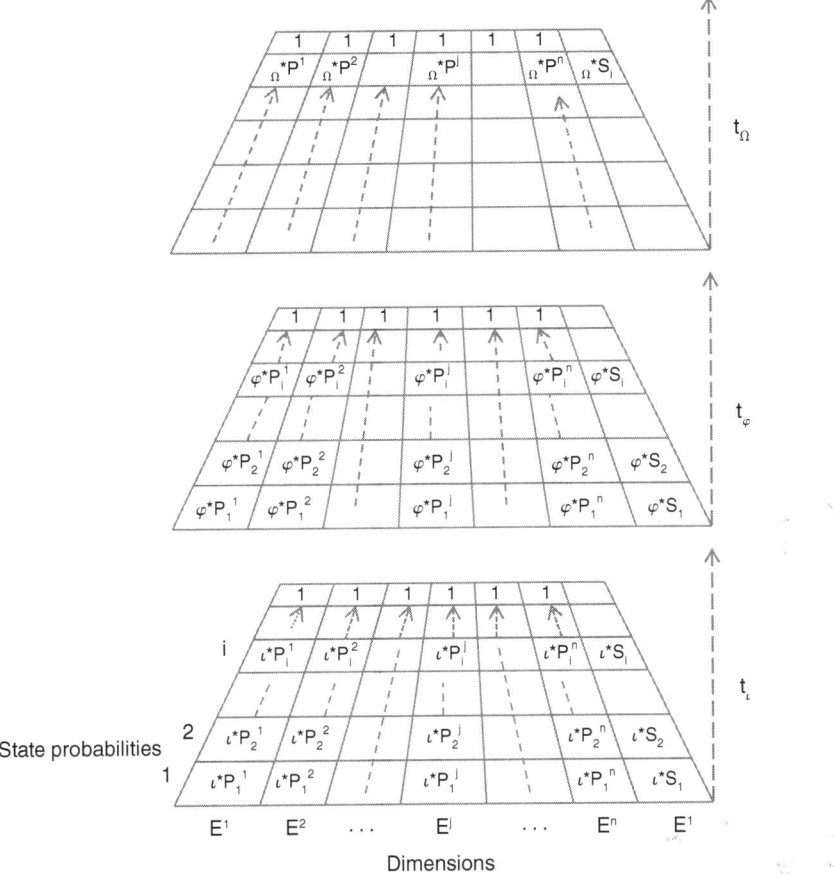

Figure 6.2 A representation in time of a multidimensional state space.

Furthermore a state S_i is some kind of function of the events of the respective dimensions, subsequently we may write:

$$S_i = F_i\{_\tau P_i^j (E^j)\} \tag{E.6.3}$$

We may think of the different dimensions $E^1 \ldots E^n$ that the probability distributions are independent, semi-dependent or dependent and whether this changes between the time slices.

In Figure 6.2 we have indicated the time slice Ω which denotes that we may make some statement about an average expected state $_\Omega{*}P^j$ ($j-1 \ldots n$) for each dimension. This "on the average" expected state that we call $_\Omega S^j$ is thus a state which is a sort of default state or whatever we may call it. Anyway the

Table 6.3 Corn prices

Weather	Oil prices		
	High – 0.4	*Medium – 0.4*	*Low – 0.2*
Sun – 0.3	0.12	0.12	0.06
Medium – 0.5	0.2	0.2	0.1
Rain – 0.2	0.08	0.08	0.04

fundamental problem is whether or not the average states at Ω really work as an average as in traditional probabilistic approaches. Let us take a small example of corn price. Two important variables for corn prices are the weather and oil prices, the latter affect the price of fertilizers. We simplify the problem as in Table 6.3.

We may now assume that weather is a bit more important for corn prices than oil prices so we have the ranking of prices, from low to high according to the following;

$$P^c_{SL} < P^c_{SM} < P^c_{ML} < P^c_{SH} < P^c_{MM} < P^c_{MH} < P^c_{RL} < P^c_{RM} < P^c_{RH} \qquad (E.6.4)$$

This ranking is in fact the function we denoted in E.6.3. In Figure 6.3 we illustrate the probability distribution over the given ranking.

From a practical point of view our mode of reasoning is relevant for many problems and from a technical point of view we apply a ranking function on the joint probabilities and if we elaborate the distributions to be continuous we may still use the ranking function, in an elaborated form.

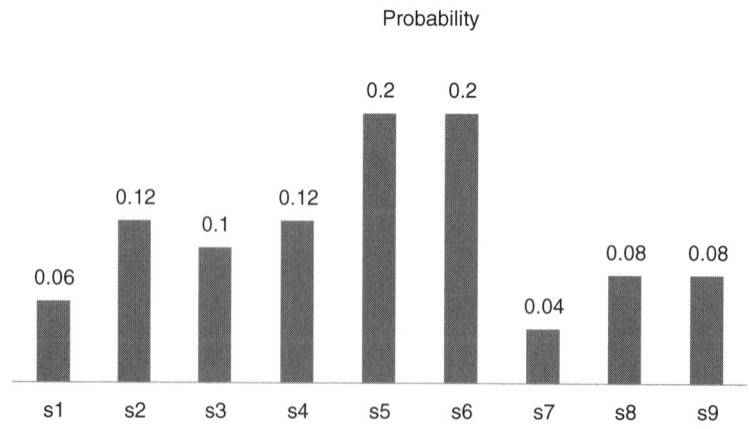

Figure 6.3 Probability distribution of different corn prices ranked from low to high.

Let us look at the expected prices of corn in Table 6.4.

We may ask if mean and variance is related to the Ω-distribution in Figure 6.2 but since we discuss a joint distribution means and variances at each time slice have little or nothing to do with the Ω-distribution and furthermore that the price information does not contain any consistent information since we cannot escape Allais' objection and we are obliged to apply a function, $\mu^2 \frown \mu$, at the variances, which might be rather tricky. Thus this relatively simple case of joint probabilities shows that a learning process using prices is indeed difficult not to say impossible: the agents should need a complete description of the multivariate problem. But given such knowledge Figure 6.3 and Table 6.4 are possible to obtain.

Figure 6.2 interpreted as in the above example is a variant of the *Copula*, which is extensively used within the financial industry to express the problem of joint probabilities.

The copula

In principle the *copula* is just an extension of conditional expectation, like:

$$P(A \mid B) = (P(A) \cdot P((B \mid A)))/(P(A)) \tag{E.6.5}$$

which may also, with respect to each dimension, be developed along the Bayesian principles. The fundamental problem is that the state space may be spanned by several dimensions which all are relevant with respect to a certain choice.

The problem with much of theoretical literature, also in fact with Debreu's text, is that when analysing expectations most examples are taken as the state space is thought of as single-dimensional events as rain/no rain. Thus if we think about the state space as a whole in Figure 6.2 and let it be spanned by n-dimensions such that we have n different probability distributions but these different events are nested with respect to the market actions the probability of a

Table 6.4 Expected prices

	Price	Probability	E(P)
s1	100	0.06	6
s2	120	0.12	14.4
s3	140	0.1	14
s4	160	0.12	19.2
s5	180	0.2	36
s6	200	0.2	40
s7	220	0.04	8.8
s8	240	0.08	19.2
s9	260	0.08	20.8

Notes
Mean E(P)=19.8, Var E(P)=17.6.

certain configuration of the state space is extremely complex. The example above concerning the expected price of corn is extremely simple in its basic setting but contained rather complex operations to receive the desired Table 6.4. Working with three dimensions increases the complexity of the problem substantially particularly with respect to the function connecting the outcomes to the goal variable, as in our case the corn price.

If we however assume continuous distributions we can define a *copula*, which presuppose inert structures, but may still be useful provided well-specified problems. We will discuss it more in detail in the next chapter on the pricing of financial assets and liabilities.

A copula, according to Sklar's theorem (1973), is a function H and describes the joint multivariate distribution formed by independent univariate distributions. In the two-dimensional case we assign the two univariate distribution functions G^1 and G^2 and then we have the copula $C: I^2 \frown I$ such that:

$$H(x, y) = C[G^1(x), G^2(y)]^8 \tag{E.6.6}$$

Given that $G^1(x)$ and $G^2(y)$ are both continuous $H(x, y)$ will be unique. Furthermore the copula obeys the same conditions as the individual distribution functions.

So as we demonstrated in our example of corn prices we have transformed a multidimensional distribution problem to a univariate distribution. Obviously we might expand the copula to be of higher dimensions but the needed power of calculations increases dramatically so there is some need for simplifying assumptions, which affects the reliability negatively. We may thus think of the state space as an *n*-dimensional copula:

$$H(x^1, \ldots, x^n) = C[G^1(x^1), \ldots, G^n(x^n)] \tag{E.6.7}$$

Linking the copula to Figure 6.2 we realize that we in fact have transformed the different dimensions to a single univariate distribution function over the states S_i and we are back to our first approach to expected utility.

However we have the problem of learning if some agents' knowledge of the space of outcome is insufficient. This learning problem includes now three elements: the mean values, the variances and the function $f^n \frown f$ and as we saw with respect to corn prices the information load with respect to prices and price variation is low, and increasing dimensionality it approaches zero.

Our discussion with respect to Figure 6.2 and Table 6.3 concerns real exchange problems and we have avoided financial pricing and risk analysis. However we ought to say some words about the difference. Risk problems in a barter economy are normally rather easy to identify. The ultimate purpose is exchanging commodities among the agents and the pricing of these commodities are depending on factors affecting production and distribution costs, as we indicated in the small example of corn prices. Pricing a financial asset is a completely different thing since it is integrated both in the microscopic and macroscopic levels and these two levels affect each other in a pretty complex way. We will discuss this in the next chapter but it is important to keep it in mind in our proceeding discussion on risk and uncertainty.

The principle of copula has received a somewhat tarnished reputation due to the financial ventures leading to the bank crash in 2008, but it is difficult to see why a perfectly legitimate mathematical method should be blamed due to misinterpretation and misuse.[9]

Used with care and in problems where we have good information about the market causality it is possible to express the matrix of Figure 6.2 as a copula. So we have in fact developed the classical formulations of the state space in a more complex way and we claim that it is a legitimate way of analysis, particularly in real exchange settings. Thus given the state space in its more complex form it is still possible to imagine a learning process like in temporary equilibrium theory such that the economy converges to a long-run equilibrium trajectory.

Consequently it is important to realize that as long as we look at the barter where money just plays a passive role as a medium of exchange we can in fact handle quite complex problems with modern statistical methods. It is apparent that our knowledge of the state space may fail but that is a different problem and also we may realize that the state space is not independent of the development in the market space but that leads us to reconsider the whole problem and the formulation of the state space.

Uncertainty of the agents' actions

Our discussion so far has concerned the barter economy and the state space, which is the exogenous structure affecting the market outcome without being affected and furthermore we interpret the barter economy in traditional neoclassical terms. We have seen that in our analysis of the state space it is rather difficult to claim uncertainty of the future in any systematic way. Even in rather complex formulations as in Figure 6.2 and the subsequent discussion uncertainty appears in the form of insufficient knowledge about the state space but it is difficult to claim that this uncertainty is an inherent quality but more something which could be eliminated by learning over time and experience. It will affect the market outcome in the form of variations in the distribution of endowments but we may on good grounds hope that these variations converge to an interval around a long-run equilibrium trajectory.

So a first step in introducing uncertainty as an inherent quality in the market economy is to scrutinize the pure barter economy as it appears in the neoclassical theory with respect to its presuppositions in relation to uncertainty and we then find that according to the analysis in Chapter 3 the two basic conditions which grant freedom from uncertainty are axiom of reflexivity and additive aggregation, which are both rejected.

As we saw from the analysis in Chapter 2 the neoclassical axiomatic structure is not a prerequisite for praxeology but works more as a norm for human decision making. The six basic axioms grant the existence of general equilibrium but that is something else. Our basic criticism of the six axioms concerned the axiom of reflexivity which implied that a function of a commodity is identical to its physical appearance. When we reject that, a commodity can very well become a multidimensional complex with respect to its functions. That is actually a necessary and a sufficient condition to imply that consumption of a certain commodity can contradict itself. That is, two consumers' different use of a certain commodity can be contradictive. This is what we have when we induce negative external effects but in fact it is a basic feature for most commodities and thus the utility aspect of a commodity is defined over both the negative and the positive utility space. That also implies that the praxeological decision making regards the commodity choice as a part of a wider purpose, hence the commodities become a mean to achieve a purpose not the purpose in itself; this is also in line with modern consumer theory.

The praxeological effect of these modifications is that the very commodity choice is related to the (unknown) purpose of the consumer, given an apprehended context, an epistemic cycle. Thus the stability of the behaviour of the agent is due to the stability of the apprehended epistemic cycles. Some cycles, like the planning of a party is of a dissipative character but some cycles, concerning such as for instance job, housing, transports and similar factors that can be of a very inert character but if they break down the instability may be affecting many aspects of life and even other agents in the environment.

The fundamental thing is that the stability of the economy is not emanating out of a certain equilibrium but from socioeconomic factors and the social development.

Our analysis in Chapter 2 concerning the praxeological character of the agents' decision making is as a matter of fact rather close to von Mises.

If we go back to our analysis of the state space many analysts are apt to let in the nature but also the behaviour of social and political structures and institutions. This however makes the state space as a dubious concept dubious. We earlier quoted from von Mises on the two sources of uncertainty: insufficiently known natural phenomena and human actions. The state space with regard to natural phenomena leads us in principle to assume an objective probability over the state space save for insufficient knowledge.[10] But following von Mises' line of reasoning social and political structures and institutions definitely belong to the realm of human actions and have to be lumped together with market actions. Thus human actions belonging to what we normally look at as the social and political sphere are eventually affecting the market as much as actions more traditionally thought of as market actions.

Thus we have a nature with a state space which in principle can be attached with an objective probability distribution along the lines of the copula and furthermore we have a seemingly complete mess of interacting social, economic and political relations dependent on human subjects.[11] Von Mises' solution to this rather complex problem seems to stem from his rationalist ideas, when he classifies probabilities:[12]

There are two entirely different instances of probability; we may call them class probability (or frequency probability) and case probability (or the specific understanding of the sciences of human action). The field for the application of the former is the field of the natural sciences, entirely ruled by causality; the field for the application of the latter is the field of the sciences of human action, entirely ruled by teleology.

(op. cit.: 107)

However in spite of his rationalist approach, von Mises' tribute to individualism prevents him from ending up in determinism and the following quote is interesting with respect to his alleged rationalism:

In the real world acting man is faced with the fact that there are fellow men acting on their own behalf as he himself acts. The necessity to adjust to his actions to other people's actions makes him a speculator for whom success and failure depend on his greater or lesser ability to understand the future. Every action is speculation. There is in the course of human events no stability and consequently no safety.

(op. cit.: 113)

Von Mises' distinction between class probability and case probability the difference between them an alleged objective frequency probability interpretation and the case probability is similar to what Keynes call "degree of rational belief" (1962 [1921]: 10), that is something like saying that due to the polls during the last months I believe the social-democratic party will form the government after the next election.

Thus the judgements concerning the future with respect to individual/social behaviour is based upon both an understanding of what is rational but also on certain perceptions of social inertia. To our understanding von Mises applies an attitude to rationality which is similar to that we express by introducing epistemic cycles.

Von Mises has a rather conventional apprehension of the monetary element of the market economy, but according to the quote above he arrives at a conclusion that the market economy as a barter economy per se is unstable due to uncertainty of the future and this result is in line with our analysis in Chapter 2.

The second pillar of inherent uncertainty in the barter economy is strictly speaking a consequence of our rejection of general equilibrium, particularly the rejection of the axiom of reflexivity as generally holding. It is the rejection of additive aggregation, which also follows from Arrow's paradox.

Our analysis in Chapter 2 showed that the aggregate levels were independently created from the underlying microscopic levels. Thus the microscopic and the macroscopic levels affect each other but they are partly independent of each other. We derived the mereological rule of thumb vis-à-vis the relation between macroscopic organizations and its contained microscopic subsystems. That means that the optimal decision of an organization on an aggregate level is to a great extent independent from the optimum decisions of its contained subsystems. The effect is that the single agents are not only affecting each other but they are part of independently working macroscopic epistemic cycles. We have earlier given examples of such macroscopic epistemic cycles and causes for changes. We have recently seen how financial distress in macroscopic bodies has caused severe changes in the conditions of living for individuals. The individuals affect those aggregate bodies but from the individual point of view the effects are very unclear and the uncertainty of individual actions becomes very high.[13]

Thus in our praxeological methodology we presuppose methodological individualism as in traditional neoclassical theory but we also comprehend the individual as a social creature.

Causality and time

Humans are subjects and thus ultimate causes. In nature we have intricate causal structures but no ultimate cause except an eventual creator. It is obvious that for a radical determinist humans are to be enrolled along the same principle. But at least with respect to humans themselves the human being fails to be analysed in the same manner as the surrounding nature and applying radical determinism on intra-human affairs is probably a bit dangerous, and from a logical point a view we relatively soon approach Gödel's paradox. So, from a practical point of view we regard humans as ultimate causes, which means, humans can start a causal chain without any detectable reason, if it is not told by the acting agent. From the point of view of the single agent there is a purpose, a context, appropriate means which together lead to an act which should ideally lead to some end, that is the *ex ante* causality. However this *ex ante* causality will be just one among many interfering causal chains and some even contradictory ones at the same time. In situations where the decisions and actions are almost simultaneous, like when buying a loaf of bread the causal structure is trivial, but accepting a new job in London when currently living in Sweden implies normally a rather complex set of decisions and actions of which some lie in the future. Accepting such a job often implies a complete change of life which might lead to unexpected consequences. Thus although the human can be regarded as an ultimate cause it is in a limited way. Decisions by fellow agents and aggregate levels may enforce reconsiderations before the expected causal chain has borne some fruits or is simply obsolete.

Decisions, actions and achievements of the ends take time but that is not a matter of calendar or clock time but of interfering causal structures. In Ekstedt and Fusari (2010) the authors discuss the time concepts and arrive (in chapter 4) at social space–time composed by the standard physical apprehension of time as relative changes and ongoing causal structures. That means in its extreme interpretation that each individual starting a causal chain creates a new time concept.

From a strictly logical point of view this means that the social (or economic) space–time is not continuous. Observe that this is different also from Samuelson's historical time:

$$x = g[t; t^0; x(t^0)] \qquad\qquad\qquad (E.6.8)$$

Events at time t_i may alter the parameters but does not per se imply a discontinuous change of the function.

Instead it will affect our approach to time. Dynamic decision analysis is often performed as a decision tree.

A decision tree analysis is much the same as a chess player has to perform in each move, but still it is possible to make an estimation of the optimal draw, that is why computers always will beat man if they have a sufficient capacity. The decision tree analysis is based on a continuous space–time and thus it is possible to calculate it with relatively simple methods, although the used algorithms are terrifying.

As an alternative to the decision tree we may use Figure 6.5, taken from Ekstedt and Fusari (2010: 122) which is a simplification, as well as a different interpretation, of Reichenbach (1991 [1956]: 41).

In Figure 6.5 we can only order these events in these quadrants through which the "time axis" runs, while events and processes in the two quadrants on the respective sides cannot be time ordered. Thus a_1 has happened before a_2 and c_1 is expected to happen before c_2. Events b_1 and b_2 however if they are at all imagined cannot be time ordered, consequently we cannot say whether b_2 has happened before a_1 or is expected to happen after c_2. In the unordered areas we are unable to define simultaneity but after we have been informed about its occurrence. This implies that new information about historical events, although old, may affect the expected causality of taken decision; concerning some type of information we can talk about skeletons in the closet, it is however more than that. During the beginning of the 2000s American consumers were seen as the growth motor of the world. The increase in the demand triggered investments, which were rational from an economic perspective given that the systemic risk was assumed to be constant. The changed behaviour of the banks however had occurred already at the end of the 1990s and implied successively increasing credit default risks, true that some individual economists understood it, but the general sentiment was such that such an understanding was regarded

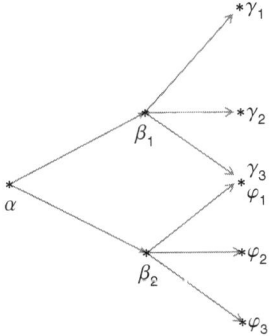

Figure 6.4 Decision tree.

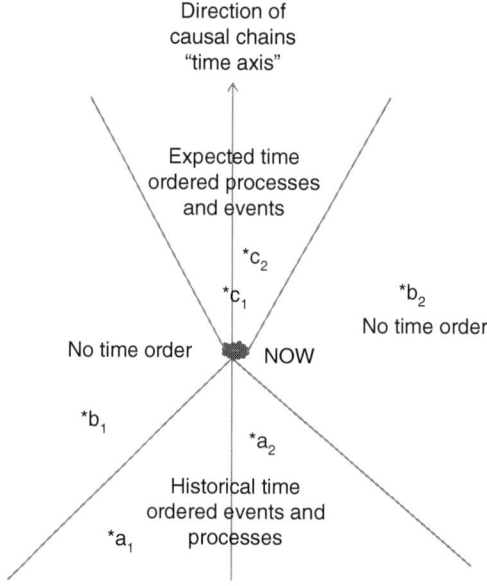

Figure 6.5 Simultaneity and evolution.

as unimportant. Thus b_2 may have occurred before a_1 but its causal effects may occur between NOW and c_1, thus completely changing the epistemic cycles for the agents.

If we compare Figures 6.4 and 6.5 we can interpret them in many ways of which some interpretations imply that there is no substantial difference in the message. However the decision tree in Figure 6.4 implies a constant epistemic cycle for the successive choices. Thus we may arrive to γ_3 and φ_1 via different routes which mean that the probabilities, per *ex ante*, are seen as independent and constant as well as the causal chains are. In Figure 6.5 the NOW is built by epistemic cycles created by the agents' different apprehension of the historical quadrant. An action/event is subsequently irreversible in the sense that it affects the structure of the epistemic cycle and thus the praxeological structure. If we relate to the decision tree the interaction between physical, socioeconomic and political structure implies that the successive steps in the decision tree will undergo changes such that an *ex post* correct decision tree presupposes perfect knowledge about the total number of epistemic cycles involved, even at higher aggregate levels.

However, the fundamental difference is that the decision tree analysis concerns discrete configurations of the state space, while we in Figure 6.5 illustrate a nested process of state space events and reactions on certain actions. This also means that an economic decision generally contains a mixture of more objective probabilities and the Keynesian expression "degree of rational belief", the latter referring to our estimation of other agents' action/reaction patterns as well as eventual aggregate effects. Consequently the *ex ante* considerations of a reality illustrated as in Figure 6.5 can never be caught by a copula approach, as in Figure 6.2. We cannot mix probability distributions with subjective degrees of rational beliefs or confidence even if we may put figures to the latter.

The real and the monetary economy

The Dominican brothers in Salamanca convinced by an ingenious analysis of St Thomas' writings that it was possible for a Christian to earn his living on money exchange, but they were well aware of the logical differences between ordinary trade and money exchange. When dealing with the two types of trade from the perspective actualized by Figure 6.5 and being implicit in Arrow's paradox, namely that the outcome of a decision to a high degree depends on actions and reactions of other agents it appears that there is a difference between profiting from real exchange and money exchange. When it comes to real exchange you are dependent on your fellow agents' judgement of your commodity in relation to their respective preferences, which you may affect with commercials and persuasion, and you can try to adapt to what you believe the preference structure to be, but you have to sell your product and its specific particulars and if the trends and technology change you might fail. When we however think of trade in the financial market we are utterly dependent to regard our fellow agents' behaviour and adapt to that. In poker the rule for winning is very simple; you bet hard when your cards are better than your co-players and when your cards are worse you do not bet. The tricky thing lies in persuading your fellows to think that they have better cards than you when they don't. In financial business you earn most money when you buy cheap and sell expensive, but that is also the tricky thing and makes you end up in Keynes' beauty contest.

Thus when analysing the real trade you have to consider whether your product induces a sufficient utility for your fellow agents so they proceed buying your commodity. For financial assets it is only its expected price which matters and that depends solely on the expectations of the fellow agents.

This means that for buying an ordinary commodity our presumption of methodological individualism holds given the modifications we have suggested. Furthermore the praxeological behaviour is fairly simple since the definition of the utility value of a certain commodity is basically an internal process. For the financial business the methodological individualism is indeed doubtful since money possesses three dimensions; medium of exchange, liquidity and valuation of future assets, which are partly at variance with each other. This also implies that the praxeological approach more or less breaks down.

We will come back to the monetary matters in the next chapter.

Three levels of uncertainty in decision making

We have so far discussed uncertainty with respect to decision making and we may make some summing up before proceeding.

Level 1. The first level of uncertainty stems from insufficient estimation of the dimensionality of the state space and the distributions, which affect the actions in the form of false trading. Hopefully this sort of uncertainty can be reduced by learning.

Level 2. A second level of uncertainty is indicated by Allais' paradox. A precise probability represents a certain risk but the character of the distribution also adds a degree of uncertainty with respect to its entropy or volatility. Thus the risk concept is two-dimensional which theoretically implies that there will be no unique price vector to a defined expected utility. We may arrange the uniqueness by assuming risk avert agents but that is a further assumption.

Level 3. A more complex form of uncertainty emanates from Arrow's paradox, which on one hand implies that agents affect each other and on the other hand that the aggregation is not an additive function and thus the aggregate levels are partly independent of the microscopic levels. That means that we must add to the problems concerning the state space judgements of fellow agents' behaviour as well as behaviour of aggregate organizations and aggregate consequences of microscopic behaviour. That means a sort of mixture between objective distributions and degrees of rational beliefs and confidence in their own judgements concerning behaviour of other agents. In a barter given appropriate inertia it will probably be possible to make reasonably good forecasts since the market only concerns commodities which are demanded for their own sake. When we however go from Figure 4.1 to 4.2 and introduce the monetary system in its complexity we will demand assets which have no value in themselves other than liquidity and an expected future price and if the information spread then increases by electronic technology the space for a praxeological attitude shrinks considerably.

Thus for financial business we end up in Keynes' beauty contest and which, as we have touched on, partly has already been institutionalized in the form of mathematical methods.

7 Inter-temporal valuation, expectations and stability

Introduction

Hume's discussion on money is interesting since he attaches other characteristics to the monetary economy than to the barter economy, thus while looking at an barter economy as more or less only concerning individual relations, the monetary economy becomes a social process. He looks at the monetary economy as a diffusion process which due to neutrality of money with respect to commodities creates new alternatives for the consumer thus increasing the dimensionality of the commodity space both for the individual as well as the society, and thus induces an economic dynamics separate from that of the barter economy.

Economic exchange is good per se but it becomes too narrow both from a social and geographical point of view and has little social long-term impact. But the monetary dynamics allow for future ventures to a much greater extent and inventions and innovations become a highly important feature in the monetary economy compared with the barter economy.

It is indeed interesting when Hume advocates a yearly increase (2 per cent) of the monetary base in order to stimulate market supply and innovations which will affect the socioeconomic and cultural transformation of the society.

Hume looks at the monetary economy as a diffusion system, which is in line with Jean Baptiste Say whose "law" emanates from such an approach on money. The particularly useful characteristic which money possesses is the neutrality vis-à-vis the different commodities, thus the consumption of an income is independent of the earning of the income. This is in fact also a basis for uncertainty which business suffers from, and it is the foundation for the so-called *paradox of thrift*, which tells us that financial saving has no certain address, either in the form of investment or in time. Obviously people cannot save all their income so an increase in saving is of temporal importance with respect to aggregate demand, which may be interpreted as a shift from current demand to future demand and as such requires adequate means of production in the future; this is the neoclassical interpretation which may be illustrated as in Figure 7.1, where an investment increases the growth of the consumption although we must sacrifice area A_1 to have A_2 in the future.

Consumption level

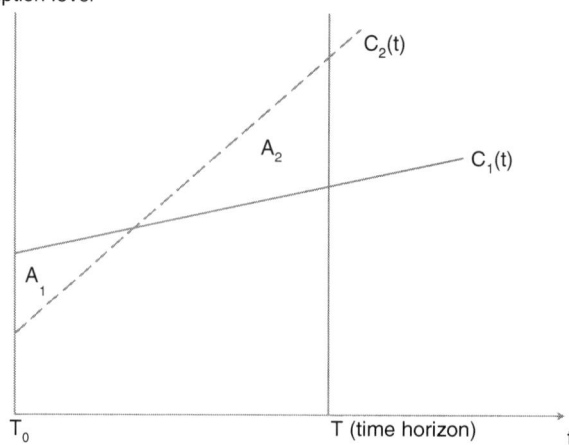

Figure 7.1 Saving, investments and growth.

Note
Eventual nominal difference between the areas denotes the expected real internal rate of return.

If we however look at such household saving from the point of view of the manufacturers like Volvo for instance, we miss an address of the saving. A family's increased saving might be aimed at financing a new Volvo car, but since the saving is in mostly financial assets the family may decide later that the Volvo might be vanquished by a trip for the family to Tahiti in Polynesia. Thus the information which is spread around by an aggregate increase in savings is that people consume less, but on the aggregate level we know quite well, and so do probably also the consumers, that the aggregate demand will in due time return to old levels, but the really tricky thing is that the agents on the microscopic level do not know if the diminished demand for *their products* will recover or if the consumers of their products will change their consumption patterns. Furthermore we know quite well from empirical studies that structural changes often take place in recessions which are prolonged for some companies which have had problems earlier. So when an economy rises from a recession its production and business structure has sometimes gone through considerable changes.

Thus the specific characteristics of money create the paradox of thrift which is displayed on the aggregate level but its effects through increased uncertainty concern the microscopic level and this in fact complicates a general economic policy of stimulating aggregate demand.

We have in earlier chapters discussed the relations between the monetary economy and its real base. In this chapter we will particularly focus on future values which makes us leave the real now for an expected future real now, hence the financial superstructure has a real base both currently as well as in the future. Worse than that, the asset and liability structures build on historical and current dreams underlying expectations and form a gigantic inertia of the society. We have earlier discussed the importance of inertia within consumption and production structures as well as institutional inertia, but this kind of inertia forms, together with earlier realized expectations and dreams, a huge inert rock which restricts the action space of the current which also in its turn gives rise to dreams and expectations of changes in the future. Like Lugi Amoroso says in his article about Vilfredo Pareto and which we in fact circle around in this book:

> The internal forces of the economic system are not susceptible of a theoretical representation as simple, elegant and universal as is the case of the applied forces. They are not only, as for the material macrocosmic systems, forces of conservation, by which – to express it elegantly – the dead city dominates *through inertia* the living city; they are also directive forces of impulsion, through which the living city *forms or attempts to form* the city of the future.
>
> (op. cit.: 6, original emphasis)

Just to make the quote clear we remind ourselves that the neoclassical model is a Newtonian system built on forces of conservation. Our emphasis on innovation, invention and social change represents the forces of the living city.

It is however important that we also realize that all expectations of the future both with respect to valuation of financial assets and liabilities as well as existing production organization are to be expressed in money flows, and thus from a theoretical point of view the expected real production and consumption take on the same characteristics as money; that is it belongs to a non-proper class. The current real affairs are made according to a precise current restriction space which has to be fitted into a currently apprehended context with respect to goals; it is also subject to real inertia in the sense that it affects its environment and it is subject to an institutional structure and finally to the current expectations of the future.

With respect to expectations of the future however these are obscure in many dimensions and mostly dependent on stability of current structures. Thus while the current decisions deal with particularities and eventually also change the real structure the expectations of the future concern the general and to a large content aggregate structures, thus affecting prices but not the real space. This implies for example that the price of a share representing a part of a real stock in a company is in fact subject to the same kind of uncertainties as a financial liability and thus we have an equalization of real stock and bonds. If we take the standard p/e-value, the stock is subject to expectations of the general demand; of course if we have extra information of particularities these may modify the expectations of the evolution of demand, and then we have general expectations of technology development which indeed may be tricky during certain periods while more relaxed during others. To these real aspects we have the financial side of the company; liquidity, currency positions, and asset and liability structures. Furthermore we have aggregate variables concerning inflation, tax matters and institutional changes which might affect the outcome of the affairs of the company. The generality of the aspects affecting the expectations of the value of the future valuation of the stock makes in fact particular information of the company less important, save for definitely agreed contracts. Furthermore the generality of the aspects affecting expectations implies that it is virtually imposs- ible to isolate a particular state space which could be relevant.

This example of valuation of a future stock value implies that we may expect a considerable volatility of the stock value. But as we see the particularities are to a great extent overruled by the generalities in importance and that also goes for financial assets and liabilities to a great extent under the same conditions: Keynes looked at shares and bonds as close substitutes.

Before we proceed with our analysis there are some features on demand that are important to keep in mind. Demand for consumption commodities is a final demand in the sense that the commodities are demanded for their use in house- holds and their creation of welfare, social position and similar purposes. Demand for investment commodities, although assigned as final use in input–output tab- leaus are to be seen as derived demand. We invest to get future incomes, split in wages and profits, which will be used for consumption demand. So although fashion may turn my jacket temporary obsolete, the concept of obsolescence is to a high degree viable with respect to investment demand.

The same holds for money and financial assets which thus are similar to investment goods; this is basically why Keynes saw shares and bonds as close substitutes. So from this very character of shares and bonds the only thing which constitutes a difference in uncertainty is the default risk, in private companies the priority order of liabilities and for public bonds the loyalty of the taxpayers. However we also have the liquidity aspect in the sense that financial contracts are not supposed to vary other than with respect to demand for liquid or near liquid assets.

We have however been used to regard shares in physical production as more volatile and even uncertain than financial assets issued by states, financial organ- izations and even by productive organizations, but that depends on the relations of the real basis of the economy and the financial superstructure; it also depends on the difference between the decrease of the individual uncertainty by spread- ing the risk through creation of financial instruments and the increase of the uncertainty on the systemic level.

There are two theoretical sources of this seemingly paradoxical statement: on one hand we have our earlier rejection of additive aggregation and on the other hand we have the concept of entropy which we mentioned in the discussion of Allais' paradox.

The concept of entropy is even more pronounced by globalization, which has implied that particularities of productions and consumption structures of single countries affect the national finances. Difference in welfare structures creates on one hand financial vulnerability and on the other hand it may affect social stability/instability. As a matter of fact the globalization of the economy has caused the same kind of phenomenon in economics as seen in astronomy, namely that spatial distances are mixed up with temporal distances. Thus we have a wide spectrum of techniques and patterns which are specific in a spatial sense but there is also a wide spectrum of techniques and patterns representing different temporal locus. That means that if we apply Hume's socioeconomic analysis on our time we may expect rather violent bifurcations both with respect to techniques and to socioeconomic patterns thus giving rise to rather substantial variations in relative prices as well as expected future prices of assets. The rejection of additive aggregation and the mereological rule of thumb, means that different aggregate levels are independent of each other with respect to optimization, while they at the same time are depending on each other since the aggregate structure affects the individual decisions and the individual decisions affect the aggregate structure.

We have earlier rejected the rational expectation hypothesis other than for well-specified markets, but the rationale for the hypothesis is interesting since it divides the macroscopic structure from the microscopic and, at least implicitly, claims that a macroscopic policy based on macroscopic variables may be compromised by actions taken by the agents on the microscopic level. In fact this is a brilliant example of Arrow's paradox.

Consequently we have a severe problem with macroscopic modelling, the stability of the macroscopic variables might be stable during periods of high structural stability in the economy but if that is not true we actually do not know what is under the variables and consequently we need more structural information.

Thus failures by individuals to close an epistemic cycle lead to reconsideration of the individual behaviour and only if all agents succeed in closing their epistemic cycles, the *ex ante* expectations are equal to the *ex post* result and we have no systematic impact on the behavioural structure. A situation where some agents are successful and some fail with respect to current actions built on the respective apprehensions of the context does not lead only to redistributions but also to revisions of the apprehended context and eventual revisions on goals. Failures by aggregate bodies to optimize the aggregate behaviour lead inevitably to individual reconsiderations which change the conditions for further aggregate actions.

Theoretically this means that we may find reversible structures at the individual level provided that the impact on the environment, in a broad sense, is negligible in a limited time period. Unfortunately negligibility always implies truncations which certainly have nasty effects under some conditions but given that we make efforts to classify the general stability of the relevant microscopic structure we may have reversibility at the microscopic level, temporary and locally. This is unfortunately not the case at the macroscopic level. Virtually all aggregate actions are irreversible, save for extremely short-run actions which are reversed.

This matter is indeed corrupted by the neoclassical theory which already in the very axiomatic structure introduces reversibility as a *prime feature*.

The second aspect with respect to entropy follows logically from rejecting additive aggregation. The working of the entropy concept can be illustrated as in Figure 7.2 in conjunction with Figure 6.5 of the preceding chapter.

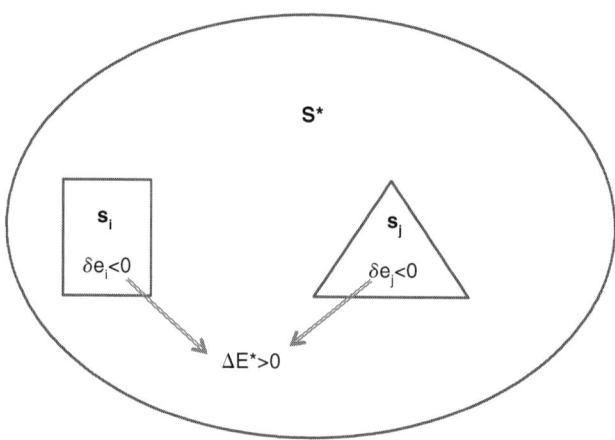

Figure 7.2 Individual and system entropy.

Let us interpret an increase in certainty which implies that we increase the possibility to order the future with respect to causal structures. We assume a closed system S^* which consists of subsystems $s_1 \ldots s_n$. Thus the decrease in entropy of the subsystems by actions by the elements s_i and s_j, implying a supposed increased possibility of ordering future causal structures as implied by Figure 6.5, implies an increase in entropy of the global system S^*; that is decreased possibility of ordering future causal structures. The increased entropy of the global system S^* obviously implies that the entropy of the agents $s_1, \ldots, s_{i-1}, s_{i+1}, \ldots, s_{j-1}, s_{j+1}, \ldots, s_n$, will have an increase in their entropy caused by the general increase of entropy in S^*. An interesting question is of course the reversal effect on the subsystems s_i and s_j. In principle the increase in entropy of the subsystems $s_1, \ldots, s_{i-1}, s_{i+1}, \ldots, s_{j-1}, s_{j+1}, \ldots, s_n$ ought to lead to reconsiderations of decisions and actions thus changing the environment of the agents s_i and s_j; whether or not this will take place is a matter of information, concerning the systemic increase in uncertainty.

An interesting example of this in the development in the financial world is illustrated by *Black Monday* in 1987.

According to Hillebrand, one of the characteristics of the stock markets in 1987, was that the financial market actors did not question the level of mean reversion in the market, on the contrary they lowered their expectations. The Brady-report pinpointed the fact that the long term upward moving market together with a short-term bull market environment as the reason to lack of scepticism concerning the level of mean reversion. . . .

The week before the "Black Monday" the market did fall due to fundamental news. As the market fell the dynamic hedge programs triggered off and started to realize their holdings, in order to secure the value of portfolios....

When the press reported the hedge programs as well as the volume, it came as a surprise to the market actors. As a result the expected level of reversion prior to the decreasing market was questioned and the investment portfolios needed to be adjusted to the new expected level of the mean reversion. This in turn led to the fact that the market plunged further, and the crash was a fact.

(Arnér and Ekstedt 2008: 33)

It is indeed an exciting story, and we realize the interactions both with respect to individual and aggregate entropy, as well as we see the crucial importance of the information structure.

It is also interesting to notice that the financial analysis has since long ago incorporated such empirical knowledge while it has had little impact on economic theory in general.

But we have also examples from the real economy, where safety is increased for certain groups at the expense of others. The (unfortunately) ancient discussion on usury and greediness hits this theme quite well when applied to the banking sector.

Valuation and expectation linked to the real economy

As we have said the current real economy is the basis for all kinds of expectations concerning the future, even those concerning financial assets and liabilities. Irrespectively of the character of dreams and expectations all these have to be somehow implemented in the real world thus affecting the real structure and also the basis for further dreams and expectations. Hence if I expect that it is possible to bring a substantial part of the moon and sell shares among the cheese lovers, this must be followed by real actions and implementations in order to change the real structure, thus affecting financial investments through some people believing in my dreams, and most probably causing future redistributions of wealth and decreased liquidity for some agents and affecting the aggregate liquidity. But due to adequate scepticism no real actions have probably taken place so the damage is most probable of little importance; but having said this we immediately remember financial bubbles causing much annoyance, as for example the famous price bubble on tulip bulbs in the early seventeenth century. It is however important to notice that this bubble emanated out of a real cause namely a disease which threatened the entire tulip growing, the same with the IT bubble in early 2000. It is important to separate speculation in unrealistically founded dreams and speculation founded in real matters, although sometimes it might be difficult. Mr Greenspan, former Governor of Federal Reserve, is said to have commented on the risk for an IT bubble, in the beginning of 2000s "I know of how to recognize a recession but not a bubble" has in fact relevance, whether he said it or not. A bubble depending on real factors is recognizable only after careful analysis based on rather comprehensive studies, while a bubble based on unrealistic dreams has more to do with education and the degree of superstition among people. The former type of bubbles will repeat themselves in new forms while the second type hopefully will converge to non-existence or at least become more and more rare.

Anyway the most common problem is the valuation of the future value of stocks. Irrespective of all complexity of the financial sector it is the stock of production capital which is of essence in the economic analysis. Marx's analysis which might be criticized for clumsiness and poor mathematical technique is a challenge already in the title *Das Kapital*. He may have underestimated the human ability of inventions and innovations but in Solow's growth analysis these factors are introduced as exogenous and without them Solow's analysis is at best a theoretical *Perpetuum Mobile*. In our macroscopic analysis we showed that the specific inertia of a production system created inflation, permanent unemployment, structural uncertainty and other kinds of annoying features characterizing the dynamic evolution of an economy.

So let us start from the simple P/E-value. In doing so we are looking at two different aspects of the company, the future incomes and the financial stability.

The future incomes discounted to current value is the basic figure and is of course dependent upon judgements on market development and technological development with respect to the company in relation to relevant sources of competition. This analysis is vastly different for different agents, some are only looking at the current and the short-run forecasts, thus looking at the shares in question mostly as some kind of semi-liquid asset. Others, mostly families who own a considerable share of the company have, at least historically, showed a more long-run concern for the company(ies) in question. There is not much to say about the judgements and valuations per se from a general point of view. Some agents are better than others are worse in making judgements about business development and mostly it comes from a combination of experience, luck and animal spirit.

However the structure of ownership is important as, already Keynes noted (1973 [1936]: 150–1). Assume a pension fund F_0, which is owned by an organization and where prospective pensioners may buy a sort of bond. The fund managers buy shares in different stock companies together with financial assets of different maturity, thus the yield of the fund has two sources, short sell of shares and financial assets and/or dividends from companies and interest rate.

The strategy of F_0, as well as the strategy of the prospective pensioners and the production companies, is obviously to maximize its profit, but this maximization problem of the fund is different from the maximization problem of the prospective pensioners and one of the productive companies. This difference may affect the behaviour of the firm, if the stock ownership in a specific company is substantial and calls for membership in the board, with respect to its financial position vis-à-vis the stock market as well as the financial market by introducing a different time preference.

Furthermore the portfolio management of intermediary funds may affect the total stock market. Risk management induces complementary relations among

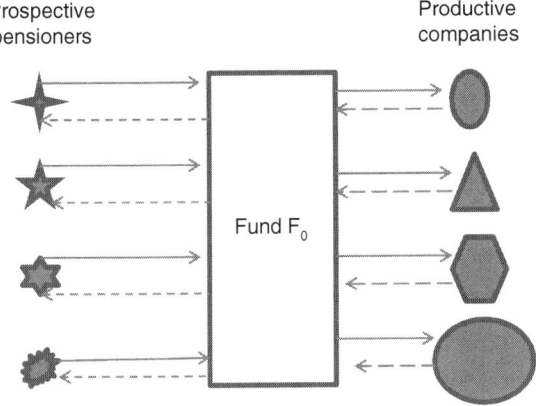

Figure 7.3 Fund ownership.

different stock shares implying both an increase in the systemic risk as well as potential leverage effects.

The paper by Blanchard and Plantes wrote with respect to expectations and uncertainty is an interesting paper. Their main derived theorem is explained like this:

> Thus, for financial assets to be gross substitutes, all partial correlation coefficients must be nonnegative. In particular, all asset returns must be non-negatively correlated. (Note that implying "similarity" between two assets, i.e., a positive correlation, is clearly far from implying substitutability between them.) Such a stringent set of conditions seems unlikely to be satisfied in practice.
>
> (1977: 770)

The gross substitutability condition is necessary if we want to integrate the financial analysis into a general equilibrium framework. It is built on an implicit assumption of some kind of Solowian growth combined with an endogenous growth approach. The assumption dismisses completely the changing commodity space and structural changes in demand and production technology, which are the main uncertainty creating factors with respect to the expectations of the future. However for short-run analysis it may work due to inertia but that is of the same quality as "the weather will be the same tomorrow as today".

Real performance and the financial sector

Our version of the economic circular flow of the monetary economy in Figure 4.2 makes us rather convinced that the complexity of the money transactions gives rise to profit augmenting financial innovations which in principle have little or nothing to do with the real sector. Our example above on financial inter-mediation implies that we impute an agent who can affect the real investment decision but we cannot say that the agent improves the efficiency of the financing of investments nor can we say if the investment decision efficiency is improved. During a certain period it was claimed that the financial growth during the first years of the 2000s was an increased efficiency of the financial market caused by financial innovations. After 2008 such opinions have more seldom been heard.

One of the most influential economists in analysing the anatomy of financial crises is Hyman Minsky. He claims:

> Innovational activity in the financial sector is a response to the profit oppor-tunities which are generated within an inherited financial structure as sus-tained growth takes place and will be related to the real sectors that are, figuratively speaking, "powering" the growth. The pace of financial innova-tion is a market induced reaction to the pace and direction of economic growth; however, the nature of the financial innovation that occurs will in turn affect the pace and direction of economic growth.
>
> (Friend *et al.* 1964: 174–5)

We have earlier suggested that there is a qualitative difference between the barter economy and the monetary economy; this difference is mainly due to its features of medium of exchange and, according to for instance Hume and Say, implies a closer inter-relation between the economy and the surrounding socio-political structures. The content of the above quote suggests other relations; monetary market flows may augment the effects of real changes, but they may also affect the direction of the real changes.

Before we go further into this let us illustrate the economy in the form of an enlarged input–output tableau.[1] Consequently we complete the input–output chart with a financial matrix F and the corresponding financial asset vectors R, and financial liabilities, R', in Figure 7.4 we give an overview. The matrix A denotes the flows of intermediate products and Y and B the incomes and finished products respectively. The X and X' vectors are the gross costs and gross deliver-ies respectively.

We may now more closely look at the financial matrix and the corresponding matters in Figure 7.5

We have on the left side and above the opening liabilities and assets respectively while we have the closing liabilities and assets correspondingly to the right and below.

If we assume that we cut out a piece of an equilibrium trajectory *à la* Neumann-Gale with endogenous growth the reasoning according to the matrix in Figure 7.5 is straightforward. Given that the government is regarded partly as a production and a consumption sector and the outstanding money volume is

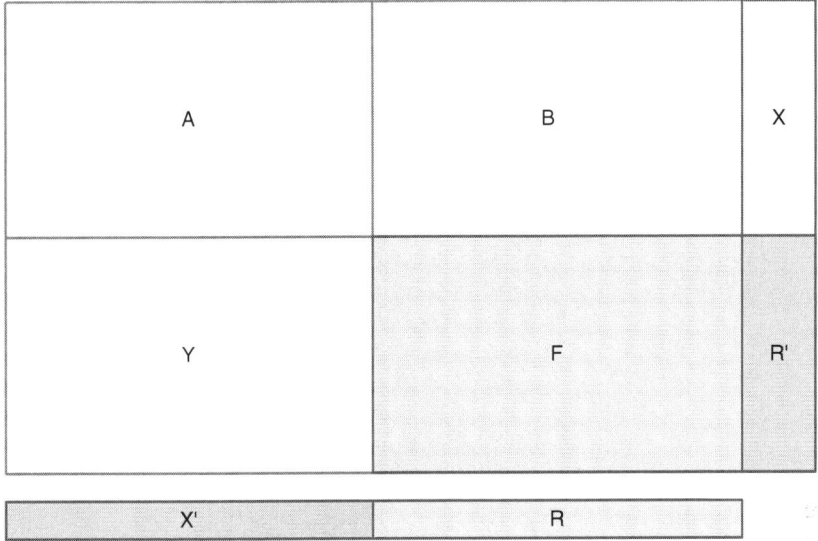

Figure 7.4 Outline of an input–output system completed with financial transactions.

regarded as a financial debt which renders a service to the agents, we will have that the financial flow adds to the financial resources and liabilities such that the stock-equilibrium is prevailed and in correspondence with the real flows. Unfortunately with respect to such an interpretation there has been imputed two awkward vectors V^A and V^L which denote eventual revaluation of the assets and liabilities respectively, but given that such revaluations are based on expectations of future directions of the real flows and consequently they change the stock values; however if these expectations are based on an environment where the space of outcome is known and the subjective probability distributions are within a reasonable frame, as we discussed in relation to the temporary equilibrium theory, we will most probably have a stable trajectory given some fluctuations.

However inducing uncertainty into the scheme, which not only concerns the environment of the market but the market process in itself, in manners we have earlier discussed, will influence on the vectors V^A and V^L respectively in a way which is not coherent to the real exchange.

If we try to illustrate the dynamics of the charts in Figures 7.4 and 7.5 we may cut out three time discs at $t-1$, t_0 and $t+1$ and look at the connections.

Given the development of consumer demand the links between the time discs relate to production factors in conjunction with investments in fixed capital and the stocks of financial assets and liabilities affecting current financial activities. Expressed in this way we will have a connected socioeconomic space–time of the same character as the Einstein-Minkowski space–time illustrated in Figure

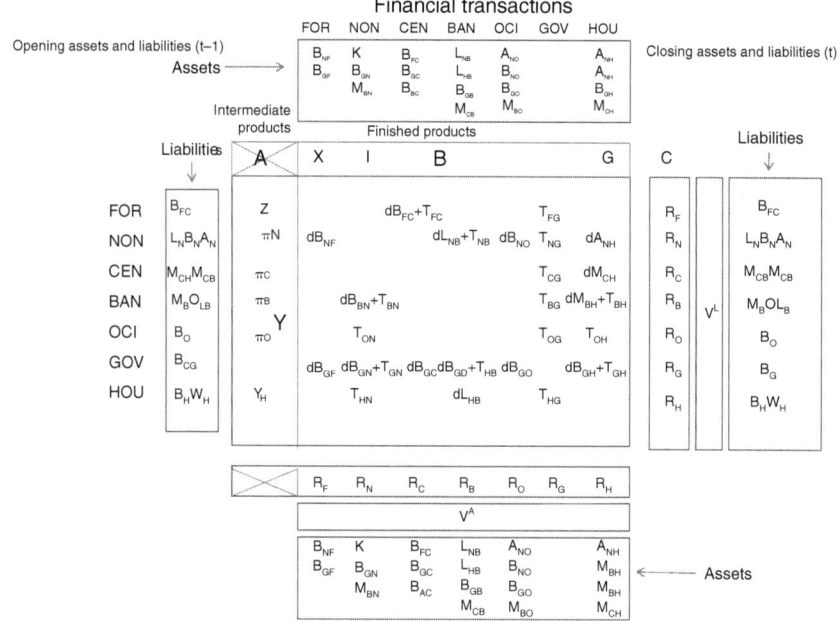

Figure 7.5 Detailed financial matrix.

Notes
FOR – foreign sector; NON – non-financial business; CEN – central bank; BAN – banks; OCI – other credit institutions; GOV – government; HOU – households.
Entries in the matrix:
B – bonds; T – transfers, interest and taxes; L – loans; M – money.

5.3. However unfortunately from a technical point of view, we have been forced to add the revaluation vectors V^A and V^L to the right in Figure 7.6, and this causes the time discs to be principally unconnected. If we look at Samuelson's analysis of different time models, not even the historical time can catch the problem we describe, provided a standard interpretation. Historical models may express shifts in parameters which cause kinks in the development, like the time curve A'B'C'D'A″ in Figure 5.3, the curve is probably not differentiable but still it can be connected in space–time. This is relevant for a real side analysis. If we think of a bankruptcy, the production organization/capital undergoes a major revaluation but it still exists. You may, if interested, make a good deal and proceed with the operations under modified financial conditions. Thus the real side as such is mostly a point of connectedness in the social space although conditions as differentiability do not hold. However looking at this event from the financial point of view the revaluation actually implies that the wealth of some agents' wealth will vanish and this may also indirectly affect their liquidity position. So we then have the interesting problem, from a technical/

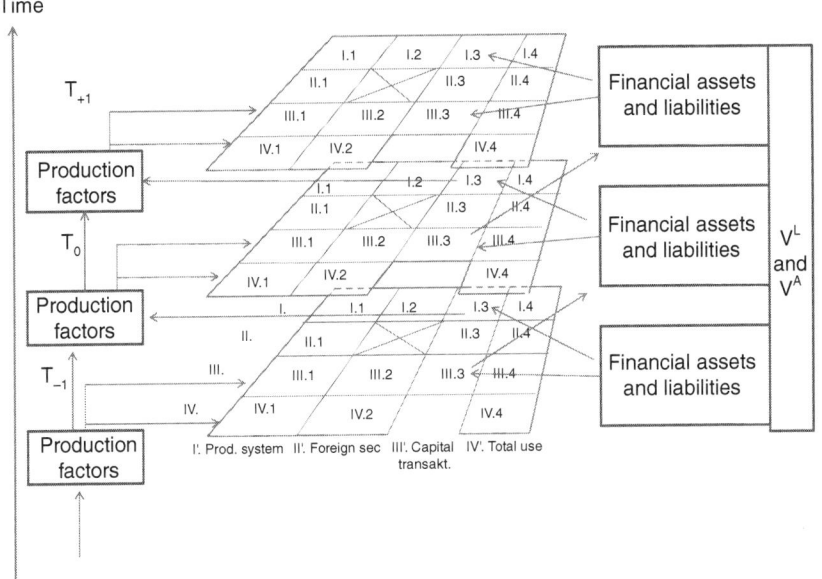

Figure 7.6 Illustration of evolution of the total input–output system.

Notes
We have four sectors in the rows and transposed to columns: I – internal production system; II – foreign sector; III – capital transactions; IV – income use.
We have also added a box of the revaluation vectors V^A and V^L to the right.

Entries:

Table A

I.1 I/O-system	**I.2** Export	**I.3** Gross investment	**I.4** Consumption
II.1 Import	X	**II.3** Net foreign	**II.4** Current net foreign
	(empty)	Assets	transfers
III.1 Consumption of	**III.2** Capital transfer	**III.3** Internal financial	**III.4** Saving
capital	from abroad	transactions	
IV.1 NDP	**IV.2** Net capital	X	**IV.4** Disposable NDP
	income from	(empty)	
	abroad		

methodological point of view that while the assumed bankruptcy might have only minor effects on the real development its financial effects might be quite considerable, not only with respect to the distribution aspect among agents, but eventually also with respect to the aggregate system liquidity. Thus from a theoretical point of view we have an asymmetry between the real and the financial side.

Consequently the key question is: what causes revaluations of assets and liabilities?

The Minsky problem

Basic to the Minsky problem is the Miller–Modigliani principle that given an efficient financial market the mode of finance will not affect the value of a firm (Modigliani and Miller 1958). This means that a higher debt ratio will impose a higher financial risk to the firm thus requiring a higher desired return on equities.

As such the principle is relatively harmless and in a general equilibrium setting evident. However going back to the above quote from Minsky he claims that financial innovations are generally a feature of what he calls *sustained growth*. We have earlier taken an example of a period of sustained growth which we called the greenhouse effect and it occurred from the end of the Second World War to the middle of the 1960s. After that there have not been any such long periods for a large number of countries, but during the first decade of the 2000s a combination of the strong growth in China and the financial innovation in the US, creating a strong consumption growth together with the expansive war finance, created a strong growth of demand overlapping the "normal" business cycle variations in many western countries.[2]

Anyway during such a period the Miller–Modigliani principle evolves from a principle to a temptation, and the financial structure in Figure 7.3 may well trigger such a policy.

The Miller–Modigliani theorem is based on rather simple calculations of the relations between debt and equities for firms and debts and wealth for households. Let us first say that when discussing these matters we come close to a wide diversity of accounting frauds, the ill-famous Enron scandal is an educative example, and other forms of economic criminality, but we dismiss such perversities and discuss only the problems which are well inside what is legally accepted in western countries.

We thus have the *accounting identity*:

$$TK \cdot r_t \equiv W \cdot r_w + D \cdot r_d \qquad \text{(E.7.1)}$$

where TK is total capital, W is wealth, D is debt, r_t is current interest on total capital, r_w is desired interest on (wealth) equity capital, r_d is exogenously given interest on debt.

Firms' profit and yield on wealth is *ex post* to be seen as a residual although we may express it as short-run maximization resulting in the optimal capacity utilization given each level of demand. But if we according to Minsky assume that we are in a kind of sustained growth which affects expectations upwards we may utilize revaluation of equities and wealth, housing capital for instance, to a proportional increase of debt. Obviously there occurs excesses in these matters but we do not need to take such into consideration.[3]

We may write E.7.1 as:

$$W \cdot r_w = TK \cdot r_{tk} - D \cdot r_d \qquad \text{(E.7.2)}$$

which we may write:

$$W \cdot r_w = (W + D) \cdot r_{tk} - D \cdot r_d \qquad \text{(E.7.2')}$$

This gives us an expression for the desired interest on wealth (equity capital):

$$r_w = r_{tk} + \frac{D}{W} \cdot (r_{tk} - r_d) \qquad \text{(E.7.3)}$$

We may thus conclude that as long as $r_{tk} > r_d$ we may increase the debt to wealth ratio with a limit ratio of 1, while in the opposite case reduce the ratio, with a limit ratio of zero.

This is more or less the Miller–Modigliani theorem when we assume constant wealth (equity capital) and in such a case it is obvious that the risk of wealth/ equity capital increases, which makes us suspect that the behaviour is not particularly smart even if we have a sustained growth *à la* Minsky.

But it is here that the revaluation vectors V^A and V^L in Figure 7.4 come into the picture. The revised expectations in a sustained growth increase the current value of wealth/equity capital, thus the calculations in E.7.3 are not relevant since the current value of wealth/equity capital makes it possible to increase debt without disturbing the value of the ratio.

So why not impute some prudence since we know from history that sustained growth is very often limited on the microscopic level.[4] But that is indeed problematic since we then have the question whether we altogether shall refrain from the benefits of the sustained growth. "I can make some money and I am skilled and prudent so I know when to stop" is indeed a tough thought to fight in poker as well as in financial investments.

A process of interacting of real and financial growth as we have described is working in a rather straightforward way in a not very advanced financial technology. So going back to the quote from Minsky the financial innovations play a very active role in augmenting this process. Before we go into this in a more detailed discussion it seems appropriate to remind of the ability of the banking system to create money. In a rather animated debate on the internet at the end of March and at the beginning of April 2012, reminding to some extent of the bullionist debate at the beginning of the nineteenth century in England, monetary principles and banks' ability to create money was debated. The debate started with an article by Paul Krugman in the *New York Times* "Minsky and Methodology" and other participants were Scott Fullwiler, Steve Keen and many others.[5] We will not comment on the whole debate but a part of it referred to banks' ability to create money by raising credits. Krugman writes (nytimes blog 30 March 2012):

> As I read various stuff on banking – comments here, but also various writings here and there – I often see the view that banks can create money out of thin air. There are vehement denials of the proposition that banks' lending is limited by their deposits, or that the monetary base plays any important role;

banks, we're told, hold hardly any reserves (which is true), so the Fed's creation or destruction of reserves has no effect.

This is all wrong, and if you think about how the people in your story are
assumed to behave – as opposed to getting bogged down in abstract algebra
– it should be obvious that it is all wrong.

First of all, any individual bank does, in fact, have to lend out the money
it receives in deposits.

Krugman has more argument for his statement but for us the quote gives rise to
some comments with respect to financial innovation, except for a nice comment
a bit further in the argumentation: "Banks are important, but they don't take us
into an alternative economic universe." Well, it of course depends from which
universe we start, but if we start from the barter economy of the neoclassical
theory or the different IS-LM approaches they actually do.

Let us go back to Hume and his insistence on metal money and suspicious-
ness of banknotes which might increase the money base into infinity. Hume's
attitude is respectable since he warned against unresponsible behaviour, next to
fraud but he was well aware of the ability of the banking system. Henry Thornton and Jean Baptiste Say are among the earliest ones to discuss a system where
banks created bank money in expanding credits. Say (1834 [1803]: 284–7)
discuss paper money, which he does not entirely appreciate due to its use under
the revolution, and he describes the proper paper money as "The paper-money is
thus left in the exclusive possession of the business of circulation; and the absolute necessity of some agent of transfer, in every civilized community, will then
operate to maintain its value" (ibid.: 284).

Thornton describes in detail, but in the same spirit as Say, how a treasury bill
might be used as money and security for loans all over the world and the level of
its business use is a matter of the needs of the businessman and the pleasure of
the banks. Furthermore Thornton introduces the very constructive distinction
between *potential* and *enforced circulation*. *Potential circulation* is in principle
what we call bank money based on credits. Potential circulation is to the largest
extent dependent on economic activity and the degree of confidence in the economic system. The word *potential* means that there is an upper limit set by risk/
uncertainty and speed of information and formal handling; if that speed is
increased towards infinity as in electronic affairs the limit of potential circulation
is almost infinitely short. Thus in principle we can out of a stock of deposits
defined in money terms, create an infinite volume of credits. Enforced circulation in Thornton's time was a change in the volume of metal money. To understand the very consequence of enforced circulation in a monetary economy the
two ventures by Deutsche Reichbank in the 1920s during the super-inflation and
during the 1930s when Hitler with the help of Hjalmar Sacht constructed the so-
called MEFO-bills which replaced the official currency in internal business and
subsequently saved the official currency from inflation and depreciation.

With respect to the risk/uncertainty limit the crash in 2008 obviously is a
good example but we will take an example from Sweden where HQ Bank lost its

bank-permission. We base the example on the protocol from Finance Inspection (FI), FI Dnr 10-7854, dated 27 August 2010.

HQ Bank was a somewhat new bank concept with a much more aggressive style. Among many people on the market and also in universities it was seen as a bank of the future. They were involved in advanced and large trading of derivatives, way above its ordinary bank business. In the somewhat dry protocol from FI it is said that although the bank in March 2010 informed FI that the sufficient capital to cover trading risks was 33 million SEK, the realized loss in June same year was 1230 million SEK. With respect to the assessment of risk FI has severe complaints: HQ Bank used implicit risks for active derivative markets which means that the risk measure is based on the underlying asset. For inactive markets the HQ Bank used theoretical volatility based on historical volatility during 100 days with an assumption of mean reversion, i.e. that if the volatility occasionally is outside the historical it is explained as occasional and does not lead to revisions in the valuation. To impose such an assumption implies that the bank never attends actively to the current risk position of the trading. When reading the story of the bank it is clear that they followed the Holy Scripture quite faithfully that "not let your *left hand* know what your *right hand* is doing", in the sense that at the same time as 33 million SEK in March 2009 was considered enough to cover trading risks, the Board had taken a decision in June 2009 that the overnight limit of 150 million SEK, which means a risk level where the bank is allowed to lose in one day is 150 million SEK. Interestingly to note is that Jean Baptiste Say gives similar examples of bank papers "assignats" based on similar lax bank affairs during the French revolution (op. cit.: 284).

Anyway both Keynes in *Treatise on Money* and Wicksell in *Güter und Geldzins* discuss the banks' ability to raise credits and thereby increase "bank money" rather explicitly.

Consequently it is a bit hard to understand Krugman from a pure theoretical point of view. Another matter however is whether the central bank and the government can impose quantitative restrictions on the banks, which we will discuss later with respect to a theorem by Enthoven and Arrow. In Sweden until the beginning of the 1970s there was a system of quantitative restrictions which worked fairly well, but had to be brought to an end due to the increasing cross-border relations. Today any form of quantitative restrictions requires international agreements.[6]

Back to Minsky, he claims that the financial system and financial innovations increase the augmentation of real effects. The real effects which are interesting are due to bad performance of existing economic activities and related capital stock, in serious cases bankruptcies, misjudgements in real investments and erroneous expectations which lead to misallocation of resources. Already in a next to barter economy, that is when we just regard money as a medium of exchange, the circular flows of the real economy induce a leverage effect due to multiplier/accelerator relations. So according to Minsky the financial system somehow augments or multiplies these real leverage effects and he also means that financial innovation further augments the financial leverage effects.

The very foundation of the existence of financial leverage effects are that additive aggregation is rejected with respect to the real economy but not with respect to money and financial assets and by that also the existence of a general equilibrium. This means that individual optimizing behaviour may affect the aggregate levels in such a way that "new" effects are created which affect the individuals in a different way compared to the situation when we assume additive aggregation.

There are a multitude of leverage effects in the financial system, but let us start with a rather simple one which created some nuisance during the 1980s, namely cross-ownership by producing companies. The money preserving authorities pay nowadays some attention to this phenomenon and that also holds for banks and companies. Today cross-ownership has a different focus. Nevertheless it is to a great extent a result of what Minsky calls a sustained growth. We take the example from Sweden, and use Volvo, Skanska (a construction company) and the household sector and the cross-ownership between Volvo and Skanska was substantial.

The problem arises from the fact that the shares in Skanska and Volvo in respective company are market valued and thus affect the reverse equity valuation. In the particular case Skanska owned a building in central Tokyo which got a magnificent rise in price and affected the valuation of equities of Skanska quite substantially which had a distinct effect on the valuation of the equities of Volvo, and this was reversed like a multiplier effect. This was the prime leverage effect, the second one concerned the wealth of the households which contained the full effect of the "leverage multiplier" and thus to some extent made the households more attracted to increase borrowing according to our reasoning above. Unfortunately the story ended in the Black Monday 1987 and then the boards of Volvo and Skanska took a decision to decrease the cross-ownership, with explicit reference to the leverage effects.

Another kind of leverage effect is spreading liquidity defaults through the banking sector. These kinds of effects emanate from the concept of liquidity, which we earlier discussed; if A lends B money and B fails to pay it back A is hurt financially and this will eventually trigger real effects emanating from A,

Table 7.1 Leverage caused by cross-ownership

Volvo		Skanska		Households	
Debit	Credit	Debit	Credit	Debit	Credit
Real capital	Equity capital	Real capital	Equity capital	Housing	Wealth
Financial assets	Debts	Financial assets	Debts	Financial assets	Debts
Shares in Skanska		Shares in Volvo		Shares in Volvo and Skanska	

but normally only wealth not income is affected and in principle that is all. If however Bank Φ lends α money and α fails this will hurt the liquidity position of the bank which is dependent on the flow of funds, thus it will affect both the wealth and the flow of funds which generate income and thus in principle will affect the general public. Therefore interpersonal lending/borrowing may be covered by defining appropriate securities such that B's failure will be accompanied by transfer of wealth from B to A, in the form of a house, car etc., which normally will roughly be of the same value in A's hands as in B's, while in the relation between Bank Φ and agent α eventual real securities of the above mentioned kind, do not cover the flow of fund effect and its wealth effect is low if any due to administrative costs; presenting financial securities is from the latter point of view better but then we have security for a financial transaction which is still a part of the financial system. Thus under normal times it works quite well but in financial distress it is of little value.

An instructive, and happy, story from 2009 is when a big bank in Sweden was in real financial distress in the OSS-countries and in fact was next to bankrupt, however a state-owned export supporting organization had backed the bank against a kind of barrier option in a volume of the shares, which should be released if the share price would become lower than a certain value. This happened and the state organization suddenly became owner of a substantial part of the share capital which later implied that when the bank issued new share capital the judgement by the market actors was that the state would never let the bank go bankrupt so the emission was extremely successful and the state organization made a good profit and everybody was happy (except for some market liberal purists and some stubborn socialists).

Thus the bank's lending was way above any deposit reserves and depended solely on the trust in the bona fide of the debtors and the flows of fund. When this was broken due to mostly exogenous events (perhaps the author's kind heart underestimates the responsibility of the bank), the entrance of the state organization however restored the bona fide of the bank for future business.

Financial innovations are seldom new in the sense that they are linked to inventions but leans on old principles which are used in a new context. Particularly the market for derivatives has been rich with respect to financial innovations. The main underlying desire is to spread risks. This is highly desirable at the microscopic level but not necessarily at the macroscopic level. If we assume additive aggregation there is no difference but since we have rejected that we are in theoretical trouble with respect to the complex reality. Our happy ending example above about the adventures of the Swedish bank in the OSS-countries is a good example. Neither issuing organization nor the buyer has any idea of the worth of the derivative in question during normal business, and that was taken to its border when the so-called NINJA-bonds were issued in the US before September 2008.[7] Perhaps these bonds are the best example of Minsky's approach. The strategy was extremely simple: strip some of the outstanding claims in different risk classes and create bonds which are announced to be risky and thus of higher yield, package them into a set of different kinds of assets and sell them.

Thus they got the risky stuff off the balance sheet, which implied that they could increase the lending and involve groups which before had had little or no access to the credit market. The banks became more or less a mediator and the doubtful lending was covered so that banks' incomes were increased, but at what real price? Thus the default risk of the new borrowers did not disappear but was just transferred to a larger group of financial actors and the theoretical question is then what effect the spreading of the risk (uncertainty) implies vis-à-vis the systemic risk. As our two examples above from the Swedish bank show, the system is based on confidence, in the happy Swedish case the entrance of the state through the barrier option restored the confidence in the bank. In the case of the HQ Bank the authorities found that either the board and the management were too inexperienced to lead a bank or alternatively it was a case of fraud; the case was partially solved in the second level administrative court on 14 April 2012, but there are still legal enquiries going on.

We can thus expect that defaults by the creditors affect the confidence of the lenders and that implies an augmentation of the systemic risk in itself. When defaults as in the NINJA case become massive the system breaks down.

Going back to the flowcharts in Figures 7.5 and 7.6 we see that credits flow to real investments and consumption as it should, possibly however it is a problem when a credit expansion goes to the households as in the NINJA example. Other credit flows occur when we have revaluations of stocks in a sustained growth and there is a credit expansion directed to stock investments, real and financial, which may trigger prices of the secondary market for assets and liabilities.

Let us go back to the situation we described by Figures 4.11 and 4.12 which implies a higher proportion of liquid resources; at the same time however increasing global competition, cultural and political tensions also create a high uncertainty with respect to the future commodity space. We thus need liquid resources both for precautionary and speculative purposes as Keynes names it. However this liquidity has to be handled and it is rather ironic nowadays to see that, not seldom, the return on financial investments are higher than on real investments. We should then notice that it is a good policy by big producing firms in groups of companies, concerns, to invest in real capital out of non-distributed profits and use borrowed financial resources for hedging purposes; thus they try to separate the risks but the production capital still implies an implicit security as well as a basic uncertainty. However this policy implies that a substantial group of rather powerful actors compete with banks on the financial market and in principle withdraw important sources of profit for banks. This process explains to some extent the rather absurd circus around the NINJA bonds and the lax lending policy. It has also been a gradual evolution of conglomerates of financial organizations and producing companies of oligopoly character.

However we must note that the only way the society can gain on all levels of aggregation is via production of real commodities and their exchange on the market. This is the basic gospel of all theoretical approaches in economics. Financial transactions at best can make the production and exchange more efficient but using the financial sector as a source for profits without this efficiency dual is zero-game, and it is precisely here that the *value of money* enters. When the financial side of the economy grows and the agents need a higher rate of liquidity the inflation problem becomes rather serious. All financial assets and liabilities are in the end nominal although we may link them to certain indexes or other currencies. Emission of real priced bonds at any more substantial scale would have an effect parallel to the real balance effect and cause asymmetric deflationary consequences.

However when the nominally defined stocks of assets and liabilities grow we more or less get the same problem. These are investments in future prices.

It is a fundamental difference between a commodity and a financial asset with respect to prices. With respect to a commodity it is desirable irrespective of its price. In fact when the price is lowered we may consume more of it. Neither for real nor financial assets this is true. It has only its value through the expectation of its future price, which is subject to a great variety of risks and uncertainties. Inflation is then a fundamental danger to the value of assets in nominal prices and then it is important to remember that such inflation attacks the very fundamental insurance against uncertainty which is available, not even gold and precious stones will do, which in fact was observed by Henry Thornton and Jean Baptiste Say, as liquidity is defined in the very medium of exchange. Observe that a person may well protect the wealth through investing in gold but that does not hold for a company which has to be liquid with respect to current cash flows. The financial trading in Thornton's and Say's times was probably pursued in a rather gentle manner with no excessive hurry. Unfortunately the increased efficiency has removed most of the charm and today we are discussing speeds approaching the speed of light, thus to wait for the latest report from the Bureau of Statistics is rather meaningless. The policy authorities are not fighting current inflation but expected inflation which is a completely different business as we have previous discussed. That implies that we have to create, if possible, a general context where we can say that inflation *will not* occur.

But that means that we in principle must create a next to deflationary context in order to preserve the value of money.

It is in this general context our discussion vis-à-vis Figures 4.11 and 4.12 become sensitive and important. At the same time we must consider the nature of expectation formation. The lead time between decision and execution of a financial affair is in many cases close to zero and that implies that forming expectations cannot be built on massive information gathering and complex analysis, which takes time; it has to be built on rules of thumb, standardized measures and observed anomalies in market behaviour.[8] We discussed earlier the developments of Black and Scholes have been directed into studying actual changes in behaviour of agents rather than studying a believed theoretical state space or something similar. The general rationale of such models is that the information space contains so many dimensions that it is not even sure that the sum of all prevalent dimensions believed currently by the agents to cover some actual space; furthermore it is obvious that spreading disinformation could be as profitable as collecting right information. Thus in a context where we have derivatives to hedge our investments, the price is affected mainly by the interest rate and the perceived volatility. Thus methods like the Heston model aims at detecting and revealing the historical volatility as close as possible to the current moment of time; particularly important are the daily opening prices at different markets.

Thus expectations have become more and more volatile. In traditional economics we use many different approaches to expectation formation, rational, extrapolative, adaptive, constant and Keynes' *beauty contest*. The Heston model is to be regarded as a negative variant of Keynes' beauty contest. When the volatility of prices increases we can expect higher prices on options since the market uncertainty obviously increases. But models like the Heston model are only applicable at specific markets like option markets; when it comes to variables like inflation the explanatory variable space is rather diffuse and agents can be expected to widen the spectrum of expectation; it can be everything from a general increase in capacity utilization to a trade union leader expressing more than usual firmness to raise the labour wages or the minister of social affairs declaring concern for the inadequate social safety net. Thus normally the market actors learn about repetitive patterns but when new features appear or what is believed as normal patterns are broken the expectation formation might be rather wild, furthermore a general feeling of uncertainty has strong effects.

During 2008 more or less all market actors were aware of the rather shaky situation of the banking sector and after Bear Stearns collapse in March, the market was more or less on red alert and the sharp increase of the Chinese inflation during March to May as seen in Figure 7.7 triggered by galloping prices on oil, futures increased from 100/105 USD/barrel in March to 135/140 in June, which turned into a declining demand in general and particularly implied a sharp decline in prices of oil futures, below 80 USD/barrel end of August, which further affected financial positions. Such events in a more balanced credit system would probably have been coped with but now the system was corrupted by irresponsible lending behaviour by the banks prior to these events and undermining

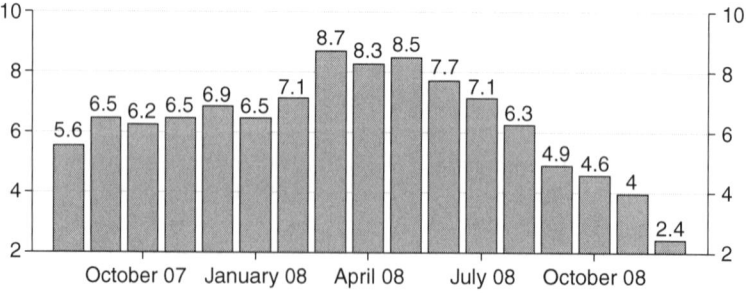

Figure 7.7 China inflation, 2008 (source: quoted from the website of the National Bureau of Statistics of the People's Republic of China, www.stats.gov.cn).

the general confidence in the prospects of the economy due to evolving liquidity distress.

Thus Chinese inflation, combined with rather extreme variations in the price of oil futures seems to have been rather important for the financial breakdown since it turned an already shaky world demand into a declining demand as to some extent illustrated in Figure 7.7.

All this affected the world demand negatively and thus sharpened an already ongoing credit crunch in the financial sector. The late summer and the beginning of autumn 2008 was in fact more or less an implementation period of the financial crises and a sort of chicken game.

Expectations

From our discussion it follows a rather standard view according to Keynes. It is obvious that we, as in the neoclassical case, have some kind of state space which we may think of as more or less inert. But beside that we have the question about how the market agents view this state space and which consequences they believe a specific event will have. That of course depends on historically taken positions which also may be matters for expectations and assumptions. On top of that we may add what Keynes calls *degree of rational belief*, which indeed is much more complex than a rational analysis (1953 [1930]: 10–11). We could describe it by the help of epistemic cycles as assumptions of some standard context which fellow agents perceive and given this some adequate time horizon which makes us able to say something of eventual rational market behaviour. However when we have done so we must ask which confidence we have in our own assumptions and that is not the same as prescribing some kind of subjective probability.

However the *concept of inertia* comes to help but that mostly concerns the real side of the economy. Real supply and demand changes but changes not that fast at the microscopic level, but from Figures 4.11 and 4.12 we understand that for the single agents their liquidity position may change quite quickly. Concerning the macroscopic level business cycles affect singular agents differently and these singular effects are, according to our discussion above spread and at least sometimes levered by the financial sector which affects the expectations of the future prices of the financial assets and liabilities and thus the financial wealth of the agents' and the companies' liquidity positions by revaluations.

Thus with respect to the future our expectations mostly concern prices on financial commitments of different kinds.

If we look at so-called adaptive expectations they are well in line with Wicksell's discussions on microscopic stability. They build on an expectation function like:

$$p_i^e = p_{i.-1}^e + \gamma \cdot (p_{i.-1} - p_{i.-1}^e)$$

and implicitly it builds on what is called a mean reversal. This is quite realistic when it comes to real processes which are subject to real restrictions. The demand for a product is a good example provided that the product is established at the market. However the more specified the product is the more doubtful is the adaptive expectation and conversely when we discuss commodity groups the wider we make the group the more realistic will the adaptive expectation function concerning the average price become.

When we pass over to financial assets however the pricing will involve not only the particulars but also the judgements about the general macroscopic situation.

Much the same can be said about rational expectations. Strictly derived from a theoretically correct model we end up in a mean reversion forecast, which as we claimed above is probably not a particularly erroneous assumption for a real market segment given the same kind of comments as we did for adaptive expectations. Consequently we have the same problem with respect to financial assets and liabilities.

It seems that with respect to financial markets the so-called extrapolative expectation behaviour is more relevant particularly taking into account the reverse kind of risk/uncertainty forecasting procedures that modern option pricing models, like Heston's model use when they actually build the uncertainty measure on the perceived volatility of prices as we said earlier some kind of reversed Keynesian beauty contest. Our earlier quote from Arnér and Ekstedt (2008) also shows some of the complex relations between microscopic behaviour and macroscopic effects.

The extrapolative expectation is a rather simple trend hypothesis, but we may say that in volatile reigns the extrapolative behaviour is more widespread in relation to some believed risk free assets. With respect to the stock market it is interesting since there are definitely other factors than the stock price and the rather rude p/e--value in order to form expectations and we may expect sophisticated investors to use more fundamental information in their expectation formation. However in this book we have described a rather complex real problem out of equilibrium, a multitude of price vectors, innovation and inventions and moreover integrated into a global economy where we have social, cultural and political tensions. All this means that fundamentals may be switching pretty quickly. Maybe the beauty contest behaviour or similar trivial rules are not that stupid. Let us look a bit more into the extrapolative expectation behaviour. The classical analysis of extrapolative expectations is Enthoven and Arrow (1956) and we will follow their discussion.

Principally the expected price is a function of the current price change:

$$p_t^e = f(p_t, \dot{p}_t) \tag{E.7.4}$$

which can be linearized to:

$$p_t^e = p_t + \eta \dot{p}_t$$

We may also write the relation between the size of excess demand and the price change as:

$$\dot{p}_t = k \cdot x_t \qquad\qquad\qquad\text{(E.7.5)}$$

implying that the price change will be a function of the effect of excess demand of a price change. They get an interesting condition for stability, a more comprehensive discussion is found in Ekstedt and Fusari (2010): 234–6). Let us define:

$$b_i = \frac{\delta x_i}{\delta p_i^e}.$$

The condition for stability is then for the *i*th commodity:

$$\frac{1}{k_i} > b_i \cdot \eta_i \qquad\qquad\qquad\text{(E.7.6)}$$

where η_i is taken from the linearized form of E.7.4 which implies that the sensitivity of price with respect to excess demand should be smaller than the total effect of the extrapolative expectations.

Important to remember is that this result concerns ordinary commodities. Fernando Vega-Redondo (1989: 513) emphasizes this (original emphasis):

> In a model of market adjustment which allows for the presence of extrapolative expectations on the future values of the *excess demands*, not on prices per se, the following conclusion is reached: if prices adjust in the direction of expected excess demands, these being formed by sufficiently sensitive extrapolation of their present rates of change, every (regular) market equilibrium is locally stable.

That is in a system of commodities with rather complex substitute and complementary relations and moreover is out of equilibrium in the sense that there exist multiple price vectors, there is reason to believe that an excess demand for some commodity does not raise the price of it very quickly and to a high degree, save maybe for some very fashionable goods.

But when we come to the financial market, it seems to be reasonable to expect that b_i and η_i with modern technology approach infinity and in such a case the constant k_i must approach zero, thus the effect of the size of excess demand must not affect the price.

The result is very interesting and may actually support those who want to induce quantitative restrictions in order to stabilize the financial market but such a policy conclusion requires that we know a lot more about the links between the real and financial parts of the economy.

The Enthoven and Arrow result has rather recently generated some discussion when the analysis is transferred to the financial analysis. James Choi (2005) developed a general equilibrium model to analyse extrapolative behaviour in relation to a more sophisticated behaviour characterized by rational expectations; furthermore the extrapolative behaviour ignored mean reversion and was therefore trigged in two directions by good and bad times. He postulated that the behaviour of the rational investors, which were assumed to be rich, while the extrapolative investors were believed to be relatively poor, thus the poor ones were triggered in good times to overestimate the equity premium.

He however finds, based on empirical testing of the model, that extrapolative behaviour is "contagious" through its strong effects on the aggregate consumption of the poor investors, since they display this "zero/one" behaviour and will thus influence the behaviour of the rich, rational investors. He also adds that "Numerous of studies have documented that extrapolative beliefs about stock returns are commonly held in the population, even among the rich" (ibid.: 17).

Hirshleifer and Yu (2012: 1) partly support Choi's findings "Extrapolative bias increases the variation in the wealth-consumption ratio; recursive preferences cause this variation to be strongly priced; and adjustment costs corporate payouts more procyclical."

Although appearing earlier than the above quoted works by Choi and Hirsleifer and Yu, Kevin Lansing in a way summarizes them:

> The flavour of the above ideas is clearly evident in the model set forth in the paper. The main contribution is to show that an individual agent can become locked-in to use of a suboptimal, extrapolative forecast if other agents (i.e. "game-players") are following the same approach. From the perspective of an individual agent, switching to fundamentals-based forecast would appear to reduce forecast accuracy, so there is no incentive to switch. A reasonably calibrated version of the model is capable of generating excess volatility, time-varying volatility, bubbles, crashes, and other well documented features of long run U.S. stock market data.
>
> (2005: 24)

All the quoted works concern stock market behaviour which is the very fundamental asset with respect to future and future expectations. When it comes to pure financial papers the recent events have indeed made us question the concept of *risk free* asset. When S&P downgraded USA, for the first time ever, in 2011, they sent a universal message that no risk free assets exist in their opinion, which is interesting for theoreticians but next to meaningless for the market traders.

Barter and the money economy

It is instructive to look at the problem of future prices and expectations from the point of view of a barter economy because it brings us back to the behavioural assumptions of the market economy in the neoclassical approach.

We have claimed that we cannot see any fundamental objection to the *behavioural content* in the axioms in a modified form which works within an epistemic cycle. The most problematic are the *reflexivity* and the *continuity* axioms. The former we revitalized through the introduction of epistemic cycles, and given social inertia we may actually use it practically locally and temporally. With respect to continuity there are two types of problems. On one hand we have the traditional indivisibility problem which is less a problem for the society as a whole as for the individual. On the other hand we have claimed that commodities are to be seen as multidimensional complexes and are thus defined differently with respect to the actual context. This will result in higher price volatility and the existence of bifurcations depending on both growth and income distribution matters and on the whole at the social development. If we use Becker's household production approach or the Gorman/Lancaster approach we can fairly well describe such volatility and such bifurcations, the classical example is Giffen's paradox. But still this is a minor problem with respect to the market as a whole and given social and economic inertia.

So we come to the conclusion that applying the behavioural content of the axioms on a process like Allais' equimarginal principle may work quite well locally.

However we must realize that the behavioural assumptions only deal with the real flows and if we assume a barter economy in real sense we can well understand the relevance of the theory. There is no medium of exchange but the commodity production is at the same time instrumental for exchange into other commodities. Environmental outcomes like drought or too much rain and similar events, will change the flows but there is a possibility to borrow against future production or at least by selling one's own work. If somebody gets an idea of for example a cattle watering machine, he has to persuade his fellows that it is useful but if he succeeds depends of the actual patterns in cattle-breeding and can be assumed to be a rather slow market process.[9] Thus in the barter economy we can expect that the revaluation vectors are linked more or less entirely to different disturbances of the current flows, which might be insured against in the neoclassical way. Technical changes are slow and, practically speaking, well announced. In this context it is important to remember Hume's rather devout praise of the market economy bringing unknown commodities and business contacts, bringing luxuries which smoothen the minds and make people more civilized; the spread of new social patterns as well as technologies in a monetary market economy is a quicker process and it evolves through changed money flows which may alter demand flows and direction of savings quite quickly which might also imply sudden shortness of resources as a result of changed directions of demand and investment flows.

As a matter of fact Hume uses the picture of the circulation of blood (1770: 59) to describe the role of money and it is an interesting picture. The blood provides the different parts with nutrition in a broad sense but when the body for example is under shock the blood is drawn back to protect the most vital parts in the body, the brain and the heart. In a way money has the same role. We have earlier mentioned how the states during the sixteenth and seventeenth centuries actively promoted a monetary economy which made it much easier to redistribute resources and thus gain control over larger parts of the countries. The same when we come to investments in new technologies and commodities even if the local demand is thin.

Thus the real market economy of the village and its close surroundings evolve by the introduction to an anonymous sort of organism, where the personal relations are replaced by transfers of money values. This was not only discussed by Hume but was clearly realized by the friars of Salamanca.

Thus when we look at the neoclassical theory it is in its theoretical fundamentals back in the medieval village of isolation, no matter how sophisticated the mathematics we use we can never transform it into covering the problems of the monetary economy. The flow chart we hinted at in Figures 4.1 and 4.2, expresses that the monetary economy is in fact a different organism compared to the barter economy. Particularly that concerns the expectations of the future since money provides us with the power of directing the allocation of resources to remote distances particularly with current technique.

So our enquiry has brought us to a conclusion that money matters, but not only matters but is of basic importance to understand the economy. Look at Walras' $n+1$th equation, look at the quantity equation, look at the neoclassical price index, look at the IS-LM model in Hicks' version; in all these cases the question of money is neutralized so money becomes unimportant.

It is interesting to read Keynes both in *General Theory* and *Treatise on Money*. In both these works he discusses the institutional arrangements of money and discusses the question of liquidity and its role vis-à-vis uncertainty and expectations, but he passes over the social role of money rather quickly. The reason is perhaps that he saw it as evident, but Hume and the friars of Salamanca were much more outspoken on this aspect of money most probably because the monetary economy was in a relative beginning and the development of transport facilities and the production technology changed the pace of its growth.

With respect to economic theory in its sophisticated form it can be seen as trivial to bring an elementary concept such as *anonymity* in the foreground of the discussions, but in fact this forces us to consider the social development and its consequences in changing production technologies, demand structures and institutional arrangements. This also widens the concepts of risks and uncertainty to contain also the agents' very market reactions. Pamela Labadie discusses anonymity and individual risk. The anonymity implies that the households are unaware of the total commodity space, the completeness axiom is thus rejected, and they can just pay attention to their own net trade. Furthermore she assumes that markets are not separated by type (we may substitute a Ferrari to a diamond ring), thus contracts are not exclusive which actually means that agents can make side arrangements, there are secondary markets locally and temporally. She arrived at the interesting conclusion for a barter economy:

> Since agents face the same budget constraint in net trades, but face different endowment distribution risk, agents will execute different net trades depending on type. The result that some states are under-insured while others are over-insured. The equilibrium has the property that the marginal rate of substitution is equalized across states in the contingent claims market. The

anonymous equilibrium is derived and shown to exist, although it may not be unique.

(2009: 2452)

In principle we can say that if there is a viable second hand market we may have a sort of constrained equilibrium although not unique but this second hand market is only local and temporal in relation to the total market.

However applying such an approach we also can see money in a radically different role, which is evident in the modern society and in studies concerning financial markets but not so much in mainstream theory as it manifests itself in mathematical modelling.

The input–output tableau in Figures 7.4 and 7.5 can easily be made completely deterministic but for the revaluation vectors when we accept money in its modern form it is more problematic.

Let us look back at Table 3.1 and Figure 3.3, we discussed there a systematic change in the conditions for a big Swedish firm. At the end of the 1980s the enquiry which brought the table got the result that the company changed its strategy and on one hand increased its foreign investments and on the other hand increased cooperation with similar companies in other countries. Thus their behaviour basically changed with respect to what could be expected from the current production flows of the company and it concerned its disposition of money and financial assets. They realized that their situation was entirely different with respect to traditional apprehension of risk and implied both a different risk structure but also elements of genuine uncertainty with respect to the dependence of different countries' specific institutional, political and social particularities.

As said in relation to Table 3.1, the discussed company was just one among many Swedish companies which experienced much the same development which in fact changed the whole basis for the economic policy. One could say that from the middle of the 1980s the Swedish government pursued an economic policy to a great part in congruence with traditions from the 1960s and 1970s which resulted in a real and financial disaster in the beginning of the 1990s, which was actually as big or even worse, at least according to figures, than the current breakdown of Greece, but it was in another international environment of course. The awareness of the crisis was delayed by the fact that the financial flows partly hid the real problems because of delayed transactions and by the fact that Sweden upheld a currency basket not relevant for the actual trade structure. When the change of the currency basket came it was evident that the situation was unsustainable.

The described development is not as much a description of the specific money problem but description of the environment of modern companies where technological advancements create on one hand increased possibilities of profits but on the other hand both an increased dimensionality of the risk space and uncertainty, where the added risk dimensions in relation to the real exchange market is within the very functioning of the market since it covers completely different social, institutional and political structures which to a larger extent are unknown to the management. So in a way we are still discussing real risks and uncertainties but they are a consequence of the *potentials* of the monetary economy and also endogenous in the monetary economy but do not exist in the barter economy.

Uncertainty and money contract

Joseph Bower (1970) studied the resource allocation and investments in private companies, where he categorized three different types of investments: cost reducing investments, capacity increasing and investments in new products. He followed 50 different investment projects in a big American company during ten years and calculated the ratio of actual return to expected return and the calculations ended up in Table 7.2.

Table 7.2 is actually rather a deterrent and gives us a picture of why a company hesitates to invest in new concepts and even to increase capacity. Cost reducing investments increase labour productivity and profit and little risk/uncertainty is added to the company. Nevertheless new products are more or less constantly introduced and if we remind ourselves of the so-called *product cycle model* we know that those who succeed are rewarded, but it has to be financed. If we return to the barter economy for a moment the discussion of Table 7.2 is virtually meaningless. Who will ever invest in a new product except nations in war which are able to use force in the allocation of resources? In a monetary economy this is possible since we have a collateral asset/liability in the form of a financial contract. This very fact makes it possible to acquire a portfolio of risky assets and end up in a lower total risk.

With this in mind we must also realize the fact that the production, the distribution as well as the consumption and the use of real items, take time and efforts makes it appropriate to induce the concepts of inertia and friction in the analysis. We are aware of this problem if we look at the financial matrix of Figures 7.5 and 7.6 where we have the revaluation matrices V^A and L^A. Changes in the expectations on the future depending on *any cause and of any character* will immediately change the revaluation vectors and thus change the financial conditions for the next period although virtually nothing has happened to the real flows.

This ability implicit in the use of money is dependent on three basic conditions: the money used is commonly accepted as money, there are sufficient

Table 7.2 Mean value of actual return in relation to calculated return in the investment plan

Type of investment	Ratio of actual return to calculated
Cost reducing	1.1
Capacity increasing	0.6
New product	0.1

grants that the money in question will prevail as the accepted medium of exchange, and there exists bank money where real and financial assets can be seen as collaterals. That of course means that the financier must share, at least partly, the expectations of the borrower but it is a vast difference between the two. While the value of the real asset is entirely defined by the flow of incomes it produces, the corresponding financial asset however apart from the debt service payments is unproductive in a real sense but can fully well work as security for further financial operations. Thus in the financial world an asset linked to a real asset is a base for further profitable business where the asset serves in a way as a shipload of coffee which can be sold several times during the transport from South America to Europe finally ending up in Lebanon, although the financial asset may go on forever in principle. Thus it is important to understand how an inert *stock* can be used to generate more profitable *transactions*.

Unfortunately the real item and its income generation underlies the whole financial superstructure and it is obvious that we must calculate with individual non-systematic failures to a certain degree and that is basically what risk calculations are about, but if we have systematic processes either on the real side which increases the risks on real capital or on the financial side which increases the risk taking for instance to increase the transaction volume, the system will sooner or later become unbalanced and we are approaching financial distress or even breakdowns.

If we then have a steady growth like we had during the 1950s until the middle of the 1970s the real development is, at least seemingly, rather homogeneously from a financial perspective and the financial organizations have a relatively easy journey. In the world of today with large cultural discrepancies, a spatial journey takes a certain clock time but culturally, socially and politically we travel through a time span of several centuries. At the same time, as all have access to virtually the same technology of information and control leading to contradictive and volatile policies, the environmental risks have been increased by magnitudes. To believe in business as usual might indeed need frequent redefinitions.

In fact physical and social organizations are inert to a certain degree but their environment need not to be and then factual effects of the organizations in question are not inert. It is however also important to remember that although we have a clear risk increase we also have an increase of new profitable opportunities. Nevertheless if we could think of this world only as a barter economy we would certainly have a slower development where risky dimensions had time to be compensated by new opportunities but unfortunately this is a dream and when money comes into consideration its almost frictionless nature aggravates and obscures the effects, and also constantly changes the financial conditions for the real productive structures.

With respect to the financial contracts there are particularly two aspects which are a bit troublesome. The first aspect we have already touched on several times and it is the inflation problem. Almost all financial contracts are written in nominal figures and that makes them sensitive to inflation, but when the states pursue an anti-inflationary policy to stabilize the economy and to calm the financial actors, they have to fight inflationary expectations which most probably requires an even tighter as well as persistent deflationary policy than just fighting a current inflation; in fact we also introduce a systemic risk increase on the underlying real assets. Thus the persistent inflationary policy increases the systemic risk of both the real production and the financial portfolios.

The second aspect is that according to the earlier discussion it is possible to use an asset as a means to increase the transactions by using it as a security. We may even have defaults in some of the assets/liabilities without serious effects, provided the defaults are non-systematic.

If we thus experience higher risks and/or want to increase profitability we may act in two ways: increase the transaction speed and the risk taking. The latter is of course a clear possibility if we at the same time increase the flow of transactions and with modern techniques it could be done ultimately to a considerable fraction of the speed of light. This is more or less what was happening in 2008.

These two strategies in conjunction are of course devastating for stability as well as for real growth.

Say's law again

In the end of Chapter 5 we considered Say's law from a somewhat different perspective and we have in this chapter showed the enormous complexity of the financial system. Furthermore we have discussed the inherent instability of future markets of financial assets and liabilities and in Chapter 6 we discussed the specific concept of uncertainty which is not per se linked to the surrounding physical state space of the market system but to the agents themselves. If we think about a totally frictionless physical system we will see that it will be completely without stability till we bring some inertia. We criticized Adam Smith in Chapter 2 when we discussed his wording in Book IV (op. cit.: 309) where he says that "as the necessity of civil government gradually grows up with the acquisition of valuable property, so principal causes which naturally introduce subordination gradually grow up with the growth of that valuable property". From a general point of view Smith is absolutely right. We have discussed epistemic cycles and their theoretical implications implying uncertainty, but we know from our daily life and from historical experiences that property and wealth imply both social responsibility as well as social status. Thus work, property and social position imply perhaps a certain uncertainty of the individual and needs of protection but with respect to the action space of the individual it is definitely the highest form of inertia we can induce in the individual. Laws and sanctions are a good help to discipline the individual but property and work is generally imperative for social stability.

Thus when we look at Figures 4.11 and 4.12 from a macroscopic point of view and with respect to social stability the concept of economic growth is less about the circulating volume of commodities and more about the fact that people's productive ability is used to full extent. Growth of the economy has to include an employment rate which is socially desired and remunerated in a decent way which is the only kind of macroscopic politics which promotes an increasing dimensionality of the commodity space in conjunction with a declining systemic uncertainty.

This means that the general belief that investments in real production are relatively uncertain while investments in securities are more secure is true at the microscopic level while at the macroscopic level it is the other way around. The conventional belief that microscopic relations are additive to the macroscopic is an unfortunate effect of the neoclassical approach. It is easy to see when we regard the very meaning of financial securitization. We decrease the individual risk by spreading it to the rest of the agents, which means that we increase the systemic risk when we add the problem of liquidity as a form of lexicographic preference. As long as this kind of securitization is parallel to growth which is socially sustainable, i.e. implies an acceptable distribution and declining permanent unemployment, it is perfectly defensible, good and necessary. In such a scenario the financial sector works in strengthening the society. If it works as we have witnessed the latest decades in earning money on money in a zero-sum game it ruins the society and the sector's protection of the value of money directly threatens the value of money in risking social unease.

For the single entrepreneur who has discovered possible ways of developing the dimensionality of the commodity basket along the social evolution takes considerable risks, but for the financial system which may create portfolios of risky projects to insure themselves the risk is in fact lower than in lending out to states for common demand policies or lending to consumption directly. The latter may be more profitable in the short run but I think we by the sharply augmented default risks have reached the end of this road.

The only thing which creates values is entrepreneurship and human industriousness and that has always been the attitude of market analysts but somehow in our time industriousness and entrepreneurship are often regarded as risky, while papers, bonds or money seems riskless even for theorists on the macroscopic level.

Some comments on the globalized economy

We have earlier in the book only occasionally touched on international topics and the effects of globalization. As a matter of fact the international dimension augments certain effects of the monetary economy but does not really change the problem in a qualitative way, but there are some points to comment on.

Development

The globalized economy takes the general equilibrium approach to its absolute limit, save for inter-galaxy ventures. It is taken to its limit in several ways since it is an upper bound for trade in every moment of time and furthermore the concept of epistemic cycles becomes really important with respect to the differences in culture, social structures and technology. As we mentioned before a journey through the world is also a journey in time covering many centuries, however an interpretation in Hume's manner leads us to think about infinite paths of growth when different societies are penetrated "in every vein" by the monetary economy. The Ricardian trade theory is probably true, given a particular moment but as a means to describe the dynamic process it fails, even with the modifications by Hecksher-Ohlin. The dynamics created by the penetration of the monetary economy goes in fact through Say's law. The key issue is the production venture which implies also a learning process and sooner or later a need for public interactions and institutions. Such a dynamic process in poorer areas, as already Hume describes, implies a higher risk level as well as uncertainty in the more advanced countries. The latter of course tries to limit the development by transforming the problem to moral obligations and offer their "help" but upholding the process will have the same effect as when we in Figure 7.2 try to save the low entropy in the systems s_i and s_j and by that increase the "cost" in the form of entropy increase in the surrounding S^*. That will lead to some form of collapse. For societies the development we see in North Africa is of course a possible form.

In this context it is important to realize that a *sustainable* development can never be a static state with respect to cultural, social and political structures but it is a constant change, which does not upset the possibilities for the individuals to compose their lives given the given set of restrictions. A thought that a Marxian synthesis, a Kantian or Platonic a priori world or an everlasting state of general equilibrium could be realized in the real world is indeed corrupting for the human mind. We are born to be changed and we are born to change and in that perspective the monetary economy is the basic social technology.

We mentioned earlier "Polsk Riksdag" (Polish parliament) which is an ancient Swedish expression for the effects of individual veto. Unfortunately the neoclassical theory in its social interpretations comes close to that and that is central to Arrow's paradox. Development starts in production and market innovations but even small business requires a certain amount of institutional stability so the successive development of public uncorrupted structures is vital for economic development. A vital "help" for the development of poor countries is that rich countries refuse to take part in corrupting administrations and political establishments. Looking around in the world today this is may be a most demanding condition.

Currencies

The global economy also takes the concept of money to its limit. We have seen that, Hume, Smith, Ricardo, Thornton and Say, although their conflicting views on money saw gold and to some extent silver as the only reliable international currency, they agreed to a large extent on the view that for *internal trade* coloured stones would do as a medium of exchange provided appropriate stamps and signatures. But international trade takes place between different legal systems and Mr Brown's signature doesn't work where M. Dupont's signature is required. Consequently gold as most commonly traded as a store of value became a suitable grant for foreign trade. It is then important to realize that Hume, Thornton and Say explicitly claimed that international trade is a sort of barter since basically the export should pay the import. This system is now granted by the integration of banking systems within a frame of international agreements it is partly granted by the volume of trade among the involved nations, partly by the holdings of baskets of currency reserves including gold to protect for trade asymmetries. But as gold, during the days of the friars of Salamanca, as well as the days of Henry Thornton, varied in price according to the national price level due to shortages and surpluses of commodities, the convertibility today is in the same way due to currency variations in relation to each other and is also due to political actions.

The currency value expressed in exchange rates is an interesting example on the difference between real aggregation and aggregation in money terms. A change in the exchange rate will have asymmetric changes on the real supply and demand irrespective of the cause of the change. It is perfectly possible that the actual development of a nation implies a systematic long-term change in the exchange rates but it may equally well happen that a change in the exchange rates is due to factors independent of the relation between the national and the international real structures.

A nice example of the latter is Sweden's remarkable performance in the aftermath of the financial crises 2008. Sweden was hit as all other countries but in the preceding boom several important export companies had displayed structural problems and a need of structural modifications. The effect of the financial crises was that financial reserves were to a high extent rerouted to big currencies particularly to the euro but also to USD. The SEK depreciated in a period of four months by approximately 25 per cent. This depreciation which should normally have taken place in a situation of severe economic difficulties, now took place without any political or other measures whatsoever; it was a pure flight to quality. The government got a golden opportunity to perform an expansive fiscal policy which actually eased the structural reconditioning of the big export companies. One particular company gave the trade unions notice of a possible need to reduce the working force with more than 400 workers as an effect of the closing down of inefficient parts of the production, but the depreciation implied that the Swedish companies when the international demand rose had a substantial price advantage and it really worked out extremely well for the mentioned company so in the end only 40 workers had to resign, but shortly afterwards they were re-employed.

The point is that if Sweden had chosen as a conscious policy to depreciate the currency there had became other nasty side effects of sinking confidence and considerably higher risk premiums but as it happened Sweden came out of the turmoil with a strengthened economy and without a stain on its character.

Unfortunately the present situation does not allow for similar lucky events for the Swedish economy.

As the example from Sweden shows the reactions of the market actors as an answer to the financial crises 2008 implies that the SEK is not regarded as international money in terms of security. The important factors which still make the USD the international money despite the shaky debt and trade situation of the United States is first that most international basic commodities, energy, metals, agriculture and so on are priced in USD. Second the USA is still the biggest market in the world although the euro zone market is rather close. That means in terms of economic distress that it is favourable having the assets in a currency of the big market and the subsequent richness of possibilities and that naturally goes for the euro zone too. However although the USD and the euro are pretty good substitutes with respect to market size and although it is possible to make international contracts in euro, the USA has a single government wholeheartedly supporting the USD while in the euro zone still local national interests are affecting the euro.

In 2011 S&P downgraded USA from AAA to AA+. Many thought it was a completely meaningless action. The relative grading should ideally be a sort of norm for the relative price of a swap between different currencies and in the case of the USD a so-called *basis swap*. That is when you for security reasons want to swap assets in one currency to assets in USD you have to pay an interest in between, since the USD is seen as the most secure currency and there is no risk premium. If you then downgrade USD, which might be fair relative budget and current accounts deficits, still the USD will be regarded as the base currency with respect to risk premium, so what is the point of downgrading? We upgrade all interest rates in the world by 500 basis points (0.5 per cent) but that will not change the fact that USD is the basic currency. Maybe the downgrading is a policy warning but in that case what does S&P know of politics? According to our earlier discussion in this book the financial organizations looking after their own interests may often force governments to actions which are against their own long-run interests, and this long run is probably not that long. If we prioritize the interests of the financial sector exclusively we do not only let the dead city rule the living city, but we also let it kill the living city.

8   Money and stability

When I was a child we often played marbles. The marbles were of a complex nature and formed a rather consistent monetary system in the local trade and valuation. They were of three different materials; there were two sizes and a multitude of colours.

The socially given intrinsic value of these different marbles was of two dimensions, the mass and the aesthetic quality. The mass was important for winning the game and the aesthetic value seemed to be a kind of social aspect for the ranking, anyway there had evolved a rather strict and consistent relative valuation of the different types of marbles.

The relative valuation of marbles could also be used in the exchange of other valuable things like sweets, pictures of famous football players and all kinds of mysterious things of the universe that adults since long have lost their ability to appreciate. We had actually developed a monetary system. Thus trading and exchange seems to be rather deep in the souls of human beings. It is also interesting to see that the marbles have in fact developed into a pretty consistent local and temporal currency built on social conventions almost aiming for a kind of law money. I have noticed that children nowadays seem to have developed similar kinds of systems.

There are other descriptions of trade and use of different money systems among children and we of course pay our deepest respect to the icon of business and entrepreneurship of all times, Tom Sawyer. He sold the rights to do boring work for him in a skilfully performed barter trade and then he used the different acquired treasures to change them into a local church currency (differently coloured pieces of paper) in order to win a bible (not the bible per se but the ceremony when it was given to him), which he needed to get to impress one Becky Thatcher and the rest of the world. His transactions were rather similar to that going on in international trade.[1]

Consequently money as a medium of exchange is not a mystery but quite natural in human societies of all kinds, irrespective of if it is gold, stones or paper. The key question is the social acceptance and the convertibility into other similar systems. The marbles, which the kids play with, obviously do not work when they go to the local candy store, so they are depending on some form of weekly allowance from their parents but once they have bought their rations they can start the local market process.

In a way such a description covers fairly well the discussions by Hume, Say and Ricardo, all these saw the money for use at the internal market basically without any intrinsic value but trading with foreign countries required a currency which was internationally accepted, gold and silver, and consequently it is necessary with a link between internal and international trade. Henry Thornton thought a bit differently since he introduced paper money as assets/liabilities in commercial trade where the trade and other commercial relations induced trust per se in the paper currency.

Thus money as a medium of exchange is not difficult to understand. The next step is to realize that the acceptance of money as a medium of exchange also gives money a value which is independent of any intrinsic value namely the value of the most liquid asset. Jean Baptist Say was advocating a currency where the basic money had an intrinsic value, mainly silver, but still he claims that even if we are prepared to pay with jewels the latter is not liquid since it lacks the official status as a medium of exchange.

Consequently when we discuss chartalism or metallism we must remember that it is not the eventual intrinsic value which creates the liquidity but it has more to do with the general trustworthiness and such matters and this was also the view of Aristotle. Subsequently the market use as such is the key issue and that implies that it is easier to trust a big currency issued by a rich country since it is part of a larger amount of transactions, compared with a currency of a small country; the quantity and size of the market transactions in a big country makes the currency more trustworthy.

In the same line the use of money coins or papers attached to gold is easier to trust than the use of iron and/or copper as a norm, since people use gold for more for valuation then for practical purposes.

Consequently when we go back to our quotes in the beginning of Chapter 2 from von Mises and Iwai we are apt to lean towards Iwai's opinion: money is to the largest extent depending upon social acceptance.

The dimensions of the concept of money

We have worked with three different dimensions of money; medium of exchange, liquidity and medium of accounting/valuation. When we look at the main stream economic theory these dimensions of the concept of money seem to go along quite well; in fact in the neoclassical economy neither of the dimensions is necessary. The quantity theory is sometimes added to the neoclassical theory but its theoretical meaning with respect to the axiomatic structure is indeed unclear.

Money as a medium of exchange is understood at least since the days of Aristotle and so is the concept of liquidity. As a medium of exchange money is the lubricating oil of the system, if we allude to Hume's wording, and does not need any intrinsic value at all. This is accepted by most economists during history. However the very fact that an item is used as a medium of exchange induces an intrinsic value to this item as long as it is used and trusted as a medium of exchange. This was emphasized already by Aristotle. We can also save some of the medium of exchange for later expenses or for security or for speculative purposes. Thus security and speculative demand for money/liquidity goes back to times long before Aristotle since he actually treats these things as known since long.

Thus the dimension of liquidity stems from the use of an item as a medium of exchange and if we at the same time claim that the item used as a medium of exchange should have an intrinsic value separate from the value it gets from the social acceptance as a medium of exchange, we actually run into a rather complex situation. A naive analysis must end up in Gresham's law and what do we do then? We have seen that gold/silver was used in international trade since it was trusted to have an intrinsic value as a sort of back up insurance, but the friars of Salamanca as well as the economists during the eighteenth and the beginning of the ninteenth century realized that it was the relative prices of commodities which gave value and completed with trade volumes decided the relative trade position of the country. Special attention was of course paid to the control and use of the gold mines in America. Thus the role of gold was actually treated as rather passive and the bullionists often regarded it as a kind of norm for measurements of *money*, as in the Bretton Woods system when USD price in gold was set to 37.5 USD/ounce gold and the other currencies were linked to USD in respective proportions. Hence from this point of view we can choose whatever item as for instance marble only that gold is more accepted.

The alternative view of this matter the *real bill approach* was advocated by Adam Smith and also von Mises, as is seen from the quote in the beginning of Chapter 2, leads in fact to two contradictive principles of valuation which is the basic rational for Gresham's law.

The concept of liquidity is however of a specific nature. We illustrated the imperative character in the form of lexicographic preferences and Jean Baptiste Say also noted that the acceptance of the liquid item must be prompt and not require any further operation. Even if we have whatever valuable items as jewels these are worth much but require considerations from both sides in the transaction; which the item which renders the status of liquidity does not do, this is also implicit in Gresham's law.

This actually is the very basic rationale for the link between liquidity and uncertainty, thus the subjective apprehension of uncertainty induces a current motive for demand for money which is independent of the demand for commodities; obviously the concern for future demand for commodities is underlying this motive and liquidity is the ultimate border between current and future demand.

How do we then understand uncertainty? According to our discussions we may say that the risk concept has a logical form which might be seen as a link between a known, at least in theory, state space and the commodity space. The uncertainty concept however is completely without any logical form and although we can simplify the concept by defining it as a situation where we do not know the space of outcome we must stress that there is no possibility to ever know of the future more than possibly some trust in locally and temporally inert spaces.

This means that uncertainty is a formless and universal state which is applicable to any real or financial structure irrespective of its structural content. Subsequently any item which shall be used as a protection against uncertainty must have as few structural links as possible to the current mode of economic affairs. Consequently money, defined as the most liquid asset, must possess a value almost completely free from particular preference and production structures.

If we allude to the bullionist discussion at the beginning of the ninteenth century the above discussion is the ultimate theoretical basis for an anti-bullionist attitude.

Having established this we turn to the third dimension intrinsic to money, the accounting/valuation aspect. This concerns assets and liabilities payable in a nearer or more distant future issued in nominal terms. Obviously bills with short time until expiration can be used as money, but not completely since it requires access to a certain institutional structure. This is a rather important issue discussed by Thornton to separate bank money from law money. Bank money implies a particular risk/responsibility structure and is thus mostly linked to particular institutional structures, which imply that bank money is not as commonly used as law money. That means that if we regard the different definitions of money, M0,..., MZM, we also have a shrinking group of agents from M0→MZM for whom the respective definition is relevant. There are groups of people for whom pure cash is the only possible medium of payment and the reader may contemplate the rest of the definitions.

Assets and liabilities with longer time to expiration are more complicated when we regard our discussions of liquidity. The assets and liabilities are defined in nominal money which means that the expiration will imply that current liquid assets are expected, but the question is at what purchasing value?

The intrinsic logical meaning of money

Uncertainty has no logical form and thus we might expect that money as liquidity should possess as few structural links to any real structures as possible and thus have a different logical form compared to real commodities.

It might seem a bit surprising and even disappointing that this evident difference between real commodities belongs to proper classes and money belongs to non-proper, is the most important part of the explanation to all the frustration about "a serious theory of money". Our earlier investigations have shown that apart from the necessary introduction of epistemic cycles the axiomatic postulates of the neoclassical theory have to be rejected as an axiomatic structure but nevertheless the behavioural assumptions they describe are not unreasonable and they also approximately hold in Keynesian theories. The one concept which is frustrating is *uncertainty of the future*. The only way uncertainty of the future can affect both the direction and the volume of real exchange is by the accumulation of liquid assets, which in most cases are attached to money in an ordered society by contractual and accounting relations which are based on nominal values. On the other hand fear of a considerable inflation may lead to instant consumption as we have witnessed in many countries falling apart socially and politically.

The reason why economic theory has failed to include these aspects is, if we go back to Wittgenstein's proposal 6.211 illustrated in Figure 1.1, the transforming of the reality into mathematical models and enough attention has not been paid to the two translation arrows in Figure 1.1 and when the models then have been extended to include other questions in the economy the researcher has accepted the basic mathematical picture and other researchers have been interested in the abstract development of the models and overlooked the basic question about in what way the model is a reasonable picture of the reality and in what way it is not.

Much criticism has been directed to the extensive use of mathematics in economy and some may be relevant. In general however mathematics is an indispensable tool for logical analysis but a by-product of the use is the fact that we by translating a real problem into a mathematical form also get some peculiarities in the sense that we have to observe the "rules" of mathematics. Problems which are well posed and restricted can normally be rather easily analysed but when we try to generalize modelling and increase the complexity it is more difficult to see where we stretch the pure mathematical conditions in an imprudent way.

The problem of friction and non-friction is interesting in the sense of mathematical modelling. We have mentioned somewhat about pricing modelling on particular options. These models have evolved into a clearly interesting direction where we actually have an (at least implicit) effort to work out an adequate modelling for the Keynes' beauty contest, although in a negative way, and we have got models for a practically frictionless world. It started with the Black and Scholes model originally based on heat propagation, developed by Samuelson (1965) and McKean (1965). The development of Black and Scholes follows the same principles but releases some of the original assumptions; nevertheless it builds on a physical reality where friction is brought down to a minimum which is correct in the case of money flows in the modern economy. In fact this shows the very problem of economic theory; what is realistic in the modelling of the financial flows is not so when we deal with the real economy. This is perhaps the most treacherous point in modelling economic theory, and this is why we have to pay attention to the fact that the neoclassical axiomatic structure transforms the real economy to a frictionless Euclidian space. The particular neoclassical modelling methodology is in its turn to a great extent kept by those working with Keynesian models.

Diffusion of money and equilibrium

David Hume, Jean Baptiste Say and to some extent also Henry Thornton regarded the monetary economy as a diffusion process, which in fact follows from the specific logical character of money. The simplicity of using money as a medium of exchange, its easiness in business, its almost infinite divisibility was not only a lubricating oil, it was an important means to expand the market and to expose new enterprises and commodity dimensions and consequently it was also seen as an important factor in the *socialization of the society*. Through the money system the society could be penetrated with all kinds of commodities thus changing social structures. The mentioned economists saw money as a means of civilization, as the economic market process became a never ending dynamic process; all of them saw with excitement upon the future.

But the mercantilist thinking fought back and economic theory was developed which locked up the theoretical picture of the society in a closed equilibrium system like Newton's and its simple logic appearance was interpreted as the true scientific road. It seems like the theoretical development made a full stop from Ricardo, save for Wicksell, Keynes and some other heterodox economists, in a world looking like a medieval village with barter. This world was promoted to an example of highest mathematical complexion with the so-called Arrow and Debreu economy. Money was forgotten completely or thrown away as an unimportant theoretical concept. The economy was not seen as a diffusion process but as an everlasting unmoving equilibrium or an equilibrium trajectory built on a logical time model in Samuelson's meaning.

The equilibrium feature as we have discussed in this book has three particular features; (i) equilibrium in relation to some definition generally implies a fairly simple logic and a good possibility to derive useful hypothesis, (ii) the equilibrium concept seems to cover the market process in the meaning that the customer and the supplier have to come to an agreement, (iii) the equilibrium concept provides us with an efficiency norm which is attractive when we deal with economics, i.e. the allocation and distribution of scarce resources.

However we have seen that those early economists which were aiming towards an equilibrium theory, Aristotle, Smith and Ricardo, all implied that the labour value, land rent or even the price of corn was the hub around which the prices moved. If we add the thoughts in temporary equilibrium theory we might illustrate a kind of model which expresses Smith's and Ricardo's approaches, a so-called Hopf-bifurcation, illustrated in Figure 8.1, actually a bit similar to a

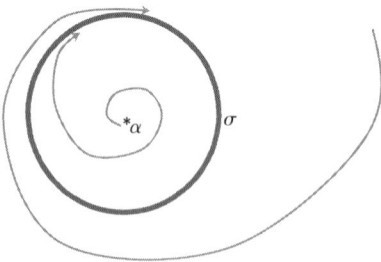

Figure 8.1 Hopf-bifurcation.

Volterra-Lotka equation about competing species, but more apt to describe an economy with exogenous shocks.

In Figure 8.1 the equilibrium point α is unstable, exogenous events, erroneous information or expectations throwing the economy out of equilibrium but out of equilibrium there are equilibrating processes such as a priori fixed values, fixed price relations or similar factors which if the economy leaves the equilibrium α too much brings the system back nearer the equilibrium. The result is that we will have a trajectory σ illustrating the border where the equilibrating forces are bigger than the dis-equilibrating ones. In economic theory we might think of an accelerator model with predefined maximum/minimum values.

The labour (land rent) theory of the early economists was replaced by the utility theory in the neoclassical theory, but then replaced by preferences in the modern Arrow/Debreu approach, which also replaced the theory of decreasing marginal utility with a combination between the axiom of reflexivity and the axiom of convexity. This implied that the equilibrium got a more general outlook but in fact it made the axiomatic structure equally or more restricting. Smith and Ricardo linked their reasoning to actual social structure while the neoclassical theory transformed the agents to automatons.

We have claimed that given a reasonable inertia we might locally and temporally look at economic exchange processes as almost deterministic but this only applies to the microscopic world and the logical result of the neoclassical theory with respect to the macroscopic world the additive aggregation has to be rejected.

With respect to money the rejection of the neoclassical theory means nothing. In equilibrium money is a redundant concept and the inducement of money in a meaningful way in economic theory implies that we accept an out-of-equilibrium economic dynamics.

Early theoreticians such as the friars of Salamanca, David Hume, Jean Baptiste Say and Henry Thornton did not see the economy as an equilibrium system but a social process which in depth transformed the society. Money was of extreme importance in diffusing inventions and innovations, fashion and modes of living. Money streamlined business even with remote parts, and Thornton's description of how bank money could penetrate the country and the empire and bring new possibilities of trade is a homage to entrepreneurship and industriousness. In the world of these economists there were equilibrating forces but no equilibrium.

Wicksell took, as we told in Chapter 2, a seemingly not particularly important example of a ball in an urn and on the table respectively to illustrate microscopic and macroscopic equilibrium. We do not underestimate his other contributions when saying that this little example is of utmost importance to understand the difference between the macroscopic and microscopic theories and it places Wicksell strictly outside the realm of neoclassical theoreticians; it is also easy to understand why Wicksell had real troubles to understand the quantity theory of money.

When we reject the axiomatic structure of the neoclassical economy we still can assume the agent to be rational. The Austrian School particularly Ludwig von Mises has introduced the concept of *praxeology* which can be further developed by introducing epistemic cycles. Thus all agents, save for pathological cases and situations, panic and similar, are rational given a set of epistemic cycles. Given this we can show that there does not exist any additive aggregation and further that optimizing behaviour is possible on all levels of aggregation but an optimum on a given level of aggregation does not imply that underlying aggregate levels obtain an optimum simultaneously; we called the principle a *mereological rule of thumb*.

This principle implies that we impose a generic source of uncertainty in economic behaviour. The different levels of aggregation are interlinked but their mutual dependence is unclear and asymmetric and this is the basic rationale for Wicksell's example where he separates microscopic from macroscopic stability. Thus on the microscopic level there may exist local and temporal inertia but not so on the macroscopic level which is a function of the underlying levels; this function can however hardly be assumed to be constant but probably dissipative.

With respect to money this implies that money works with respect to all the inherent features, medium of exchange, liquidity, accounting/valuation although we are in an out-of-equilibrium situation. This means however that we also arrive at an internal conflict between the inherent concepts of money. Thus the very feature of money as a medium of exchange endows liquidity and the accounting figures with a value, but this is the actual point where the concept of inflation is a bit devastating.

The modelling problem

Obviously our distinction between real transactions and money transactions implies a huge problem. As long as we distinctly attach money to real flows as just a medium of exchange, we treat money as a representation of the real items. Basically this is the reason why we claimed that our analysis of the neoclassical theory only concerns the macroeconomic conclusions vis-à-vis the effects of additive aggregation. The use of the theory at the microeconomic level is not at stake as a consequence of our distinction. However if we use the microeconomic technique for an aggregate welfare analysis we utilize the reversibility correlate of *revealed preferences*, which is not valid in non-equilibrium; it is only valid in a prevailing equilibrium. Thus even if we to a large extent have accepted the axioms in a modified form this is not sufficient. If we also add the theoretical content of Arrow's paradox the economic welfare theory is definitely an insufficient theoretical tool. Observe that Arrow's paradox does not present a problem in the reality but a problem in modelling the reality.

Thus our distinction concerns macroeconomic theory and the main difficulty both from a technical and a psychological point of view is that we cannot use additive aggregation for commodities or epistemic cycles but we can use additive aggregation of money values. This implies that when we regard efficiency measures in money terms these can be used for enterprises the sole goal of which is to maximize the financial surplus given a time horizon. We may only partly use it for enterprises producing an output which must be defined with respect to multidimensional qualities in non-monetary terms but aiming at cost minimizing. This requires of course that we construct appropriate measures for these different qualities, for example within health care, education, defence, infrastructure, environmental matters and the like.

The latter type of enterprises is not disqualified for private production organizations per se but since we add the cost-minimizing aspect we have, given a more complex restriction space, an efficiency criterion possible to express in financial terms, which implies that we may separate the financing from the production. However it requires a precise definition of qualities and a regulation and control system.

It is important to remember that from a strictly theoretical point of view, no aggregate goals can be expressed only in money terms in a non-equilibrium economy. Thus for example the aggregate labour productivity increase is not saying anything particular with respect to some efficiency dimension of the aggregate since it is a function of technology improvements, capacity utilization and substitution of labour. An increase for example of the permanent unemployment as a consequence of a particular structural change in the production sector increasing its financial surplus as well as its productivity could hardly be measured as an increase in some kind of efficiency goal for the entire economy since it affects social structures. It is the same with economic growth. Since we have no unique price vectors even at a singular point of time we have even less so in inter-temporal studies. Thus a measure like GDP at current prices is to be seen as a measure of the total turnover of commodities in the current economy and our earlier discussion of inflation measures implies that we doubt that fixed price measures produce some more substance save for shorter periods where we can expect sufficient social and technological inertia.

The neoclassical inability to treat money as we earlier discussed is not due to a lack of understanding of the role of money but to the fact that commodities and agents are transformed to exactly the same logical class of elements namely as belonging to non-proper classes. As we have showed in Chapter 2 the commodity space is transformed to a Euclidian space where the agents are elements. This is why prices are just an index and this index is unique with respect to each and every equilibrium, a conclusion which we can accept, but it increases the confusion about money as a medium of exchange as well as a measure. Money terms are used to represent both nominal and real quantities but if so what is then inflation from a theoretical point of view? Does it appear in equilibrium or is it a non-equilibrium phenomenon? Representing the economy with an equilibrium model obeying the neoclassical axiom forces us into accepting that inflation solely depends on excess money supply but if so either revaluation of financial contracts are symmetric, and thus irrelevant in real terms, or the Walrasian nth or $(n+1)$th (whatever notation we use), which is the numeraire, is not of degree zero and the same with the Arrow and Debreu price index and we arrive at the result that the price vector is a linear transformation increasing the utility of cash holding due to inflation, a result which takes us outside the axiomatic structure, since in equilibrium we can use any multiple of the price vector as the standard one.

We may also ask how the answer to these questions affects monetarist and Keynesian theories. Other intricate questions with respect to the input–output tableaus in Figures 7.5 and 7.6 touch on the problem of the revaluation vectors; a revaluation caused by changed real flows is understandable but what can we expect from revaluations based on expectations on future production, which is the general investment problem? The latter case obviously creates a time distance between the current state of affairs and when the real processes actually take place. There are many examples, for instance from the IT bubble at the beginning of the early 2000s when shares were highly priced although no production took place. Mr Greenspan the former head of the Federal Reserve is said to have remarked "I know how to recognize a recession but I do not know how to recognize a bubble" which is on the spot with respect to describing the phenomenon. Equity has a monetary value but is it real? Are expectations to be regarded as real entities? Obviously they lead to monetary flows, which affect real variables.

Returning to Vespasian's expression about the lack of smell of money, we have two well-known aspects of money, on one hand we can currently trade the future without any real flows involved but *money contracts* might imply future restrictions of the real exchange when the uncertainty of the future is different from the current character of the uncertainty.

This means that all future contracts are not only in monetary terms but also concern only monetary values and can be traded as such provided that the expected value at the date when the contract reaches maturity is above zero. Keynes said "For the importance of money essentially flows from its being a link between the present and the future" (1973 [1936]: 293), but if it is possible to earn money on expectation we can try to move the future ahead in financial terms by trading liquidity. Cash is king is true to some extent but it is hard to eat, and sacrificing the real growth for this king is a long-term high-risk project.

The selling of the future has thus no real limits in a multidimensional economy, although the money sums involved affect the current real business. Thus comparing the real flow chart of Figure 4.1 and the flow-chart of the monetary economy in Figure 4.2 the occurring monetary flows have little to do with the real flow-chart but they affect the real flows in the monetary economy.

The second aspect of the fact that money does not smell concerns, a bit drastically expressed, the fact that money earned from a robbery is equivalent to money earned from life saving sea-operations by the coast guard. That is, in neoclassical theory we assume that the commodities traded on the market are gross substitutes and have at least a semi-positive (strictly positive in standard theory) value for all agents. Thus the commodities span a strictly positive Euclidian space, so there are no contradictions among the dimensions. This guarantees in fact the happy solution of the general equilibrium. With our modifications of the behavioural contents of the neoclassical axioms we allow even for the fact that the use of a commodity in one epistemic cycle contradicts the use of the same commodity in another epistemic cycle. If I buy a gun for hunting, given that I fulfil relevant laws and responsible behaviour, the result may be positive for me and my family without affecting the neighbours or society, but if I use the gun for robbery my purchase was obviously of negative value for my fellow citizens. To treat this problem as external effects is meaningless since the phenomenon is not linked to the commodity but to the agents. Technically we may therefore treat commodities as multidimensional items with respect to their use and the way the individuals use the commodities may be positive as well as negative for the social welfare.[2]

Anyhow this means that while a real analysis must regard these matters in terms of institutional arrangements and control systems which in fact well may decrease the general welfare, but such restrictions systems as well as on producing commodities for both good and bad has an equivalent principle of value in money terms. This fact was actually the reason why economics originally was seen as a moral science. Aristotle dealt much with economic problems in the Nicomachean Ethis. Adam Smith was a moral philosopher, Hume, a broader philosopher dealt deeply with moral questions. Wicksell in his non-economic writings was active in moral questions. In the neoclassical economy such problems have completely disappeared.

We have arrived at the conclusion that for the aggregate level general models of traditional character add little to the very common understanding of elementary economy. Sure the IS-LM model provides a certain basic understanding of the principal skeleton of the economy. However to gain further knowledge we must know such things as the liability structures of business and households, internal market structures of a country in relation to the structure of its foreign affairs, the structure of labour demand in relation to demographic and educational information of the potential stock of labour and so on. Much of these studies are already done but they give partial information which is difficult not to say impossible to combine in a kind of universal model although they add to a more fundamental understanding of the economy which is lost if we want to construct mathematically consistent models. The reason for this is that many causal links to events upsetting the economic stability go through the minds of the acting subjects and their particular apprehensions of what is going on as grounds for their actions.

Thus a universal model for the economy should consist also of psychological and sociological equations as well as equations covering dreams, idiosyncrasies and prejudices; even dreams, idiosyncrasies and prejudices are to be taken seriously as they are expressed in money flows.

This means that the prospects for general models are not very good since we then either have to mix variables belonging to different mathematical classes which require information which is outside what we get from models expressed in money terms, or we have to transform them into the same kind of mathematical variables. We then however lose an important aspect of the reality particularly the role of money and if we try to add that we are back again to the first option.

A further theoretical conclusion of these considerations is that it might well be so that a barter economy is relatively stable in a temporal sense, save for structural upheavals, but the monetary economy is to its very character unstable in itself, since the agents always can go for liquidity or invest in future ventures with high uncertainty or they can earn money on trading liquidity or dreams and expectations of the future. All these types of behaviour are still within the realm of what we might call rational behaviour but we can see the relevance of what we called the *mereological rule of thumb*. The deepest meaning of this is that any stability is created by general social structures and developments, where the economic development certainly is an important part and as such dependent on the surrounding social stability as well as vice versa, thus any economic structure threatening the social stability is not sustainable in the longer run.

Finally, Adam Smith, Ricardo and later economists made a huge job to explain the barter economy and they have maybe also explained some of the benefits of the monetary market economy. The analysis is however most suitable for a relatively isolated medieval village and although it has a mathematically advanced form, the modern neoclassical theory has not reached beyond that.

It may have played a positive role in the scientific development although we can see alternative ways of thinking which more or less have been suppressed by the alleged scientific theorization in terms of a kind of Newtonian modelling. In the modern society the neoclassical a priori general equilibrium theory has no scientific role in explaining the modern economy. All practical suggestions are relatively simple and follow naturally from the axioms but this also means that consequences of such suggestions in a broader perspective are overlooked as a consequence of the closed axiomatic reasoning.

But most of all it completely misses the role of money.

Production and its conditions

In our discussions we have claimed that the production activities are subject to considerable inertia, both with respect to heterogeneities and complementarities. We have also discussed the fact that all kinds of investments give rise to nominal contracts which give rise to risks and uncertainties with respect to future prices and production volumes. Thus the production organization per se is inert and gives rise to uncertainty, but it has also caused nominal contracts which if broken have repercussions not only on the owners of the production organization but on the liquidity position of creditors and by extension it might affect the entire credit system. The sanguine discussion of flexible prices and wages dismisses the financial consequences of such flexibility, thus real inertia as caused by the behaviour of the agent, as opposed to inertia caused by physical and technical factors, has most probably its origin on the financial side. The expressions "let bygones be bygones" and "never throw good money after bad" are generally sound advice not to be too sanguine, but if the financial consequences are judged to be widespread we have a reversed risk calculus; what is the chance that we may restore the organization or at least give us more time to plan our default strategy, and what is good money and what is bad money and what are the bygones?

We have seen that liquidity is a separate factor for the companies to account for under certain conditions and this requires holdings of money or financial assets next to money to protect the production organization. Thus the security demand for money evolves to a virtual insurance motive. It is in this perspective that the concept of inflation has its most devastating consequences. It is also with respect to this that we have the most serious intrinsic contradiction in the concept of money. An increased liquidity demand for money affects the volume of money as a medium of exchange and furthermore a protection of the purchasing power of contracts in nominal money also may harm the money stock for commodity exchange. This intrinsic conflict in the money concept per se has nothing to do with whether we discuss chartalist or metallist money; it has to do with the very definition of money as a medium of exchange and the intrinsic features created by that.

It is illustrative to look at the financial disaster 2008 and the causes behind it. The banks had increased the volume of bank money in order to increase profits and the bank money was in a way properly met by securities. The problem was that the securities were based on lax risk analysis and rather tiny information to the holders; thus the default risk increased disproportionally evolving into an increased systemic risk. When the disaster was a fact it did not occur in the form of inflation but in the form of real failures and diminished credits. This is in fact rather close to Henry Thornton's distinction between potential and enforced circulation and his opinion that an increase in potential circulation is met by default risks. When we however look at the *law money* an increase in its supply might cause inflation but the very problem is that real events may also cause inflation as we discussed earlier.

Inflation is basically a macroscopic concept. Thus we only speak of that in conjunction with aggregated real concepts as consumption, investments, exports and imports, and we then mean the very real items or processes (service production) underlying the concepts, but unfortunately there are no such real aggregate items or processes but their eventual monetary valuation. This is perhaps where the neoclassical general equilibrium concept has made the most damage. We have seen how the axiomatic structure mixes the monetary valuation of commodities with the real items or processes. This means that commodities become dimensions in a Euclidian space which implies that the problem is transformed to a smooth mathematical problem with measurable functions. Our rejection of the reflexivity axiom is a frank denial that a commodity could be a real number, which implies that in reality commodities are not atomistic items that could be aggregated additively as real numbers. In fact commodities are parts of consumption and production technologies where there are complementarities, heterogeneities and inertia. In the almost fruitless discussion of relative price and wage flexibilities at aggregate levels one fails to realize that this is dependent on real structures which have to be seen as real structures not as their monetary representations.

We showed that money and real commodities were from a strict mathematical point of view of two fundamentally different logical classes. Money belonged to non-proper classes and real commodities to proper classes. In the neoclassical theory this is jumbled when real commodities are transformed to non-proper classes. This implies that the entire dream of the existence of general equilibrium is based on this fundamental logical misconception.

Thus when we discuss the evolution of the real economy we cannot use additive aggregation and we cannot think of market equilibrium where we have a Pareto optimum which is also valid on the aggregate level. When we insert money into this more complex world it works fine locally and temporally as both a medium of exchange and a local and temporal measure, provided it is socially accepted. But we then also must accept the intrinsic conflicts of the concept of money. The reason is that the real economy is endowed with generic uncertainty and this basically comes from the two theoretical approaches; (i) humans are subjects, and thus to be seen as final causes, (ii) commodities are multidimensional complexes with respect to their functions, thus they are partially defined by the context.

This means that, as Arrow's paradox indicates, there is a rather complex relation between aggregate levels and their parts, which ends up in the *mereological rule of thumb*.

When we thus come to the value of money this concerns strictly a relation of the current structure of the economy to earlier or later structures depending on whether we discuss past or expected inflation, the concept of *purchasing power* is a key issue. The problem is that the concept of purchasing power constantly changes its structure and so the definition of purchasing power and inflation. The quantity identity of money indicates a relation between money supply and inflation which we can accept for extreme cases which we have seen in history, but history has also shown that there are other sources of inflation. Furthermore the difference between the real commodities and their monetary representation is in itself a complex which when we add changing commodity space makes measurement of inflation indeed complicated from a logical point of view. Measurement of growing new dimensions of the commodity space should normally imply a seemingly increased inflationary pressure.

A still more serious example is when we have the problem that the average optimal capacity utilization is below the level of production where the employment level is socially desired. We have shown how this may trigger a rather ugly development as illustrated in Figure 4.12, where we actually have a conflict between technology growth and employment, which Ricardo claimed but Wicksell denied. Both are right. There is no necessary conflict but it might be. When we are so convinced that there is a separate economic value from the one produced that we are willing to sacrifice people and resources to save the value of financial assets and liabilities we actually live in a dream world. The true story we tell in economic analysis of the market economy is that the only value which exists beside what God has given us *is that which is produced*.

But more than that we have also said that the only way money can work is that it is socially accepted. When we in our eagerness to save a highly theoretical future value of financial assets and pursue a development where we close the entrance to the labour market for young people, where we throw out people from the labour market in a vain hope of productivity increase we build a massive social debt which will come upon us in the form of social unease and the value of money is really at stake.

When looking at inflation it is obvious that it has negative effects if taken too far but in a situation where the optimal capacity utilization is substantially below the socially desired level we cannot save future purchasing power if we do not increase real growth in the meaning that more people get access to the labour market and this also holds for the financial sector with respect to their self-interests. In such a reign a certain inflation due to an acceptance of high demand in times of prosperity combined with social investments puts higher risks on monetary transactions in a zero sum game of price revaluations of existent assets of different kinds. Edvard Munch's painting *The Scream* was recently sold at a record price and when such things happens out of a development of general growth and prosperity it is normal but when it is due to a search for security for the future, as a part of a general attitude, it is a logical contradiction.

We quoted Matthew 6:24 in the beginning of Chapter 1 and asked how we can be servants to money? One, and the usual, interpretation is that we waste our resources on useless pleasures and depravities. Following our discussions however we may interpret it as we forget that money used as a medium of exchange is promoting industriousness and entrepreneurship which create the value of money but instead we serve money in the sense that we try to keep a value it does not have and consequently we let the dead city rule the living city and we even may allow the dead city to kill the living city.

Notes

1 Introduction, scopes and methods

1 In his book *The Human Use of Human Beings: Cybernetics and Society*, Norbert Wiener (1952) makes a nice metaphor that in the natural sciences the scientist meets an honourable opponent while in social science this is not the case.
2 Hume discusses eight specific "Rules by which to judge of causes and effects" in section 15 of Part 3: Of knowledge and probability, in David Hume (2002 [1740]: 116–17).
3 Given variations in demand, prices and incomes given the neoclassical axioms, we can "reveal" the utility function.
4 The congress archives are available at www.dalidimension.com.
5 On these matters D'Arcy Wentwort Thomson has written an inspiring book, first published 1917, which has inspired many scientists among others René Thom and Ilya Prigogine. The book is available in abridged version from 1961 *On Growth and Form*, Cambridge: Cambridge University Press, reprinted 1997.
6 We base our discussion on Stěkin (1963/1999).

2 The understanding of money: a retrospective glance

1 We will discuss these achievements in Chapter 6.
2 Whether or not there exists a market economy which is non-capitalistic is to a large extent an ideological question. We will not have a clear opinion on this, since from our point of view it is a matter of definition of concepts.
3 Bno refers to the Berlin enumeration.
4 In fact that was quite a task and St Thomas was for some time on the brink of being excommunicated.
5 The letter can be found at www.ourcivilisation.com/smartboard/shop/smitha/hume-dead.htm.
6 Hume is by many ranked as the first modern philosopher. From him we have the ruling scientific understanding of causality and for empiricists his scepticism of empirical studies through using inductive reasoning as a stumbling block, which until current time has been easy to dismiss in natural sciences but the latest development of quantum physics has revealed the difficulties. In social sciences Hume's scepticism should always be considered depending on the fact that humans must be regarded as subjects. For Hume it was an impossibility to develop a closed equilibrium system of a social science like economics; he links the economic development of the society to a vulnerable relation between classes and between the people and its rulers.
7 Adam Smith was seen as moral philosopher and published *Theory of Moral Sentiments* in 1759. He was strongly influenced by the German/Swedish philosopher Samuel von Pfufendorf, who became professor at the University of Lund, Sweden,

1668 and made also some contributions in economics. Von Pfufendorf developed a kind of civil philosophy splitting civil ethics from religious ethics, and he was strongly influenced by René Descartes, who was in Stockholm during the middle of the seventeenth century and they are supposed to have met. It is probable that Smith was more influenced as a philosopher than in his economic thinking by von Pfufendorf, which also made him sympathetic to Newtonian thoughts. Hetherington (1983), Sandelin (1990) and Saurette (2005: 42).

8 A more comprehensive discussion on such matters are found in Ekstedt and Fusari (2010: ch.4).

9 The bullion, normally gold, was defined according to weight and purity. A gold coin was defined by weight and purity but had a stamp which showed its nominal value. Thus in the latter case the nominal value could be different from the "bullion value" of the coin, which is the fundamental reason for Gresham's law. Real bills, which Adam Smith was a proponent for, implied that all paper money should be one to one convertible into gold. Thus a 10 shilling bill should be an equivalent to 10 shillings in gold.

10 This was an answer to Charles Bosanquet, who criticized the report of the Bullion Committee from a real bill perspective.

11 The convertibility implied that banks could strengthen their reserves and merchants could use gold in foreign affairs. However gold was not liquid as the paper money in everyday affairs. With respect to real bills gold was the liquid asset.

12 As a matter of fact Henry's father, John, and grandfather, Robert, were both directors of the Bank of England while his brother, Samuel, became the governor of the Bank of England. Henry Thornton was a member of parliament from 1784 to his death in 1815 and was also the co-author of the Bullion Committee Report 1810.

13 Say, although very appreciating of Adam Smith, meant that many of his ideas were already contemplated by Hume and that Smith learnt much from his correspondence with Hume (Say 1834 [1803]: xlii). Interesting is also that Say's grandson Jean Baptiste Léon Say edited Hume's economic writings "Oeuvre économique de David Hume", 1852 and where he claim in the introduction that Hume's publication of his *Essays* "à une époque où l'économie politique ne formait pas encore une science, mais où elle sortait déjà de son berceau. Adam Smith est son élève" (Diemer 2005: 14n.).

14 Chapter XXI, section I "General Remarks".

15 There were many others during the ninteenth century having the same thoughts but we limit the discussion to those appearing in our exposé.

3 Money, value and prices in neoclassical economic theory

1 This was solved by Johannes Keppler, who imposed elliptic orbits and so also varying speed; Arthur Koestler (1979 [1959]).

2 The second law of thermodynamics says that it is impossible to make a heat transfer from a state of lower temperature to a state of higher temperature without changes elsewhere. This is the ground for the concept of entropy which is a measure of the energy needed to make such a transformation. We will later on use the entropy concept as some kind of measure of order/disorder.

3 It is interesting to note that Friedrich Engels reacted rather hard against the entropy concept since it undermined the Marxian historical theory.

4 This part builds on Ekstedt and Fusari (2010).

5 An excellent presentation and proofs is found in Makarov and Rubinov (1977).

6 These endowments can be in the form of productive capacities, physical and mental.

7 The concept of equivalence relation plays a fundamental role in the axiomatic structure as a mathematical concept and its interpretation as a definition of rationality is a posterior interpretation.

8 Arrow (1950).
9 For a comprehensive non-technical discussion of these axioms see Ekstedt and Fusari (2010: ch. 2).
10 We may ask if we can reverse the link and propose that the six axioms concerning the individual are true given that the four axioms defining the social welfare function. The answer is obviously yes.
11 Paul A. Samuelson wrote a very amusing article on these matters in *Canadian Journal of Economics*, February 1968.
12 See Debreu (1982) and Radner (1982).
13 This has actually given rise to the Temporary Equilibrium Theory which we later will discuss.
14 Table 3.1 is taken from a seminar work at the School of Public Administration, University of Gothenburg, 1989. The table also appears in Ekstedt and Fusari (2010: 218–19).
15 There is obvious empirical evidence that some parts hold locally and temporally but that has nothing to do with the model in its global form.
16 However as we have mentioned elsewhere Keynes' criticism had the fortunate effect that one of the dimensionality problems of the neoclassical theory was illuminated. It is also important to realize that the axiom of non-satiation taken apart from the axiomatic structure is relatively harmless.
17 It is interesting to observe that the friars of Salamanca discussed these aspects when discussing the difference between the place where the contract was concluded and the place where the commodities or the commodity exchange was located.
18 This aspect is very important in legal proceedings. A person able to behave rationally with respect to planning and the performance of a crime is basically in such a mental state to be regarded as responsible for the crime.
19 We will in Chapter 4 have more comprehensive discussion of Russell's paradox with respect to money.
20 *Mereology* concerns the relation between the whole and its parts.
21 Two sets X and Y are homomorphic if an element x_i in X can be uniquely linked to an element y_i in Y.
22 An additional problem of dimensionality with respect to money in particular, will later be discussed in relation to other features of money as a measure of liquidity and using money for accounting measures with respect to inter-temporal assets.
23 See, www.sociologyguide.com/sociology_of_fashion/fashion_in_modern_society. php.
24 Observe that the characteristics matrix does not need, probably in the normal case is not, to be a square matrix. But for illustrative purposes it is simple and shows the necessary points. Thus when we have j characteristics and i commodities we end up in

$$\frac{i!}{j!}$$

solutions and furthermore, when $i>j$ satisfying the consumer needs to a outlay means that some commodities will not be consumed and when $i<j$ consuming any commodity combination means that some characteristics will not be satisfied. The simplest case when $i=j$ gives us also difficult problems so let us look at this case a bit more, since this will be basic when i differs from j.
25 Lavoie and Liu (2007).
26 Warmdinger (2004).
27 We will base our presentation on Grandmont (2006, 1977 and 1982).
28 Obviously we have the problem about what is true. If everybody but one agent has erroneous expectations acts upon this, will this not affect prices in such a way that the one with the "right" expectations will be worse off? This problem is however

excluded since we basically define the agents according to the neoclassical axiomatic structure and furthermore look upon the state space as a once for all given.

4 Money, value and prices in the Keynesian and monetarist theories

1 Keynes (1973 [1936] ch. 5), "The State of Long-term Expectation" is to a great extent built on Keynes' Treatise on Probability (1962 [1921]). The problem of the time concept involved is extensively discussed in Ekstedt and Fusari (2010: ch. 2), "On Time and Ethics".

2 The discussion is mainly based on Arnér and Ekstedt.

3 Keynes (1973 [1936]) makes a reference to Wicksell at page 242 in chapter 17, "The Essential Properties of Interest and Money".

> In my Treatise on Money I defined what purported to be a unique rate of interest, which I called the natural rate of interest, which, in the terminology of my Treatise, preserved equality and the rate of investment. I believe this to be a development and a clarification of Wicksell's "natural rate of interest", which was, according to him, the rate which would preserve the stability of some, not quite specified, price-level.

4 See, http://web.mit.edu/krugman/www/ and www.wws.princeton.edu/~pkrugman/.

5 The beauty contest appears at op. cit.: 156.

6 He actually writes this in his discussion of Wicksell's natural rate of interest "the rate which would preserve the stability of some, not quite clearly specified, price-level". The stability discussion by Wicksell, which we discussed in Chapter 2, appeared in his "lecture notes" which were published in Swedish 1906 revised 1911 and German 1922, but not available in English until 1929 *Lectures on Political Economy vol. II*, (Macmillan, London) and *vol. I* in 1934 (Routledge, London). It is probable that Keynes never had seen it in the English translation. Given this the text quoted here is quite close to Wicksell.

7 This is not an opinion which is always accepted; some analysts claim that the production activities grant a cash flow which is the base for the financial operations which are the prime source of profits. Here we thus stick to a more conservative opinion.

8 From a practical point of view it may matter, as was the case in Argentina during the 1990s when they divided all prices by 10 000 to facilitate for the computers.

9 I will refer to the quantity *identity* in order not to be involved in different theoretical approaches depending on different assumptions concerning the involved variables.

10 It is definitely not supported by for instance David Ricardo who distinctly discussed different qualities of labour and the subsequent remuneration problem.

11 The result in the form of tables is also reproduced in Ekstedt and Fusari (2010: 188).

12 Such a development is discussed in Ekstedt and Fusari (2010: 227–9) as well as in Keynes (1973 [1936]: 295–8).

13 In Chapter 7 we will however discuss the occurrence of an increased instability in recent development. This is however not definitely proved but some signs can be seen.

14 Generally speaking the difference between Europe and the US was that the European nations were more dependent on exports to pay their imports than the US was since USD was the world currency and also that the cold war promoted a kind of "political trade"; this together with the necessity of promoting the defence production, made the US in the end extremely dependent on imported commodities. Seymore Melman has discussed these factors comprehensively during the decades from the 1950s to when he died 2004. Melman's thesis is that the civilian export sector more or less was sacrificed: (Melman 1985 and 1992).

15 A more detailed analysis can be found in Ekstedt and Westberg (1991: 42–66 and

158–66), and in Ekstedt and Fusari (2010: 221–9), there is a basically theoretical analysis of the phenomenon.

16 Government Proposition 1982/83: 150.

17 Figures 3.9 and 4.11 and the subsequent analysis are based on Ekstedt and Westberg (1991: ch. 2), and Ekstedt and Fusari (2010: ch. 6).

18 Observe that we may here talk about demand inflation since we are dealing with an asymmetric demand and production structure out of equilibrium.

19 The super-inflations in Argentina at the end of the 1970s and Russia in the early to mid 1990s were obviously caused by excess supply but it was in states institutionally more or less ceasing to exist.

5 Concluding comments on the nature of money in economic theory

1 Please do not interpret me as I mean money is something comparable to a contagious dicease.

2 The latter problem was partly touched on in Chapter 3 with respect to temporary equilibrium theory and Allais' equimarginal principle.

3 Op. cit.: 405–6, Appendix C: Fixed-point theorems and related combinatorial algorithms.

4 For further discussions we recommend Hammond (1997), Ehlers (2001), Knoblauch (2003).

5 Obviously such effects of commodities reject the neoclassical axioms and we will have piecewise concavities.

6 In business, small- and medium-sized companies when experiencing such a situation the owners often have to reduce their control by selling parts or even the whole of the company.

7 Keynes' critique of Say's law is based on a neoclassical misunderstanding. In the preface to the French edition of *General Theory* however he discusses this misunderstanding, which is very interesting and enlightening way and he explicitly enters the dimensionality problem. It is also of value to stress that Say's rejection of any form of "true" measures implies that he analyses an out-of-equilibrium economy seen from a neoclassical perspective.

8 *Pecunia non olet* – money doesn't smell; *rem acu tetigit* – he has touched the point with a needle.

9 The so-called "household production approach" is an example of commodities belonging to disjointed Euclidian spaces, so is also the characteristics model by Gorman/Lancaster.

10 According to Luigi Amoroso this depends on the fact that Pareto's sociology was as mechanical as the economic equilibrium theory. Amoroso's article from 1938 provides an excellent reading into Pareto's approach to sociology and economy.

11 Keynes claims that this description shows that Hume has "a foot and a half in the classical world" but as far as I can see Hume's description is more a rule for a growing economy and more similar to the process which Allais names the *equimarginal principle*. Furthermore Hume recognizes a dynamic interaction between the market and social development, which induces me to doubt "a foot and a half", particularly with respect to Hume's otherwise sceptical philosophy.

12 The easiest way to get rid of the concept of unemployment is to define the market economy for those who have a current endowment vector above zero. Thus in Debreu's setting we get that all agents participating in the market economy are defined as $(\lesssim_i, e_i \mid e_i > 0)$. Ekstedt and Fusari (2010: 46) discuss this kind of market.

13 See Ekstedt and Fusari (2010: 46) for a more comprehensive discussion.

14 Frisch (1965). Frisch received the Economic Price in Memory of Alfred Nobel 1969. See also for example Albrecht and Hart (1983). An interesting paper is also Lasky (2003).

15 Hume's causality analysis is from a scientific point of view the ruling approach to causal dynamics.

16 This discussion is to a large extent built on Hans Reichenbach (1991 [1956]), particularly chapter 11 on "Determinism Versus Indeterminism in Classical Physics", 82ff.

17 Ekstedt and Fusari (2010, ch. 3 and 4).

6 Uncertainty, money and liquidity

1 Kant's ethical imperative goes like this: "You shall always act in such a way that your action can be made a general law."

2 Gresham's "law" can be expressed as: coins with a higher intrinsic metal value will vanish from circulation and be replaced by coins of a lower intrinsic value but the same face value.

3 The necessary prerequisites for this is found in von Neumann and Morgenstern (2002 [1944]: ch. 1, 1–45).

4 In Jane Austen's works the land rent plays an overwhelming social role and matrimonial prospects were chiefly ranked with respect to land rent of the men involved. Even Miss Elizabeth Bennet (*Pride and Prejudice*) who claimed to be free from such calculations, as it happened chose Mr Darcy, granted for £10 000 a year and a charming castle, and herself granted only a fortune of £1000 by her father.

5 Constructed in this way we may create an insurance system which is a complete cover for changes in the state space. The completeness is heavily dependent on the assumptions of constancy of the state space and reversibility (Arrow and Hahn 1971: 119–21).

6 The entropy concept is often used as a measure of relative uncertainty. The late Henri Theil (1967) for example developed the entropy measure as a measure of income distribution. Increasing entropy means then an increasing degree of disorder, and if we apply it to income distribution a decreasing concentration of incomes.

7 This discussion is to a large extent built on Reichenbach (1991 [1956]), particularly chapter 11, "Determinism Versus Indeterminism in Classical Physics", 82 ff.

8 Weisstein (2000), entry "Sklar's Theorem".

9 Salmon (2009) is a rather violent attack on the use of the copula and he blames particularly Li's development of a formula for forecasting credit defaults. The formula which was used was developed by Li (2000) and contained some bold assumptions on Gaussian distributions but handled with care and prudence as one of several tools it is hard to see any problems with those assumptions. It is in these circumstances easy to claim the necessity for the financial agents to get quick results due to competitive reasons but then they also put all the eggs in the same methodological basket, which is exactly as doubtful as it sounds.

10 It is worth mentioning that Ludwig von Mises, the economist which we discuss, had a brother, Richard von Mises, philosopher and mathematician. Ludwig was a rationalist and Richard was a logical empiricist, thus they were philosophical and methodological opponents. The author is not completely convinced that Ludwig was a particularly orthodox rationalist but displayed a sort of mixture between rationalism and empiricism.

11 It is important to emphasize that von Mises regarded the individual as a subject. He violently attacked all kind of social planning "It is customary nowadays to speak of 'social engineering'. Like planning this term is a synonym for dictatorship and totalitarian tyranny" (von Mises 2007 [1949]: 113).

12 Reading Ludwig von Mises carefully it is hard to see him as a rationalist in the Kantian way. Thus the quote might fit rather well into Hume's attitude that reason is the humble servant of passion.

13 It is also important to remember that decisions in macroscopic organizations are both taken and executed by individuals who, by their specific apprehension and perception, affect the macroscopic organization.

7 Inter-temporal valuation, expectations and stability

1 The charts are taken from Westberg (1983). These charts are also discussed in chapter 1 in Ekstedt and Westberg (1991). However basically Figures 7.4, 7.5 and 7.6 and much of the discussion is founded on lecture notes by Professor Tor Fernholm (1964). I found these lecture notes two years ago and they are a veritable gold mine. I probably possess the only two copies remaining but if I find a publisher I will try to publish them.

2 In South America there has been a relatively prolonged growth but more on a regional level during the latest decade.

3 When there are financial crises of a major format mostly excessive behaviour is reported in media along with criminal activities, but we have to remember that it is the rather normal behaviour of ordinary people which creates the foundation of financial crises although excessive and criminal behaviour may occasionally play important roles.

4 If growth is limited on the highest macroscopic level is very hard to say. Technically we can change the measure by changing the "commodity basket" and from a philosophical point of view we have probably been in the reign of some kind of sustained increase of the ability to utilize natural resources as long as human beings have existed. Whether this will go on is more a matter for metaphysical speculations.

5 Articles and comments appear on http://krugman.blogs.nytimes/2012/03/27/minsky-and-methodology-wonkish/, http://krugman.blogs.nytimes/2012/03/30/banking-mysticism-continued/, http://krugman.blogs.nytimes/2012/04/02/oh-my-steve-keen-edition/, www.debtinflation.com.blogs.nytimes/2012/04/02/ptolemaic-economics-in the age-of-einstein/. Comments also appear in *Heterodox Economics Newsletter*, Issue 129, 9 April 2012. It is also instructive to read "Scott Fullweiler: Paul Krugman – The Conscience of a Neo-Liberal?" appearing at http://www.nakedcapitalism.com/2011/03/scott-fulwiler-paul-krugman%E2%80%94the-conscience-of-a-neo-liberal.html.

6 A unilateral system of quantitative rules in an open economy is as difficult as believing in tax-incomes from unilateral taxation on air-fuel.

7 NINJA – **N**o **I**ncome **N**o **J**ob **A**ssets.

8 I have been told that using the Heston model, which is the most sophisticated, with appropriate number of decimals, 34 implies three days computer time to create a decent set of simulated development path for option prices. Reducing the decimals to 28, an increased calculation uncertainty about 1 000 000 times, reduced the calculation time to less than six hours. That means that the calculations can be done before the opening of trading next day. It should however be noted that I was told this approximately one year ago so improvements may have taken place.

9 The example is taken from Heron's invention of a cattle watering machine around AD 80 which didn't come into use before the early 1870s when a British engineer happened to discover Heron's drawings in the collected works of Heron which was published in the middle of 1860s (Ekstedt and Fusari 2010:180).

8 Money and stability

1 This is to be read about in Mark Twain's *Tom Sawyer*, chapters 1 to 4. For the local church currency an illustrated bible was comparable to gold bullion. Thus one bible=ten yellow paper pieces, one yellow piece of paper=ten red, one red=ten blue pieces and one blue piece=the ability of reciting two bible verses. We thus see that the ruling principle was Adam Smith's real bills, since the supply of bibles was in principle unlimited. We also understand why Tom Sawyer chose the quicker way of market operations in acquiring the bible although unfortunately he failed when the reverend asked him a question from the bible.

2 In the 1980s it was prohibited in Sweden to carry knives publicly and as the law was

formulated in the first version, there were no exceptions or writings to that effect. Our children were then active in scouting which implied that a sheath knife and a small axe were normally carried at the belt. Thus the scouting organizations protested and got the government to choose different formulations. But still is it the knife or the person handling the knife who is the problem? This question is actually meaningful to ask with respect to the neoclassical axiomatic structure. Postulating the axiom of reflexivity we lay the responsibility at the knife.

Bibliography

Albrecht, J.W. and Hart, A.G. (1983). "A Putty-Clay Model of Demand Uncertainty and Investment", *Scandinavian Journal of Economics* 85(3), 393–402.

Allais, M. (1953). "Le comportement de l'homme rationel devant le risque: Critique des postulates et axiomes de l'ecole amricaine", *Econometrica* 21(4), 503–46.

Allais, M. (1987). "The Equimarginal Principle: Meaning, Limits and Generalization", *Rivista Internazionale di Scienza Economica e Commerziale*, 34(8), 689–750.

Amoroso, L. (1938). "Vilfredo Pareto", *Econometrica* 6(1), 1–21.

Aquinas, Thomas St. (1998 [1271]). "What Makes Actions Good or Bad", in *Summa Theologiæ*, 1–2, 18–20, pp. 565–611, in *Selected Writings*, London: Penguin Classics.

Aristotle (1990 [original around 334–324 BC]). Politics Bno. (1257a), in *The Works of Aristotle vol II*, Chicago, IL/London: Encyclopædia Britannica, Inc. p. 452, Bno. 1258b (Bno refers to the Berlin enumeration).

Arnér, M. and Ekstedt, F. (2008). "Option Pricing and Volatility: A Study of Four Contiuous-Time Models", Master Thesis in Mathematics, Dept. of Mathematical Sciences, Division of Mathematics, Chalmers University of Technology and Göeteborg University, Göteborg, Sweden.

Arrow, K.J. (1950). "A Difficulty in the Concept of Social Welfare", *Journal of Political Economy* 58(4), 328–46.

Arrow, K.J. and Hahn, F.H. (1971). *General Competitive Analysis*, San Francisco, CA: Holden Day Inc.

Austen, J. (1988 [1813]). *Pride and Prejudice*, Oxford/New York: Oxford University Press.

Becker, G.S. (1964). *Human Capital: A Theoretical and Empirical Analysis, with Special Reference to Education*, Chicago, IL: University of Chicago Press.

Becker, G.S. (1976). *A New Economic Approach of Human Behaviour*, Chicago, IL: University of Chicago Press.

Bergson, H. (1912). *Tiden och den fria viljan* [Time and the Free Will], Stockholm: Wahlström & Widstrand.

Black, F. and Scholes, M. (1973) "The Pricing of Options and Corporate Liabilities", *Journal of Political Economy* 81(3), 637–59.

Blanchard, O.J. and Plantes, M.K. (1977). "A Note on Gross Substitutability of Financial Assets", *Econometrica* 45(3), 769–71.

Boltho, A. (1982). "Growth", in ed. Boltho, A., *The European Economy: Growth and Crises* (pp. 9–37), Oxford: Oxford University Press.

Bonar, J. (1923). "Ricardo's Ingot Plan", *Economic Journal* 33(131), 281–304.

Bower, J.L. (1970). *Managing the Resource Allocation Process: A Study of Corporate Planning and Investment*, Boston, MA: Irwin.

Brody, T. (1994). *The Philosophy behind Physics*, Berlin/Heidelberg/New York: Springer Verlag.

Choi, J.J. (2005). "Extrapolative Expectations and the Equity Premium", Harvard University, available at: www.stanford.edu/group/SITE/papers2005/Choi.05.pdf.

Commons, J.R. (1990). *Institutional Economics: Its Place in Political Economy*, New Brunswick/London: Transaction Publishers (originally published: New York: Macmillan, 1934).

Debreu, G. (1982). "Existence of General Equilibrium", in eds Arrow, K.J. and Intrilligator, M.D., *Handbook of Mathematical Economics vol. II* (pp. 697–743), Amsterdam/New York: North-Holland Publishing Company.

Debreu, G. (1987 [1959]). *Theory of Value*, New York: Wiley.

Diemer, A. (2005). "David Hume et les économists français", Hermés, Université de Reims, May, pp. 1–27.

Downs, A. (1957). *An Economic Theory of Democracy*, New York: Harper.

Drèze, J.H. (1985). "Second-best Analysis with Markets in Disequilibrium: Public Sector Pricing in a Keynesian Regime", *European Economic Review* 29(3), 263–301.

Ehlers, L. (2001). "Multiple Public Goods and Lexicographic preferences: Replacement principles", Centre Recerce et développement en économique, Cahier 25-2001.

Eichengreen, B.E. (1995). *Europe's Post-War Recovery*, Cambridge: Cambridge University Press.

Ekstedt, H. (2006). "Some Comments on the Concept of Rationality", Paper presented at the EAEPE conference in Istanbul, 2–4 November.

Ekstedt, H. and Fusari, A. (2010). *Economic Theory and Social Change: Problems and Revisions*, London/New York: Routledge.

Ekstedt, H. and Westberg, L. (1991). *Dynamic Models for the Interrelations of Real and Financial Growth*, London/New York: Chapman & Hall.

Enthoven, A.C. and Arrow, K.J. (1956). "A Theorem on Expectations and the Stability of Equilibrium", *Econometrica* 24(3), 288–93.

Fernholm, T. (March 1964). "Samhällsekonomisk Orientering" [An Overview of Political Economy], Lecture notes, mimeograph.

Fleming, J.M. (1962). "Domestic Financial Policies under Fixed and Floating Exchange Rates", IMF Staff Papers 9: 369–79.

Friend, I., Minsky, H.P. and Andrews, V.L. (1964). *Private Capital Markets*, Englewood Cliffs, NJ: Prentice-Hall, Inc.

Frisch, R. (1965). *Theory of production*, Dordrecht, Holland: D. Reidel.

Gorman, W. (1980). "The Demand for Related Goods: A Possible Procedure for analyzing Quality Differentials in the Egg Market", *Review of Economic Studies* 47; first circulated as Journal Paper no. 2319, Iowa Agricultural Experiment Station November 1956, 843–956.

Grandmont, J.M. (1977). "Temporary General Equilibrium Theory", *Econometrica* 45(3), 535–72.

Grandmont, J.M. (1982). "Temporary General Equilibrium Theory", in eds Arrow, K.J. and Intrilligator, M.D., *Handbook of Mathematical Economics, vol. II*, Amsterdam, New York, Oxford: North-Holland Publishing Company.

Grandmont, J.M. (2006). "Temporary Equilibrium", no 2006-27, Institut National de la Statistique et des Etudes Economiques, Série des Documents de Travail du CREST (Centre de Recherche en Economie et Statistique), www.crest.fr/doctravail/document/2006-27.pdf.

Green, J.R. (1973). "Temporary General Equilibrium in a Sequential Trading Model with Spot and Future Transactions", *Econometrica* 41(6), 1103–23.

Grice-Hutchinson, M. (1952). *The School of Salamanca*, Oxford: Clarendon Press.

Hammond, P.J. (1997). "The Efficiency Theorems and Market Failure", a preprint of a chapter which appeared in Kirman, A. ed., (1998) *Elements of General Equilibrium Analysis*, New York/London: Wiley-Blackwell. Available at: www.citeseerx.psu.edu. www.crde.umontreal.ca.

Hansen, A.H. (1949). *Monetary Theory and Fiscal Policy*, New York: McGraw-Hill.

Heston, S.L. (1993). "A Closed-Form Solution for Options with Stochastic Volatility with Applications to Bond and Currency Options", *Review of Financial Studies* 6(2), 327–43.

Hetherington, N.S. (1983). "Isaac Newton's Influence on Adam Smith's Natural Laws in Economics", *Journal of the History of Ideas* 44(3), 497–505.

Hicks, J.R. (1937). "Mr. Keynes and the Classics: A Suggested Interpretation", *Econometrica* 5(2), 147–59.

Hicks, J.R. (1980–81). "IS-LM: An Explanation", *Journal of Post Keynesian Economics* 3(2), 139–55.

Hirshleifer, D. and Yu, J. (2012). "Asset Pricing in Production Economies with Extrapolative Expectations", available at: http://papers.ssrn.com/sol3/papers.cfm?abstract_id=1785961.

Hobsbawm, E. (1994). *The Age of Extremes: 1914–1991*, London: Abacus.

Hume, D. (1770 [1752]). *Essays and Treatises on Several Subjects, vol. II, containing Essays, Moral, Political, and Litterary*, printed for T. Cadell (successor of Mr Millar) in the Strand; and A. Kincaid and A. Donaldson, at Edinburgh.

Hume, D.A. (2002 [1740]). *A Treatise of Human Nature*, Oxford: Oxford University Press.

Humphrey, T.M. (1982). "The Real Bills Doctrine", *Economic Review*, September/October, Federal Reserve Bank of Richmond.

Iwai, K. (2009). "The Second End of Laissez-Faire: Bootstrapping Nature of Money and Inherent Instability of Capitalism", Faculty of Economics, University of Tokyo. Paper presented at the Interdisciplinary Workshop on Money, Berlin Free University, 25–28 June 2009.

Keynes, J.M. (1920) *The Economic Consequences of the Peace*, London: Macmillan and Co., Ltd.

Keynes, J.M. (1953 [1930]). *A Treatise on Money. Volume I: The Pure Theory of Money*, London: Macmillan & Co,

Keynes, J.M. (1962 [1921]). *A Treatise on Probability*, New York: Harper & Row Publishers.

Keynes, J.M. (1973 [1936]). *The General Theory of Employment Interest and Money*, Cambridge: Macmillan, Cambridge University Press.

Knoblauch, V. (2003). "Continuous Lexicographic Preferences", Economics Working Papers 200331. Available at: http://digitalcommons@uconn.edu.

Koestler, A. (1979 [1959]). *The Sleepwalkers*, Bugay, UK: Richard Clay Ltd.

Labadie, P. (2009). "Anonymity and Individual Risk", *Journal of Economic Theory* 144(6), 2440–53.

Lancaster, K. (1966). "A New Approach to Consumer Theory", *Journal of Political Economy* 74(2), 132–57.

Lansing, K.J. (2005). "Lock-in of Extrapolative Expectations in an Asset Pricing Model", Federal Reserve Bank of San Francisco Working Paper 2004-06, available at: www.frbsf.org/publications/economics/papers/2004/wp04-06bk.pdf.

Larsson, L.-G. (May 2010). "On the Law of Demand. Is it Compatible with any Choice

Bbehaviour? A Descriptive Approach with no Giffen Good" (First Draft) Department of Economics and Statistics, School of Business and Law, University of Gothenburg.

Lasky, M. (2003). "A Putty-Clay Model of Business Fixed Investment", Technical Paper Series 2003-9, Congressional Budget Office, Washington, DC. Available at: www.cbo. gov/sites/default/files/cbofiles/ftpdocs/45xx/doc4573/2003-9.pdf.

Laver, M. (1997). *Political Action: An Invitation to the Politics of Rational Choice*, London: Sage Publications Ltd.

Lavoie, N. and Liu, Q. (2007). "Pricing-to-Market: Price Discrimination or Product Differentiation", *American Journal of Agricultural Economics* 89(3), 571–81.

Li, X.D. (2000). "On Default Correlation: A Copula Function Approach", *Journal of Fixed Income* 9, 43–54.

Lucas, R.E. Jr (1972). "Expectations and the Neutrality of Money", *Journal of Economic Theory* 4(2), 103–24.

Lundberg, E., Ohlin, G. and Werin, L. (1975). "Dags för tillväxt? Konjunkturrådets Rapport 1975–76", Studieförbundet Näringsliv och Samhälle (SNS), Stockholm.

McCulloch, J.R. (1888). *The Works of David Ricardo: With a Notice of the Life and Writings of the Author*, London: John Murray.

McKean, H.P. Jr (1965) "A Free Boundary Problem for the Heat Equation Arising from a Problem in Mathematical Economics", Appendix to Samuelson, P.A. (1965) "Rational Theory of Warrant Price", *Industrial Management Review* 6(2), 13–39.

Makarov, V.L and Rubinov, A.M. (1977). *Economic Dynamics and Equilibria*, Heidelberg, Berlin: Springer Verlag.

Mankiw, G. (2003). *Macroeconomics*, 5th edn, New York: Worth Publishers.

Markowitz, H.M. (1959). *Portfolio Selection: Efficient Diversification of Investments*, New York: John Wiley & Sons.

Melman, S. (1985). *The Permanent War Economy: American Capitalism in Decline*, New York: Simon & Schuster.

Melman, S. (1992). *Rebuilding America: A New Economic Plan for the 1990s*, Westfield, NJ: Open Media.

Mitchell, W.C. (1916). "The Role of Money in Economic Theory", *American Economic Review* 6(1), 140–61.

Modigliani, F. and Miller, M. (1958). "The Cost of Capital, Corporation Finance and the Theory of Investment", *American Economic Review* 48(3), 261–97.

Mundell, R.A. (1963). "Capital Mobility and Stabilization Policy under Fixed and Flexible Exchange Rates", *Canadian Journal of Economic and Political Science* 29(4), 475–85.

Muth, J.F. (1961). "Rational Expectations and the Theory of Price Movements", *Econometrica* 29(3), 315–35.

Nicolis, G. and Prigogine, I. (1977). *Self-Organisation in Nonequilibrium Systems: From Dissipative Structures to Order through Fluctuations*, A Wiley-Interscience Publication, New York/London/Sydney/Toronto: John Wiley & Sons.

Radner, R. (1982). "Equilibrium under Uncertainty", in ed. Arrow, K.A., *Handbook of Mathematical Economics* (pp. 923–1006), Amsterdam/New York/Oxford: North-Holland Publishing Company.

Reichenbach, H. (1938). *Experience and Prediction*, Chicago, IL: University of Chicago Press.

Reichenbach, H. (1991 [1956]). *The Direction of Time*, Berkeley, CA/Oxford: University of California Press.

Ricardo, D. (1815). "On Profit", in *Essays on the Principles of Political Economy and*

Taxation. Available at: www.econlib.org/library/Riccardo/ricP2.html. This version is based on 3rd edn, London: John Murray, 1815.

Ricardo, D. (1821 [1817]). "On the Principles of Political Economy and Taxation", London: John Murray. Available at: Library of Economics and Liberty, www.econlib.org/library/Ricardo/ricP.html.

Russell, B. (1992 [1903]). *The Principles of Mathematics*, London: Routledge.

Russell, B. (1996 [1946]). *History of Western Philosophy*, London: Routledge.

Salmon F. (2009). "Recipe for Disaster: The Formula that Killed Wall Street", *Wired Magazine:17.03*, www.wired.com/techbiz/it/magazine/17-03/wp_quant.

Samuelson, P.A. (1947). *The Foundations of Economic Analysis*, Cambridge, MA: Harvard University Press.

Samuelson, P.A. (1948). *Economics: An Introductory Analysis*, New York: McGraw Hill.

Samuelson, P.A. (1965). "Rational Theory of Warrant Price", *Industrial Management Review* 6(2), 13–39.

Samuelson, A.P. (1968). "What Classical and Neoclassical Monetary Theory really Was", *Canadian Journal of Economics* 1(1), 1–15, and (1972) *Collected Scientific Papers*, III, 529–43.

Sandelin, B. (1990). "Samuel von Pufendorf", in eds Jonung, C. and Ståhlberg, A.-C., *Ekonomporträtt: Svenska ekonomer under 300 år* [Portrait of Swedish Economists during 300 years], Stockholm: SNS förlag. Available at: http://www.nek.lu.se/pdf/hist_pufendorf.pdf.

Saurette, P. (2005). *The Kantian Imperative: Humiliation, Common Sense, Politics*, Toronto/Buffalo/London: University of Toronto Press.

Say, J.B. (1834 [1803]). *A Treatise on Political Economy: Or the Production, Distribution, and Consumption of Wealth*, Philadelphia, PA: Grigg and Elliot.

Sklar, A. (1973). "Random Variables, Joint Distribution Functions and Copulas", *Kybernetika* 9(6), 449–60.

Smith, A. (1952 [1776]). *An Inquiry into the Nature and Causes of the Wealth of Nations*, Chicago, IL/London/Toronto: Encyclopedia Britannica Inc.

Solow, R.M. (1971). *Growth Theory an Exposition*, Radcliffe Lectures Delivered in the University of Warwick 1969, Oxford: Clarendon Press.

Stěkin, S.B. (1963/1999). "Theory of Functions of a Real Variable", in eds Aleksandrov, A.D., Kolmogorov, A N., Lavrent'ev, M.A., translation by Gould, S.H. 1963, *Mathematics: Its Contents, Methods and Meaning* (pp. 3–36), Mineola, NY: Dover Publications, Inc.

Stolpe, S. (1982). *Drottning Kristina* [Queen Christina], Borås, Sweden: Askild & Kärnekull.

Theil, H. (1967) *Economics and Information Theory*, Amsterdam: North-Holland Publishing Company.

Thornton, H. (1939 [1802]). *An Enquiry into the Nature and Effects of the Paper Credit of Great Britain*, London: George Allen and Unwin. Available at: http://oll.libertyfund.org/index.php?option=com_staticxt&staticfile=show.php%3Ftitle=2041&layout=html.

Twain, M. (1974 [1876]). *Tom Sawyer* (Swedish translation of *The Adventures of Tom Sawyer*), Stockholm: Tidens Förlag.

Vega-Redondo, F. (1989). "Extrapolative Expectations and Market Stability", *International Economic Review* 30(3), 513–17.

von Mises, L. (2007 [1949]). *Human Action: A Treatise on Economics*, Vol 2, Indianapolis, IN: Liberty Fund.

von Neumann, J. and Morgenstern, O. (2004 [1944]). *Theory of Games and Economic Behaviour*, Princeton, NJ/Oxford: Princeton University Press.

Warmdinger, T. (2004). "Import Prices and Pricing-to-Market Effects in the Euro Area", Working Paper Series no. 299/January, European Central Bank.

Weisstein, E.W. (1999). *CRC Concise Encylopedia of Mathematics*, Boca Raton, FL/ London/New York/Washington, DC: Chapman & Hall/CRC.

Weisstein, E.W. (2000). *Concise Encyclopedia of Mathematics*, CD-ROM version, London: Chapman and Hall.

Westberg, L. (1983). "Finansiering i ekonomisk teori" [Finance in Economic Theory], Memorandum Dept of Economics, University of Gothenburg, Sweden.

Wicksell, K. (1936 [1893]). *Interest and Prices*, London: Macmillan and Co. Ltd., p. xxiii. The original appeared in German (1893) as *Geldzins und Güterpreise*.

Wicksell, K. (1937 [1922]). *Föreläsningar i Nationalekonomi* [Lectures in Economics, 2nd part], Lund, Sweden: Andra delen, C.W.K. Gleerups Förlag.

Wiener, N. (1952). *Materia, maskiner och människor: cybernetiken och samhället*, Stockholm: Libris. In English: (1988 [1954]) *The Human Use of Human Beings: Cybernetics and Society*, Boston, MA: Da Capo Press.

Wittgenstein, L. (1974 [1921]). *Tractatus Logico-Philosophicus*, London: Routledge & Kegan Paul.

Index